Building the American Republic

VOLUME 2

Building the American Republic

A NARRATIVE HISTORY FROM 1877

Jane Dailey

The University of Chicago Press   CHICAGO AND LONDON

This is volume 2 of a two-volume narrative history of America by Harry L.
Watson and Jane Dailey. Volume 1 is written by Watson; volume 2 is
written by Dailey. To read digital editions of both volumes and more,
please visit buildingtheamericanrepublic.org.

The University of Chicago Press, Chicago 60637
The University of Chicago Press, Ltd., London
© 2018 by Jane Dailey
Published 2018
Printed in the United States of America

27 26 25 24 23 22 21 20 19 18   1 2 3 4 5

ISBN-13: 978-0-226-30079-5 (cloth)
ISBN-13: 978-0-226-30082-5 (paper)
ISBN-13: 978-0-226-30096-2 (e-book)
DOI: 10.7208/chicago/9780226300962.001.0001

Library of Congress Cataloging-in-Publication Data
Names: Watson, Harry L. | Dailey, Jane Elizabeth, 1963–
Title: Building the American republic.
Description: Chicago ; London : The University of Chicago Press, 2018. |
Includes bibliographical references and index.
Identifiers: LCCN 2017026856 | ISBN 9780226300481 (vol. 1 ; cloth :
alk. paper) | ISBN 9780226300511 (vol. 1 ; pbk. : alk. paper) |
ISBN 9780226300658 (vol. 1 ; e-book) | ISBN 9780226300795 (vol. 2 ;
cloth : alk. paper) | ISBN 9780226300825 (vol. 2 ; pbk. : alk. paper) |
ISBN 9780226300962 (vol. 2 ; e-book)
Subjects: LCSH: United States—History.
Classification: LCC E178.B955 2018 | DDC 973—dc23
LC record available at https://lccn.loc.gov/2017026856

Contents

5 · Depression, 1928–1938 139

6 · Assertion, 1938–1946 173

7 · Containment, 1946–1953 201

8 · At Odds, 1954–1965 231

11 · Right, 1974–1989   321

Preface

When Benjamin Franklin left the Constitutional Convention in Philadelphia in July 1787, a bystander reportedly asked him what sort of government the delegates had created. "A republic," he replied, "if you can keep it."

Keeping a republic is no easy task. The most important requirement is the active involvement of an informed people committed to honesty, civility, and selflessness—what the Founders called "republican virtue." Anchored by its Constitution, the American republic has endured for more than 220 years, longer than any other republic in modern history.

But the road has not been smooth. The American nation came apart in a violent civil war only 73 years after ratification of the Constitution. When it was reborn five years later, both the republic and its Constitution were transformed. Since then, the nation has had its ups and downs, depending largely on the capacity of the American people to tame, as Franklin put it, "their prejudices, their passions, their errors of opinion, their local interests, and their selfish views."

Our goal in writing *Building the American Republic* has been to craft a clear, engaging, readable, and thoughtful narrative history of the United States. In a world of increasing complexity and danger, America's civic tradition, both past and present, is a vital public asset and a continuing source of national renewal. Those who want to build a better America, however they define it, must understand the nation's history, its place in the world, the growth of its institutions, and their own role in preserving and reinvigorating the Republic.

Harry L. Watson
Jane Dailey

FIGURE 1. *The Bosses of the Senate*, by J. Ottmann Lith. Co., after Joseph Keppler, published in *Puck*, January 23, 1889. Courtesy of the United States Senate, catalog no. 38.00392.001.

CHAPTER 1

Incorporation, 1877–1900

On July 2, 1881, the 20th president of the United States, James A. Garfield, was shot in the back as he walked through a railway station in Washington, DC. His deranged assassin, Charles Guiteau, is frequently described as a "disgruntled office-seeker," and indeed he was: Guiteau considered himself responsible for Garfield's election and demanded repeatedly to be appointed consul to Paris. The stricken president lingered through the summer heat, suffering from infection, blood poisoning, and pneumonia. He succumbed to a massive heart attack on September 19, 1881.

Garfield's death was deeply disturbing to a nation still governed by the Civil War generation. Poet Walt Whitman, who had spent the war caring for wounded soldiers, captured the apprehension occasioned by the second presidential assassination in fewer than 20 years. Of the tolling bells that announced "the sudden death-news everywhere," Whitman wrote

> The slumberers rouse, the rapport of the People,
> (Full well they know that message in the darkness,
> Full well return, respond within their breasts, their brains, the sad
>   reverberations,)
> The passionate toll and clang—city to city, joining, sounding,
>   passing,
> Those heart-beats of a Nation in the night.

Americans who had lived through the Civil War were not easily rattled. They pulled up roots and settled the continent their fathers had claimed but never truly conquered. They endured colossal loss of life to achieve monumental feats of engineering such as the transcontinental railroad and the Brooklyn Bridge. They adapted to shifting, even convulsive, economic conditions, spurred by a deluge of inventions (like electricity). They tolerated if not necessarily celebrated the strange languages and customs tucked away in the bags of millions of newcomers to the nation's shores.

What *did* frighten many Americans was anything that undermined the fragile mutual understanding—the rapport—of the people. This was especially true of future Supreme Court Justice Oliver Wendell Holmes Jr., one of the most influential American thinkers of his (or any other) time. Holmes saw the worst of the worst during his three years with the 20th Regiment of the Massachusetts Volunteer Infantry, which suffered more battle deaths than all but four Union regiments. Wounded three times himself, Holmes survived, but the war convinced him that certitude is dangerous, and that only democracy can prevent competing conceptions of how to live from overheating and leading to violence. Whereas some—for example, white supremacists and opponents of woman suffrage—worried that expanded access to democracy would destroy American civilization, Holmes was convinced that the only way to *preserve* the Republic, restored through the sacrifice of millions, was to make sure that the political playing field was as accessible and even as possible. Everyone must have a say.

For Holmes, participatory government—government of the people, by the people, and for the people, as Lincoln had put it at Gettysburg—*was* the Republic, not a means to it. Lose one and the other disappears. The fundamental unity of the people was maintained through the democratic process. Threats to that process, whether violence, corruption, unchecked power, overbearing wealth, or disenfranchisement, endangered that sense of unity. Holmes understood that today's losers have to believe that victory is possible tomorrow. Loss of faith in the system imperils the Republic itself.

A higher percentage of eligible voters participated in American politics during the last third of the nineteenth century than any time before or since. In presidential election years, turnout averaged 78 percent, and this takes into account the suppression of black and white Republicans by white supremacists in the South. Voters perceived fundamental differences between the two political parties. Democrats, dominated by their southern wing, argued for the rights of the states against an ever-expanding federal government. Republicans, empowered by the war and Reconstruction, embarked on a 40-year crusade of nation-building. The future of that nation depended, in great measure, on the capacity of the American political system to absorb newcomers—African Americans, immigrants, women—into the political system, and keep the peace.

In Motion

During the last third of the nineteenth century, the United States underwent a rapid and profound economic revolution. This economic transformation was rooted in abundant natural resources (e.g., land, lumber, coal, and oil), an expanding market linked by new transportation and communications networks (railroads and telegraphs), a brimming pool of labor constantly restocked from abroad, new forms of business organization that facilitated both economic growth and contraction, and a strong federal government determined to incorporate into the nation the territory (if not necessarily the indigenous peoples) of the great American West.

IRON HORSES

The importance of railroads to late nineteenth-century American history cannot be overstated. US railroad mileage tripled between 1860 and 1880, and tripled again by 1920, opening vast western expanses to commercial farming, facilitating a boom in coal and steel production, and creating a truly national market for manufactured goods and staples like beef and grain. Railroad cars transported the army that "pacified" the Indians, and then unloaded the settlers who organized and incorporated the West into the nation. No models of efficiency or rationality themselves, railroads nonetheless created the conditions that allowed other industries such as steel, grain, and meat-packing to incorporate and innovate a new capitalist logic. Railroads came to symbolize American progress. In his book *Triumphant Democracy* (1886), steel magnate Andrew Carnegie declared, "The old nations of the earth creep on at a snail's pace; the Republic thunders past with the rush of the express."

Railroads changed everything they touched, beginning with space. The transcontinental railroads effected a massive spatial turn: the axis of North America, which had previously run North–South, was turned East–West. Railroads altered people's sense of time and space. Because people experience distance in terms of time, linked by rail, places grew closer together: what German philosopher Karl Marx called "the annihilation of space by time." It took less time in 1880 to travel from Boston to Montana (a distance of circa 2,000 miles) than to Charleston (a mere 1,017 miles). Together, railroads and telegraph systems, whose lines were strung alongside tracks, "shrank the whole perceptual universe of North America."

Beyond people's understandings of time and space, railroads reorganized time itself. Before 1883, clocks were set locally according to the sun. Noon was the moment when the sun stood highest in the midday sky, which varied according to longitude. When clocks read noon in Chicago, it was 11:50 a.m. in St. Louis, 11:27 a.m. in Omaha, and 12:18 p.m. in Detroit. Two trains running on the same tracks at the same moment but with clocks reading different times could find themselves suddenly occupying the same space, with deadly consequences. In November 1883, the railroad companies carved the continent into four "standard" time zones, in each of which clocks would be set to exactly the same time. Not that this meant the trains ran on time. As one rider complained, the train "was seldom there when the schedule said it would be, but occasionally it was, and [people] were amazed and angry when they missed it."

Railroads even liberated people from weather. When the Great Lakes were frozen and nothing could move by ship, the railroads ran. As one railroad promoter announced, "It is against the policy of Americans to remain locked up by ice one half of the year." Railroads allowed an entrepreneurial butcher named Gustavus Swift to "store the winter" by transporting ice, a large-bulk, low-value commodity, to the stockyards in Chicago, where meat-packers used it to create refrigerated boxcars, which enabled them to ship beef and pork in all directions.

By the 1890s, five transcontinental rail lines linked western mines, ranches, farms, and forests with eastern markets. The South, which laid track even faster than the rest of the nation, became integrated into this national market economy. With the trains came towns. Previously dominated by plantations, the southern landscape was dotted with villages, whose numbers doubled between 1870 and 1880, and then doubled again by 1900.

"VAST, TRACKLESS SPACES": THE TRANS-MISSISSIPPI WEST

What Walt Whitman referred to as the "vast, trackless spaces" of the Trans-Mississippi West was first an extension of the Mexican North.

The expansive territory that became the American West was nearly all acquired from Mexico in 1848: California, Arizona, New Mexico, Nevada, Colorado, and Utah. Many people were included in this transfer, among them several major Indian nations, including the Papago, Navajo, Puebloan, and Apache, as well as approximately 75,000 Mexicans. The frontier experience of the American West was never an encounter with virgin land. It was, instead, a process in which new wilderness zones were created in places where civilizations had once existed.

At first, Indians remained in their homelands. Americans were quickly incorporated into the extensive Indian agricultural and trading networks that characterized the southwestern United States. For example, the Pima and Papago "River People" who dwelt along the Gila and San Pedro Rivers supplied the US Army with a million pounds of wheat in 1862, plus cotton, sugar, melons, beans, corn, and dried pumpkins.

In 1869, Congress created the Board of Indian Commissioners, which was composed of prominent evangelicals and humanitarians, including old abolitionists, to oversee what President Ulysses S. Grant and others termed the nation's "Indian problem." The commission recommended replacing the treaty system, which had treated Indian tribes as akin to sovereign nations, with a new legal status for "uncivilized Indians" as "wards of the government."

In a departure from the prior policy of Indian removal en masse to another location, the commission recommended the creation of reservations located far from ancestral lands as well as other population centers. The goal was to isolate Indians from outside influences. Under this plan, missionaries were in charge of Indian life. They replaced Indian languages, practices, and religion with English, American models of domestic agriculture, and Christianity. They sent Indian children away to boarding school. In addition to supplanting native cultural practices, the reservation arrangement also undercut the ability of Indians to sustain themselves through trade or employment off the reservation.

What was called the "Peace Policy" was welcomed with hostility by many Indian nations. War with the Apaches broke out in Arizona. In the Great Plains and on the West Coast, the US Army battled the Lakota, Cheyenne, and Modoc Indians. President Grant remained unperturbed. In his opinion, Indians—even the warlike Apaches—could "be civilized and made friends of the republic."

Republicans considered tribal sovereignty incompatible with the national unity forged in the Civil War. In 1871, Congress stopped negotiating new treaties with Indians and refused to recognize the independent nation status of tribes. Under the terms of the 1887 Dawes General Allotment Plan, Indians were required to distribute communal land among individual families. Those who cooperated became US citizens. So-called surplus land was sold to whites.

Indians held 138 million acres in 1887. During the following 47 years, 60 million acres were declared to be "surplus." All told, nearly two-thirds of tribal land was conveyed to Americans through a variety of devices. Commissioner of Indian Affairs Francis Amasa Walker, the government's guardian for the native peoples, declared in 1872, "The westward course of population is neither to be denied nor delayed for the sake of the Indians. They must yield or perish." Most tribes did both.

MANIFEST DESTINY

Americans settled more land between 1870 and 1900 than in all their previous history. The population of the territory to the west of Illinois and Missouri mushroomed from 300,000 in 1860 to 5 million in 1900. Much desirable land was beyond the reach of homesteaders, however. Enormous grants of public land to subsidize railroad construction, the distribution of land to Union veterans, and the use of dummy corporations allowed speculators (who acquired land not for its use but for its resale value in a rising market) and mining, timber, and cattle companies to acquire land under falsified claims. Under the terms of the Railway Act of 1864, railroad companies received 12,800 acres of public land for every mile of track they laid. This land could serve as security for bonds, or be sold to settlers, who paid for land their government had given away to the railroads.

Article 3 of the Northwest Ordinance of 1787 stipulated that "the utmost good faith shall always be observed towards the Indians; their lands and property shall never be taken from them without their consent." Americans never lived up to this ideal. Instead, they negotiated treaties that pushed Indians westward, broke those treaties to expand farther, and killed Indians who resisted. Sometimes white settlers wanted Indian land to farm. Other times, they coveted water or right-of-way (in the case of railroads) or minerals. In California, white settlers fought a genocidal campaign against the native peoples there.

Of some 150,000 Indians in California when gold was discovered there in 1848, only 30,000 remained by 1860.

With Native American control weakened in the West, settlers poured into the vast central plains. European immigrants, particularly Scandinavians and Germans, established themselves in the northern territories of Wisconsin, Minnesota, and the Dakotas. During the period of mass immigration, one out of every two western settlers was foreign-born.

American-born settlers also set out across the continent, including large numbers of white and black southerners. Many rural blacks migrated west to Kansas, Indiana, and Oklahoma, where land was plentiful and cheap. "The Negro exodus now *amounts to a stampede*," exclaimed one North Carolina white in 1890. African Americans also gravitated toward industry, particularly mining. "It was easy," one miner recalled. "All you needed was a pair of gloves, overalls and experience and you could get hired anywhere." The West had another advantage over the South: as one settler wrote to a friend in Louisiana, "They do not kill Negroes here for voting."

Mass influx of settlers from the South and East provoked conflict with Indian nations, some of whom defended their land fiercely and resisted relocation to reservations. In 1876, during the Sioux Wars, Cheyenne and Lakota warriors defeated an overconfident Lieutenant Colonel George Armstrong Custer, killing him and all his men at the Battle of Little Bighorn.

In the midst of a serious drought in 1889, Congress cut food aid to several Indian nations, including the Lakota. Deaths from hunger and disease rose on the reservations. Instead of an armed uprising, starving Native Americans turned to the Ghost Dance, a spiritual movement associated with the teachings of the Northern Paiute spiritual leader Wovoka. The circle dance of the Ghost Dance represented a broad credo of working the land, Anglo education, and, above all, nonviolence.

In 1890, the US Army massacred more than 150 Lakota, mainly women and children, at Wounded Knee Creek in South Dakota. Some of the Lakota at Wounded Knee were among those who had routed George Custer at Little Bighorn. The massacre has been associated with the Ghost Dance, but in fact was unrelated. The Ghost Dance continued into the twentieth century, practiced by Indians across the country.

IMMIGRATION, MIGRATION, AND URBANIZATION

The population of the United States quadrupled in the half century following the Civil War. High birth rates and wave after wave of immigrants pushed the population to more than 75 million by 1900, leaving America the second-most populous nation in the world.

Immigrants gambling on the wonders of America flooded embarkation centers in New York, Galveston, and San Francisco. Some were pulled by the prospect of a higher standard of living. Others were pushed by one or more of several factors, including political oppression, religious persecution, war, and interethnic rivalries. Still others were simply trying to escape overbearing parents. Between 1879 and 1915, 25 million immigrants arrived "yearning to breathe free," in the words inscribed on the Statue of Liberty. By then, immigrants made up nearly 15 percent of the American population.

Although some immigrants joined the stream of western settlement, most gravitated to the jobs, educational opportunities, and ethnic communities of urban America. In a relatively brief period, America's population shifted from one with predominantly British (including Scots and Irish) and German roots to a much more heterogeneous mix. Over half of the 3.5 million immigrants who entered the United States in the 1890s came from Italy and the Russian and Austro-Hungarian Empires of central and eastern Europe. The vast majority of them were Catholic. However, hundreds of thousands were Jews, the first major influx of non-Christian immigrants to the United States.

Increasingly "exotic" immigrants and their American-born children constituted a majority in the nation's largest cities—a fact that worried many native-born Americans. Some charged that immigration diluted American society by allowing "inferior" races to outnumber the Anglo-Saxons. New immigrants, wrote Commissioner of Indian Affairs Francis Amasa Walker in 1880, were "beaten men from beaten races."

One immigrant group concerned white Americans more than any other: the Chinese. The first federal legislation designed to discourage immigration was the Page Law of 1875, which was aimed at single Chinese women on the assumption that they were prostitutes. Pressed by nativists in California, Congress passed a more comprehensive law in 1882 that banned further immigration of Chinese laborers. The Chinese Exclusion Act criminalized what had been a normal movement of global labor and stigmatized Chinese Americans as unassimilable—as incapable of ever becoming truly "American."

Urban immigrants were joined by millions of native-born farm boys and girls. Between 1879 and 1920, nearly 11 million Americans moved from rural areas to the burgeoning cities of New York, Chicago, St. Louis, San Francisco, Los Angeles, and Houston. Newcomers and native-born alike streamed into the industrial labor force, which grew even faster than the general population. By century's end, industrial workers constituted more than a third of the American population. Class boundaries increasingly ran along ethnic, religious, and racial lines.

Between 1860 and 1890, America went from a predominantly homogenous nation to one defined as much by difference as by similarity. The United States was largely an agricultural nation through the Civil War, but by 1880 a majority of the American workforce was engaged in nonfarming jobs. Thanks to a host of technological innovations, those who remained on the land farmed on a scale unimaginable a generation earlier. Cities exploded, buoyed by a constant stream of newcomers. In those cities, the outlines of a new American working class—one dominated by immigrants—were already visible.

The Labor Question

What was referred to euphemistically as "the Labor question" was *the* political issue of the late nineteenth century. The political economist Henry George observed in the 1870s, "Work is the producer of all wealth. How does it happen that the working class is always the poorer class?" In the fifty years that followed, this statement lost none of its force.

The juxtaposition of a new industrial class and a growing army of workers raised questions about the relationship between the Republic's economy and its political system. Walt Whitman posed the question starkly: "If the United States, like the countries of the Old World, are also to grow vast crops of poor, desperate, dissatisfied, nomadic, miserably-waged populations, such as we see looming upon us of late years . . . then our republican experiment, notwithstanding all its surface-successes, is at heart an unhealthy failure."

FREE LABOR

In 1870, most industrial workers still subscribed to the free-labor ideology of antebellum America. This system, with its explicit promise of economic upward mobility for those with the character and diligence to earn it, was premised on the idea that wage labor was not a permanent condition. Labor was a means to self-improvement: today's workers were tomorrow's farmers and shopkeepers. As long as the boundary between wage earner and property owner seemed permeable, workers remained confident in their own ability to succeed.

Faith in advancement muted criticism of industrial working conditions. The average workweek in the 1870s was 59 hours, or six 10-hour days. America was the only industrial nation in the world with no workers' compensation program to support workers injured on the job. Predictably, the United States had the highest accident rate in the world. Thousands inhaled toxic gases in fetid coal mines or lint in cotton mills, were burned working with molten steel, and lost fingers and limbs in factories to machines with unguarded moving parts. Between 1890 and 1917, 230,000 railroad employees died on the job, and close to 2 million more were injured. Laws to improve safety conditions were denounced by owners as "class legislation" that favored one group (workers) at the expense of another (employers).

Divided along regional, occupational, ethnic, and linguistic lines, labor was slow to organize. After the Civil War, a group of craft unions, local ethnic associations, and unskilled workers united in the National Labor Union (NLU). The NLU condemned wage labor as enslaving and undemocratic. Calling themselves "masters of their own time," the NLU's 600,000 members devoted themselves to winning the eight-hour day. The NLU's demand for "eight hours for work; eight hours for rest; eight hours for what we will!" announced the determination of the new industrial working class to assert their independence from their employers and bolster their authority as citizens.

The Noble and Holy Order of the Knights of Labor left a more enduring imprint on American labor politics than the NLU. Founded in 1869, the Knights combined the social network of a fraternal order, the labor focus of a trade union, and the reform instinct of a political party. The constitution of the Knights of Labor announced, "We declare an inevitable and irresistible conflict between the wage-system of labor and the republican system of government." After a successful and well-publicized railroad strike in 1885, membership skyrocketed. By 1886, as many as 20 percent of American workers were affiliated with the Knights, united under the motto "An Injury to One Is an Injury to All." The Knights of Labor were active in the South as well as the North, enrolling blacks as well as whites, women as well as men. In the West, however, the Knights were deeply involved in the anti-Chinese movement.

The American Federation of Labor (AFL), founded in 1886, provided an alternative to the Knights' cooperative vision. Led by Samuel Gompers, a cigar-chomping pragmatist from London, the AFL accepted the new economic reality that most workers would be permanent wage earners rather than proprietors. Eschewing the class-conscious language of the Knights, Gompers spoke of "working people" and explained that he wanted workers understood as "real human beings . . . with the same desires and hopes of a better life" as other Americans. Preferring to practice "pure and simple unionism," meaning a narrow focus on wages, hours, and working conditions, the AFL did not run candidates for office. Unlike the Knights, which welcomed unskilled workers, the AFL focused on organizing skilled labor. Gompers positioned union members as "average"—literally in the middle of the social spectrum between an impoverished and potentially dangerous mass below and an unworthy elite above.

RISK MANAGEMENT

Gilded Age America (so dubbed by Mark Twain, for the era's flamboyance and seeming superficiality) was marked by an unprecedented expansion of economic output. The gross national product quadrupled from $9 billion to $37 billion between 1869 and 1901. Steel production increased from 77,000 tons in 1870 to 11,270,000 tons in 1900. Exports surged from $234 million in 1865 to $1.5 billion by 1900. Vast fortunes were made—and lost—overnight.

Celebrants of cutthroat capitalism explained vast divergences in fortune among groups and individuals through what they called Social Darwinism, after English naturalist Charles Darwin. Darwin's transformative 1859 book *On the Origin of Species* argued that the diversity of life on earth had evolved from a common source through a process of natural selection that privileged and perpetuated species that adapted to changes in environment.

Darwin did not use the phrase "survival of the fittest"—that was coined by British philosopher Herbert Spencer, who adapted Darwin's concept to his own thinking on social and economic competition: In a process as natural as cream rising to the top of the milk bottle, those with talent, industry, and perseverance would succeed while others would fail. Whether nations, races, or individuals, those who succeeded would be rewarded with wealth, power, and acclaim. Winners deserved what they got—they earned it. So did losers.

Spencer's ideas resonated with America's entrepreneurs, whose vast and ever-expanding wealth was so unprecedented that a new vocabulary had to be coined to describe them: "tycoons," "Robber Barons," "magnates." In New York City, the number of millionaires increased from a few dozen in 1860 to hundreds by 1865. By 1890, the wealthiest 1 percent of the population had the same total income as the bottom half of the population and owned more property than the remaining 98 percent combined. Scottish-born steel tycoon Andrew Carnegie, who began his career at age 13 in a cotton mill, dedicated a chapter of his autobiography to "Herbert Spencer and His Disciple." The owner of Standard Oil of Ohio, John D. Rockefeller, showcased his own adaptive talents when he combined Spencerian insights with Baptist doctrine and insisted that "the growth of a large business is merely survival of the fittest, the working out of a law of nature and a law of God." Other denominations agreed. "The race is to the strong," pronounced the Episcopal bishop of Massachusetts, who assured rich men, "Godliness is in league with riches." Competition was good; it weeded out the weak and assured the survival of the strong.

Sometimes. But competition could also be destructive. Railroads overbuilt and then undercut each other's freight rates to the point where they were *all* losing money. Fierce competition in the emerging oil industry was creating "a state of chaos," complained Rockefeller.

At the end of the nineteenth century, during the great merger movement that created the trusts and gave antitrust law its name, "socialism" meant an imposed absence of competition, not public ownership. Business fluctuations were understood to be the result of a lack of economic coordination. The key to limiting industrial risk was to eliminate "ruinous" competition through corporate consolidation. Like life or fire insurance, the corporation was designed to manage risk.

FROM STRIFE TO COOPERATION

A corporation is a legally sanctioned fiction that a group of people collectively constitute a single legal entity—a corporation. Like individual citizens, corporations can hold property, sue and be sued, and enter contracts. Unlike citizens, corporations cannot participate in political life by voting, serving on juries, or running for office. Corporations have two chief advantages over other forms of ownership: they ease access to capital by pooling assets, and they distribute risk across multiple shoulders. Centralized managerial control allows for effective negotiation (with labor, suppliers, transportation), administrative efficiency, and industrial integration.

Integration comes in two shapes: vertical and horizontal. Horizontal integration is the merging of competitors into one big company—what people in the nineteenth century called "trusts." Mergers benefit the corporation by limiting competition. Taken to the extreme, they can create a monopoly—a business with so much market share that it need not price its goods or services competitively. Vertical integration combines multiple entities involved in different stages of product creation and delivery to accomplish in one massive corporation what had previously involved the combined efforts of many different businesses. When today's computer companies make everything but their processors, they engage in a form of modified vertical integration.

Rockefeller was the master of both forms of integration. By 1879, Standard Oil controlled over 90 percent of American oil production. A congressional investigative committee found "that the Standard Oil Company brooks no competition; that its settled policy and firm determination is to crush out all who may be rash enough to enter the field against it; that it hesitates at nothing in the accomplishment of this purpose." Portrayed as heartless, Rockefeller was no more ruthless than his competitors. He was more organized, more efficient, more far-sighted. The key to business success in these years was not only individual striving but effective combination. "The incalculable," tutored Rockefeller, "must give way to the rational, strife to cooperation."

Cooperation proceeded apace in the 1880s and 1890s. Trusts proliferated as businesses became aware of their effectiveness. Large companies like American Telegraph and Telephone (AT&T), General Electric, and the American Tobacco Company followed Standard Oil's example and virtually monopolized their respective industries. The bigger the company, the more capable it was of buying its competitors or running them out of business. The bigger it got, the easier it became to set its own prices, unencumbered by competition.

The immense power wielded by the trusts was not lost on small businesses and farmers, consumers and workers, who came to regard the trusts as potent agents of undue power and unfair advantage. Widespread worry about the concentration of economic power led to the passage of the Sherman Antitrust Act in 1890. The act was designed to protect consumers by prohibiting various practices considered to be anticompetitive.

Like industrialists, farmers were exposed to the unpredictability of the market. As American agriculture shifted from subsistence farming to the production of cash crops, farmers were exposed to new risks.

By the 1890s, entire regions farmed a single crop, such as cotton or wheat, which left everyone exposed to fluctuations in market prices. This market was becoming more international, too. American farmers might see high wheat prices owing to a drought in Poland, or low ones caused by a bumper crop in Argentina or Canada.

LABOR POLITICS

Many Americans worried that economic inequality and workplace antagonism would divide the nation's citizens along class lines and spill over into politics. It did. Those who had recently fought a war that eradicated slave labor and the political economy it built understood that politics and economics were part of the same system. Because even noncitizen white men could vote almost everywhere, the potential political power of American workers was always a factor to consider.

By the late nineteenth century, the independent artisan and the skilled industrial worker had all but disappeared. In their place stood deep ranks of unskilled workers, including agricultural laborers, industrial "pick and shovel men," miners, and assembly-line factory workers. In industry after industry, workers with specialized knowledge and skills were replaced with machines that could be operated by unskilled workers, including children. The 1880 census counted more than one million wageworkers under the age of 16. Unskilled workers earned less than half the daily wage of skilled workers. Depending on the state of the economy, between 20 percent and 50 percent of unskilled workers found themselves out of work for three or more months each year.

A new term was coined in 1887 to describe the growing phenomenon of widespread involuntary joblessness: "unemployment." Whereas employers were content to maintain a "reserve army" of labor available to be called up at any time, working-class leaders began to ask if there was a right to work—or if there was at least a right to some hedge against the overwhelming anxiety of providing for oneself and one's family during periods of unemployment.

The decade known as the Great Upheaval was marked by thousands of strikes involving more than a million workers that culminated in a nationwide general strike for the eight-hour day on May 1, 1886. The eight-hour day movement addressed both workers' quality of life and unemployment by spreading jobs around. "Never before has anything of the kind occurred," observed *Banker's Magazine* in 1886. "The strikes now raging are like a huge wave rolling over the land."

In Chicago, a parade of 40,000 for the eight-hour day merged with a strike at the McCormick reaper factory in which four workers were killed by police. A small, mostly German anarchist group called a mass meeting for the following night in Haymarket Square to protest police brutality. As the final speaker concluded on the evening of May 4, a large group of policemen arrived and ordered the crowd to disperse. Suddenly, a bomb of unknown origin exploded among the police, killing one officer and fatally injuring seven others. The police fired into the crowd, killing a half dozen and wounding approximately 100, including 60 of their own officers.

In the first-ever Red Scare in America, Chicago police raided the meeting places of anarchists, socialists, and other labor leaders indiscriminately, detaining hundreds. Eight defendants, seven of whom were anarchists and all but one of whom was German-speaking, stood trial for the bombing in the summer of 1886.

Although testimony showed that six of the eight defendants were not in Haymarket Square when the bomb was thrown, the state insisted that whereas "perhaps none of these men personally threw the bomb, they each and all abetted, encouraged and advised the throwing of it, and are therefore as guilty as the individual who in fact threw it." Exhorted by the state attorney general to hang the defendants and "save our institutions," the jury found all eight defendants guilty of murder, and sentenced seven to death. Of the eight, one committed suicide in jail, three had their sentences commuted in 1893, and four were hanged on November 11, 1886. Two hundred thousand Chicagoans lined the street to witness the funeral procession.

LABOR WARS

In the 1890s, industrial workers waged a series of strikes so brutal on both sides that historians have dubbed them the "labor wars." In eastern Tennessee, coal miners struck to protest the use of convict labor. The militant Western Federation of Miners was born in Coeur d'Alene, Idaho, in a bloody battle with management. The port of New Orleans was closed down by an interracial strike of dock workers. In the context of yet another raging depression resulting in millions of unemployed, labor fought for the right to organize and bargain with bosses collectively through unions for higher wages, better working conditions, shorter hours, and control of the work process.

In the 1870s, steel king Andrew Carnegie wrote that "the right of the workingmen to combine and form trades-unions is not less sacred

than the right of the manufacturer to enter into association and conferences with his fellows." By 1892 he had changed his mind. A strike
at Carnegie's Homestead Mills led by the Amalgamated Association of
Iron and Steel Workers pitted the rights of labor, including the right
to organize, against the rights of private property. Carnegie's manager
Henry Clay Frick employed a "take no hostages" approach to the striking workers, and sicced a large force of private Pinkerton detectives on
them. When the workers fought off the Pinkertons and occupied the
factory, Frick demanded National Guard troops to protect the mills.

The presence of National Guard troops in Homestead raised a question labor and capital encountered often in the 1880s and 1890s: how
far would the state go to protect private property? The answer to this
question depended in good measure on who was running the state,
and which branch of government was involved.

The drafters of the 1890 Sherman Antitrust Act intended the law to
check corporate power. But courts found that labor strikes and boycotts were forms of market restraint, and turned the act against labor.
Under the common law, it had once been a tort—an act that caused
someone harm—for an employer to lure away another employer's
workers. Judges now applied this thinking to labor organizations
that encouraged sympathy strikes, in which workers for Company B
walked off the job in support of the striking workers of Company A.
Courts began to issue injunctions—court orders that forbid specific
actions—against labor organizers. Judge and future president William
Howard Taft explained the difference between a lawful strike, which
was for the "purpose of selling the labor of those engaged in it" for
a good price on good terms, and an illegal boycott, in which other
workers withdrew their labor in solidarity with striking workers in an
effort to induce a third party—the bosses of the striking workers—to
act. Labor leaders who disobeyed injunctions risked contempt charges
and jail.

After four and a half months, the Amalgamated capitulated. The
mills opened in November. The company slashed wages, reinstated the
12-hour day, and fired 500 people associated with the union. Homestead's production tripled and its profits rose tenfold between 1892
and 1900.

Enlightened Selfishness: Reforming Politics and People

In a time of massive social and economic change, Americans questioned the role and purpose of government. There was no returning to

the antebellum world of a federal government that consisted of a small army and a large post office. It was clear to everyone that government *could* do many things. The question was, what *should* it do? What were the practical and constitutional limits to its authority? James G. Blaine, a highly influential Republican senator and perennial presidential contender, wrote in 1884 that "the basis of much that is wisest in legislation" was "enlightened selfishness." Americans spent the last third of the nineteenth century trying to determine the correct balance between those two words.

PATRONAGE POLITICS

Nineteenth-century political parties and their supporters inhabited a world of mutual obligation. Voters turned out for their party in droves. The winning party gained access to thousands of state and federal jobs, and parceled them out to their faithful supporters. Growing federal agencies such as the Pension Bureau and the Post Office employed thousands of men and women. Some government posts, such as the head of the New York Custom House (which collected millions of dollars in duties on imported goods), exercised considerable commercial power. State-level political machines employed thousands of workers in government positions and "get out the vote" organizations, and had operating budgets that rivaled the largest corporations.

Capturing the patronage required winning elections. Political campaigns were funded through a combination of state and federal patronage and assessments levied on officeholders (effectively a tax on those who held patronage positions). Parties were a vital mechanism of government. As British observer Lord James Price explained in 1895, "Party organizations in fact form a second body of political machinery, existing side by side with that of the legally constituted government, and scarcely less complicated. Politics, considered not as the science of government, but as the art of winning elections and securing office, has reached in the United States a development surpassing in elaborateness that of Britain or France."

Political machines were especially powerful in the cities. The machines indoctrinated new immigrants and found them jobs. On Election Day, the machines paid voters' poll taxes, marched them to the polls, distributed premarked ballots, and passed out cigars and whiskey. Supporters of the secret ballot and other electoral reforms considered this sort of reciprocal politics corruption. The parties and their supporters called it loyalty and friendship.

Congress made no sincere effort to reform the patronage system until President Garfield's assassination, when his successor, Chester A. Arthur, insisted on change. No one was better situated for this task than Arthur. A classic product of the spoils system himself, Arthur's cronyism in the 1870s was so overt that President Hayes stripped him of his post as head of the New York Custom House. The reformist 1883 Pendleton Act established a Civil Service Commission, implemented entrance exams for incoming government employees, and prohibited political assessments.

The end of the spoils system of jobs and assessments eroded party loyalty and forced politicians to find alternative sources to fund their campaigns. Federal and state officeholders turned to their "friends" in business. Railroad lawyers, insurance executives, and corporate managers stalked the floor of Congress. By 1888, the Senate was accurately described as a "Millionaire's Club," whose members—elected by state legislatures, not directly by the people—represented various "principalities and powers in business."

Municipal politicians found revenue in city services. The Tammany machine in New York City charged patrolmen upwards of $500 for the privilege of joining the police force. Patrolmen, in turn, levied "taxes" on both legal and illegal businesses. Licensed liquor dealers paid between $5 and $20 a month. Pushcart vendors were charged $60. At a charge of $250 and up, unlicensed saloons paid dearly for the drinks they poured. An 1894 report estimated the annual cost of police "fees" in New York at $7 million.

Such endemic corruption characterized American party politics because the Constitution, which provided for elections, offered no advice about how to conduct them or fund campaigns. Torchlight processions cost money, as did treating voters to rounds of drinks in saloons. Assessing the period, historian Gary Gerstle concludes that "the vulnerability of the American democratic system to graft was chronic and even systemic."

THE BUSINESS OF GOVERNMENT

Money questions arising from the Civil War preoccupied Americans for the final third of the nineteenth century. Like the Confederacy, the Union government financed the war through a combination of currency expansion (literally printing money, known as "greenbacks" for their color), bonds (government debt), taxes, and tariffs (duties) on imported goods. In 1866, Congress resolved to "retire" the greenbacks by buying them with gold coin. The trouble was, greenbacks were a depreciated currency. It took $130 in greenbacks to acquire $100 in gold. Although the dollar bill claimed to be worth one dollar, the market treated it as if it were worth only 77 cents. Rather than buy gold with their greenbacks, debtors used them to pay off their loans. Lenders, understandably, were unenthusiastic about this arrangement.

Postwar Congresses eliminated or lowered many wartime taxes, but held firm on the tariff, which generated most of the revenue necessary to run the government and reduce the national debt. Like taxes, tariffs were a government-mandated redistribution of economic resources — in this case, from consumers to producers. The tariff protected American manufacturers from foreign competition by effectively raising the price of imports. Tariff reduction became the lodestar of progressive politics because it revealed so clearly the ways in which federal economic policies could favor or harm specific regions and interests, and expand or limit the activities of the government.

Before 1873, gold and silver coins circulated alongside the greenbacks and private banknotes. When the market price of silver exceeded its mint price, however, people stopped using silver dollars and melted them instead. The Coinage Act of 1873, which ended the production of silver dollars, reflected this reality. But when rich new silver mines in the West glutted the market and the price of silver fell a few years later, silver producers demanded repeal of what they called the Crime of '73. The Bland-Allison Act of 1878 allowed the Treasury to purchase limited quantities of silver and produce silver coins once again. Congress overrode Republican president Benjamin Harrison's veto.

Silver promised to make a capitalist economy that seemed rigged in the interest of manufacturing and finance through the tariff more equitable. Farmers and workers joined in the chorus for "free silver" (the free supply of silver coins) because they understood that it would increase the money supply, and therefore lower the real burden of their debts — which, after all, were inflated because of protective tariffs. They were taken aback by the fervent opposition to free silver by business and manufacturing interests, and their representatives in government.

The silver question was only one facet of a broader debate about the role and responsibility of government. To what extent, if any, could government, whether state or federal, attempt to manage the economy? To what ends? "There should be some things to which the whole people of the United States shall accustom themselves to look to the General Government as a benefactor," insisted Republican senator George F. Hoar of Massachusetts. Democrats disagreed, arguing instead that government aid was paternalistic and tempted the people to a "pitiful calculation of the sordid gain to be derived from their Government's maintenance."

FARMERS

The currency issue was relevant to everyone, but was especially important to farmers. Collectively, farmers produced more goods, paid more taxes, and cast more votes than any other group of Gilded Age Americans. Yet their voices seemed to go unheard in Washington, and they felt exploited and abused by business at every level. This was particularly the case when it came to transporting, storing, and selling their crops. Cotton and grain farmers in the South and Midwest were perennially at the mercy of railroads and commodity storage and exchange systems, which often monopolized routes and set their own prices. "We have three crops," lamented a Nebraskan, "corn, freight rates, and interest. The farmers farm the land, and the businessmen farm the farmers."

Like workers, farmers with little bargaining power as individuals banded together. The Patrons of Husbandry, or the Grange, peaked in the 1870s with 1.5 million members. To increase the bargaining power of its members, the Grange established its own warehouses, cotton gins, and grain elevators in an effort to encourage collective buying and selling. The Granger Laws, a series of laws passed at the state level, asserted the right of government to regulate grain elevators and railroad rates.

In *Munn v. Illinois* (1877), the Supreme Court of the United States ruled 7–2 that the state of Illinois could constitutionally regulate a private business in the public interest. When one "devotes his property to a use in which the public has an interest," the court declared, "he, in effect, grants to the public an interest in that use, and must submit to be controlled by the public for the common good." Because both grain elevators and railroads constituted virtual monopolies, they were vulnerable to regulation by the people. *Munn v. Illinois* opened the door to state regulation of the boundary between private interest and public good on economic matters.

Congress has the power to regulate commerce among the states. In

1887, Congress passed the Interstate Commerce Act and created the first independent regulatory agency, the Interstate Commerce Commission (ICC), to ensure that railroad rates were "reasonable and just." The act prohibited discriminatory pricing mechanisms, required that railroads both publish and honor their rates, and forced the railways to submit their account books (what historian Richard White considers "one of the nineteenth century's great fictional genres") to annual financial reporting. The law lacked teeth, however, which suited the railroad companies just fine. "It satisfies the public clamor for a government supervision of railroads," wrote corporate lawyer Richard Olney, "at the same time that the supervision is almost entirely nominal."

The Farmers' Alliance, which succeeded the Grange, continued to ask questions about how to fund government and about the role of government in regulating commerce. In the 1890s, the federal government had two main sources of funding: the tariff and the liquor tax. In 1894, farmers tired of subsidizing the government through the tariff succeeded in pushing the first-ever federal income tax through Congress. The Supreme Court nullified it a year later. The majority opinion called the law a "communistic" assault on property. In an impassioned dissent, Justice Henry Billings Brown characterized the court's decision as "nothing less than the surrender of the taxing power to the moneyed class."

THE FARMERS' ALLIANCE

By 1890, the Alliance movement had outposts from California to New York. The 1.5 million members of the Alliance—at least one-quarter of whom were women—were joined by an affiliated Colored Farmers' Alliance with over a million members. The slogan of the Southern Alliance captured the essence of the movement: "Equal rights to all, special privileges to none." A chief goal was to free working Americans, including farmers, from a demeaning dependence on those who otherwise controlled the economy.

Organizing agricultural workers was daunting. The Farmers' Alliance spread its message through traveling lecturers and sympathetic newspapers. Alliance organizers were most successful in places, such as Texas, that had experienced rapid population growth in the 1870s and 1880s with the advent of commercial agriculture. Landowners (as opposed to agricultural wage workers and sharecroppers) dominated the order and set its agenda.

In 1890, Alliance members met in Ocala, Florida, and issued the Ocala Demands. The farmers' manifesto expressed deep distrust of "the money power"—banks and corporations whose financial power allowed them to manipulate a supposedly "free" market. As Mary Lease lectured across Kansas, "Wall Street owns the country. It is no longer a government of the people, by the people and for the people, but a government of Wall Street, by Wall Street and for Wall Street." Alliance members called on government to even the economic playing field and reduce tariffs on imported merchandise, regulate railroad rates, and expand the currency supply through bimetallism (silver). In addition, the platform called for a federal income tax to support the functions of government, and popular election of US senators.

In 1891, delegates from the many Alliances, the Knights of Labor, the AFL, and other reform groups (100 of them African American) met in St. Louis to discuss forming a third national political party. In the presidential election year of 1892, more than a thousand like-minded delegates met in Omaha, Nebraska, to form the independent People's Party. Representing the "producing classes" of small farmers and wage laborers, the Populists, as they were known, denounced a nation "brought to the verge of moral, political, and material ruin" by economic inequality and political corruption, and announced that "the fruits of the toil of millions are boldly stolen to build up colossal fortunes for a few, unprecedented in the history of mankind."

The Omaha platform proposed a coherent program of far-reaching economic change through government action. Declaring that the time had come "when the railroad corporation will either own the people or the people must own the railroads," the party called for public ownership of transportation (railroads) and communication (telegraphs). The Populists demanded a flexible national currency and banking system that favored the credit needs of producers, a graduated federal income tax, postal savings accounts, the popular initiative and referendum, popular election of US senators, and opposition to "any subsidy or national aid to any private corporation for any purpose." The Populists' proposed Subtreasury Plan was a national system of farm credit, warehousing, and marketing with a confusing name.

The Populist manifesto pit collective ownership and control against private ownership of vital sectors of the economy having to do with exchange, especially money and transportation. More noteworthy than any of its specific proposals was its insistence on government responsibility for the economic well-being of the nation, and the need to establish reliable democratic controls over corporate capitalism. Populists were not backward-looking—far from it. Their grasp of the interlocking nature of democratic politics and government regulation of the economy was as far-seeing as it was unprecedented.

Upheavals

ORGANIZED WOMEN

The Fourteenth Amendment (1868) required a reduction in representation in Congress for any state that denied the right to vote to any of its *male* citizens. This left womanhood the primary marker of disenfranchisement in the United States. Supporters of woman suffrage adopted two very different approaches to address this problem. The American Woman Suffrage Association (AWSA), led by Bostonians Lucy Stone and Henry Blackwell, formulated a race-based "Southern strategy" designed to allow white women access to the polls while denying it to black women. The National Woman's Suffrage Association (NWSA), led by Elizabeth Cady Stanton and Susan B. Anthony, made the case for female enfranchisement through the language of male despotism. Turning to familiar republican language about caste, Stanton and Anthony argued that the white man's democracy of the antebellum years had been replaced by "an aristocracy of sex." Stanton was not above making racist and nativist arguments—why should a black man or an Irish immigrant vote when noble Anglo-Saxon American women such as she could not? Her main argument, however, was that democracy should not exclude women.

Woman suffrage got nowhere during the 1870s, especially after the Supreme Court held in *Minor v. Happersett* (1875) that women's rights as citizens did not include the right to vote. In *Bradwell v. Illinois* (1873), the court upheld the notion of coverture, in which "a woman had no legal existence separate from her husband, who was regarded as her head and representative in the social state." Elizabeth Cady Stanton, married and the mother of seven, was livid: "In crowning all men with this dignity, denying it to all women, we have established here the most odious form of aristocracy the world has ever seen—an aristocracy of sex . . . that exalts . . . the son above the mother who bore him."

With woman suffrage stymied, temperance became the main vehicle for women's rights. Dating back to the 1820s, the temperance movement was always associated with women's rights, because the campaign against alcohol was designed to protect women and children from abusive male power. Focused initially on changing individual behavior, by the mid-1870s the movement aimed to abolish the liquor trade. The Woman's Christian Temperance Union (WCTU), founded in 1874, was the most powerful women's organization in the country. The WCTU was led by Frances Willard, the first Dean of Women at Northwestern University. Happily unmarried, Willard was a staunch woman suffragist. "If we are ever to save the State," she declared, "we must enfranchise the sex. . . . Give us the vote, in order that we may help in purifying politics."

"Purifying politics" was a far cry from liberating womankind from the tyranny of men. The WCTU did not challenge male authority. Instead, it concentrated on changing men—the source of so many of women's problems—by teaching them to honor and respect women. The organization's agenda went far beyond shutting down the liquor trade and the other vices that found a home in saloons: gambling, tobacco, and prostitution. WCTU women wanted to abolish the "white slave trade" (sexual trafficking), eradicate venereal disease, and encourage men to share power and resources with their wives. "It is her income as well as yours," the organization lectured, and urged husbands not to drink away the family's resources. In the hands of the WCTU, temperance and woman suffrage were designed to make women better mothers. The WCTU, concludes historian Christine Stansell, made suffrage safe.

By 1890, Christian redemption replaced the Constitution as the centerpiece of the suffrage campaign. While appealing in many ways to many people, this politics of redeemed women and unredeemed men was easily adaptable to antidemocratic uses. It could be turned against racial, ethnic, and religious minorities ("backward" peoples, "inferior" civilizations). And even as the WCTU scorned male weakness and depravity and celebrated female moral superiority, it left unchallenged the legal and economic bases of male privilege. The focus on motherhood as the central value of the women's movement perpetuated the "sentimental nonsense" (in Stanton's words) that women were "above men, celestial, ethereal."

ONWARD CHRISTIAN SOLDIERS

A financial panic in 1893 stimulated by a European business contraction and poor harvests led to a banking panic in the United States. When the banks called in the loans to overextended railroads, more than 70 railroads fell into bankruptcy. By 1894, more than four million jobs had been lost. Nearly 25 percent of American workers were unemployed by 1894. Soup kitchens sprang up in cities, and homeless families slept in the streets.

As the railroads convulsed in 1894, a wealthy Ohio businessman named Jacob Coxey led a cross-country march of unemployed men to the steps of the US Capitol to demand public works and an eight-hour day. The march produced no concrete change, but it helped draw attention to unemployment. Coxey was arrested for walking on the grass.

The official name of Coxey's Army was the Army of the Commonweal in Christ, which reflects an important truth about the ways Americans responded to the class polarization of the 1880s and 1890s. Many churchgoing Christians found it hard to square their religion, with its condemnation of avarice and selfishness and its egalitarian inclinations, with what they saw happening around them. Civic action offered a way to ease Christian consciences strained by the realities of poverty and injustice. By the late 1880s, many devout Protestants like Jacob Coxey believed that to inherit the Kingdom of God they must first improve their own world.

Adherents of what was eventually dubbed the Social Gospel movement advocated a government of Christian decency, with the Golden Rule ("Do unto others as you would have them do unto you") supplemented by Jesus's repeated command to care for the poor and vulnerable. The two most prominent exponents of the Social Gospel, ministers Washington Gladden and Walter Rauschenbusch, endorsed workers' rights and exhorted Christians to combat social injustice. For them, salvation was not purely an individual matter but was achieved in part by striving to construct a just society through collective action at the level of government. They were joined in 1891 by Pope Leo XIII, whose encyclical "Rights and Duties of Capital and Labour" criticized greed, endorsed workers' right to unionize, and urged governments to care for the poor.

As the pope's encyclical suggests, the labor question transcended national boundaries in the new age of global capital. At the end of the century, a new form of transnational politics based on the social landscapes carved by industrial capitalism developed on both sides of the Atlantic. A new vocabulary evolved around the term "social": the social question, the social problem, social politics, and, most pressingly in the context of ongoing strife between labor and management, social peace.

Creating social peace meant understanding the links between economic and political power and building a state in which, as the Republican governor of New York Theodore Roosevelt put it, "Property shall be the servant and not the master of the commonwealth." Utopian novelist Edward Bellamy's 1887 best-selling book *Looking Backward* imagined this world through the eyes of a wealthy Bostonian who falls asleep during the class conflict of the Gilded Age and awakens in the year 2000 to an America of communal property, plenty, cooperation, and full employment. Bellamy was no more a communist than Theodore Roosevelt; his future Americans were moved by nationalism, patriotism, and altruism, not class-consciousness. But like the "marching petition" represented by Coxey's Army, Bellamy connected economic and political power and the health of the republic, and asserted a role for the government in each.

PULLMAN

The labor wars of the nineteenth century culminated in a national boycott in support of striking workers against the Pullman Palace Car Company in 1894. This epic insurgence paralyzed the economies of 27 states and territories, pitted the United States Army against the American Railway Union, and generated the most destructive civil violence since Reconstruction.

In the 1860s, George Pullman developed a patented railroad car that incorporated pulldown platforms with mattresses. This luxurious "hotel room on rails" was an immediate hit with long-distance travelers and established for Pullman a virtual monopoly on sleeping cars. By the early 1890s, the company was worth over $36 million and had weathered economic ups and downs sufficiently to pay robust dividends to stockholders for over 20 years.

In 1881, Pullman built a state-of-the-art factory and planned community outside Chicago. The company town was designed to create an environment conducive to steady work, good morals, and industrial peace. The streets of Pullman were smooth and shaded. The homes, which could be rented but not purchased by workers, were a pleasing diversity of architectural style, with indoor plumbing and electricity. The town had a school, a public square, a market, and a library with plush upholstered chairs and books chosen carefully by George Pullman. Rents were higher in Pullman than in surrounding towns. Employees were not required to live there—but George Pullman was not required to state a reason for firing anyone, either.

In the midst of the worldwide economic depression of 1893, George Pullman laid off more than half his workforce of 5,800 employees, and cut wages by 25–40 percent. He did not, however, lower rents in Pullman, cut corporate salaries, or reduce stockholders' dividends. When Pullman refused to negotiate with a workers' grievance committee, the company town staged a walkout on May 11, 1894.

Pullman workers who had joined the American Railway Union (ARU) turned to its leader, the charismatic Eugene V. Debs. To support the Pullman workers, the ARU refused to run trains that included the ubiquitous Pullman Palace cars, shutting down railroads across the Midwest. Federal judges issued injunctions from coast to coast against the railroad strike. Debs shrugged them off and wired a supporter, "It will take more than injunctions to move trains." Declaring that "we have been brought to the ragged edge of anarchy," US attorney general (and influential railroad lawyer) Richard A. Olney advised President Grover Cleveland to send federal troops to Chicago. Olney also advised against informing the governor of Illinois and the mayor of Chicago, both of whom sympathized with the strikers. An outraged Governor John P. Altgeld learned of the troops only after their arrival in Chicago.

Under the pretense of upholding the federal obligation to deliver mail, which traveled by train, President Cleveland ordered US Army troops fresh from fighting Indians to break the strike in Chicago. What had been a largely peaceful strike turned violent within a day. Mobs tipped and set fire to railroad cars. The military responded with bayonets, cavalry charges, and, finally, guns. *Harper's Weekly* warned that in defeating the nationwide strike, the nation was "fighting for its own existence just as truly as in suppressing the great [Confederate] rebellion." The *New York Times* had a different take. The Pullman strike and boycott, the *Times* told its readers, was "in reality . . . a struggle between the greatest and most important labor organization and the entire railroad capital." Chicago reformer Jane Addams agreed with the *Times*, and wondered at the speed with which "the ugliness of the industrial situation" was revealed.

THE GREAT COMMONER

Prosperity was still out of view as Americans prepared to elect a new president in 1896. Neither the Republicans nor the Democrats could ignore the threat of the People's Party, which was poised to siphon off significant numbers of votes from both of the major parties. Silver was the dividing issue, with large numbers of people adamant that the free coinage of silver was the key to restoring prosperity, while others were equally certain that only fidelity to the gold standard would guarantee the future.

Arguments about currency were stand-ins for broader disagreements about economic policy, especially monetary policy and government regulation of business. The Democrats were in open rebellion against their incumbent president, Grover Cleveland. The Republicans looked forward to recapturing the White House. Their nominee, William McKinley, was a former congressman from Ohio popular with business interests and industrial workers for his support of a high protective tariff. He was also a solid gold man, which alienated western silver Republicans, who walked out of the GOP convention. Aided by his brilliant campaign manager, Marcus (Mark) Alonzo Hanna, a wealthy Ohio businessman, McKinley promised Americans social harmony and "a full dinner pail," and hinted darkly that jobs would disappear if the Democrats were returned to power.

The divided Democrats floundered until southern and western delegates came together at the convention to nominate the 36-year-old former Nebraska congressman and outspoken silverite William Jennings Bryan. An unabashedly Christian man, Bryan's speech to the delegates in Chicago is famous for its finale, in which he declared that the Democrats represented "the producing masses of the nation," as opposed to the Republican's business elite, and declared that the people would answer the GOP's demand for a gold standard by saying to them: "You shall not press down upon the brow of labor this crown of thorns, you shall not crucify mankind on a cross of gold."

The "cross of gold" crescendo was first-rate political theater, but it did not represent the substance of Bryan's message to the Democratic delegates. This was contained in his meditation on the role of government in regulating the economy in the interest of the people ("the cause of humanity") rather than in the interest of the elite. "There are two ideas of government," he told the Chicago convention. "There are those who believe that, if you will only legislate to make the well-to-do prosperous, their prosperity will leak through on those below. The Democratic idea, however, has been that if you legislate to make the masses prosperous, their prosperity will find its way up through every class which rests upon them." For Bryan, the truly democratic government—the truly Christian government—wrote laws that protected the interests of the masses against the prosperous, powerful few.

THE ELECTION OF 1896

Bryan's nomination posed a quandary for the Populists. Should they "fuse" with the Democrats and support Bryan? Or should they nominate their own third-party candidate and run the risk of a McKinley victory? In the end, they threw in their chips with Bryan—but many mourned that they had doomed their party, and their principles, in the bargain.

Bryan's convention speech electrified the Democratic masses and terrified the Republican elite, who, prodded by Hanna, poured unprecedented amounts of money into GOP campaign coffers. In the pre–Pendleton Act era, all Democratic officeholders would have paid an assessment to subsidize Democratic nominees. In the new world of private political contributions, Hanna raised more than ten times the amount of campaign funds available to Bryan. Most of this was spent on campaign literature and to send forth thousands of speakers to sing McKinley's praises. McKinley himself remained sedately, one might say presidentially, on his front porch in Canton, Ohio, where he chatted with small groups of voters handpicked by Hanna.

Bryan, meanwhile, stormed the country, regaling hundreds of thousands with homely stories from his rural youth. Known ever after as "the Great Commoner" for his expansive faith in the plain people, Bryan was unrivaled as an orator and had an unerring capacity to articulate political issues in ways that connected with ordinary Americans. For example, here is how Bryan explained the need for a regulatory state to a Labor Day crowd of 150,000 in Chicago: In Iowa recently, recalled the candidate, he had seen "a number of hogs rooting in a field and tearing up the ground." This reminded him of how, as a boy, he had kept the family's hogs tethered so that they would not destroy the land. "And then it occurred to me," he continued, "that one of the most important duties of government is to put rings in the noses of hogs. . . . We submit to restraint upon ourselves"—through laws—"in order that others may be restrained from injuring us."

The hogs were not amused. Outspent by an energized and unusually united GOP, Bryan lost to McKinley by 500,000 votes out of an estimated 14 million cast. The Republicans were solidly in power and, with the exception of Woodrow Wilson's two terms between 1912 and 1920, would remain in control of the federal government for the next 36 years.

The election of 1896, in which nearly 80 percent of eligible voters cast a ballot, concluded an era of closely contested national elections and divided government. The People's Party, and with it agrarian politics, was mortally wounded. William Jennings Bryan, however, was just getting started. To some, Kansas journalist William Allen White recalled, Bryan seemed "the incarnation of demagogy." But the *demos*—the people—were grateful. White acknowledged, "It was the first time in my life and in the life of a generation in which any man large enough to lead a national party had boldly and unashamedly made his cause that of the poor and the oppressed." Of more lasting structural importance, Bryan shed his party's legacy of considering federal power always and everywhere a threat to the liberty of the people. Bryan would never be president, but he made an eloquent case for the regulatory state as the only entity strong enough to create the conditions for business prosperity while still, as he would have put it, tethering the swine.

Race and Equality in the Turn-of-the-Century South

At the 1893 World's Columbian Exhibition in Chicago, Ida B. Wells, a young African American journalist, teamed up with the venerable abolitionist Frederick Douglass to author a pamphlet titled *The Reason Why the Colored American Is Not in the World's Columbian Exposition*. The pamphlet documented the extent of American racism and explained that the fair's organizers had refused to include African Americans in the US exhibits. Douglass, who had been ambassador to Haiti and now served as the island nation's representative to the fair, delivered a blistering speech from the portico of the Haitian Building. When white hecklers interrupted him, Douglass turned his steely eyes upon them: "Men talk of the Negro problem. There is no Negro problem. The problem is whether the American people have loyalty enough, honor enough, patriotism enough, to live up to their own constitution." White southerners were already failing the test.

WRESTLING WITH THE FOURTEENTH AMENDMENT

The Civil War settled the question of whether a state could secede from the Union, and the Thirteenth Amendment ended slavery. But the critical question of whether individual citizens had any federal constitutional rights against the states remained unsettled. Prior to the Civil War, the Constitution guaranteed individual rights only against the federal government. This was, indeed, an essential element of the original constitutional compromise. After the Civil War, however, the Fourteenth Amendment (1868) expressly defined national citizenship and prohibited any state to deprive any person of "life, liberty or property without due process of law," to deny any citizen the "privileges and immunities" of citizenship, or to deny any person "the equal protection of the laws." Section 5 of the amendment authorized Congress to enforce these guarantees through "appropriate legislation." The Fourteenth Amendment therefore clearly altered the balance of power and responsibility between the states and the federal government. The question was, how much?

In the 15 years after the enactment of the Fourteenth Amendment, the Supreme Court interpreted its guarantees in a way that sharply limited its potential effect. In the *Slaughter-House Cases* (1873), the court, in a bitterly divided 5–4 decision, defined the "privileges and immunities" of citizenship that were guaranteed by the Fourteenth Amendment against state infringement in a way that rendered the clause almost meaningless. According to Justice Samuel Miller, who wrote the majority opinion, the phrase did not include such fundamental rights as freedom of speech, freedom of religion, freedom from cruel and unusual punishment, and freedom from unreasonable search and seizure, but only a small set of rights connected directly to *national* citizenship, such as the right to travel from one state to another or to be protected on the high seas. The justices also suggested that the Fourteenth Amendment was designed primarily to protect the rights of former slaves, and therefore it could not be invoked by other citizens. In a powerful dissent, Justice Stephen Field accused the majority of having illegitimately rendered the Fourteenth Amendment a "vain and idle enactment."

Two years later, Congress enacted the Civil Rights Act of 1875, which prohibited private individuals from discriminating against African Americans on the basis of race in public accommodations, such as inns, restaurants, and theaters. In the *Civil Rights Cases* (1883), the Supreme Court ruled the act unconstitutional. The Fourteenth Amendment, said the court, did not itself prohibit discrimination against African Americans by private individuals, and it did not authorize Congress to enact legislation prohibiting such private discrimination. Rather, the majority concluded, the amendment was directed only against discrimination by the *states* themselves. Thus, the federal government had no constitutional authority to prohibit a private restaurant owner or innkeeper from refusing to serve blacks. The most it could do was to prohibit the states themselves from discriminating on the basis of race.

The state action doctrine enunciated in the *Civil Rights Cases* effectively prevented the federal government from prohibiting private racial discrimination and therefore allowed "local custom" to continue unmolested. The decision was emphatically denounced by proponents of racial equality, who argued that there was no principled distinction between racial discrimination by the state and racial discrimination by private individuals, especially in those domains in which the government routinely licensed and regulated private businesses, such as restaurants, theaters, and public transportation. Together, the *Slaughter-House Cases* and *Civil Rights Cases* sharply limited the potential impact of the Fourteenth Amendment.

THE POLITICS OF WHITE SUPREMACY

Politics in the post–Civil War era was exceptionally fluid across the nation, but particularly in the South, where newly enfranchised black men shook up the party system. After 1877, with the Republican Party in retreat throughout the South, black voters there had two options: accede to Democratic plans to marginalize them politically, or form interracial alliances ("fuse") with the few remaining white Republicans and a larger group of disenchanted white Democrats.

What united black and white voters in the postwar South? Like the Populists who succeeded them, interracial coalitions in the 1880s stressed the benefits of popular democracy and an active government that provided important services such as public education. Threatened by interracial third parties, southern Democrats appropriated their platforms and crushed them with violence and election fraud. At the same time, Democrats looked for more legitimate ways to squelch the competition. As one Mississippi newspaper observed, "There must be devised some legal defensible substitute for the abhorrent and evil methods on which white supremacy lies."

Outside of the Fifteenth Amendment's prohibition of voter limitations based on race, color, or previous condition of servitude, states can define their electorates for themselves. Between 1890 and 1908, all 11 states of the former Confederacy rewrote their constitutions to eliminate the votes of black men and those white men misguided enough to support African American political power. The electorate was slashed by literacy tests, complicated registration procedures, multiple ballot boxes, racially restricted primary elections (white primaries), poll taxes, and "understanding clauses" designed to protect the votes of illiterate whites capable of offering a "reasonable understanding" of the state constitution. In 1898, the Supreme Court ruled in *Williams v. Mississippi* that poll taxes and literacy tests did not violate the Fifteenth Amendment, because they applied to whites as well as blacks.

In the 1880s, more than two-thirds of adult southern men voted. That proportion rose to nearly three-quarters in the 1890s in states that had not yet limited the franchise. By the early 1900s, fewer than one man in three, white or black, voted in the South.

The consequences of disenfranchisement were catastrophic. Although the South as a whole suffered from an uncompetitive party system, African Americans paid the greatest price. If black men could not vote, they could not be elected to office. If they could not be elected to office, they could not shape or administer the laws that governed them. In 1873, 64 African Americans sat in Mississippi's state legislature; none served after 1895.

African Americans divided over the white supremacist campaigns of the late nineteenth century. Some educated middle-class black southerners suggested that limiting suffrage to the literate might not be such a bad idea. The most influential black man in America, Booker T. Washington—a former slave and the founder of the Tuskegee Institute, a vocational school in Alabama—implied in an 1895 speech in Atlanta that African Americans should leave politics to white men and focus instead on economic advancement. Suffrage was only one avenue to power, said Washington; labor that resulted in savings, he explained, amounted to "a little green ballot" that "no one will throw out or refuse to count." Dubbed the Atlanta Compromise by more radical African Americans, Washington's position was later ridiculed by northern black scholar and activist W. E. B. Du Bois, who remarked acidly that "the way for a people to gain their reasonable rights is not by voluntarily throwing them away and insisting that they do not want them."

MAKING JIM CROW

In 1890, the Louisiana state legislature passed a law requiring "equal but separate" railway cars for black and white passengers. Railroads resisted the separate car law on economic grounds (separate cars meant more cars and trouble for the conductors). African Americans insisted that the law violated the Thirteenth and Fourteenth Amendments by establishing an "insidious distinction and discrimination between citizens of the United States, based on race." In an 1892 test case initiated by the New Orleans Citizens' Committee for the Annulment of the Separate Car Act, Homer Plessy, a mixed-race man who was to all appearances white, violated the law by riding in a coach set aside for whites.

In *Plessy v. Ferguson* (1896), the Supreme Court, in an 8–1 decision, upheld the constitutionality of the Louisiana law. Segregation did not treat blacks unequally or even differently than it treated whites: blacks had "black" cars and whites had "white" cars, which were, theoretically, the same. In a key passage, the court explained: "We consider the underlying fallacy of the plaintiff's argument to consist in the assumption that the enforced separation of the two races stamps the colored race with a badge of inferiority. If this be so, it is not by reason of anything found in the act, but solely because the colored race chooses to put that construction upon it."

With the Supreme Court's blessing, southern states and municipalities enacted a proliferation of laws separating blacks and whites in nearly every aspect of life. Blacks and whites were required by law to drink from different water pails, use separate toilets, and walk through separate entrances and exits. They were nursed in separate hospitals, educated in separate schools, buried in separate cemeteries, and forbidden to marry each other in the majority of American states. Jim Crow's power over African Americans came not only from segregation, however, but also from exclusion: exclusion from voting booths, juries, neighborhoods, unions, higher education, restaurants, theaters, hotels, and the professions. Racial hierarchy was backed up by white economic and political control and secured through the power of the state.

For segregation to work, laws racially categorizing people had to exist. State laws varied and were revised repeatedly. Depending on the state and the decade, people who were more than 1/4 black, or 1/8 black, or 1/16 black, or even 1/32 black, were categorized for the purpose of Jim Crow as "nonwhite." Bureaus of Vital Statistics registered births, marriages, and deaths, and classified and cross-checked people according to race. Yet even as the color line solidified, it became more porous. Untold numbers of light-skinned blacks migrated across the country and across racial boundaries — they "passed" for white. Many other southerners either challenged or defended their racial identity in court, which forced the judiciary to police the color line.

The deep discrimination of the Jim Crow order was marked through the practice of segregation, but it went deeper than that. As Justice John Marshall Harlan, the lone dissenter in *Plessy* argued, segregation was a "badge of servitude," a marker of inequality. A landmark in the history of Jim Crow, the *Plessy* decision embraced the reasoning of white supremacy and haunted efforts on behalf of racial equality for the next 75 years. Jim Crow laws were an essential element of white supremacist consolidation of political power at the end of the nineteenth century. By 1900, white supremacy and racial purity had become articles of civic faith.

THE NEW SOUTH

The architects of the Jim Crow South called their creation the New South, which in their eyes was a South bursting with entrepreneurial energy, abundant natural resources, and cheap labor, primed for northern industrial investment. According to the author of *How to Get Rich in the South*, the region abounded in "tempting inducements to the capitalist for profitable investments."

Although still rooted in agriculture, the southern economy diversified after the Civil War. To encourage industry, southern state legislatures kept taxes low and provided few public services. Those they did provide, such as public schools, were underfunded, racially segregated, and wholly unequal. Draconian penalties for petty crimes, such as theft and vagrancy, combined with racially discriminatory law enforcement, resulted in inflated, and disproportionately black, prison populations in every southern state. Mines, railroads, and lumber companies leased large numbers of convict laborers and housed them in primitive camps that were hotbeds of disease. The availability of cheap prison labor kept the wages of white workers artificially low, which contributed to the overall poverty of the region. In 1900, southern per capita income stood at a mere 60 percent of the national average.

The New South was also characterized by a sickening rise in mob violence directed at African Americans. Between 1882 and 1946, white southern mobs murdered 4,715 black men, women, and children. Composed of respectable citizens as well as the rabble, defended in the press and frequently in the pulpit, lynch mobs acted without fear of punishment. Local sheriffs colluded with the mobs and released black prisoners to them. White grand juries refused to indict anyone, insisting that lynching victims "died at the hands of persons unknown." Impervious to outside criticism, the white southern establishment considered lynching a regrettable but necessary evil.

Although there were broader social and political goals to lynching, the primary rhetorical justification for white mob violence was the supposed need to protect white women from allegedly predatory black men who, no longer governed by whites, were "regressing" as a race and indulging their base "primal instincts." This rationale persisted despite the pioneering work of black journalist Ida B. Wells, who demonstrated that not even a third of black men lynched had been *accused* of rape. Instead, Wells linked white violence to fear of black economic and political advancement.

Mob violence embarrassed elite southern whites, who argued that if interactions between blacks and whites resulted in such horrors, the only logical solution was to limit still further the contact between the races. In tacit recognition of the political nature of mob violence, white southerners justified the segregation by race of streetcars and other public spaces as necessary to establish "public peace and good order" in the South. Others stressed more sinister reasons for both lynching and segregation. In a 1902 article in the *Atlantic Monthly* describing a black man who had been burned at the stake, a professor at Emory College in Atlanta observed that the purpose of such "savagery" was to "teach the negro the lesson of abject and eternal servility," to "burn into his quivering flesh the consciousness that he has not, cannot have, the rights of a free citizen or even of a fellow human creature."

*

In 1886, political economist and philosopher Henry George reflected on the state of the Union: "We plow new fields, we open new mines, we found new cities, we girdle the land with iron roads and lace the air with telegraph wires; we add knowledge to knowledge and utilize invention after invention." Yet despite this progress, he declared, "it becomes no easier for the masses of our people to make a living. On the contrary, it is becoming harder." All the transformations of mechanization and mass production had broadened rather than narrowed the gulf between the employed and the employer. "Social contrasts," George observed, "are becoming sharper; as liveried carriages appear, so do barefooted children."

Henry George was not alone in this observation. As the United States approached the line of the new century, many leaders worried about the paradox of immiseration amid massive production. In his opinion in an 1895 antitrust case, Supreme Court Justice John Marshall Harlan worried about avarice. "Combination governed entirely by the law of greed," Harlan pronounced, "threatens the integrity of our institutions." If Harlan was right, what should government do? What *could* it do? What was the relationship between the state and the economy?

PUTTING THE SCREWS ON HIM.

FIGURE 2. *Putting the Screws on Him*, by Udo J. Keppler, published by J. Ottmann Lith. Co., in *Puck*, November 2, 1904. Prints and Photographs Division, Library of Congress, Washington, DC, LCCN 2011645581. Theodore Roosevelt Digital Library, Dickinson State University, http://www.theodorerooseveltcenter.org/Research /Digital-Library/Record.aspx?libID=0277869.

CHAPTER 2

Interconnected, 1898–1914

City health officers found the children wracked with fever, headache, and severe back pain, vomiting, and covered with telltale lesions. The officers quickly removed the patients and searched All Nations Block for more victims. The most thickly populated block in the most concentrated city in the United States, All Nations Block was a short walk from Manhattan's fashionable Central Park West neighborhood. A rough conglomeration of Irish, Italian, German, Austrian, Jewish, Swedish, and African American day laborers, domestic servants, seamstresses, bootblacks, and waiters packed into tenements, the block was a perfect petri dish for disease.

New Yorkers would remember Thanksgiving 1900 as the beginning of the city's first smallpox epidemic of the twentieth century. Smallpox was already epidemic in the American South, where it had spread quickly among workers in coal mines, railroad camps, and crowded and unhygienic urban neighborhoods in New South cities like Atlanta. With an incubation period of approximately two weeks, during which time the infected person remained asymptomatic but contagious, smallpox, like so many viral vagrants, hopped the boxcars of industrializing America and traveled far and wide, from western mining camps to immigrant districts in the urban East, from Washington, DC, to America's new imperial outposts in Puerto Rico, Hawai'i, and the Philippines. No class, race, or region was untouched.

The new mobility of American life made quarantine—the public health solution of previous centuries—implausible. As the *New York Times* explained, smallpox could no longer be confined to poor neighborhoods like All Nations Block: "Public conveyances and places of public assembly bring all classes together to such an extent that only the recluse can feel quite safe, and not even the recluse if ministered to by servants who visit friends in the infected districts."

This recognition of what historian Michael Willrich calls the "inescapable interdependence of modern urban life" instigated a wave of turn-of-the-century reform measures to protect the public health. In the South, black and white women driven by "the democracy of the microbe" worked together to improve sanitation in otherwise neglected African American neighborhoods in order to eliminate flies, which transmitted typhoid and acknowledged no color line. Everywhere, reformers urged vaccination against smallpox as the only reliable preventative measure against this ancient scourge.

Appealing to a sense of community, civic obligation, and enlightened common sense, advocates of universal vaccination maintained that individual liberty was subordinate to the collective interests of society. Vaccination "is not only a wise measure of personal precaution," argued the *Times*. "It is a public duty which every citizen owes to those with whom he comes in daily contact." Rather than rely on voluntary vaccination, the *Times* endorsed compulsory vaccination of everyone by public authorities.

Americans responded with a range of reactions, across a spectrum that extended from ready compliance to violent resistance. Opponents organized anti-vaccination societies, fought to repeal state vaccination laws, and flooded the courts with lawsuits challenging compulsory vaccination as a violation of constitutional rights. This response may have been antisocial, but it was not irrational. The introduction of live cowpox virus into the human arm left it sore. Workers who relied on their brawn complained of lost work and wages. In some instances, the vaccine spread deadly tetanus, which could steal the lives protected against smallpox. Christian Scientists, who rejected modern medicine, considered compulsory vaccination a violation of their religious freedom. Some parents resented school vaccination mandates because they encroached on parental authority and violated their children's bodies.

Compulsory vaccination raised a broad set of questions about the nature of institutional power and the bounds of personal liberty in a modern urban-industrial nation. How could individual freedom be balanced against the claims of society? What was the role of the state in striking that balance? Progressive reformers such as philosopher John Dewey argued that individual rights existed not for themselves but because they served important social interests. Other Americans disagreed and challenged the increasing reach of state power into areas of personal freedom. Did individuals have the right to refuse vaccination even if that refusal could make them and therefore others susceptible to a deadly disease? Did the state have the right to bar unvaccinated children from public schools? As the nation entered a new century, the question of how to balance the tension between individual liberty and the people's collective welfare moved to the forefront of American politics.

Into the Open Arena of the World

"No war ever transformed us quite as the war with Spain," the president of Princeton University, Woodrow Wilson, wrote in 1902. "The nation has stepped forth into the open arena of the world." In 17 years, between 1888 and 1915, the United States acquired colonies in oceans bounding both sides of the continent. In 1898, Hawai'i, home to many white missionaries and entrepreneurs, was formally annexed. That same year, as part of the Spanish-American War, America seized Cuba, Puerto Rico, Guam, Wake Island, and Manila in the Philippine Islands. The rest of the Philippines was captured in 1902.

At the height of the age of steam, these island possessions created for America a line of coaling stations that fueled American political, economic, and cultural influence all the way to China. They also raised vital questions about the possible effects of colonization on American democracy. Expansionists maintained that exporting democracy abroad would strengthen it at home. Anti-expansionists insisted that imperial territories and subjects constituted a dagger pointed at the heart of the Republic.

THE SPANISH-AMERICAN WAR

The Spanish-American War grew out of American involvement (Spain characterized it as interference) in Cuba's effort to liberate itself from Spanish colonial rule. Begun in 1895, the Cuban rebellion was stalled by 1898. In three short years, a combination of disease, malnutrition, and fierce fighting between Spanish soldiers and Cuban rebels reduced the island's population by a fourth. This story, which was reported with gusto by two New York newspapers with national readerships, caught the imagination of Americans, who sympathized with the revolutionaries' political goals and the Cubans' plight.

Business leaders worried too. America had important commercial interests in Cuba. More than $50 billion was invested in sugar alone.

Moreover, the strife in Cuba threatened American trade in the Pacific, because Spain controlled the islands of Guam and the Philippines, which were gateways to China. It was clear that the teetering Spanish Empire would soon collapse. The question was who would reap the benefit: the United States or Germany, which was, like America, an energetic latecomer to colonialism.

Since the 1880s, European nations had engaged in a mad scramble for political and economic control of "unclaimed" areas of the globe: unclaimed, that is, by other European powers. Joined by the French, Germans, Belgians, and Italians, the British competed for colonies in the Middle East, North and sub-Saharan Africa, East and Southeast Asia, and, to the alarm of Americans, the Caribbean and Latin America.

With public opinion divided on the wisdom of intervention in Cuba and President McKinley hesitant to act, a young assistant secretary of the Navy took it upon himself to order the US fleet to the Philippines in April 1897. A forceful advocate of "the strenuous life" of "toil and effort, of labor and strife," Assistant Secretary Theodore Roosevelt believed that America faced a turning point. It could join the "civilized nations" in their joint stewardship of the earth, or it could allow itself to be eclipsed by "some stronger, manlier power," such as Germany.

Not to be outdone by his audacious underling, the president dispatched the battleship *Maine* to Cuba. On the night of February 15, 1898, the ship was destroyed by an explosion that killed 267 crewmembers. The press pinned the event on the Spanish government. Rallying to the cry "Remember the *Maine*," Congress declared war on Spain. Americans still suffering from the economic depression that had begun in 1893 rushed to enlist in the army. Less than a week after McKinley signed Congress's war resolution, a navy squadron led by Admiral George Dewey destroyed the Spanish fleet in Manila Bay. Aided by Filipino revolutionaries led by Emilio Aguinaldo, 11,000 American troops captured Manila on August 13, 1898.

The war in Cuba lasted barely a month, from the first landing of American troops on June 22 to the Spanish surrender on July 17. Most volunteers never made it off US soil, but Theodore Roosevelt did. He resigned his position in the Navy and joined the First Volunteer Cavalry Regiment, known popularly as the "Rough Riders." Composed of western ranchers, cowboys, and a few Ivy League polo players, the Rough Riders fought in the decisive Battle of Kettle Hill. Under the cover of Gatling guns (machine guns), the Riders joined the all-black

10th Cavalry regulars in an assault on the hill. Their horses collapsed from heat exhaustion; the volunteers and the African American regulars battled their way up the hill on foot. Together, these "Buffalo Soldiers" (named for their service fighting the Indian wars in the West) and Roosevelt's Rough Riders took the heights—although it must be said that they outnumbered the Spaniards four to one.

AMERICAN EMPIRE

In the Treaty of Paris, signed on December 10, 1898, Spain ceded the Philippines to the United States, along with Guam and Puerto Rico, in exchange for $20 million. This was a fire sale price: as recently as April 1898, the United States had offered Spain $300 million for Puerto Rico alone. Cuba was declared nominally independent, although the 1901 Platt Amendment to the new Cuban constitution granted the United States the right to intervene to protect that "independence" whenever necessary. America also empowered itself to oversee Cuban debt so that European creditors would have no excuse for future intervention. Finally, as part of the treaty, the United States secured a 99-year lease on a naval base at Guantanamo Bay.

The treaty encountered fierce resistance in the Senate, which ultimately ratified it on February 4, 1899, by a margin of only one vote. Opinions on the treaty, and the American empire it initiated, broke down along partisan lines, with sharp regional differences. Republicans, influenced by commercial interests, favored expansion across the globe. Many of the nation's new imperialists also argued that the United States had a moral obligation to spread the benefits of American civilization beyond the nation's borders, especially to those who occupied lower rungs on the ladder of racial hierarchy.

On the other side of the debate were those who resented the influence of eastern financial elites in the cause of American imperialism, feared a radical expansion of federal power, worried about the injection of so many people of color into the American body politic, and challenged the morality of American imperialism. Idaho senator William Borah warned that the acquisition of an empire would sacrifice the principles fought for in the Revolution—namely, "that colonies exist for their own benefit, and not for the advantage of the mother country."

These objections led to a further question: if a republic could have colonies, what rights, if any, had its subjects? "What about the people?" demanded William Jennings Bryan. "Did we purchase them? If not, how did we secure title to them? Were they thrown in with the land?" As Bryan put the question when he ran against McKinley for a second time in 1900, "Does the Constitution follow the flag?" Does an individual who lives in an American colony have the same constitutional rights as an individual who lives in the United States proper?

The answer provided by Congress was "not quite." In 1900, Congress passed the Foraker Act, which established Puerto Rico as an unincorporated territory of the United States, ruled by Congress and an appointed governor. In a series of sharply divided decisions between 1901 and 1922 known collectively as the Insular Cases, the Supreme Court held that the people of the so-called unincorporated territories possessed certain undefined "fundamental rights," but not all the rights of Americans. Were Puerto Rico, Alaska, and Hawai'i foreign countries within the meaning of the tariff laws? (Sometimes.) Did the people who lived there have the right to trial by jury? (No.) Did the Fifth Amendment's prohibition of double jeopardy (being tried twice for the same crime) apply in the territories? (No.) Could Puerto Rico extradite criminals from the states? (Yes.) As Secretary of State Elihu Root remarked approvingly of one of the court's decisions, "As near as I can make out the Constitution follows the flag—but doesn't quite catch up with it."

THE CIVILIZATION TRUST

In the eyes of Filipinos, who had been fighting for independence since 1896, the Treaty of Paris transformed Americans from allies to occupiers. The Philippine-American War began in January 1899, when rebel leader Emilio Aguinaldo declared the independence of the Philippine Republic. By the time the war ended in 1902, 4,200 Americans had died, another 2,800 had been wounded, and $400 million had been expended. Enraged by their inability to conquer the Filipino guerrilla forces, American commanders turned to a scorched earth policy. General Jacob H. Smith demanded that the island of Samar be made "a howling wilderness," and ordered the burning of villages and killing of all persons capable of bearing arms—defined as age 10 and up.

Gruesome details of American torture of Filipino troops and atrocities against civilians outraged and emboldened opponents of American imperialism. Dozens of respected figures rejected American expansion overseas, including two former presidents, one from each party (Republican Benjamin Harrison and Democrat Grover Cleveland), AFL head Samuel Gompers, William Jennings Bryan, the presidents of Stanford and Harvard, reformer Jane Addams, corporate titan Andrew Carnegie (who offered to buy the Philippines and give them their independence), and public intellectuals like philosopher William James and author Mark Twain.

Most anti-imperialists believed, along with expansionists, in white racial and cultural superiority and considered Anglo-Saxons uniquely qualified to rule the "lesser" races. They did not necessarily reject Theodore Roosevelt's assessment that Filipinos were "utterly unfit for self-government." But they disagreed vehemently about the benefits of empire for America. Expansionists argued that a global empire was the logical next step for a nation whose boundaries already stretched from sea to sea. Anti-imperialists like William James dismissed this argument as worshipping "the idol of a national destiny, based on martial excitement and mere 'bigness.'" In the face of Theodore Roosevelt's disdain for anti-imperialists as those "who cant about 'liberty' and the 'consent of the governed,'" critics like Mark Twain insisted that what he dubbed "the Blessings-of-Civilization Trust" imperiled fundamental American values only recently affirmed in the Civil War.

In a blistering critique of American policy written for distribution by the Anti-Imperialist League of New York in 1901, Twain argued that the goal for America in the Philippines ought to have been solely to liberate the islands from Spain and to support the infant Philippine Republic. "The game was in our hands. If it had been played according to the American rules," Twain wrote, "Dewey would have sailed away from Manila as soon as he had destroyed the Spanish fleet," and left the islands in the capable hands of Aguinaldo and his rebels.

Instead, commercialism reigned supreme, leading Twain to conclude, "There must be two Americas: one that sets the captive free, and one that takes a once-captive's new freedom away from him and picks a quarrel with him with nothing to found it on; then kills him to get his land." The nation that obliterated slavery in its own midst was now, mourned William James, "openly engaged in crushing out the sacredest thing in this great human world—the attempt of a people long enslaved to attain to the possession of itself."

AMERICA IN THE WORLD

The war with Spain inaugurated a conversation that would span the twentieth century, as the United States became ever more involved in global affairs. What was the proper role of America in the world? To spread democracy? To expand its commercial and military interests? To fulfill an imperial mission begun in 1776? Arguing for the annexation of Cuba, Major General James Harrison Wilson combined all the arguments when he exclaimed, "Let us take this course because it is noble and just and right, and besides because it will pay." The severity of the depression of 1893 had reinforced popular arguments about the need to "overcome the limitations of U.S. markets" by securing access to foreign markets and promoting American business, especially in the Far East and Central and South America. American overseas investments grew from $700 million in 1897 to $2.5 billion in 1908.

American international businesses and the individuals who ran them had to be protected militarily. One legacy of the Spanish-American War was a permanent change in the size and focus of the American armed forces. A commercial, seagoing power depended on an enlarged and modernized navy that, in turn, relied on the construction of naval bases in places like Pearl Harbor in Hawai'i and Guantanamo Bay in Cuba. Lines of trade depended on open lines of communication, which meant free access to, if not downright command of, the sea. "Freedom of the seas" was a vital national interest and not an empty mantra; asserting this right would eventually pull the United States into a world conflagration sparked by incessant commercial and territorial competition by European empires.

Joining Britain, Germany, and France on the imperial stage meant joining an arms race as well as a race to territorial acquisition. Far-flung territories demanded a large standing army ready to spring into action at short notice. Guided by the ever-present Elihu Root, now serving as secretary of war, the army quadrupled in size and modernized its command structure. The 1903 Dick Act designated the National Guard as the backup for the army and made it accountable to the federal government as well as the states. In the three years after the Spanish-American War, the overall military budget increased by more than 300 percent.

Commercial and strategic goals were deeply interrelated in America's rise to a world power. "There is a fundamental danger which arises from our rapid growth economically," Massachusetts senator Henry Cabot Lodge wrote to Theodore Roosevelt. "We are putting terrible pressure on Europe, and this situation may produce war at any time. The economic forces will not be the ostensible cause of trouble, but they will be the real cause, and no one can tell where the break will come."

The demise of the Spanish Empire and the simultaneous rise of the United States, Germany, and Japan (whose status as a "civilized" nation Americans and Europeans questioned) upset the established international order. This new state of affairs aroused anxiety among the great colonial powers (Britain, France, Russia, Italy, and Belgium), fed colonial rivalries and shifting alliances, and raised the fearsome possibility that a crisis anywhere in the world could plunge Europe into war.

The Republican Roosevelt

On September 14, 1901, for the third time in 36 years, an American president was assassinated in office. William McKinley was shot by native-born anarchist Leon Czolgosz in Buffalo, New York. McKinley's vice president, former assistant secretary of the Navy and New York governor Theodore Roosevelt, ascended to office. Only 42 years old, Roosevelt was irrepressible and uninhibited, a voracious reader and prolific author, an outdoorsman addicted to hunting, horseback riding, hiking, and bird-watching. The product of an old and moderately wealthy Manhattan mercantile and banking family, Roosevelt's decision to enter politics was unusual for a well-heeled graduate of Harvard. His sense of noblesse oblige, imbibed from his southern mother, was not. He rose quickly through the ranks from civil service commissioner to New York state legislator to New York City police commissioner to governor of New York to the White House. Described by one contemporary as a "steam engine in trousers," Roosevelt's effervescence and energy were legendary.

TAKING ON THE TRUSTS

Roosevelt assumed office in the midst of an economic boom. From 1896 to 1901, the gross national product grew by an astonishing 60 percent, from $13 billion to $21 billion. But even as profits skyrocketed, three-quarters of all Americans were classified as either poor or very poor.

These years also saw extensive corporate consolidation. Mergers and takeovers were common. Giant corporations commanded key sectors of the economy, including the railroads and coal, which was the chief source of industrial fuel and domestic heat. Some industries, such as oil and steel, were oligopolies controlled by a handful of large firms. This enormous concentration of industrial economic strength was entangled in a web of banks, insurance companies, and brokerage houses—what reformers called the "Money Trust"—that empowered a small cohort of wealthy and highly influential financiers.

Roosevelt's presidency, which lasted from September 1901 through March 1909, was defined by his need to grapple with the social extremes produced by relations between capital and labor, and the balance of power between business and government. The "absolutely vital question" facing the nation in 1901, Roosevelt wrote to a friend, was "whether or not the government has the power to control the trusts." The power of the trusts was so great, the wealth of their owners so monumental, and their appetite for profit so voracious that the question of how to balance private enterprise against the well-being of the nation commanded increasing attention.

The trusts question was political as well as ethical. As a Republican, Roosevelt was concerned that many workers who had supported McKinley in 1896 now insisted that William Jennings Bryan was "the only man who can control the trusts; and that the trusts are crushing the life out of the small men." As long as Republicans resisted any regulation of the trusts, he warned, workers who had suffered "a good deal of misery" would drift toward the "the quack." Bryan's Democrats had policy proposals. Rather than resisting all regulation of business, "the party of property," argued Roosevelt, should move toward a more "enlightened conservatism."

Enlightened conservatism, he said, demanded that "corporations should be managed with due regard of the public as a whole." To do this, the public needed an advocate and corporations needed a sovereign. The federal government, Roosevelt believed, could play both roles. "The great corporations which we have grown to speak of rather loosely as trusts," he explained in 1903, "are the creatures of the State [through law], and the State not only has the right to control them, but it is in duty bound to control them wherever need of such control is shown. The immediate necessity in dealing with trusts," he continued, "is to place them under the real, not the nominal, control of some sovereign to which, as its creatures, orders may be enforced. In my opinion," he concluded, "this sovereign must be the National Government."

In 1901, three large railroads owned by J. P. Morgan, John D. Rockefeller, William H. Harriman, and James J. Hill had combined to form a single vast firm, the Northern Securities Company, which cemented control over the railway market in the Northwest. Morgan had already consolidated the steel industry the previous year (US Steel); Rockefeller's Standard Oil had made him the wealthiest man in the world. Journalist Mark Sullivan worried that these men were "more powerful than the people, more powerful than Congress, more powerful than the government," and therefore "presented to Roosevelt a challenge such as his nature would never ignore."

TRAINS AND COAL

On February 19, 1902, the Justice Department announced its intention to file an antitrust suit against Northern Securities. This shocked Wall Street; when a friend of Attorney General Philander Knox complained that he had not been given "a friendly tip in advance," he received the curt response, "There is no stock ticker in the Department of Justice." Morgan, accustomed to treating the federal government as a junior partner in industry, was dumbfounded that the president had filed suit and not resolved the matter personally, man-to-man.

In a controversial 5–4 decision in 1904, the Supreme Court, which had previously wielded the Sherman Antitrust Act chiefly against labor, held that the Northern Securities Company had violated the act. Emboldened, the president went on to wield the Sherman Act against 43 different trusts, striking at the tallest trees in the forest: American Tobacco Company, Du Pont, and Standard Oil. Rather than nationalize key industries, as many European and Latin American nations did during this period, the United States tried to limit the power of immense private firms and to require them to be as attentive to the needs of the people who relied on their services as they were to their stockholders.

The principle of government regulation of industry had already received considerable backing by the time the Supreme Court vindicated it in *Northern Securities Co. v. United States.* In the fall of 1902, the coal industry was embroiled in labor strife. With winter coming and panicky mayors calling for nationalization of the coal industry to prevent a "coal famine," President Roosevelt personally intervened in a strike begun the previous spring. He was impressed by the dignity and seriousness of purpose of United Mine Workers leader John Mitchell and the discipline of the 147,000 miners Mitchell represented. "I strongly favor labor unions," the president declared. "If I were a wage worker . . . I would certainly join one."

The president was less impressed by the sanctimoniously uncompromising stance of the mine owners, who insisted that "the rights and interests of the laboring man will be protected and cared for—not by the labor agitators, but by the Christian men whom God in His infinite wisdom has given the control of the property interests of the country, and upon the successful Management of which so much depends." These Christian men had, among other things, paid their workers with company scrip good only in company stores, refused to recognize collective bargaining by unions, and resisted a shorter working day. Rather than send the army to end the strike, as Grover Cleveland had done in Chicago in 1894, the president mediated between the parties and negotiated a federal coal strike commission to resolve the dispute. The commission reached an agreement that reduced the workday from ten hours to nine and instigated a 10 percent wage increase, but denied official recognition of collective bargaining.

Roosevelt's arbitration earned him acclaim as the first head of state to confront the largest problem of the new century. He was cheered in the French Chamber of Deputies and hailed by the *Times* of London. "In a most quiet and unobtrusive manner," gushed the *Times*, "the President has done a very big and entirely new thing. We are witnessing not merely the ending of the coal strike, but the definite entry of a powerful government upon a novel sphere of operation." The central question of progressive politics for 25 years—whether the federal government could regulate the economy—was decided.

THE PEOPLE'S WELFARE

"The permanent lesson" of the coal strike, Roosevelt said later, was that the public had "vital interests and overshadowing rights" in negotiations between capital and labor, and that the state, as the representative of the public, had a place at the bargaining table. Responding to accusations of a federal power grab, Roosevelt explained that he had merely given the people, through their government, a voice in a battle that concerned their vital interests. "The Government is us. . . . You and me!" the president exclaimed, and any influence generated by its involvement in the coal strike accrued not to him but to the people as a whole.

Roosevelt's regulatory interventions were aided by scandals uncovered by a new breed of investigative journalist known collectively as "muckrakers" for their propensity to root around in dirty politics and business. *McClure's* magazine set the standard, publishing such leading lights as Ida Tarbell (who wrote a scathing exposé of Standard Oil), Danish immigrant Jacob Riis (whose photo-essay on urban poverty, *How the Other Half Lives*, shocked middle-class sensibilities), Ray Stannard Baker (author of *Following the Color Line*, an investigation of race in America), and Lincoln Steffens (whose essays detailed the corruption of municipal government).

The breathtakingly corrupt three-way bargains struck among industry, state legislatures, and US senators documented in David Graham Phillips's 1906 series "The Treason of the Senate" energized demands for popular election of senators. Public outcry following the publication (and verification) of Upton Sinclair's riveting if nauseating exposé of the meat-packing industry enabled passage of the Pure Food and Drug Act and the Meat Inspection Act, which established federal inspection of meat and other products and set sanitation standards in stockyards.

Roosevelt had learned the disinfecting potential of transparency while serving as New York City police commissioner. He became close to Riis, who took Roosevelt to see the appalling conditions of the city's overcrowded tenements, with their lack of fresh air, sweatshops, and avaricious landlords and commercial interests determined to evade regulation. "It is one thing to listen in perfunctory fashion to talks of overcrowded tenements," Roosevelt said, "and it is quite another actually to see what that overcrowding means." The experience stuck: "I became more set than ever in my distrust of those men, whether business men or lawyers, judges, legislators, or executive officers, who seek to make of the Constitution a fetish for the prevention of the work of social reform" through invocation of "liberty of contract."

As president, Roosevelt justified government regulation of free enterprise as preferable to other solutions, including nationalization of modes of transportation and communication and revolutionary violence. Neither was out of the question. Germany's model of state and federal co-ownership of railroads was potentially adaptable to American conditions. President McKinley's assassin was an anarchist. Revolutions in China, Mexico, and Russia in 1905 shook the propertied classes everywhere. That same year, a new organization, the Industrial Workers of the World (IWW), convened a "Continental Congress of the working class" in Chicago. The IWW echoed earlier labor movements in its belief that "the working class and the employing class have nothing in common," but departed from them by declaring war on the

wage labor system itself. Strongest in the West, where struggles between workers and employers were frequently settled by gunfire, the
IWW organized the unskilled workers neglected by the AFL, especially miners. Wobblies (as they were known) eschewed politics and
embraced direct action, such as strikes, boycotts, and demonstrations.
In its inclusion of Asians, women, African Americans, and immigrants,
the IWW was the most inclusive labor organization since the Knights
of Labor.

"ENGLISH ECONOMICS" AND ITS CRITICS

What Americans understood as "laissez-faire" economics (French
for "leave alone") or the "free market," Germans called "English economics." The German name historicized laissez-faire economic theories by tying them to Britain's meteoric rise to world economic domination in the eighteenth century. In historicizing notions of economic
"freedom," the Germans rebutted Scottish theorists like Adam Smith
who considered laissez-faire economics a "natural" phenomenon of
individual actions and private desires, and elevated the place where
this natural phenomenon occurred, the "market," to a special realm of
autonomous and automatically self-regulating processes. Instead, German economists of the late nineteenth century reimagined economics
in the language of policy and politics, and considered economic action
in the marketplace the product of social activities—in other words,
constructed by people and not by Nature or God.

Laissez-faire government never meant, as it was later asserted,
a state that merely guarded its people and their interests as a night
watchman. Indeed, the nineteenth-century British state was the model
administrative state, molding all sorts of issues, from military and imperial policy to sanitary regulations to mine inspections to limits on
the work of women and children. The maxim of classical economic
liberalism, which equated liberty with decentralized institutions and
minimal state intrusion into the economy, in practice sustained a state
capable of fining management for violating safety rules, sending children to school, and demanding vaccination against infectious disease.
If there was room for government in laissez-faire economics, however, state action was nonetheless considered "outside" of an "organic"
market composed of individual actions and private desires: hence the
notion of the "interventionist" state.

As a cultural outpost of Britain, the United States had an early and lasting education in English economics. Germany did not share this legacy. What it *did* share with the United States, and with Britain by 1900, was the reality that "free market" economic theories hindered rather than helped efforts to address the social problems caused by industrial capitalism. Social unrest, in turn, fomented political unrest. At the turn of the twentieth century, Wilhelmine Germany (so called after its king, Wilhelm II) constructed a social welfare state unmatched in Europe while simultaneously leaping to the front of the pack in commercial success.

During these years, a generation of American scholars trained in Germany brought back the German critique of laissez-faire economics as well as new ways of thinking about how the state, through politics, could pursue social justice and, hopefully, social peace. Americans were both admiring of German social welfare policies, such as state-run insurance systems that addressed issues of health, old age, unemployment, and industrial accidents, and alarmed by German social and economic advancement.

The fear that the United States was falling behind in the international race of social and economic progress gave American reformers an added sense of urgency and helped protect them from charges of political utopianism. Theodore Roosevelt fumed in 1908 that the United States was constantly singled out as a laggard at international congresses on industrial work and social reform. How was it, asked progressive writer Walter Weyl in his influential book *The New Democracy*, that "the tortoise Europe" had "outdistanced the hare?"

PERPETUAL CENSORS

While progressives attacked laissez-faire economic theory, the justices of the United States Supreme Court worked overtime to prop it up. Their instrument was the due process clause found in both the Fifth and the Fourteenth Amendments, which provided that no person shall be deprived of "life, liberty or property without due process of law."

In the *Slaughter-House Cases* (1873), a divided Supreme Court acknowledged the power of government to pass laws for the common good that impinged on individual lives, liberty, and property, as long as the laws had a "reasonable" relation to a legitimate legislative purpose, such as the protection of public health or safety. Anything else, said the majority, would "fetter and degrade the State governments" by subjecting them to federal oversight in realms, such as public health, traditionally left under local jurisdiction and turn the Supreme Court into "perpetual censors" of every law passed by state legislatures.

When states established safety rules designed to protect workers and consumers and passed laws regulating minimum pay and maximum hours, however, the Supreme Court changed its mind. In a series of highly controversial decisions beginning in the 1890s, a conservative majority of the justices held unconstitutional a broad range of progressive laws, including those guaranteeing a minimum wage, prohibiting child labor, and regulating the banking, insurance, and transportation industries.

Relying on what came to be called substantive due process, the court elevated "liberty," particularly liberty of contract, above other rights. This trend came to a head in 1905 in *Lochner v. New York*, in which a five-justice majority denied the constitutionality of a state-mandated 60-hour workweek for bakers. According to the majority, the pertinent question was, "Is this a fair, reasonable and appropriate exercise of the ... power of the State, or is it an unreasonable, unnecessary and arbitrary interference with the right of the individual to his personal liberty?"

In a stinging dissent, Justice Oliver Wendell Holmes criticized the majority's reliance on laissez-faire thinking, and insisted that the US Constitution does not "embody a particular economic theory." Although the majority might find workers' protection laws "novel and even shocking," that shock "ought not to conclude our judgment upon the question whether statutes embodying them conflict with the Constitution of the United States." Warning that the majority was substituting its own values for the Constitution, Holmes reminded them that only a few days earlier the court had upheld the constitutionality of a mandatory vaccination law, despite the claim that it, too, impinged on the liberty of the individual.

Lochner enshrined liberty of contract as the very essence of individual freedom. Logically, this argument should apply to all workers. Did it? What about child laborers? What about adult women workers?

In 1908, the Supreme Court upheld an Oregon law that limited the number of hours women could work in a day. The court ruled in *Muller v. Oregon* that women's procreative powers differentiated them from men, and that the state had a legitimate, reasonable interest in protecting the future of "the race" by protecting women's health, even if that limited their contract rights. Following *Muller*, 39 states enacted women's working hours legislation as well as a stack of new child labor statutes. Considered a victory for reform in its day, *Muller's* acceptance of differential treatment on the basis of sex reinforced the common view of women workers as weak, dependent, and undeserving of the same economic rights—such as equal pay—as men.

America in the World, 1901–1912

The Spanish-American War marked the beginning of what would later be called the American Century, as the United States dipped its toes into the deep waters of great power politics. In 1901, the colonies and protectorates of the six European great powers covered two-thirds of the earth's surface and one-third of its population. As President McKinley announced that year, American "isolation was no longer possible or desirable."

DUTY, DOLLARS, AND DESTINY

Because the ongoing war in the Philippines had soured many Americans on colonies, nonisolation took the form of expanding and safeguarding American commercial interests. Although the United States solidified its influence in the Caribbean and the Pacific Basin, it did not acquire new colonies or join any of the alliances that marked European politics in the years leading up to World War I.

Acquisition of the Philippines nonetheless led the United States to play a more active role on the Asian mainland. Following China's loss in the Sino-Japanese War (1894–1895), Britain, Germany, Russia, and Japan all staked out spheres of interest there—what diplomats referred to as "slicing the Chinese melon." Worried about being locked out of the lucrative China market, the McKinley administration issued in 1899 the Open Door Policy, which urged the imperial powers not to discriminate against the commerce of other nations within their spheres of influence in China, while at the same time leaving open the possibility of acquiring an American sphere of influence there. "May we not want a slice, if it is to be divided?" inquired McKinley.

The man who as assistant secretary of the Navy ordered the fleet to the Philippines was predictably uninhibited as president when it came to foreign affairs. Always appreciative of sea power, Roosevelt was himself a shrewd naval strategist. "In a dozen years," he predicted in 1904, "the English, Americans and Germans, who now dread one another as rivals in the trade of the Pacific, will have each to dread the

Japanese more than they do any other nation." The United States, he decided, needed a stronger navy.

It also needed to assert control of its neighborhood. Having heeded British poet Rudyard Kipling's admonition to "take up the white man's burden" and join the imperial club of "civilized" nations in 1898, the United States relied on a combination of diplomacy and military and industrial strength to protect its international interests, which were mostly commercial. "Speak softly but carry a big stick" was how Roosevelt described his strategy, and he followed his own advice assiduously.

In the Caribbean, Roosevelt jealously guarded America's sphere of influence. In 1902, he risked war with Germany to prevent it from establishing a military presence in Venezuela. Two years later, he announced what was immediately dubbed the "Roosevelt Corollary" to the Monroe Doctrine: the United States would respect the sovereignty of Latin American and Caribbean nations as long as they conducted their affairs with "decency," but would intervene in cases of "brutal wrongdoing," such as defaulting on debts to European nations and nationals. The Roosevelt Corollary made the United States the policeman and debt collector of the Western Hemisphere.

Defending a transoceanic empire required a link between the Atlantic and the Pacific. When the Colombian Senate rejected the United States' offer to buy a narrow strip of land running through the state of Panama in 1903, Roosevelt let it be known that the United States would support a rebellion if Panama seceded from Colombia. The revolution promptly materialized, an American gunboat appeared to prevent Colombian reinforcements, and work on the Panama Canal— just the sort of heroically difficult task Roosevelt loved—began.

THE BEST HERDER OF EMPERORS SINCE NAPOLEON

In February 1904, Japan, convinced that Russian influence in East Asia threatened its imperial ambitions in Korea and China, launched a surprise attack that crushed the Russian fleet at Port Arthur in southern Manchuria. Japan occupied Korea and pushed the Russians deep into Manchuria, to the north. As the tiny Asian nation pummeled inept Russian troops, Roosevelt worried about the global balance of power as well as theories of racial supremacy that he and his associates took for granted. The president stepped in and convinced the combatants to negotiate their differences at a peace conference in Portsmouth, New Hampshire.

The treaty negotiated by Roosevelt in August 1905 left Japan in control of Korea and Port Arthur, and Manchuria open to both powers. Russia lost territory, but escaped having to pay compensation to Japan for costs incurred in the war. Henry Adams pronounced Roosevelt "the best herder of emperors since Napoleon." The president became the first American honored with a Nobel Peace Prize. To demonstrate that America was now an international force to be reckoned with, Roosevelt sent 16 navy battleships on a "goodwill mission" around the world. The Great White Fleet was received warmly in ports on both sides of the Pacific, including Japan, whose admirals decided to expand their own navy.

Having negotiated peace between Japan and Russia, Roosevelt was furious when the United States' good relations with Japan were jeopardized in 1906 by San Francisco's creation of separate public schools for whites and "Orientals." Acknowledging Japan's new status as a world power, Roosevelt remarked acidly that San Franciscans had been happy to accept $100,000 in emergency aid from Japan after the devastating earthquake earlier that year, and suggested that anti-Japanese sentiment was rooted in resentment "of their efficiency as workers." The president smoothed Japan's feathers by convincing San Francisco to repeal the school segregation law in exchange for a voluntary agreement with Japan to limit immigration to the United States. The 1907 Gentlemen's Agreement saved Japanese face while placating nativist sentiment in California.

The imperial herder had another opportunity to exercise his negotiating talents when French efforts to dominate Morocco threatened German interests there and brought the two nations to the brink of war. Roosevelt intervened, he said, to prevent a possible "world conflagration." At this time, elaborate treaties connecting France, Britain, and Russia, on the one hand, and Germany and Austria-Hungary on the other, obliged each nation to defend its allies in case of war. No one expected France to invade Germany anytime soon; these interlocking treaties focused on imperial possessions in Africa and Asia, and were designed to prevent what had happened to Russia in the war with Japan. Asserting the right of the United States to intervene in European matters when they endangered its own national security, Roosevelt nudged France and Germany toward the peace table.

The American national security threats Roosevelt referred to were not in Europe or Africa: they were in Latin America and the southern Pacific, where German machinations had begun to worry the Roosevelt administration. At the conference of Algeciras, in southern

Spain, Roosevelt backed France, flattered the touchy German kaiser Wilhelm II, and, when the kaiser appeared ready to abandon the talks, threatened to publish private correspondence in which Germany had pledged to compromise. France got what it wanted, and the kaiser received Roosevelt's fulsome praise for his "epoch-making political success" and "masterly policy." War was averted, but Germany was angry and the kaiser still spoiled for a fight.

DOLLAR DIPLOMACY

Secretary of State Richard Olney's declaration in 1895—three years before the onset of the Spanish-American War—that the United States was ready "to realize its great place among the powers of the earth" and "to accept the commanding position belonging to it," was aimed at two targets: domestic isolationists, and Germany and Britain, whose continued commercial and military forays in Latin America irritated a series of occupants of the White House. By 1904, when the Roosevelt Corollary was announced, the United States had solidified its influence in its own neighborhood, as Roosevelt would have put it.

When William Howard Taft succeeded Roosevelt in 1905, the administration promoted a new form of "dollar diplomacy," which aimed to replace European political and economic influence, especially in Latin America, through dollars rather than bullets. The Taft administration treated Latin American nations like failing corporations, injecting capital and reorganizing management. American bankers loaned foreign governments the funds they needed to pay off European creditors. American experts then tied the debtor nation's currency to the dollar, redesigned its tax structure, budgets, and tariffs, and set the terms of its foreign trade. When the Senate and some Central American countries balked at treaties containing these terms, the government turned to "colonialism by contract" through agreements with private businesses and foreign governments minded by the "benevolent supervision" of the State Department.

This neocolonial approach provoked nationalist opposition in some of the "rotten little countries" (as Woodrow Wilson put it) south of the border. Guatemala refused the American proposals; Costa Rica refinanced its debt through European banks. Honduras's congress refused American terms, but Sam "the Banana Man" Zemurray, an American entrepreneur already busily converting Honduras into a "banana republic," financed a rebellion against the Honduran government led by an American soldier of fortune and backed up by a US warship. In the Dominican Republic, rebels furious with the government's acquiescence to US terms seized control of several customshouses, leading Taft to send in the US Marines. Similar policies spurred a revolution in Nicaragua as well. Members of the US Senate, distressed by this state of affairs, revolted and refused to ratify Taft's treaties.

Woodrow Wilson, who followed Taft as president in 1912, continued his predecessor's dollar diplomacy policies, most dramatically in Haiti. In the midst of a bloody anti-American revolt in July 1915, President Wilson sent 330 marines to occupy the island. Within six weeks, American representatives controlled Haitian customshouses, banks, and the national treasury, and negotiated the repayment of French and American debts. American advisors controlled Haiti, backed up by the US Marines, for the next 19 years, until President Franklin D. Roosevelt (who had been assistant secretary of the Navy under Wilson when Haiti was first occupied) withdrew American troops in 1934.

These heavy-handed American interventions in Latin America permanently altered relations between the United States and its neighbors to the south. What Theodore Roosevelt and Taft considered "benevolent supervision" was experienced as an arrogant attempt to impose American values and institutions on other nations. Economic manipulation and the military occupations that often followed destabilized a region the United States sought to calm and damaged America's long-term interests. The nation that in the nineteenth century had inspired republican revolutions in South and Central America became by 1910 "the Colossus of the North," a domineering neighbor that, in the words of poet Rubén Darío, yoked "the cult of Mammon to the cult of Hercules."

AMERICANS ABROAD

Not all adventures abroad were conducted by the state. Americans increasingly left their own shores. In 1900, it took only a week to cross the Atlantic by steamship. Americans built railroads and mines in Mexico, sold life insurance to Russians, and planted sugar in Hawai'i. American students flooded European universities, and American heiresses married English nobility long on castles but short on cash. Protestant missionaries, who often served as an advance guard for commercial interests while spreading the Gospel, fanned out across the world, especially to China and Japan. Missionary work offered opportunities for women, who also took a leading role in the creation of international relief programs.

Others stayed home but turned their attention beyond American shores. Women segued easily from work on suffrage and temperance to international causes, including a burgeoning world peace movement. Organized women campaigned for disarmament and joined conferences in The Hague on international arbitration of disputes. In 1905, the American Red Cross was chartered as a semiofficial government agency and led many emergency humanitarian operations. African Americans such as antilynching activist Ida Wells-Barnett reminded the world that the United States was not immune from barbarism.

Groups of organized citizens also inserted themselves directly into American foreign policy. For example, after hundreds of anti-Jewish pogroms (organized massacres of an ethnic, religious, or racial minority group) took place in Russia between 1903 and 1906, American Jews conducted mass protests in New York and Chicago and demanded government action. President Roosevelt declined to act, but he did pass on a petition to the Russian government—which resulted in a rebuke from the Russian ambassador, who considered the petition "unbecoming" coming from a nation that lynched African Americans and beat up Chinese.

The president's hand was forced after more than 3,000 Jews were killed during the 1905 revolution in Russia, however. In New York City, 50,000 Jewish Americans marched, and leading financier Jacob Schiff called for military intervention in Russia. When this was, predictably, rejected, Schiff and other Jewish bankers blocked US and European loans to Russia for its war with Japan and helped the Japanese secure funds—hoping that a Russian military defeat might provoke revolution. In 1906, the protesters formed the American Jewish Committee (AJC) to further their goals.

Since the great majority of the world's Jews lived in the Russian Empire (which included parts of Poland), it is not surprising that an organization concerned with anti-Semitism and Jewish life would focus on Russia. In an effort to improve conditions for Russian Jews, the leaders of the AJC focused on the Russian-American commercial treaty of 1832, which called for equal treatment for citizens of all countries, and argued that the treaty should either be honored or ended. In December 1911, responding to pressure by American Jews, the House of Representatives passed a resolution 300–1 favoring abrogation of the treaty. Critics complained that a minority group had influenced foreign policy; American Jewish leaders hailed their "great victory for human rights." Both claims were true—as was the fact that the United States was the only great power to speak out against Russian treatment of Jews.

The Progressive Era

Early twentieth-century Americans confronted a host of social and political problems generated by what journalist Ray Stannard Baker described as "industrialism forcing itself into politics." Industrialism entered politics through many doors: through labor disputes such as strikes and lockouts, through the explosive growth of American cities, through new conceptions of economic citizenship and understandings of its relationship with political equality, and, above all, through visible and disturbing social extremes. Animated by the belief that economic and social conditions could not be divorced from politics, reformers sought collective solutions to what they considered inescapably collective problems.

THE PROGRESSIVES

Between about 1895 and 1920, an emerging class of educated middle-class Americans attacked the social problems they saw all around them. More an ethos than an organized movement, the people dubbed "progressives" had at least one thing in common: an unshakeable faith in the ability of people to change the world for the better. "There are no necessary evils," explained one progressive minister. "There are no insoluble problems. Whatever is wrong cannot be eternal, and whatever is right cannot be impossible."

Progressives were as varied as the causes they championed. They cut across political, religious, gender, race, and regional boundaries. What bound progressives together was a shared belief in scientific inquiry (they had a voracious appetite for data) and strategic, rational state regulation. Politically, they were nonpartisan: "progressive" was an adjective attached to the nouns "Democrat" and "Republican." By 1910, the progressive movement had made significant gains, especially in the South (under the Democrats) and the far West and Midwest (under the GOP). Progressive state legislatures enacted limited woman suffrage, direct ballot initiatives and referenda, regulatory restraints on railroads and insurance companies, corporate taxes, and laws restricting some of the most extreme industrial employment practices, such as child labor. The criminal justice system was overhauled; probation, parole, juvenile courts, and specialized family courts were all Progressive Era innovations.

Some progressive reforms were structural, aimed at the machinery of governance itself. In many midsized cities across the country, campaigns for municipal home rule liberated city governments from state overseers. City managers with planning and administration experience replaced elected mayors, and municipal at-large voting schemes diluted the power of party machines. The new nonpartisan governments lost no time in establishing administrative oversight and regulation of vital utilities such as streetcars, gas, water, and electricity. Other states followed California's lead and required nonpartisan elections for certain specialized positions, such as judges and school boards. Wisconsin, with its lively university in Madison and its German socialists in Milwaukee, pioneered so many progressive reforms that it became known as the "laboratory of democracy."

While progressive leaders theorized a new conception of government, their "new democracy," in the words of an influential book, exposed the ambivalence of many reformers about popular self-government. Progressive political innovations such as referenda and initiatives empowered voters to decide policy questions directly for themselves through the ballot. Recall elections enabled them to "throw the bums out." Primary elections shifted the selection of candidates from the back room to the polling booth. In 1913, the Seventeenth Amendment to the Constitution transferred the power of appointing United States Senators from state legislatures to the people, through popular election.

At the same time, though, these self-proclaimed champions of the people often harbored a barely concealed disdain for the political capacity of many of their fellow citizens. In their view, what was needed was an *enlightened* electorate, rather than merely an expanded one. Elaborate registration processes, literacy tests, poll taxes, and the secret ballot reduced the immigrant vote in the North, the Asian vote in the West, and all but eliminated the black vote in the South.

PETTICOAT POLITICIANS AND SEWER SOCIALISTS

As government power expanded into previously "private" realms, "private" actors entered the public sphere. The most numerous and obvious example of this was the energetic involvement of middle-class women in reform movements of all stripes. Still barred from formal politics but increasingly the beneficiary of higher education in high schools and women's colleges, the organized and ambitious "New Women" of the turn of the century spearheaded a great deal of the era's search for social peace and rationality.

In the last decade of the nineteenth century, new female-dominated institutions fostered an atmosphere of experimentation, learning, and social progress. In 1889, college graduates Jane Addams and Ellen Gates Starr established Hull House in a poor immigrant neighborhood of Chicago. There, they offered everything from seminars in breast-feeding to English-language classes, concerts, and lectures, and sought to create "Americans" out of widely diverse communities divided along ethnic, racial, and religious lines. By 1900, there were nearly 100 settlement houses in major cities; most were founded by women who were fast on their way to creating a new profession: social work.

Women justified their growing public presence in civic affairs by appealing to their "natural" roles as wives and mothers. Demanding that government accept some responsibility to provide basic services like clean drinking water, sewers, and schools, female reformers developed a new and sophisticated conception of the role of the state, particularly in areas considered woman's provenance and an extension of her home: hunger, housing, health, sanitation, children, and education. So long as the state was thought to exist principally to make war and regulate commerce, male rule was, in the words of one champion of woman suffrage, "inevitable, natural and beneficent." But as soon as the state "took upon itself any form of educative, charitable or personally helpful work [social work]," it entered the realm of female expertise, and "therefore became in need of the service of women."

In addition to their efforts to achieve woman suffrage, women's clubs across the nation advocated legislation limiting the working hours of women and children, improving municipal housing codes, restricting the sale of alcohol, expanding public education, and promoting public health, including campaigns for uncontaminated milk, classes in infant care and nutrition, and women's health education designed to help mothers limit family size. In New York, the nurse and social activist Lillian Wald pioneered the role of public nurses by bringing her expertise to the crowded Lower East Side, where she traveled from one building to another by rooftop to avoid streets teeming with people and the inevitable by-product of horse-drawn trolleys.

White southerners thought they had removed "the Negro" from

politics after disenfranchisement. But "politics" itself was transformed by progressives, who, in the South as elsewhere, created clients of the state by expanding its operations. Like white women, African American women participated in progressive campaigns to improve education, public health, or city life. Civic leagues organized by black women joined white women in community cleanup days that planted seeds of interracial cooperation and offered black women access to municipal resources lost with black men's votes.

Dismissed as "petticoat politicians" by the Right and "sewer socialists" by the Left, organized women took up causes that ranged far and wide. Although "municipal housekeeping" arguments created an opening wedge for organized women in politics, they also reinforced traditional notions of "women's role" in society and reaffirmed the sexual division of labor that had long limited workingwomen's options (and earnings) and undermined women's efforts to achieve political and economic equality.

THE PANIC OF 1907

In mid-October 1907, Montana copper magnates Otto and F. Augustus Heinze tried to raise the stock price of their company, United Copper, by purchasing as many shares as possible. They were backed by Wall Street banker Charles W. Morse, who in turn was backed by Charles T. Barney, president of the Knickerbocker Trust Company, the third-largest bank in New York City.

At first, the plan worked as intended. But after a brief rise, the value of United Copper stock plummeted. Shareholders were ruined, including the State Savings Bank of Butte, Montana, which held United Copper stock as collateral for many of its loans. "Banks Totter," screamed a headline of the Boston Post, as the panic spread to Morse's Mercantile National Bank in New York and Barney's Knickerbocker Trust, which closed its doors on October 22 after investors withdrew the staggering sum of $8 million in three hours.

That afternoon, leading New York bankers met with Treasury Secretary George B. Cortelyou at the Madison Avenue mansion of John Pierpont (J. P.) Morgan, the most powerful banker in the nation. To halt the cascading bank collapse, Cortelyou agreed to deposit government funds in the Trust Company of America, which Morgan declared sound, and the bankers pledged to shore up several New York banks to keep investment moving on the stock exchange. To build public confidence, John D. Rockefeller—the richest man in America—announced that he would back the banks with as much as half of his accumulated wealth.

Learning that New York City was on the brink of bankruptcy, Morgan agreed to buy $30 million worth of municipal bonds. He also arranged a rescue of one of the stock market's largest brokerage houses, Moore & Schley, which had borrowed recklessly, using its stock in the Tennessee Coal, Iron and Railroad Company (TCI) as collateral. If panicked banks called Moore & Schley's loans, it would have to sell off its shares of TCI, which would ruin both it and TCI, and exacerbate and prolong the crisis.

Morgan proposed that his firm, United States Steel, which controlled roughly 70 percent of the steel industry, would stabilize Moore & Schley by buying its shares of TCI—*if* the federal government would agree not to challenge its actions under the Sherman Antitrust Act. On November 4, President Roosevelt accepted the deal, praising "those conservative and substantial business men in this crisis who have acted with such wisdom and public spirit." Further crisis was averted, but Roosevelt was worried.

The Panic of 1907 was caused by bankers and solved by them. Both facts revealed the extent to which the national economy was controlled by a small coterie of immensely wealthy private individuals, and the extreme vulnerability of the nation to their actions. For Roosevelt and other reformers, the panic demonstrated the vital necessity of governmental oversight of the financial systems—not simply to police what Roosevelt called "successful dishonesty," but to recalibrate the relationship of government to big business as one of superiority rather than negotiation. A balance must be struck between "the people and their governmental agents" and those men of vast wealth who were otherwise answerable to no one but themselves.

REPUBLICAN FRACTURE, 1908–1912

In 1904, Theodore Roosevelt pledged to respect the "wise custom" that presidents serve no more than eight years in office. By 1908, when his time was up, he regretted that pledge. But if he would not run for re-election, at least he could handpick his Republican successor. Roosevelt turned to his good friend Secretary of War William Howard Taft. Believing his legacy in good hands, Roosevelt handed the reins to Taft and left to go big game hunting in Africa. "Let every lion do his duty," growled J. P. Morgan.

Taft was less progressive than his predecessor in the area that most preoccupied Roosevelt: the danger concentrated economic power posed to political democracy. While Theodore Roosevelt occupied the White House, the progressives made headway at the national level through the Republican Party. But Taft was unable and unmotivated to tame the conservative wing of his party, which was anchored in East Coast banking and industry. This wing steadfastly opposed rethinking the relationship between democratic politics and government regulation of the economy, which was the core concern of both Democratic and Republican progressives.

In 1909, conservative Republicans in the Senate, dominated by a group of men transported by state legislatures directly from the boardroom to the Senate such as Simon Guggenheim of Colorado (mining), Henry DuPont of Delaware (chemicals), and financier Nelson Aldrich (who was John Rockefeller's son-in-law) of Rhode Island, alienated their progressive brethren by passing the protectionist Payne-Aldrich Tariff of 1909. Wisconsin senator Robert "Fighting Bob" La Follette protested the new tariff to little effect.

In the congressional elections of 1910, Democrats campaigning on tariff reform and expanded public power won a majority in the House and effective control of the Senate through alliance with progressive Republicans. This was too much for Roosevelt, who returned home and set his sights once again on politics.

In January 1912, convinced that only he could win the support of the people and reunite the Republican Party, Roosevelt announced his availability as a presidential candidate. When Taft nevertheless secured the GOP nomination, Roosevelt and his followers marched out of the Republican convention and formed the Progressive Party (referred to later as the Bull Moose Party, after Roosevelt proclaimed himself "strong as a bull moose" following an assassination attempt).

While the Republicans fractured, the Democrats gained strength and discipline. Their 1912 ticket was headed by the progressive governor of New Jersey, Woodrow Wilson. The Georgia-born son and grandson of Presbyterian ministers was raised in postwar Virginia. Possessed of a minister's oratorical powers but lacking a pastoral calling, Wilson attended Princeton University and then earned a doctorate in political science and American history from Johns Hopkins. In 1902, he became president of Princeton, where he attacked social privilege and stressed scholarly achievement. In 1910, hard-pressed by muckrakers and reformers, the Democratic bosses of New Jersey made Wilson their candidate for governor. The bosses soon learned what the trustees of Princeton already knew: Wilson was independent minded, sure of himself, and stubborn. In the two years he governed New Jersey, Wilson implemented an anticorruption reform agenda that included business regulation, workplace safety, and limits on campaign spending.

Tutored by William Jennings Bryan, Wilson campaigned for president in 1912 as anti-tariff and antitrust. With the Republican vote split between Taft and Roosevelt, Wilson won easily. Roosevelt came in second, Taft third, and Socialist Eugene Debs doubled his showing from 1908, polling just under one million votes (6 percent of the total), mostly from the West.

New Freedoms

Making good on his campaign vision of "New Freedom," Woodrow Wilson worked closely with Democratic congressional leaders, laid out a legislative program in his first inaugural address, held press conferences every week, and became the first president in more than a century to address Congress personally rather than by presidential message. During his first term in office, Wilson inaugurated what historian Michael Kazin has called "the greatest rush of reform legislation in U.S. history until the New Deal."

THE REVOLUTION OF 1913, PART 1: MONEY

The new president made tariff reform his first priority. With a disciplined party caucus behind him, Wilson denounced high tariffs as a subsidy to large manufacturers, "class legislation" for a class that needed no extra help. The Underwood Tariff Act of 1913 slashed rates by more than a quarter, pushing them back to the pre–Civil War level (the last time agrarians had shaped national economic policy). To pay for the reduction in revenue, Congress turned to a longstanding Democratic proposal: a federal income tax on the wealthy.

Because the Supreme Court had cut off the statutory avenue to a federal income tax with its decision in *Pollock v. Farmers' Loan and Trust Company*, Democrats proposed an amendment to the Constitution, which passed easily and was quickly ratified by the states. The federal income tax implemented under the Sixteenth Amendment left most workers and farmers untouched. It established a 1 percent tax on corporate income and on individual income over $3,000 ($4,000 for a couple), a graduated 1–3 percent surcharge on income over $20,000, and a 4 percent charge on income in excess of $75,000. Guided by Bryan, who knew when to compromise, congressional Democrats who wanted higher rates went along. Conservative Republicans complained that the new tax would "plunder" successful families of the industrial East and Midwest, and they had a point: four states—New York, Pennsylvania, Massachusetts, and Illinois—supplied almost 60 percent of the combined new income and corporation taxes. Andrew Carnegie (who supported the tax) and John D. Rockefeller (who did not) each wrote six-figure checks to the Treasury.

The Sixteenth Amendment permanently altered federal fiscal policy, but it was not only about revenue. In targeting highly concentrated wealth, the income tax addressed the broader Progressive Era concern about growing income inequality, which increasing numbers of Americans considered a menace to democracy. Both the income tax and lower tariff rates had been at the heart of Democratic politics since Grover Cleveland's presidency, and represented 25 years of relentless focus by Bryan and other progressives. Wilson's secretary of agriculture David F. Houston exulted, "Tariff revision downwards. . . . A progressive income tax! I did not think we would live to see such things!"

Brushing aside his peers' complaints of creeping communism, Justice Oliver Wendell Holmes embraced the new tax. "I like to pay taxes," he announced. "With them I buy civilization." By "civilization," Holmes did not mean museums and public libraries, although he enjoyed both. He did not mean government. He meant the civic peace and sense of national community necessary for *American* civilization to flourish. Holmes's enthusiasm for taxes begs a question, however: given the reality of income disparity under capitalism, how did taxes preserve the democratic process in a way that the tariff—also a form of government redistribution of economic resources—did not? The answer for Holmes and for other supporters of a graduated income tax was that a tax on wealth revealed and reinforced the nation's dedication to a spectrum of inequality that had limits. The definition of those limits would change over time, but the role of the federal government in policing them in the interest of national political community would endure.

THE REVOLUTION OF 1913, PART 2: BANKS

The Bankers' Panic of 1907 convinced even bankers that the nation's banking and credit institutions needed reform. As with the income tax and the tariff, congressional debate over monetary policy triggered regional competition for control over the regulatory processes of economic life and, ultimately, over the distribution of wealth. Bankers, represented in Congress by northeastern senators, favored a central bank under private (ideally, their own) control. Members of Congress from nonindustrial regions, on the other hand, sought to limit the economic power and influence of northeastern commercial interests. Southerners in particular remained deeply suspicious of any form of central bank, but clamored for a banking system that would put the farmer and small businessman only "a train's ride away" from loan approval.

In the midst of this debate, a congressional investigation into the banking industry led by Louisiana congressman Arsene Pujo pulled back the curtains on a national banking and industrial empire controlled by the directors of a half dozen New York and Boston banks. The growing power of a small number of investment bankers over the nation's industrial, transportation, and communications corporations alarmed many. J. P. Morgan was, unsurprisingly, the most powerful of all. By 1910, the House of Morgan and its associates controlled the nation's ten great railroad networks, three largest life insurance companies, and US Steel, General Electric, International Harvester, Western Union, and AT&T — corporations whose market dominance approximated monopoly control.

The Pujo Committee's charts and diagrams illustrating the multiple and intersecting roles played by the "Money Trust" set the stage for passage of a major piece of Democratic reform legislation: the Federal Reserve Act of 1913. This act provided for the creation of up to 12 regional institutions to serve as "bankers' banks" that would pool deposits and loan money to smaller banks, and established a single new United States currency, the Federal Reserve note (known as the US dollar). The banks would be overseen by the Federal Reserve Board, whose members would be appointed by the president. Republican Senator Nelson Aldrich and other representatives of banking interests assailed the bill, which they denounced as "this preposterous offspring of ignorance and unreason . . . covered all over with the slime of Bryanism."

The 1913 Federal Reserve Act, or the Glass-Owen Bill (after Virginia senator Carter Glass and Oklahoma representative Robert Owen), established an unprecedented level of "government intervention in the most sensitive area of the capitalistic economy." Rather than turn the management of the reserve system over to the bankers themselves, Congress created a powerful public institution with wide discretion to set monetary policy by controlling the supply of money and credit. Denounced as "socialistic" by the banking elite and conservative Republicans, the act was a signal victory for President Wilson, who, with Bryan's help, overcame southern Democrats' reflexive dislike of a central bank. The result was a federal banking system that reflected agrarian interests while at the same time protecting banks and their depositors by backing the system with the power of the Treasury. Another piece of financial legislation, enacted over the vociferous objections of mortgage bankers, was the Federal Farm Loan Act, which created a network of Federal Land Banks, 12 in all, that provided desperately needed farm credit. Taken together, the Sixteenth Amendment, the Federal Reserve Act, and the Federal Farm Loan Act constituted a significant reallocation of economic power from private to public hands and a recalibration of the previously dominant influence of the industrial Northeast.

THE REVOLUTION OF 1913, PART 3: JIM CROW COMES TO WASHINGTON

Although Woodrow Wilson came to Washington via New Jersey, he was a true son of the white South. The first southern president since the Civil War, Wilson brought five white southerners into his cabinet, including William G. McAdoo (secretary of the Treasury), Thomas W. Gregory (attorney general), Josephus Daniels (secretary of the Navy), and Albert S. Burlson (postmaster general). Nebraskan William Jennings Bryan, the new secretary of state, was a hero to many in the South. The president's brilliant right-hand man, Colonel Edward M. House, whom Wilson referred to as "my second personality," hailed from Texas.

The southern orientation of the administration quickly became apparent when toilets, lunchrooms, and work areas were segregated in the Treasury Department and the Post Office. Photographs were required on applications for federal civil service jobs, to facilitate discrimination. Many African American officeholders were displaced, and America's traditionally black diplomatic representatives to Liberia and Haiti were replaced with whites. Wilson's response to complaints by the National Association for the Advancement of Colored People (NAACP), formed in 1909, that he "honestly thought segregation to be in the interest of the colored people," fell on deaf ears. William

Jennings Bryan, in so many other ways the conscience of the Democratic Party and the Wilson administration, had a noticeable blind spot when it came to race. Capable of orating passionately on the unjustness of American racism in the Philippines, Bryan had little to say about the cruel and unequal treatment of African Americans at home.

The Republicans were not much better. Despite their antislavery origins, the Republican tradition of supporting at least some measure of racial equality had largely eroded by the time William McKinley entered office in 1896. Theodore Roosevelt's record on race was mixed. On the one hand, he looked away when the army blamed a riot in Houston on black soldiers and allowed them to be court-martialed and dishonorably discharged. On the other hand, Roosevelt enraged white supremacists in the South when he dined with black educator and power broker Booker T. Washington at the White House in October 1901.South Carolina senator Benjamin Tillman thundered, "The action of President Roosevelt in entertaining that nigger will necessitate our killing a thousand niggers in the South before they will learn their place again." Shocked by the violence this invitation provoked, Roosevelt determined to speak out against lynching. He did, while visiting the South, in 1903. But he did not dine with another African American in the White House.

White supremacist politics in what had become the one-party South colored national Democrats' positions on other questions as well, particularly woman suffrage. Wilson refused to support a constitutional amendment allowing women to vote. Although Bryan had long championed the cause, southern Democrats preferred to disenfranchise their wives and sisters than to offer an opening to black political power through the ballots of black women, who were as a group more educated than black men and thus more likely to pass a literacy test administered fairly.

THE REVOLUTION OF 1913, PART 4:
FOREIGN POLICY

Neither well-traveled nor especially interested in foreign affairs, Woodrow Wilson appointed William Jennings Bryan, who was both, as his secretary of state. A devout Presbyterian like the president, Bryan believed that God had singled out the United States to teach other nations how to "walk in the paths of liberty," and that the best way to do this was to promote peace through international initiatives.

Although skeptics dismissed such initiatives as futile conversations about "how future wars should be conducted in the best interests of peace," many influential Americans backed new organizations that were dedicated to preventing armed conflict, such as the World Peace Foundation, the Women's International League for Peace and Freedom, and Andrew Carnegie's Endowment for International Peace. Confronted by the competing imperial aspirations of European nations, an arms race, and the thicket of interlocking treaties that had so alarmed Theodore Roosevelt at Algeciras in 1905, the new president chose a pacifist as America's face to the world.

As Europe rushed headlong toward war in 1913–1914, Secretary of State Bryan negotiated a series of bilateral treaties in which each side pledged to submit quarrels to international arbitration and eschew armed conflict. By the summer of 1913, every major nation in Europe had signed a "cooling off" treaty, with two ominous exceptions: Germany and Austria-Hungary.

Turning their attention to Latin America, Wilson and Bryan sought to mend fences. They negotiated a treaty with Colombia apologizing and offering monetary compensation for the US role in the Panamanian revolution. The treaty provoked howls from Theodore Roosevelt and failed in the Senate. But it earned the president favor south of the border, as did a major speech in October 1913 in which Wilson disavowed US economic imperialism in Latin America, linking the exploitative commercial interests there to the bankers and corporate interests he was fighting at home.

Vowing to replace the "degrading policies" of dollar diplomacy with a new policy of "sympathy and friendship," the United States remained unable to take its own best advice when dealing with its hemispheric neighbors. Wilson and Bryan aspired to respect "our political children," as Bryan called them, but neither man could overcome his own impulse toward paternalism and, frequently, racism. The result was a period of military interventionism that exceeded even Roosevelt's exploits. During Wilson's two terms in office, he sent American troops to Cuba once, Panama twice, and Honduras five times. Nicaragua became a protectorate; the Dominican Republic was occupied by marines in 1915, as was Haiti, after an especially bloody revolution in which the Haitian president was killed and his dismembered body dragged through the streets. When the marines finally went home, they left behind dictatorial military regimes in both nations.

Wilson also intervened militarily in Mexico, where $600 million worth of American investment was imperiled after 1911 by a revolution against the regime of Porfirio Díaz, who had ruled in the interest of capital for decades. In 1913 Wilson, vowing to teach America's neighbors to "elect good men," occupied Veracruz in an effort to shape the outcome of the first great revolution of the twentieth century. It was not as easy as he imagined. The lesson he learned—the futility of trying to "direct by force . . . the internal processes of a revolution as profound as that which occurred in France"—had lasting consequences when applied four years later to the civil war in Russia sparked by the Bolshevik revolution in October 1917.

*

By the midpoint of Woodrow Wilson's first term, the United States had passed through three decades of extraordinarily divisive economic, political, and social upheaval. The reforms of 1901–1913 had moved the nation in a new direction, and most Americans were optimistic about the future. Although there was more work to be done, progressives were pleased with the compromises struck between personal liberty and collective coercion in the form of the state. Conservatives were resigned, for the moment at least. The news that Austrian archduke Francis Ferdinand and his wife had been assassinated in Sarajevo by an American-born Serbian nationalist on June 28, 1914, was of only passing interest to most Americans. "The Hapsburgs were always getting themselves killed," remarked one observer.

In the summer of 1914, no one on either side of the Atlantic was prepared for catastrophe. In the United States, President Wilson presided over the 50th anniversary of the Battle of Gettysburg with soothing platitudes about the commensurate valor of the men who wore the blue and the gray. "War fell upon us late in the summer of 1914 as a terrible surprise," recalled one reformer. Within a matter of months, the world was unrecognizable.

FIGURE 3. Virginia Arnold holding "Kaiser Wilson" banner, ca. August 1917. Photograph by Harris & Ewing, Washington, DC. Records of the National Woman's Party, Manuscript Division, Library of Congress, Washington, DC, http://hdl.loc.gov/loc .mss/mnwp.160030.

CHAPTER 3

War, 1914–1924

Woodrow Wilson disclaimed any interest in foreign affairs. The former professor of government was fascinated by domestic policy. "It would be the irony of fate," he remarked, "if my administration had to deal chiefly with foreign affairs."

Fate, as they say, can be a cruel mistress. Only 18 months into his term, President Wilson was confronted with cataclysm in Europe. His initial impulse was to steer clear of the slaughter. He recognized both the necessity and the danger of attempting to mobilize a diverse and potentially divided democracy for war. He understood that going to war in such circumstances would require more than persuasion. It would require repression.

Wilson had defeated not one but three adversaries in the 1912 presidential election. Two of them, progressive Republican Theodore Roosevelt and Socialist Eugene V. Debs, hovered constantly in the wings, offering diametrically opposed advice about the war in Europe. Roosevelt was predictably bellicose and itched to enter the fray. Debs was a pacifist determined to uphold the ideals of the international brotherhood of man and create a "workers' republic" of political and economic equality at home. Debs's Socialist Party opposed American intervention in the conflict, even after the president called for legislation equating criticism of the war with treason. In proposing the Espionage Act of 1917, the first federal legislation against disloyal expression since the Sedition Act of 1798, Wilson insisted that disloyalty "was not a subject on which there was room for . . . debate." Disloyal individuals, he explained, "sacrificed their right to civil liberties."

The question, of course, was, what constituted "disloyalty"? Was it disloyal to question the government's conduct of the war? To wonder whether any vital interests of the nation were at stake in the European conflict? To express doubt about the need for conscription? Wisconsin senator Robert La Follette, who had his doubts about the wisdom of joining the European conflict, conceded that "in time of war the citizen must surrender some rights for the common good," but he argued that this did not include "the right of free speech." To the contrary, it was even more important in time of war than in time of peace that "the channels for free public discussion . . . shall be open and unclogged." It was no solution, he concluded, "to say that when the war is over the citizen may once again resume his rights," for "now is precisely the time when the country needs the counsel of all its citizens."

In June 1918, a few months after American troops arrived in France, Eugene Debs visited three Ohio Socialist leaders who had been arrested for obstructing registration for the draft. Afterward, he addressed a cheering crowd of more than a thousand. "Three of our most loyal comrades," Debs began, had discovered the danger, "in a country fighting to make democracy safe in the world," of exercising their "constitutional right of free speech." He continued: "They tell us that we live in a great free republic; that our institutions are democratic; that we are a free and self-governing people. This is too much," he said bitterly, "even for a joke. But it is not a subject for levity." Debs exhorted his listeners to join the Socialist Party. He referred to the war only once.

Nevertheless, Debs was promptly arrested and convicted for violating the Espionage Act, and sentenced to 10 years in prison. Six years earlier, Eugene Debs had received nearly one million votes as a candidate for president of the United States. Now he was on his way to prison. For critics of the war, Debs's arrest, conviction, and imprisonment revealed just how profoundly the war had corrupted the political landscape of America. Emma Goldman, known as "the High Priestess of Anarchism," who was herself imprisoned and then deported for her views, was livid: "We say that if America has entered the war to make the world safe for democracy," then "she must first make democracy safe in America. How else is the world to take America seriously, when democracy at home is daily being outraged, free speech suppressed, peaceable assemblies broken up by overbearing and brutal gangsters in uniform; when free press is curtailed and every independent opinion gagged? Verily, poor as we are in democracy, how can we give of it to the world?" Such was the political challenge presented America by the First World War.

The War to End All Wars

The First World War, which pitted the "friendly alliance" of Britain, France, and Russia against the Central Powers of Germany, Austria-Hungary, and the Ottoman Empire, shattered a system of colonial rule and world trade that characterized the Age of Empire. Of the five great European empires that entered the war—the Ottoman, Austro-Hungarian, German, Russian, and British—only the British survived. For Europe, the war was an epic disaster that destroyed a generation and inaugurated a half century of impoverishment, debilitation, and political revolution. The United States, which suffered no war damage, sustained relatively few casualties, and benefited economically from the war, emerged from the struggle the richest and most powerful nation on earth.

A LESS-THAN-PRINCIPLED NEUTRALITY

By 1914, the United States had been tested by three decades of divisive economic, political, and social upheaval. President Woodrow Wilson's reluctance to enter the European conflict reflected his belief that the progressive reforms of the previous decade would be the first casualty of war. "Every reform we have won," he declared in 1914, "will be lost if we go into this war. We have been making a fight on special privilege. We have got new tariff and currency and trust legislation. We don't yet know how they will work. They are not thoroughly set." Calling for impartiality "in thought as well as in action," the president and his top advisors, with the significant exception of Secretary of State William Jennings Bryan, nevertheless favored the Allies.

Both sides in the war relied on American money and material; each wanted to restrict the other's access to it, regardless of consequences to noncombatants. A British naval blockade denied the Central Powers essential supplies and resulted in the death by starvation of over 500,000 German civilians. The population of neutral Belgium, occupied by the Germans in August 1914, was saved from the same fate only through the intervention of the Commission for Belgian Relief. Headed by mining engineer and humanitarian Herbert Hoover, the "piratical state organized for benevolence" circumnavigated the British blockade and fed an estimated nine million people a day at a cost of over one billion dollars.

Whereas Britain could deny Germany outside aid by mining shipping lanes and blockading the European coast, Germany had to resort to submarine warfare to cut off shipping to England and France. Germany's policy infuriated the United States, which maintained its right under international law to trade freely with all belligerents. American trade with Germany and Austria fell from $169.2 million in 1914 to a mere $1.1 million in 1916. During the same period, American trade with the Allies rose from $828.8 million to $3.2 billion. "Freedom of the seas" meant, in practice, freedom of trade—with England.

On May 7, 1915, a German submarine sank the British passenger liner *Lusitania*, en route to Liverpool from New York. Among the 1,200 dead were 128 Americans. President Wilson's response was to order his cabinet to prepare for rearmament. Secretary of State Bryan asked, "Why be shocked at the drowning of a few people if there is no objection to starving a nation?" And he wondered, correctly, as it was later revealed, if the British government had transported arms in the hold of the luxury liner. When the president rejected Bryan's plea that the United States denounce Britain's violation of US neutrality as loudly as it did German U-boat attacks, the secretary of state resigned in protest—a principled act that removed the only dissenting voice in the cabinet.

The divergent impulses of Wilson and Bryan reflected those across the country, where opinion on the European war broke down along regional, class, and ancestral lines. By 1910, one out of three Americans had either been born abroad or had at least one foreign-born parent. Of the 32 million Americans with close foreign ties, more than 10 million came from the territory of the Central Powers. German Americans alone made up almost 25 percent of the population in 1917.

It was expected that German Americans would side with the Central Powers, but they were not the only critics of the Allies. Socialists and progressives associated Germany less with spike-helmeted Prussians than with progressive social programs like workers' compensation insurance and mothers' pensions. Irish Americans rooted openly against Britain, particularly after the brutal suppression of the Irish independence movement following the Easter Uprising of 1916. Russian immigrants, especially Jews, cheered the kaiser's armies when they defeated the forces of the czar. President Wilson did not exaggerate when he remarked in 1914, "We have to be neutral, since otherwise our mixed populations would wage war on each other."

BE PREPARED

Few Americans believed that the war in Europe imperiled vital interests of the United States. Germany nurtured that view by scaling back its submarine warfare after the sinking of the *Lusitania*. Internationalists of varying stripes opposed joining the fight. American Socialists maintained that the war had been contrived by industrialists to promote armament sales and enforce social order, and argued that it could bring only misery and death to the working class that would inevitably bear the burden of fighting it. At the other end of the spectrum, the League to Enforce Peace, founded by former president William Howard Taft and other eastern Republicans, promoted the creation of a world parliament to resolve international disputes through arbitration while also supporting expansion of US military power.

An articulate minority of Americans rejected war on principle. Some pacifists rejected violence on religious grounds, such as Quakers and Mennonites; others objected on ethical and moral grounds. Women were prominent in the latter group. Jane Addams's 1907 book, *Newer Ideals of Peace*, imagined a world order in which international cooperation and a "concert of nations" replaced nationalism and military alliances. In January 1915, 165 women's organizations formed the Woman's Peace Party, presided over by Addams. The following March, Addams sailed to The Hague to chair a meeting of 1,336 women from 12 nations, belligerent and neutral alike, to demonstrate the possibility of peaceful discussion in time of war.

At the other end of the spectrum stood East Coast industrialists and financiers, who recognized the enormous profit potential in financing and outfitting the war. Before quitting the cabinet, Bryan begged Wilson to "make money a contraband of war." The president declined, and by the fall of 1915 he had joined the advocates of military "preparedness," mainly northeastern Republicans and Anglophile financiers. Bryan joked about the "scaredness" program, but he did not laugh when Wilson asked Congress to fund 100 new warships and to quadruple the ranks of the army to 400,000 men. Anticipating a renewal of the draft for the first time since the Civil War, progressives demanded that the government also "conscript wealth."

In 1914, J. P. "Jack" Morgan Jr. advised President Wilson that "the war, by cutting down the trade of other countries, should be a tremendous opportunity for America." The war produced 42,000 new millionaires, mostly from New York City and its environs. For the first time in its history, the United States lent out more than it borrowed, becoming overnight a creditor nation. Between 1914 and 1917, American banks loaned billions of dollars to the Allies, most of which was spent in the United States on food and war supplies, functioning effectively as a stimulus bill for Americans. Flush with new jobs and high wages, the AFL muted the antimilitarism that had always been central to labor's code.

War finance tilted heavily toward the Allies, especially England. By 1917, the Allies had borrowed $2.25 billion from the United States, while Germany had borrowed only $27 million. The banks' economic interest clearly lay in an Allied victory. Wilson insisted that America's financial power over Britain and France would translate to political leverage later: "When the war is over we can force them to our way of thinking." Otherwise, he explained to Jane Addams, a persistent critic of the war, America would have no seat at the inevitable peace treaty table and would be forced instead to "shout through a crack in the door."

AMERICA ENTERS THE WAR

Campaigning on the slogan "He kept us out of war" in the 1916 presidential election, Wilson was reelected by a narrow margin over former New York Republican governor Charles Evans Hughes. Before Wilson could take his second oath of office, however, Germany announced a resumption of submarine warfare—something Wilson had worked hard to prevent. In a special address to Congress on January 22, 1917, the president called on the combatants to accept a "peace without victory" based on democratic rule and general disarmament. Both sides rejected Wilson's overture, and on February 3, 1917, the United States severed diplomatic relations with Germany.

William Jennings Bryan called for a national referendum on the question of whether America should enter the war. Denounced as "unpatriotic," Bryan was defended by George Huddleston, a progressive Alabama Democrat, who insisted that "in a time like this . . . it takes a lion-hearted courage for a man to stand up on his feet and dare to speak for peace."

Desperate to defeat the Allies before the United States could intervene, German submarines sank more than a million tons of Allied shipping in the first two months of 1917. On March 1, American newspapers published an intercepted telegram sent by German foreign secretary Arthur Zimmerman that offered to return to Mexico "lost territory" in New Mexico, Texas, and Arizona if it joined Germany in war against the United States. In his second inaugural address on March 5, 1917, President Wilson warned of the European war that "our own fortunes as a nation are involved, whether we would have it so or not." Less than a month later, a somber president asked Congress to declare war on the Central Powers—or, as Wilson put it, to "formally accept the status of belligerent which has thus been thrust upon it." He called for a compulsory draft and expanded executive power to organize and oversee economic production, and proposed paying for the war through a combination of government borrowing (by issuing bonds) and increased taxation on the wealthy.

The question of who should pay for the war was shaped by expectations about who would benefit from it. In 1916, southern and western legislators led by La Follette and North Carolina representative Claude Kitchin had managed to raise the income tax on the wealthy on the principle that if bankers and manufacturers wanted war, they could pay for it themselves. "What do Morgan and [Charles] Schwab care for world peace," demanded La Follette, "when there are big profits in world war?" (There were dangers as well as profits: Jack Morgan survived a serious assassination attempt in 1915.) Three years of official neutrality undercut Wilson's sudden insistence that American participation in the war would "make the world safe for democracy." More credible, or at least more reassuring, was the belief that the United States could not influence the peace if it did not help win the war.

Arguments about future American leadership in the world reinforced the opposition to American entry into the war. Congressional critics of the president's war message did not mince words. Drawing the same connection between commercial interests and military intervention that Mark Twain and other anti-imperialists had made during the Philippine-American War, George Norris mourned that "we are about to put the dollar sign upon the American flag." Never a man to be questioned, much less crossed, Woodrow Wilson cautioned Congress that disloyalty would be received "with a firm hand of stern repression." In the end, 6 senators and 50 representatives voted against the declaration of war.

A WAR OF IDEALS

The war that America joined was hopelessly bogged down. Five million men had died by December 1916, but the battle lines had barely moved in more than two years. In the Battle of Verdun alone, 800,000 French and German soldiers laid down their lives—more than were killed during the entire American Civil War. Still the front did not move.

The war in Europe quickly became a war of production rather than mobility. Production and distribution of everything from rifles to food required labor peace, which in turn required acceptance of collective bargaining, minimum wage and maximum hours laws, old-age pensions, health insurance, and government housing for workers. The need for such policies opened the door to left-leaning politicians. In Germany, Social Democrats forced the kaiser to abdicate and flee to Holland. Britain finally opened the vote to all men and a third of women. In France, one government after another fell, and peace advocates distributed antiwar literature to troops bound for the front, where they mutinied. In Russia, food riots in March 1917 turned into a general strike in Petrograd (St. Petersburg). When the army refused to fire on the people, Tsar Nicholas II abdicated. Russia became a republic on March 17, 1917—just in time for Woodrow Wilson to claim that the Allies were fighting a war to promote democracy.

In the United States, the Wilson administration confronted the need to cultivate, even manufacture, public support for the war. Only months earlier, Wilson had won reelection as the peace candidate. Now he trumpeted the new American posture as not only necessary but inevitable and even desirable. This was no ordinary war. This was a historical *opportunity*: to advance democracy and to protect liberalism and individual freedom. It was a crusade to redeem the Old World from its own most corrupt impulses. It was a "war to end war," in which America sought a "peace without victory." Many a conscience crossed from opposition to support for the war across this shaky explanatory bridge, recalled philosopher John Dewey, who stowed his own pacifism in 1917 in response to this "plastic juncture" in history.

Wilson's idealism appealed to many African American leaders, who embraced the "war for democracy" rhetoric to challenge racial discrimination at home. The white supremacist system that the Wilson administration itself had encouraged seemed suddenly vulnerable. NAACP founding leader W. E. B. Du Bois allowed himself to hope that the tide was finally turning, writing in December 1917, "From now on we may expect to see the walls of prejudice gradually crumble before the onslaught of common sense and social progress." In July 1918, Du Bois advised blacks to "forget our special grievances" and "close ranks" behind the war effort.

Not everyone was prepared to cross to Wilson's side, however. Despite the provocative Zimmerman telegram, Germany had not attacked the United States. Of the 175 American lives lost to U-boat attacks since 1914, all but three had been traveling on belligerent (Allied) ships. Anxious about going to war against an enemy defined through what it represented (autocracy) rather than for anything it had actually *done*, Republican senator William E. Borah of Idaho denounced Wilson's rationale for American participation in the European war: "I join no crusade. . . . I make war alone for my countrymen and their rights."

Perilous Times: The United States at War

"Any great war," Secretary of the Treasury (and Wilson's son-in-law) William McAdoo explained, "must necessarily be a popular movement. It is a kind of crusade; and, like all crusades, it sweeps along on a powerful stream of romanticism." The Wilson administration cultivated popular support for the war through a combination of exhortation, negotiation, and intimidation. Neither McAdoo nor Wilson seems to have appreciated what Senator Borah sensed from the start: that wars for ideals, in which the goal becomes the transformation or annihilation of the opposition rather than the defeat of an enemy, tend to break through military lines: 3,000 miles from the front, Americans looked for enemies within.

THE ESPIONAGE ACT OF 1917

For nearly 120 years, from the expiration of the Sedition Act of 1798 until America's entry into World War I, the United States had no federal legislation against seditious expression (speech designed to incite disaffection with the authority of the government). Even during the Civil War there was no systematic silencing of dissent. Unlike Abraham Lincoln, who tolerated constant criticism of the Union war effort, President Wilson warned his fellow citizens that "disloyalty" would meet "a firm hand of stern repression." Indeed, Wilson presented Congress with legislation to suppress disloyal activities *before* American entry into WWI—a curious request for a nation officially neutral, and one ignored by Congress until it voted a declaration of war in April 1917.

Although the Espionage Act was directed primarily toward protection of military secrets, the act also made it a crime while the nation was at war for any person to (*a*) willfully "make or convey false reports or false statements with intent to interfere" with the military success of the United States or "to promote the success of its enemies"; (*b*) "cause or attempt to cause insubordination, disloyalty, mutiny, or refusal of duty, in the military or naval forces of the United States"; or (*c*) "obstruct the recruiting or enlistment service of the United States." Violations were punishable by imprisonment for up to 20 years. The act also authorized the postmaster general to exclude from the mails any writing or publication that contained any matter that violated the substantive provisions of the act.

The Espionage Act as enacted by Congress was intended to address very specific concerns. South Dakota senator Thomas Sterling assured his colleagues that "there is in this bill no prohibition on criticism" of the government or its representatives. Representative Meyer London, the only Socialist in Congress, went further and defended free speech, even in wartime. "If there are any treasonable thoughts in the minds of the American people," he declared, "I want them expressed; if there is any discontent with the war, I want to hear it."

President Wilson did not share this sentiment. Under his leadership, the Justice Department and the federal courts interpreted the Espionage Act to enable suppression of a broad range of political dissent, including any criticism of the draft, the war, or the military. Dissent became disloyalty, and disloyalty became crime. During WWI, the federal government prosecuted some 2,000 people under the Espionage Act, and routinely sentenced them to terms up to 20 years in prison. A New Hampshire man who complained that "this was a Morgan war and not a war of the people" got 3 years. Filmmaker Robert Goldstein was convicted for including the Wyoming Valley Massacre, in which British soldiers bayoneted women and children, in a movie about the American Revolution.

For his part, Postmaster General Albert Burleson interpreted the "nonmailability" clause broadly, and excluded from the mails the leftist magazines the *Masses*, the *International Socialist Review*, and the *Irish World*, and scores of other books and newspapers. The moderate *New York World* accused the post office of inaugurating an "intellectual reign of terror," and Theodore Roosevelt complained that Burleson had made it dangerous "for any man . . . to speak the truth, if that truth be unpleasant to the governmental authorities." But the authorities were not satisfied. A set of amendments to the Espionage Act known as the Sedition Act of 1918 forbade any person when the United States was at war to "utter, print, write, or publish any disloyal, profane, scurrilous, or abusive language" about the government or to use any language intended to bring the government, the flag, the uniform, the military, or the Constitution of the United States into "contempt, scorn, contumely, or disrepute."

FORGING CONSENSUS AT HOME

The reach of the Sedition Act troubled some congressmen. Senator Gilbert M. Hitchcock of Nebraska asked whether advocates of woman suffrage brought the Constitution "into disrepute" because they criticized it for not granting women the right to vote. Georgia senator Thomas Hardwick insisted that it was unnecessary and unprincipled to sacrifice American liberties in order to win a war for democracy.

To build public support for the war, Wilson established the Committee on Public Information (CPI). Under the direction of George Creel, a progressive journalist and public relations expert, the CPI manufactured a flood of pamphlets, speeches, newspaper editorials, political cartoons, and motion pictures that defended the war in the broadest of terms, as a contest between civilization and barbarism, the bearers of the torch of liberty against autocratic Huns.

Alongside the CPI strode the agents of the Treasury Department peddling war bonds, cleverly dubbed "Liberty Loans" by Treasury Secretary McAdoo. Charged with explaining the war and selling bonds in four-minute speeches, 75,000 multilingual Four Minute Men were dispatched across the country. "We went direct to the people," McAdoo recalled. "We capitalized on the profound impulse called patriotism." In fact, he did more than that. In California, McAdoo snarled, "Every person who refuses to subscribe or who takes the attitude of let the other fellow do it, is a friend of Germany. . . . A man who can't lend his government $1.25 per week at the rate of 4% interest is not entitled to be an American citizen." Ad campaigns compared wounded soldiers with "Mr. Stay-at-Home," and lectured the public that although America had "the Hun on the run," it took time to "beat defeat into the thick skulls of the baby-killing beasts from the Rhine." A Socialist coal miner who refused to buy a bond was lynched in Terra Haute, Indiana, Eugene Debs's hometown. When Ohio senator Warren G. Harding called the loan drive "hysterical and unseemly," he was hooted down on the Senate floor.

At the same time that Creel unleashed a torrent of propaganda, Wilson turned to censorship and coercion. In a nationwide raid in September 1917, federal agents raided offices of the Industrial Workers of the World (IWW), and destroyed the organization by trying and imprisoning its leaders. Attorney General Thomas Watt Gregory demanded that loyal Americans ferret out disloyalty. Voluntary organizations like the Knights of Liberty, the Boy Spies of America, the Sedition Slammers, and the Terrible Threateners targeted pacifists, suffragists, ethnic minorities, trade unionists, and socialists. They reported thousands of individuals to the authorities on the basis of hearsay, gossip, and slander. The largest of the citizen groups, the American Protective League, boasted over 250,000 members. Max Eastman, the editor of the banned *Masses* magazine, complained, "If you stopped to collect your thoughts, you could be arrested for illegal assembly."

Citizen groups strayed far beyond their supposed mandate. In Oklahoma, they tarred and feathered a minister who opposed the sale of Liberty Bonds; in Texas, they horsewhipped six farmers who declined to contribute to the Red Cross. Frank Little, an antiwar Wobbly leading a copper mining strike in Montana, was kidnapped, castrated, and hanged from a railroad trestle. In Illinois, Robert Prager, a German American socialist who had registered for the draft, was wrapped in an American flag and murdered on a public street. An uneasy president remained silent. Rather than condemn the mob, the Justice Department demanded more power to punish persons "making disloyal utterances."

AMERICA'S MOMENT

It took more than a year to raise, equip, train, and transport to Europe a US army that would fight under its own command, as an "associated power," rather than be integrated into Allied armies. Between spring of 1917 and November 1918, the American army went from 379,000 to 4.8 million men. In the meantime, Germany almost succeeded in winning the war. In Russia, the new Bolshevik government negotiated a separate peace with Germany that freed 40 German divisions on the Eastern Front for an assault on the west.

The first US troops landed in France in the spring of 1918. In June, 85,000 Americans helped halt the German drive toward Paris. In September, more than 1 million troops of the American Expeditionary Forces (AEF) pushed an exhausted German army back to the fortified Hindenburg Line constructed in 1916. All in all, 48,000 Americans were killed in action in WWI, 2,900 were listed as missing, and 56,000 died of disease. These numbers pale in comparison to the losses of Germany (1.8 million), Russia (1.7 million), France (1.4 million), Austria-Hungary (1.2 million), and Britain (947,000). But the presence of the Americans tipped the balance in the Allies' favor in the fall of 1918, and thus determined the outcome of the war.

Before Russia left the war in March 1918, the new Bolshevik government published a collection of Allied secret treaties dividing the anticipated spoils of war, and called for an international conference to discuss "peace without annexations or indemnities on the basis of the self-determination of peoples." Opposed to the imperial designs of Britain and France, Wilson nonetheless embraced their demand for the complete destruction of the Central Powers—a "total victory" the Allies were incapable of achieving on their own.

George Creel's CPI, so vital to persuading Americans to fight, turned now to convincing the world, as Creel put it, "that hope for the future lay in Wilson alone." American troops arrived in Europe "under a covering barrage of leaflets, speeches, and films" seeking to gain the support of the people, "over the heads of their own governments, for a peace of moderation and hope, not a peace of vengeance and Old World nationalism." This was the high ground Wilson regained from the Bolsheviks in his Fourteen Points address of January 8, 1918, in which he set out his vision of a future based on international free trade, democracy, national self-determination, transparent diplomacy, and collective security arrived at and defended by a "general association of nations." It was an inspiring and bold vision, but by articulating it as an alternative to Bolshevik ideals, Wilson alienated the European liberals best able to help him achieve his goals and energized conservative American opponents at home.

Worse, Wilson violated his own Fourteen Points even before the war was over. Provoked by the fanatically anti-Communist British war secretary Winston Churchill, Wilson sent 20,000 American troops in the summer of 1918 to prop up anti-Bolshevik forces in the civil war then raging in Russia. He also refused to recognize the legitimacy of the Bolshevik regime, supported an economic boycott designed to undermine it, and abetted the Allies' decision to bar the Russians from the peace negotiations. It was not an auspicious beginning for a new age of open diplomacy.

MEESTER VEELSON

The war ended on November 11, 1918, with the unconditional surrender of Germany. Woodrow Wilson traveled personally to the Paris suburb of Versailles to represent the United States and his own diplomatic vision at the Peace Conference. No sitting American president had ever left the country before. Although greeted triumphantly in France by enormous crowds, "Meester Veelson" was weakened by the undistinguished peace commission that accompanied him and by the 1918 midterm election, in which Republicans gained a majority in both houses of Congress—which looked to Europeans like a parliamentary vote of no confidence.

Europe in 1919 was, in the words of Czech leader Thomas Masaryk, "a laboratory resting on a vast cemetery." The revolutionary potential of the working classes both thrilled and terrified, especially after Communist uprisings in Hungary and Bavaria. The Austro-Hungarian and Ottoman Empires, whose combined boundaries stretched from the Danube to the Arabian Sea, lay in ruins. The postwar nations of central Europe (Poland, Czechoslovakia, Hungary, Austria) were conceived around a table at Versailles, where British, French, and American diplomats did their best to carve independent nations out of local identities rooted in overlapping and competing languages, ethnicities, religions, and historical memories.

The peace negotiated behind closed doors at the 1919 Versailles Conference in Paris was draconian. France wanted Germany dismembered and permanently disarmed. Britain wanted Germany's colonies and markets, plus reparations, including the full cost of pensions for Allied soldiers. Both insisted on pinning the blame for the carnage exclusively on Germany (the notorious War Guilt Clause).

Although Wilson's presence in Paris helped soften Allied wrath, the crushing defeat of Germany secured by two million American soldiers enabled a harsher settlement than if the Europeans had been left to their own fate and had collapsed into a less definitive peace of exhaustion.

Wilson returned to the United States with a treaty that included two personal victories: the establishment of a mandate, or trustee, system to govern the former German and Ottoman colonies, preventing their outright transfer to the victors; and the League of Nations, an international body empowered to encourage peaceful resolution of disputes through arbitration and adjudication, to employ economic and military sanctions against aggressors, and to call on a collective security mechanism that obliged league nations to defend each other against external aggression.

Discussions in the United States about the Versailles Treaty were heated. Its punitive nature offended American progressives, while conservatives objected to the league's collective security measures. A two-thirds majority of the Senate was constitutionally required in order to ratify the agreement, and most members accepted the league. But the chairman of the Senate Foreign Relations Committee, Wilson's implacable personal enemy Henry Cabot Lodge, opposed the league on the grounds that it compromised American sovereignty, and orchestrated a massive anti-league propaganda campaign.

Desperate to save the treaty, Wilson took his fight to the nation. In a 10,000-mile speaking tour, the exhausted president defended the league to generally enthusiastic crowds. On September 26, 1919, Wilson collapsed in Pueblo, Colorado, and returned to Washington. A week later, he suffered a massive stroke that left him partially blind and paralyzed on one side. He was, said Lloyd George, "as much a victim of the war as any soldier who died in the trenches." The Versailles Treaty was defeated in the Senate on November 19, 1919. It was left to Republican President Warren G. Harding to proclaim a formal end to hostilities with the Central Powers in the summer of 1921.

Progressives at High Tide

Excited by what John Dewey called "the social possibilities of war"— the prospect of reshaping domestic political and class relations in a wartime environment—progressives, including many women, flooded into government service and stepped up campaigns for expanded democracy. It was as if the war and progressives "had been waiting for each other," commented a more skeptical progressive, Randolph Bourne, who asked, presciently, "If the war is too strong for you to prevent, how is it going to be weak enough for you to control and mould to your liberal purposes?" As in Europe, World War I created a national state in America with a vastly expanded portfolio. Aside from Bourne, few progressives paused to consider the potential drawbacks of a wartime government of unprecedented size and power.

THE WARTIME STATE

The temporary absorption of economic and industrial relations within the swollen sphere of the wartime state offered Americans the chance to experiment along lines already established by the "war-socialized" European nations. Nearly 5,000 agencies were established to manage particular economic sectors. The War Industries Board established sweeping authority over manufacturing. The War Labor Board guaranteed collective bargaining and mediated labor disputes. Membership in the American Federation of Labor skyrocketed, with a wartime increase of 2.3 million members. The War Revenue Act of 1917 raised personal and corporate income taxes and imposed an excess profits tax (the closest the United States came to "conscripting wealth"). The 1917 Lever Food and Fuel Act empowered the president to control fuel prices and set the price of wheat in order to boost production. The federal government took over telephone and telegraph companies, warehouses, and, warming the hearts of old Populists, the railroads.

British leaders argued that industrial nations engaged in a struggle for existence must support their working populations or face economic and, eventually, military defeat. Americans soon understood that, in the words of Theodore Roosevelt, an army composed of "the human wreckage which a scrap-heap system of industrialism" produced would be no match for the Huns. It was therefore necessary "to bring the United States abreast of Germany and other European countries" in legislation that benefited and protected the working class—which had now become the soldier class. Progressive initiatives such as workers' compensation insurance (in case of industrial accidents), old-age pensions, health insurance, limits on child labor, and woman suffrage had been derided before the war. Now they were repackaged as national security measures.

All these things, plus the war, had to be paid for. The cost of the war was staggering: by May 1918, the federal debt approached $1 billion a month—an amount greater than the annual federal budget before the war. The federal debt leapt from $1 billion in 1915 to over $20 billion by 1920. Government spending went in two directions: toward the Grain Belt of the Midwest, whose farmers fattened on skyrocketing (and government supported) wheat prices, and toward East Coast industrialists who were all, confessed one steel executive, "making more money out of this war than the average human being ought to." The stock of Bethlehem Steel, a Morgan interest, went from $33 to $600 a share between 1914 and 1916.

Progressives wanted to fund at least half the war through taxation, which they considered more equitable than large-scale borrowing likely to increase the money supply and fuel inflation. In May 1918, President Wilson made a rare appearance before a joint session of Congress to urge higher taxes on "war profits and incomes and luxuries." But by the time the War Revenue Act of 1918 was ready for a vote in November, the war had ended.

World War I triggered a fiscal revolution in the United States. The principle of progressive taxation—laying the burden on those most able to absorb it—was woven into the tax system and generally accepted until challenged by Republicans in the 1980s. Before the war, nearly 75 percent of federal revenue came from customs and excise taxes, which weighed heavily on less affluent Americans. After the war, 75 percent of revenue derived from income taxes, profits, and estates.

MOBILITY AND MOBS, LAW AND LAWLESSNESS

African Americans had hoped that their participation in the Great War would cement their claim to equal status at home. Instead, 350,000 African American soldiers were shipped off to Europe under strict Jim Crow conditions and relegated to labor battalions. Only 40,000 black soldiers saw combat. The few commissioned black officers were treated as incompetent, and black troops were undersupplied, over-disciplined, and occasionally shot and killed by their own officers in battle. Future NAACP legal strategist Charles Hamilton Houston spoke for many when he recalled later, "I felt damned glad I had not lost my life fighting for this country."

Nonetheless, the war contributed to demographic and political shifts that furthered the cause of black equality. The sudden end to immigration from Europe in 1914, combined with increased wartime production, opened thousands of industrial jobs to black workers and precipitated a dramatic movement of African Americans from the South to the North. Many motives and circumstances combined to produce the Great Migration: higher wages in northern factories (even if black laborers were limited to unskilled positions), better schools for children, access to the suffrage and political influence, escape from the ever-present threat of violence in the South, an end to the back-breaking work of sharecropping, and, for black women, the prospect of indoor jobs as servants and laundresses. At least 330,000 African Americans abandoned the South for northern cities like Chicago, Detroit, and New York between 1915 and 1918, where they found work in homes, factories, stockyards, and railroads.

White workers resented the newcomers, seeing them as a threat to white living standards, social status, and political power. When an aluminum ore company in East St. Louis, Illinois, used black migrants to break a strike and destroy a labor union in July 1917, white workers went on a murderous rampage. Mobs beat, shot, hanged, and burned black people caught on the sidewalks or pulled off streetcars.

The striking white workers who became the mob in East St. Louis were themselves often the target of organized violence. War mobilization and labor shortages sparked labor unrest across the country. Strikers and their families were often confronted with violence, particularly in the West, where isolated mining communities were run like company-owned fiefdoms outside the reach of the law. In June 1917, 1,200 men, women, and children associated with a striking Arizona mine workers' union affiliated with the IWW were packed into cattle cars and left to bake in the desert by 2,000 members of the local Citizens' Protective League and Workmen's Loyalty League.

The war transformed previously private struggles between labor and management into battles in which the state had a commanding stake. On July 26, 1918, President Wilson condemned mob rule and insisted on the rule of law. The mob spirit, he insisted, was irreconcilable with American democracy; every American, he said, "who takes part in the action of a mob . . . is no true son of this great Democracy, but its betrayer." Organizations that had struggled against extralegal repression like lynching were quick to realize the sea change in the government's attitude. In 1919, Moorfield Storey, a prominent Boston attorney and president of the NAACP, lectured a graduating law class that the belief "that all men must obey the law is the doctrine on which free governments rest."

OPERATION OCCUPY THE WHITE HOUSE:
MILITANT WOMAN SUFFRAGE

At the turn of the twentieth century, a new generation of women turned a polite, ladylike suffrage movement into a contentious, confrontational one. Between 1910 and 1915, suffrage spectacles swept the nation. Suffragists staged dances, outdoor concerts, and vaudeville shows; they launched hot-air balloons; they barnstormed states in automobiles; they dumped suffrage flyers out of airplanes. It wasn't all fun and games, however. One 1912 parade generated a hostile crowd and hate mail. "I don't wish you any bad luck," wrote one opponent, "but I hope the sidewalk falls through and you all go to Hell."

The outlandish public behavior of suffragists was matched by intensive lobbying efforts at the federal and state levels. The National

Woman's Party (NWP), organized by radical suffrage leader Alice Paul, targeted politicians who opposed votes for women. Theodore Roosevelt's Progressive Party endorsed woman suffrage in 1912.

The first victories came in the West, where women were already often enfranchised in local elections. But then the war interrupted the campaign. Carrie Chapman Catt, the president of the National American Woman Suffrage Association (NAWSA), was a pacifist like Jane Addams and deeply committed to international cooperation among women. She nonetheless threw herself and her organization into war work after April 1917 to illustrate women's vital contribution to the nation. President Wilson, who thought that "the only women interested in woman's suffrage were aggressive and masculine with harsh voices," tepidly endorsed woman suffrage, but also lectured them that the vote was something "for which you can afford a little while to wait."

Alice Paul had waited long enough. On January 11, 1917, Paul did something no American had ever done before: she and a small group protested in front of the White House. Their banner read, "How long must women wait for liberty?" At first the president was amused; he sent hot coffee on winter days and waved at the women, who passed the hours singing and knitting socks for soldiers. But when Paul unfurled a banner proclaiming "This Nation Is Not Free" and then, later, one denouncing "Kaiser Wilson," the group was roughed up by an outraged crowd and arrested for disorderly conduct.

By November 1917, dozens of radical suffragists had been jailed in Washington, where some of them suffered solitary confinement, psychiatric treatment, and forced feeding when they staged a hunger strike. The spectacle of respectable white women attacked by mobs and arrested for criticizing the president caught the attention of the national media and embarrassed the White House.

Wilson broke first. He sent a message through a sympathetic journalist to Alice Paul in jail: if she would call off her picketing, he would support a constitutional amendment forbidding the denial of suffrage on the basis of sex. Paul's sentence was commuted, the picketing stopped, and on September 30, 1918, the president stood before the Senate to personally urge speedy passage of the Nineteenth Amendment, arguing that if Americans "wish to lead the world to democracy," they must demonstrate "that democracy means that women shall play their part in affairs alongside men and upon an equal footing with them." The amendment, he concluded, "is a vitally necessary war measure" and "is vital to the right solution of the great problems which we must settle . . . when the war is over." Although stymied initially by southern Democrats, the new Republican Senate elected in 1918 passed the bill and sent it to the states for ratification. In August 1920, American women finally gained the right to vote.

PROHIBITION

American women got the vote when they did partly because another divisive social issue, prohibition, had already been resolved through the Eighteenth Amendment, passed in December 1917 and ratified in January 1919. Prior to this, the prominence of woman suffragists in the temperance movement had inspired the fervent opposition of many men, particularly those in the liquor business, to woman suffrage.

The push to outlaw the sale of "intoxicating liquors" at the state and local level was carried forward by the activists of the Woman's Christian Temperance Union (WCTU, founded in 1874) and by the all-male, well-heeled Anti-Saloon League, which initiated the drive for a national constitutional amendment in 1913. Whereas the WCTU linked liquor to temptation and sin and focused on the evils of alcohol consumption for families (including domestic violence), the Anti-Saloon League targeted the "saloon evil" and the liquor trade rather than personal alcohol consumption. The WCTU and the Anti-Saloon League saw success in the South, where white supremacists worried about "Negro dives," and Midwest farm country. But they encountered fierce resistance in cities, especially among immigrant workingmen—who insisted, correctly, that anti-saloon laws were aimed at them.

More than simply places to have a quick drink, saloons were centers of political and social life for working-class men. Saloonkeepers were often active in local politics. One Milwaukee saloon owner described his place as, effectively, an "educational institution." The number of saloons in the United States tripled in the last third of the nineteenth century, which also saw the largest immigration boom in the nation's history. Beer consumption exploded, as did public drunkenness.

By 1910, about half of Americans already lived under some form of local liquor-prohibition legislation. These Americans had voted to limit their own behavior. The prohibitionists wanted to limit the behavior of people who lived outside their jurisdiction—namely, urban workingmen and their families, who were unlikely ever to vote against alcohol. The Anti-Saloon League's campaign for a constitutional amendment was resisted by its targets, but also by others concerned about such a vast expansion of central state authority. Former president William Howard Taft opposed the amendment on the grounds that it would undermine the federal nature of the republic and "call for a horde of federal officials" to enforce it.

Opponents of the proposed Eighteenth Amendment, which was the first constitutional amendment to limit rather than protect liberty, would almost certainly have prevailed were it not for the war. Prohibitionists leapt at the opportunity to trade on the popular association of beer with immigrants, particularly Germans, and to portray saloons as nests of un-American activities. Breweries that carried the names of their German American founders were easily associated with the Central Powers. At a time when sauerkraut was renamed "liberty cabbage," what chance did Pabst and Schlitz have?

The Eighteenth Amendment's enabling legislation, the Volstead Act, criminalized the manufacture and sale of alcohol, but not its possession or consumption. Assailed as a violation of individual liberty and derided and disobeyed by millions, prohibition did succeed in lowering the consumption of alcohol by about half.

More than most issues, prohibition revealed an urban-rural split in American life. Immigrants, clustered in cities, resented the amendment as aimed at them—which it was, in good measure. Urbane WASPs clucked that the yokels of the South and Midwest had fastened their own moral code on the nation. The issue divided the Democratic Party, which strained to encompass both white southern drys and urban immigrant wets, and remained a charged political question throughout the 1920s.

Reconstruction

The transition to peacetime was monumental and messy. "In every direction," wrote author John Dos Passos, "the countries of the world stretched out starving and angry, ready for anything turbulent and new." Determined to protect wartime gains, nearly four million American workers (approximately one in five) walked out on strike in 1919. Convinced that the federal government was a better employer than their former bosses, railroad workers demanded government ownership of the railways. Coal unions urged a federal takeover of the mines. Chicago, Washington, and Detroit erupted in murderous race riots in which African Americans returned fire: precisely the worry of white supremacists who had opposed infantry training for black soldiers. The Bolsheviks' call for global revolution found receptive ears in the United States, which fed fears of insurrection at home. All of this occurred in the shadow of an influenza pandemic that within six months killed three-quarters of a million Americans, most in the prime of life: six times the number of soldiers who died in the war.

RIVAL UTOPIAS

The immediate postwar United States was a bedlam of conflicting ambitions and rival utopias. President Wilson's most trusted domestic advisor, Joe Tumulty, pressed on the president a federal domestic program that paralleled the one offered Britons by Prime Minister Lloyd George: old-age pensions, health insurance, minimum wage and maximum hours laws, recognition of the right of collective bargaining, and permanent industrial dispute arbitration machinery along the lines of the War Labor Board. "The real antidote for Bolshevism," said Tumulty, voicing the preoccupation of every postwar government, "is social reconstruction."

Tumulty's prescription for postwar domestic peace consisted of reforms that had been championed by progressives for two decades. Had Theodore Roosevelt presided over the wartime American government—as he ardently desired—the postwar reconstruction might have turned out differently. But the war had not lasted long enough to create a sense of its own normalcy. Wilson, preoccupied by foreign policy, left the government leaderless at the top.

Into the void rushed labor and business. The year following the armistice brought ground-shaking industrial battles in coal, steel, textiles, and shipping, as workers fought to make the emergency gains of the war permanent and employers resisted to the utmost. During the war, unemployment had dropped dramatically, and wages had mushroomed. Rising incomes were eroded by skyrocketing inflation, however. The cost of living in 1920 was more than double what it was before the war. The first general strike in American history occurred in Seattle in January 1919, when the Seattle Central Labor Council shut down the city in support of 35,000 striking shipyard workers. Schools were closed, and streetcars were sidelined. Rather than herald a new revolutionary moment, however, the Seattle General Strike replayed an old theme when federal troops marched in and crushed the strike after five days.

Employers who had never reconciled themselves to treating their labor force as partners used every weapon at their command to roll back the progress of workers. In Boston, police struck after 19 officers were fired for union membership, leaving the city defenseless against crime. President Wilson denounced the strike as "a crime against civilization," and Massachusetts governor Calvin Coolidge became a national hero when he backed the police commissioner's decision to fire the entire force, declaring that "there is no right to strike against the public safety by anybody, anywhere, anytime."

The police strike was followed quickly by a nationwide strike among steelworkers. Confronted by 365,000 strikers, US Steel magnate Elbert Gary denounced them as Communists and refused to recognize the union or address any of its demands, which included one day off per week and a daily 20-minute lunch break. The men returned to work after two months without a single gain.

Coal miners, whose control over the nation's fuel supply gave them unique leverage, were less cooperative. Defying the owners (who, predictably, tagged them as Bolsheviks) as well as United Mine Workers leader John Lewis, 400,000 coal miners waged a massive strike despite a government injunction. President Wilson, who had denounced the strike as "a grave moral and legal wrong," finally intervened personally (as Roosevelt had done in 1902) and secured a substantial wage increase to end the walkout.

WE RETURN FIGHTING

Having fought for democracy abroad, African Americans were resolved to defend and expand it at home. W. E. B. Du Bois announced in the NAACP newspaper the *Crisis* that "by the God of Heaven, we are cowards and jackasses if . . . we do not marshal every ounce of our brain and brawn to fight . . . against the forces of hell" in America. "We return. We return from fighting. We return fighting."

Black veterans carried back from Europe broadened horizons and, in some cases, combat experience. "Beyond a doubt," reported a military intelligence analyst monitoring the situation, "there is a new negro to be reckoned with in our political and social life." African Americans wanted access to the polling booth, equal educational opportunities, fairer treatment in court, an end to lynching and to employment discrimination—an end, in general, to Jim Crow. "It would astonish you to know the depth of the bitterness that is in the hearts of the negroes in the South today," reported one white participant in an interracial meeting.

African American organizations surged after the armistice. Black workers joined whatever unions, such as the United Mine Workers, that would accept them. The Universal Negro Improvement Association (UNIA), founded in New York by Jamaican immigrant Marcus Garvey, called on blacks to present a united front as a people against the "white devils" who robbed African Americans of their citizenship rights and dignity. NAACP membership surged nationwide, but especially in the South. In Phillips County, Arkansas, black sharecroppers and tenant farmers, tired of being fleeced by white landlords, organized the Progressive Farmers and Household Union of America.

Government officials who considered labor organizing an insurrectionary activity among whites were doubly concerned when blacks unionized. When violence broke out in Phillips County in September 1919, 600 federal troops helped local whites "round up and disarm" suspected revolutionaries. An unknown number of blacks died at their hands. The army admitted to killing "about twenty negroes" for refusing to halt when ordered. In addition to those killed, 122 black men were indicted, 73 of them for murder, and 12 received death sentences.

The Phillips County bloodshed capped a summer of racial violence so extreme that NAACP leader James Weldon Johnson dubbed it the "Red Summer." Southern whites targeted black veterans — one soldier was lynched for the offense of wearing the uniform of the United States in public. Scores of race riots left untold numbers dead, wounded, and homeless. In July, a riot in Chicago rooted in competition over jobs and housing claimed 38 lives. Chicago's politicians and commercial leaders concluded that only strict residential segregation could prevent racial violence.

Widespread intimidation slowed and then reversed the growth of the NAACP in the South. The Commission on Interracial Cooperation, an integrated, all-male middle-class group founded in Atlanta in 1919, filled some of the void, but did not replace the mass movement. After John R. Shillady, the NAACP's first executive secretary, was beaten savagely by three white men, including a county judge, in broad daylight outside his hotel room in Austin, Texas, he expressed an understated despair about the future of America. "I am less confident than heretofore," he wrote, "of the probability of overcoming, within a reasonable period, the forces opposed to Negro equality." He returned to New York and died in 1920.

RED SCARE

On May 1, 1919, bombs were sent to 30 prominent Americans, including J. P. Morgan Jr. and Oliver Wendell Holmes. The unlucky maid of Georgia senator Thomas Hardwick lost both hands. This was but the prelude. On June 2, bombs exploded in seven eastern cities. Two people were killed. In Washington, DC, a blast sheared off the front of Attorney General A. Mitchell Palmer's house and damaged the home of his neighbors, Assistant Secretary of the Navy Franklin Roosevelt and his wife, Eleanor.

The June 2 bomb plot convinced many Americans that violent radicals posed a threat to the nation, and led to a new wave of state repression. A Senate subcommittee convened to investigate "anti-American radicalism" declared that Bolshevism was the "greatest current danger facing the Republic." On June 3, 1919, Attorney General Palmer announced a new campaign to rid the country of its "anarchist elements" through deportation. Calling for a peacetime sedition act, Palmer launched an all-out war against the "disease of evil thinking." He established the General Intelligence Division (GID, dubbed the "Radical Division") within the Bureau of Investigation to keep tabs on political dissent. Led by 24-year-old John Edgar Hoover, the GID infiltrated left-wing organizations and amassed a list of 200,000 suspected radicals. The Red Scare had begun.

The first of the Palmer Raids occurred on November 7, 1919, and targeted the Union of Russian Workers, an anarchist organization composed mainly of Russian immigrants. On January 2, 1920, Palmer cast the net more broadly. The government raided "radical hangouts" in 33 cities and rounded up 4,000 suspected subversives. Virtually every leader of every local communist organization was taken into custody. The experience of the government raiding a peaceable union meeting was described vividly by an outraged federal judge in Montana in 1920: "There was no disorder save that of the raiders. [Acting without a warrant, these agents], mainly uniformed and armed, overawed, intimidated, and forcibly entered, broke, and destroyed property, searched persons, effects and papers, . . . cursed, insulted, beat, dispersed, and bayoneted union members. . . . [They] perpetrated a reign of terror, violence and crime against citizen and alien alike."

The chilling effect of such government activity on political expression was noteworthy. Surveying the scene, the *New Republic*'s Walter Lippmann raged in November 1919, "At this moment the man who in domestic policy stands about where Theodore Roosevelt stood in 1912 and in foreign affairs where Woodrow Wilson stood when he first landed in Paris . . . is certain, absolutely certain to be called pacifist, pro-German and Bolshevist."

The attorney general was right to fear the anarchists. There *were* proponents of political violence (what anarchists called "the propaganda of the deed") in America; they *were* responsible for the spate of postwar bombings. But the rush to link the anarchists with all leftist political organizations, particularly the Socialist Party, was misguided. That organization had already split in September 1919, at its party convention in Chicago, over the question of tactics: would Socialists run for election or engage in direct action? Although those who scorned electoral politics, who joined either the Communist Party or the Communist Labor Party, called for the revolutionary overthrow of the government, they considered acts of individual terrorism like mail bombs self-defeating. Socialist Party membership fell dramatically, from a postwar high of 109,000 to 36,000 by 1920. The party's leader, Eugene Debs, remained imprisoned.

DISCOVERING THE FIRST AMENDMENT

In the spring of 1919, the Supreme Court decided several cases involving the conviction under the Espionage and Sedition Acts of people who had opposed the draft or the war. In unanimous decisions written by Justice Oliver Wendell Holmes, the court considered, for the very first time, the First Amendment's promise that "Congress shall make no law abridging the freedom of speech, or of the press." Was the government *absolutely* forbidden to prohibit speech? Surely not, Holmes decided: the authorities would be quite right to punish a man who caused a panic by raising a *false* alarm of fire in a crowded theater. But when *was* the government forbidden to punish speech?

In *Schenck v. United States,* the defendant Charles Schenck was convicted for attempting to obstruct the draft by distributing leaflets that called the draft unconstitutional and urged people to "Assert Your Rights!" The court upheld Schenck's conviction, reasoning that his speech could cause at least *some* people to unlawfully refuse induction into the army. A week later, the court upheld the conviction of Eugene V. Debs, the national leader of the Socialist Party, who had been sentenced to ten years in prison for delivering a speech that criticized the war and praised the courage of draft resisters.

Schenck and *Debs* effectively gutted the First Amendment guarantee by ruling that if speech could have bad consequences, such as hindering the draft, it could be prohibited under the Espionage and Sedition Acts. But the justices paid close attention to the ongoing free speech debate of a distinguished group of constitutional law professors and jurists. Holmes corresponded with several of them, including the author of the federal court decision overturned in *Schenck*, Judge Learned Hand.

In *Abrams v. United States*, a group of Russian Jewish émigrés distributed leaflets that criticized American military intervention in the Russian Civil War and called for a general strike. They were convicted and sentenced to prison terms ranging from 10 to 20 years. Predictably, the Supreme Court upheld the convictions, holding that the issue had been resolved in its decisions in *Schenck* and *Debs*.

Unlike the earlier decisions, however, *Abrams* was not unanimous. Influenced by critics of his earlier opinions, including Hand, who had written in 1917 that "the spirit of liberty is the spirit which is not too sure that it is right," Justice Holmes, joined by Justice Louis D. Brandeis, dissented. Holmes argued that the First Amendment was premised on the understanding that "the best test of truth" was the ability of the thought "to get itself accepted in the competition of the market." This "marketplace of ideas," Holmes reasoned, was vital to democracy, and the government should therefore not be able to limit free expression unless it posed a "clear and present danger" to the very existence of the government. Americans, Holmes concluded, "should be eternally vigilant against attempts to check the expression of opinions that we loathe and believe to be fraught with death, unless they so imminently threaten immediate interference with the lawful and pressing purposes of the law that an immediate check is required to save the country."

The position set forth by Holmes and Brandeis in a series of dissenting opinions eventually carried the day, with the court and the nation. In the meantime, though, Schenck, Debs, and the *Abrams* defendants, as well as thousands of other Americans, remained behind bars.

ILLEGAL ACTIVITIES

New York assemblyman Clayton R. Lusk, who convened a committee on radicalism in New York in 1919, was no more inclined to differentiate among critics of the government than Palmer. Egged on by the Lusk Committee, the New York State Assembly denounced the Socialist Party as "a disloyal party of perpetual traitors," and revealed its plan to expel five recently elected Socialist assemblymen. This naked assault on the democratic process provoked considerable outrage, to the bewilderment of Lusk, who defended "repression carried on by and with the consent of the . . . majority."

The depth of antiradical hysteria concerned Congress, which declined Attorney General Palmer's request to enact an even more oppressive version of the Sedition Act of 1918. Responding to the argument that the attorney general's actions were justified because of public fear "of the spread of bolshevism" and the "dastardly bomb outrages," Montana senator Thomas Walsh observed that it is "in such times that the guarantees of the Constitution as to personal liberties" are of special value. The congressional spine was stiffened by the May 1920 publication of *To the American People: Report upon the Illegal Practices of the United States Department of Justice* authored by a group of distinguished lawyers and law professors. The report documented and condemned the "utterly illegal acts which have been committed by those charged with the highest duty of enforcing the laws—acts which have caused widespread suffering and unrest, have struck at the foundation of American free institutions, and have brought the name of our country into disrepute."

Passions ebbed as the presidential election campaign of 1920 got underway. Ohio Republican senator Warren G. Harding was the heavy favorite, running against Democrat James Cox and Eugene Debs, who had reluctantly accepted the Socialist nomination although he was still imprisoned. In a special election on September 16, 1920, in New York, the voters returned all five Socialist assemblymen.

That same day, a bomb went off outside the Morgan bank on Wall Street, killing 38 people and seriously wounding another 143. The *New York Times* warned against "yielding to panic," and recommended that the explosion be treated as an ordinary criminal case. Warren Harding was elected six weeks later by the largest majority in the history of presidential elections, which he secured by winning the votes of a combination of opposites: those who thought the peace too harsh as well as those who thought it too lenient; those who believed that Wilson had betrayed internationalism and those who thought he had undermined national sovereignty; workers who blamed Wilson for the high cost of living and businessmen who damned him for coddling workers. "We have torn up Wilsonianism by the roots," exulted Henry Cabot Lodge: precisely the president's fear in 1914 when confronted with the war.

Eugene Debs was at last released from prison on December 23, 1921, when President Harding, following the recommendation of the

Justice Department, commuted Debs's sentence (something Wilson had refused to do). His first stop was the White House, where Harding greeted him by saying, "I have heard so damned much about you, Mr. Debs, that I am now very glad to meet you personally." On December 13, 1920, Congress quietly repealed the Sedition Act of 1918. The Espionage Act remains in effect.

*

Alone among the nations that fought World War I, America in 1920 was stronger than it had been in 1914. Its armed forces were larger and more advanced. The economic stimulus of the war not only had generated jobs and unprecedented profits, but also had catapulted the United States from a debtor nation (one that borrowed from abroad more than it lent) to a creditor nation (one that lent more than it borrowed) and transformed its economy into the most powerful in the world. America was now an acknowledged world leader, although its people were uncertain of how, precisely, to play that role.

There were, however, tremendous costs to America's participation in the war. The wartime suppression of dissent and its perpetuation into peacetime scarred American politics. The successful effort of business interests to cast critiques of capitalism and oppressive labor conditions as "red" and "un-American" disarmed progressives and constrained political debate. Gone were the days of progressive Republicans denouncing the evils of the "Money Trust." The *New Republic*, which once railed against plutocracy, was reduced to noting meekly that it "would rather not" have Morgan bankers "quite so much at home around the White House." The progressives had had their turn. Now it was time to see what the Morgan bankers could produce.

FIGURE 4. Ku Klux Klan parade, September 13, 1926. National Photo Company Collection, Prints and Photographs Division, Library of Congress, Washington, DC, LC-F8-40560.

CHAPTER 4

Vertigo, 1920–1928

On August 11, 1921, Edwin Stephenson, a Methodist minister, shot and killed Father James Coyle on the rectory porch of St. Paul's Catholic Church in Birmingham, Alabama. Earlier that day, Father Coyle had presided over the marriage of Stephenson's 18-year-old daughter, Ruth, to native Puerto Rican Pedro Gussman, a 42-year-old wallpaper hanger. Independent-minded Ruth had been interested in Catholicism since adolescence; Coyle had baptized her into the church some months before her marriage. When word of the wedding reached her father, he grabbed his gun and headed for St. Paul's.

Because Coyle was unarmed, Stephenson's defense team needed to come up with a more plausible explanation for the violence than the defendant's claim of self-defense. It did. Lead lawyer Hugo L. Black argued that Stephenson had acted in a state of temporary insanity brought on by the marriage of his daughter to a "Negro."

Pedro Gussman's identity as a Negro came as news to him. Prior to the trial, he had always been regarded as white. He dated white women. He was registered to vote. Had Gussman been considered black, he and Ruth could not have acquired a marriage license, since marriage across the color line was strictly forbidden in Alabama. "No one has ever questioned my color until I became mixed up in this case," he complained.

By transforming Pedro Gussman from a tanned Puerto Rican into a "Negro," Hugo Black offered the jury, composed exclusively of white men, a credible basis to find Edwin Stephenson temporarily insane: Father Coyle had seduced Ruth Stephenson away from the true faith and her father's rightful rule and married her to a man whose religion and color marked him as inferior. Any self-respecting white man would blow a fuse under such circumstances. The jury voted to acquit.

Hugo Black's reputation grew. He joined the local chapter of the Ku Klux Klan, which paid Stephenson's legal fees.

Formally reconstituted at Stone Mountain, Georgia, in 1915 by white men inspired by the heroic portrayal of the Reconstruction-era Klan in the film *Birth of a Nation*, the Second Klan was not of the hooded-hicks-on-horseback variety. The resurgent KKK was strongest in the West and Midwest and as common in urban as in rural areas. The 1920s Klan was rooted in WWI vigilance committees and is more accurately grouped with other postwar organizations like the American Legion than its Reconstruction antecedent. Two factors distinguished the Klan from other fraternal organizations of the era, however: its use of violence and its political influence.

Numbering approximately five million at the their peak in the mid-1920s, Klansmen participated actively in politics as voters, organizers, and candidates. Militantly Protestant, the Klan was a vehicle for "old stock" Americans (those whose ancestors had arrived before the great waves of immigration after 1890) striving to reassert cultural dominance over an increasingly heterogeneous and secular society. Klansmen lived in a fractured and disorienting world. Their country, especially its cities, was swamped with clannish Jews and Catholics, who educated their children apart and voted together. Their wives were politically enfranchised and assertive, their sons were disrespectful, and their daughters ungovernable, especially in matters of sex and marriage. Skeptics derided their religion. The economy, and thus their livelihood, was unpredictable. Bootleggers and their customers flouted the law of the land. All these things left men like Edwin Stephenson off-balance and insecure, and, the Klan believed, eroded the foundation of the republic, which after all was rooted in men like themselves.

Ohio Republican Warren Harding had ascended to the presidency in 1920 by promising a "return to normalcy," by which he meant a world of stable class, race, and gender hierarchy untroubled by political agitation or labor strife or cosmopolitanism. But that world had never really existed, and even if it had, too much had changed by 1920 to return to any nostalgic prewar notion of "normalcy." In 1925, Robert and Helen Merrell Lynd published *Middletown*, an exhaustive sociological examination of "normal" Muncie, Indiana. Measured by the baseline of 1890, the Lynds found dramatic transformations in virtually all aspects of life, and concluded that "we today are probably living in one of the eras of greatest rapidity of change in the history of human institutions." Constant, unnerving change seemed to be the new normal.

The Roaring Twenties

The 1920s represented a dramatic shift from both the era of progressive government that preceded the war and the strong wartime state, as it witnessed a government dedicated to the pursuit of policies favorable to large business interests. "Never before," gushed the *Wall Street Journal*, "has a government been so completely fused with business." Republicans believed that the entire nation would benefit by allying government with business. Easy credit and a get-rich-quick attitude buoyed a rising stock market. Even William Jennings Bryan cashed in on the construction boom in Florida. The "central question in the politics of the 1920s," concluded historian William E. Leuchtenburg, was "whether the business interest, given full support by a cooperative government, could maintain prosperity and develop social policies that would redound to the benefit not merely of itself but of the whole nation."

ENGINES OF GROWTH

From 1922 to 1929, the United States experienced a period of unparalleled prosperity. Although millions remained mired in poverty and unemployment hovered near 10 percent, many Americans, particularly city dwellers, achieved a high standard of living. The real earnings of workers—what their wages would buy at the store—rose 22 percent in just seven years, while the number of hours they worked was cut. Corporate profits rose at twice that rate.

Industrial productivity almost doubled during the 1920s, thanks to enormous gains in efficiency through machine power, especially electricity, and new ways of managing production. Total industrial output soared 264 percent. The iron and steel industry grew by 500 percent and, with the discovery of new oil fields in Texas, Oklahoma, and California, the petroleum industry boomed.

But it was the automobile industry that really revved the Roaring Twenties. In 1900, 4,000 cars were produced. By 1929, 4.8 million cars were rolling off the assembly line each year. The production of automobiles stimulated the economy as a whole. Prompted by the Federal Aid Road Act of 1916, government at every level initiated ambitious highway construction, effectively providing a government subsidy to the auto industry while creating construction jobs. Roads in turn stimulated new enterprises like motels (motor hotels) and advertising billboards, and encouraged the growth of suburbs featuring homes with garages rather than carriage houses. For the first time in American history, suburbs grew faster than central cities. By the end of the decade, automobile manufacturing accounted for 10 percent of the nation's income and employed four million workers.

Mass production depended on mass markets and mass consumption. The foreign markets that had sustained the United States' economic growth through WWI were no longer sufficient to prime American prosperity. American workers who labored for a pittance 10 hours a day six days a week had neither the leisure time nor the funds to shop. Without broadly distributed purchasing power, neither domestic markets nor profits could expand. Automaker Henry Ford grasped this before most people. In 1914, when the daily factory wage was about $3, Ford paid $5. Later he established the five-day workweek.

At the same time, Ford crafted a low-price, high-volume model of manufacturing through efficient innovations such as the assembly line (adapted from the meat-packing industry) and new technology. In 1913, it took 14 hours to assemble a single car. By 1925, a Model T Ford rolled off the continuously moving production line every 10 seconds. "Machinery," Ford boasted, "is the new Messiah."

The mechanical messiah was no savior to labor, however. Technological advances undermined the skills of individual workers and left them vulnerable to replacement. Routinized and repetitive work dehumanized laborers and eroded the boundary between worker and machine—a process captured brilliantly by Charlie Chaplin's 1936 film *Modern Times*, in which an assembly line worker is consumed by and incorporated into the machine he tends. As easily replaceable as any other part of the machine, such human cogs had no job security and lived in constant dread of layoffs.

"BUSINESSMEN'S GOVERNMENT"

After 20 years of Theodore Roosevelt's insults, Taft's trust-busting, Wilson's reform, and the war's expansion of the state, conservative Republicans were anxious to curb government and promote business. They got more than they bargained for with Warren Harding, who surrounded himself with cronies who used their government positions for private gain. The head of the Veterans' Bureau received kickbacks from the sale of government supplies. Attorney General Harry Daugherty resigned in disgrace after accepting payments not to prosecute criminals. The most notorious scandal involved Secretary of the Interior Albert Fall, who received nearly $500,000 (a staggering sum at the time) to lease government oil reserves at Teapot Dome, Wyoming, to private businessmen.

Calvin Coolidge, who ascended to the presidency upon Harding's death in 1923 and won election in his own right in 1924, assembled a "businessmen's government" by and for industry. The taciturn former governor of Vermont favored industrialists because he believed they could, if left to their own devices, maintain the economic prosperity necessary to preserve social harmony.

Coolidge was one of three American presidents who, as it was said, served under Secretary of the Treasury Andrew Mellon, who held that office throughout the 1920s. The third-richest man in America (behind Rockefeller and Ford), Mellon labored tirelessly in the interests of the wealthy. Guiding the three GOP presidents of the 1920s, Mellon advanced policies that undid almost completely the progressive tax policies of the Wilson era. He recommended staffing regulatory agencies with men from the very industries the agencies were meant to oversee. Coolidge obliged. His chair of the Federal Trade Commission believed it was "an instrument of oppression and disturbance and injury." Democratic Senator George W. Norris raged that Republican subversion of regulatory commissions amounted, in effect, to "repeal of Congressional enactments. . . . It is the nullification of federal law by a process of boring from within."

The conservative cause was aided considerably by the United States Supreme Court, which issued a series of decisions that cut the legs out from under organized labor. In 1915, the court had upheld the yellow-dog contract (in which workers agreed, as a condition of employment, not to join a union). In the 1920s, it upheld injunctions against sympathy strikes and boycotts, sustained drastic restrictions on picketing, and ruled that unions could be sued for damages by businesses. In 1923, the court struck down a District of Columbia minimum wage law for women, reasoning that since women were no longer barred from voting, they no longer needed the special protection of the law in employment.

Organized labor was also undermined through "welfare capitalism," in which corporations set up "company unions" that offered dialogue with management, recreational facilities, and life insurance. Many workers were willing to trade the collective bargaining power of trade unions for these new benefits. But these benefits were provided at the pleasure of management, which could—and eventually did—revoke them. As a consequence, although unions usually grew during periods of economic growth, membership declined drastically in the 1920s.

THE COUNTRYSIDE

By 1920, the number of manufacturing and industrial workers eclipsed the number in farming. Yet 20 percent of Americans still worked the land. Over half the states remained preponderantly rural, especially in the South, where farmers muscled out city dwellers for political power. Of the 50 million Americans who lived in what the quintessential Jazz Age novelist F. Scott Fitzgerald condescendingly referred to as "that vast obscurity beyond the city," 45 million lacked indoor plumbing in 1930 and few had electricity. The widening gap between country and city life that had marked politics since the 1890s was aggravated in the 1920s by an agricultural depression that settled over the land and refused to dissipate.

The economic disparities that had marked the urban-rural divide for a generation became even more marked in the 1920s. Whole families still labored side by side in rural America, including in the southern textile industry, which employed more than one million children under the age of 15. Illiteracy rates were twice as high in rural districts as in cities. While farmers' living standards fell throughout the 1920s, real wages for industrial workers rose by nearly 25 percent. Unlike manufacturers, farmers never regained their wartime prosperity after the postwar slump of 1920–1921. In 1919, farmers produced 16 percent of the national income. By 1929, that number was 9 percent. For the first time in American history, the number of acres under cultivation declined.

The roots of the crisis lay in decisions made during WWI. When fighting broke out in Europe in 1914, American farmers dramatically increased output to supply the world market. By the time the war ended in November 1918, most American farmers were enjoying unprecedented prosperity. But there was no plan for agricultural reconversion for after the war. As battlefields reverted to wheat fields, European farmers began to recover. Americans confronted huge surpluses and prices dropped precipitously. Farm income declined from $17 billion in 1919 to only $9 billion in 1921.

By mid-1923, the industrial sector was booming, but wheat was selling for less than half its wartime price and farm foreclosures were on the rise. Secretary of Commerce Herbert Hoover insisted that an expansion of credit would ease farmers through the crisis. Secretary of Agriculture Henry C. Wallace, who favored the creation of a government export program to dump agricultural surpluses abroad, retorted that farmers needed more than "an opportunity to go further into debt."

Government aid takes many shapes. Since the late nineteenth century, farmers had often turned to the government to buffer the destabilizing effects of commodity markets. In the early 1920s, a group of western and southern senators organized the "farm bloc," which pressed for tariff reduction to lower the cost of manufactured goods. Republicans focused on protecting industry were unreceptive. The farm bloc also tried to rescue farmers by raising the price of farm products through government purchase of agricultural surpluses. President Coolidge twice vetoed the McNary-Haugen Bill, which sought to enact such a policy. To farmers, such government intervention was as justifiable as the tariff that protected industry, but the president disagreed, lecturing that "no resort to the Public Treasury will be of any permanent value in establishing agriculture."

GET RICH QUICK

Although farmers languished, industry and construction flourished, and the stock market, previously the preserve of the very wealthy few, was increasingly populated by a larger and more heterogeneous crowd. As economist J. Kenneth Galbraith remarked, the stock market became "central to the culture." The volume of sales on the New York Stock Exchange leapt from 236 million shares in 1925 to 1.125 billion in 1928. In that year, industrial stocks rose by more than 40 percent. General Motors stock sold at $99 in 1925; three years later it sold at $212. Who could resist? Individuals borrowed money, bought stock, watched it rise, and borrowed more money and bought more stock.

Even so, only about three million Americans—less than 2.5 percent of the population—owned securities in 1928. So where did all the money come from? It came mostly from corporations, whose profits increased at twice the growth of productivity in the 1920s, leaving them with large cash reserves. With their tax bills lowered by Andrew Mellon and their costs held steady by an eviscerated labor movement, businesses had more money than they knew what to do with. With the stock market booming, the "smart" move was market speculation rather than reinvestment in plants and machinery.

Even more money came from the banking system, which plunged

into the stock market and real estate investments rather than fund commercial ventures or municipal bonds to underwrite public transportation and school construction. The Federal Reserve's cheap money policy allowed banks to borrow cash at a low interest rate and then lend it at triple the rate to brokers, who gave securities as collateral. One critic described a financial system in which the banks "provided everything for their customers but a roulette wheel." When demand for loans to buy stocks exceeded the banks' capacity, corporations stepped in and acted as banks. John D. Rockefeller's Standard Oil of New Jersey loaned some $69 million a day in 1929. As before the Panic of 1907, everyone relied on stocks as collateral.

The get-rich-quick fantasies that fueled the explosive rise in stock prices during the 1920s spurred the supersaturation of daily life with consumer items and the sudden barrage of advertising that heralded their arrival. There were radios, vacuum cleaners, fur coats, cigarettes, and cars. For Protestants worried about riches as an impediment to salvation, a new band of revivalists reassured that God wanted everyone to get rich. In California, Aimee Semple McPherson reached tens of thousands of people through the airwaves, spreading her message of faith healing and personal miracles. Bruce Barton's runaway best seller *The Man Nobody Knows* (1925) described Jesus's teachings as "the most powerful advertisements of all time" and portrayed him as a far-sighted entrepreneur who had "picked up twelve men from the bottom ranks of business and forged them into an organization that conquered the world."

Future New Deal secretary of agriculture Henry A. Wallace viewed the giddy economic expansion of the 1920s with alarm. "It was a false prosperity," Wallace wrote, that denied the farm crisis and the potential political repercussions of significant economic imbalance between industry and agriculture. Secretary of Commerce Herbert Hoover was also uneasy. Hoover worried about the "orgy of speculation." There were signs that the bubble might burst. Construction rates, always a bellwether of economic strength, took a downward turn, and business inventories began to accumulate. But in the rush to make money, these signs were shrugged off. "The only problem with capitalism is capitalists," Herbert Hoover remarked. "They're too damn greedy."

Modern Women

In 1892, Elizabeth Cady Stanton argued against the habit of defining women principally through their relationships with others. "In discussing the sphere of man we do not decide his rights as an individual, as a citizen, as a man, by his duties as a father, a husband, a brother, or a son, some of which he may never undertake." The speech, later published as "The Solitude of Self," made the case for the right of individual women to control their own individual destinies. "To guide our own craft," Stanton explained, "we must be captain, pilot, engineer; with chart and compass to stand at the wheel; to watch the winds and waves, and know when to take in the sail, to read the signs in the firmament over all."

Women's lives had changed dramatically since the late nineteenth century. Women's advance into public life through voluntary organizations and participation in politics and the workplace challenged assumptions about women's proper role in life. Changing sexual mores transformed ideas about the nature of womanhood and recast notions of marriage. The 1920s did not see a revolution in gender roles. But women challenged conventions across many fronts, in both the public and the private spheres, sparking reaction in many quarters.

FROM WOMEN'S RIGHTS TO FEMINISM

Elizabeth Cady Stanton's call for self-sovereignty in all things anticipated the early twentieth-century turn from discussion of "the woman question" to feminism. Borrowed from the French, the English word was rare prior to 1910, frequent by 1913, and unremarkable thereafter. The new term signaled a broadening of the nineteenth-century women's movement, and specified an awakening of individual consciousness. Carrie Chapman Catt, who had helped lead the campaign for woman suffrage, defined feminism in 1914 as a "world-wide revolt against all artificial barriers which laws and customs interpose between women and human freedom."

Feminists operated on many fronts, including education, employment, legal and civic rights, social reform, and personal behavior. Feminists affirmed both women's human rights and their distinctive needs and differences. Those differences, though, divided women themselves. Enacting the Nineteenth Amendment in 1920 removed a central cause around which women could rally. There were other issues on which they disagreed.

The Equal Rights Amendment was one of them. The National Woman's Party (NWP), run with an iron fist by Alice Paul, put all its muscle behind the push for a constitutional amendment that would forbid discrimination by sex ("Men and women shall have equal rights throughout the United States and every place subject to its jurisdiction"). Other women's organizations, however, worried that the ERA would deny the real differences between men and women and invalidate sex-based protective legislation (such as limiting the working hours of women). In fact, sex-based protective legislation was invalidated by the Supreme Court *without* the ERA. Although the Supreme Court had upheld a maximum hours law for women in *Muller v. Oregon* in 1908, in 1923 the court ruled in *Adkins v. Children's Hospital* that women no longer needed special protection because they had gained the vote.

The divide between supporters of the ERA and proponents of protective legislation reflected serious conflicts about women's nature and the meaning of equality. Could full equality before the law coexist with recognition of women's unique capacity to bear children? As sociologist Charlotte Perkins Gilman acknowledged, feminism was "a movement in more than one general direction."

Attempting to bridge the difference-equality gap, the lawyer-feminist Crystal Eastman reached back for the autonomy advocated by Elizabeth Cady Stanton and applied it to women's bodies. "Birth Control," wrote Eastman, "is an elementary essential in all aspects of feminism." Whether followers of Alice Paul or Charlotte Perkins Gilman, Eastman declared, "we must all be followers of Margaret Sanger," the birth control crusader who had declared in a 1920 book, "No woman can call herself free until she can choose consciously whether she will or will not be a mother."

Such reproductive consciousness highlighted revolutionary changes in notions of female sexuality. Signs of the new morality were apparent even before WWI; as one journal declared in 1913, "sex o'clock" had struck. Parental control of sex diminished. "The veriest schoolgirl today knows as much as the midwife of 1885," columnist and cultural critic H. L. Mencken wrote unapprovingly. One observer remarked that "the word 'neck' ceased to be a noun; abruptly became a verb; immediately lost all anatomical precision." In 1914, most middle- and upper-class young women were chaperoned in public places. In what one historian has termed the movement "from front porch to back seat," by the mid-1920s young women were venturing out alone on "automobile dates" with men. Probably not coincidentally, women born after 1900 were two-and-a-half times more likely to have had premarital intercourse than women born before 1900.

OBSCENE LITERATURES AND
ARTICLES OF IMMORAL USE

Conscious decisions about childbearing required specialized knowledge as well as cooperative partners. Evidence of each could be seen in the nation's ever-declining birth rate. Between 1800 and 1900, average family size in America fell from roughly eight children per family to three, despite advances in infant and maternal health. Already in 1867 a journalist could conclude that "a large family" was no longer "treated as a cause of congratulation" but rather as "an indication of recklessness."

Nineteenth-century Americans used a variety of methods of birth control, including abortion, to limit family size. Until the 1870s, contraception and information about contraception were generally unregulated in the United States. Rubber condoms, pessaries, diaphragms, intrauterine devices (IUDs), and douching syringes were advertised widely and sold by pharmacists and mail-order businesses. Daily newspapers ran ads for products that promised to "cure" pregnancy and/or "restore menses." It is estimated that by the 1870s, 20 percent of all pregnancies were purposefully terminated. Abortion before "quickening" (when the mother could feel the baby, which occurred around 16 weeks) was common yet dangerous.

The 1873 Act for the Suppression of Trade in, and Circulation of, Obscene Literatures and Articles of Immoral Use, known popularly as the Comstock Act after its proponent and chief enforcer Anthony Comstock, changed all of this. The act established a broad ban on all items deemed "obscene, lewd, lascivious, or filthy," but failed to define any of these terms. The law authorized severe penalties, including hard labor, and empowered the Post Office to censor and confiscate objectionable material.

The Comstock Act made it a crime to send through the mail any drug or article designed to prevent conception and any information about birth control. Freethinker Ezra Heywood, who advertised and distributed a douching syringe he called "the Comstock," was sentenced to two years in prison in 1876 for his pamphlet *Cupid's Yokes: The Binding Forces of Conjugal Life*. Heywood condemned Comstock as a "religious mono-maniac," and denounced government intervention in the home. "If government cannot justly determine what ticket we shall vote, what church we shall attend, or what books we shall read, by what authority does it watch at keyholes and burst open bedchamber doors to drag lovers from sacred seclusion?" he demanded.

By 1900, doctors in most states could not lawfully instruct their patients about contraception. States with high concentrations of Catholics passed especially restrictive laws. Connecticut declared it unlawful for any person to purchase, possess, or use contraceptives. At the same time, prodded by the new American Medical Association, whose (all-male) doctors were replacing midwives at women's bedsides, states also began to outlaw abortion. By the turn of the century, there were more than two million abortions per year and one-third of all pregnancies ended in abortion.

A majority of the women seeking abortions were married. In most cases, too many pregnancies, not pregnancy itself, was the issue. Few women approved of an interruption of pregnancy (as they would have put it) after quickening, but most viewed an interruption before then as harmless. Advocates of "voluntary motherhood" asserted sovereignty over their bodies and rejected the notion that motherhood was the only "course marked out for [women] by Providence."

REPRODUCTIVE POLITICS

There is nothing inherently political about sex. What has placed sex at the center of politics at various moments in American history has been its regulation by the state. Certain sexual acts (e.g., oral sex) were illegal in many places throughout the twentieth century. Most states forbade both marriage and sex across the color line before 1960. Prosecutions of homosexuals increased dramatically in the late nineteenth century, and the policing of gay life escalated considerably in the first decades of the twentieth. But the most widespread debate relating to sexuality concerned contraception.

Margaret Sanger trained as a nurse and dedicated herself to women's health care. Already attuned to the physical and emotional toll of too-large families—Sanger's mother had 11 children and died of tuberculosis at age 50—Sanger was shocked by the suffering caused by unwanted pregnancy among her obstetrical patients on New York's Lower East Side. The poor immigrant women crowded with their families into two-room apartments beseeched Sanger to reveal to them the "Yankee tricks" that well-do-do women used to keep their families small. After watching patients die from self-inflicted abortions, Sanger determined to learn more about reproductive control.

In 1913, Sanger wrote a series of articles, "What Every Girl Should Know," for a socialist daily, *The Call*. Anthony Comstock ordered her final essay suppressed because it included information about venereal disease and masturbation. In the space the magazine usually devoted to Sanger's essays, the *Call* printed, "WHAT EVERY GIRL SHOULD KNOW — NOTHING! BY ORDER OF THE POST-OFFICE DEPARTMENT."

Undaunted, in 1914 Sanger founded a journal, *The Woman Rebel*, in which she discussed birth control and urged her readers to "speak and act in defiance of convention." Indicted under the Comstock Act, Sanger fled the country and triggered a new round of public discussion of birth control. In March 1915, suffragist Mary Ware Dennett, Free Speech League vice president Lincoln Steffens, and other prominent liberals founded the National Birth Control League. In May, an overflow crowd of 2,000 attended a meeting on birth control at the New York Academy of Medicine to hear doctors call for a fundamental change in public policy.

Anthony Comstock died in the fall of 1915. By then, birth control leagues had been established in cities across the nation. The charges against Margaret Sanger were dismissed, and she returned from exile. Joined by her sister, Ethel Byrne, also a nurse, Sanger opened the nation's first birth control clinic in a working-class neighborhood in Brooklyn in October 1916. The sisters were promptly arrested and imprisoned.

Despite the fervent opposition of the Catholic Church, which blocked legislation that would have repealed the state and federal Comstock acts, the birth control movement gained steam in the 1920s. Journalist Ruth Millard recalled that "methods of birth control were discussed over tea cups," and the Comstock laws "were violated hourly, but no charges were pressed." The birth rate fell by 30 percent from 1895 to 1925, despite increasing government regulation of reproduction. The great majority of workingwomen and even most Catholic women practiced some form of birth control, but any public information about more sophisticated means of contraception remained unlawful.

WORK AND HOME LIFE

By the end of the 1920s, 10 million American women (one in four) worked for wages. The vast majority were young and single. Workingwomen were concentrated in a handful of occupations including teaching, domestic service, clerical work, and the garment trades.

Most married women in cities still did not work outside the home, but millions in the countryside joined their husbands in agricultural labor. For example, Japanese women on the West Coast provided the unpaid labor that was crucial to the remarkable success of Japanese farmers.

The attention paid to working wives was out of all proportion to their numbers, as only 10 percent held down jobs. Magazine writers agonized that wage-earning women eroded their husbands' power. One marriage expert cautioned, "When the woman herself earns and her maintenance is not entirely at the mercy of her husband's will, diminishing masculine authority necessarily follows." Whether they worked outside the home or not, wives were still expected to run the household. Caring for the home was easier in the 1920s than it had been before, thanks largely to electricity. In 1907, less than 10 percent of American households had electricity. By 1920, more than half did, although that half was disproportionately urban. Appliances like washing machines, sewing machines, and irons sped up housework. On the other hand, as electric lights illuminated dusty corners, standards of cleanliness increased dramatically.

Housekeeping had always been *work*; now it was touted as a job. A key component of that job was to spend money—but wisely. Women's purchases represented two-thirds of the $44 billion Americans spent annually. Women's new importance as consumers was vital to the economy, in which mass consumption sustained mass production. Women's consumption could also become a political weapon in the form of economic boycotts, as African American women demonstrated in "don't buy where you can't work" campaigns directed at stores.

The percentage of married Americans increased in the 1920s. But so did the number of divorces, indicating a challenge to traditional views of the sanctity of marriage. In 1880, 1 in every 21 marriages ended in divorce. By 1890 the figure was 1 in 12, and by 1924, 1 in 7. Concerned observers blamed emancipated women, but more important was the development of the affectionate family and companionate marriage. Victorian women had considered marriage a duty and sought happiness outside the family within circles of female friendship. Their granddaughters saw marriage and the family as a source of personal fulfillment and looked to their husbands for friendship and emotional support. The heightened expectations of marriage led to frequent disappointment and contributed to the rising divorce rate as partners looked elsewhere for satisfaction.

Women's styles changed as well. By 1920, hemlines were raised to below the knee; long curls gave way to short "bobbed" haircuts. Pleasure-seeking "flappers" (an English term once applied to prostitutes) drank, danced, and smoked their way through life. The heightened emphasis on female sexuality was not entirely emancipatory, however. As movies and magazines became more popular, standardized ideals of physical attractiveness took root. Sales of cosmetics increased from $17 million in 1914 to $141 million in 1925, as the goal of achieving perpetual youthfulness underwrote a cult of beauty and consumption. Flappers' rejection of curves led to women binding their breasts and dieting to look boyish. The bathroom scale first appeared on the scene in the 1920s, and cigarette ads targeted women with such slogans as "Reach for a Lucky instead of a sweet."

Social Control

If the government can draft young men, ban contraceptives, separate the races, and insist on compulsory vaccination in the name of the common good, what else can it do? Can it prevent certain people from reproducing? Can it deny a workingman a beer after a long day's work? Can it jail people for dressing as the opposite sex? Can it commandeer children and expose them to knowledge and belief systems that conflict with those of their parents? Even as government intervention in the economy was scaled back after the war, the state intervened more aggressively in other ways in everyday life. Some Americans who earlier had trumpeted government regulation in the interest of the common good discovered the wisdom of James Madison's warning that unrestrained majority rule can endanger individual liberty. Conversations about the balance between personal freedom and government authority reverberated throughout the 1920s and nurtured a deeper understanding of the nature and importance of civil liberties.

"THREE GENERATIONS OF IMBECILES ARE ENOUGH"

In the 1920s, many Americans embraced the popular doctrine of eugenics, which fused Darwin's theory of evolution with Swiss botanist Gregor Mendel's research in plant heredity to take the first shaky scientific steps toward genetic engineering. Eugenicists claimed that "unfit human traits" such as "feeblemindedness, epilepsy, criminality, insanity, alcoholism, pauperism" ran in families and were inherited "in exactly the same way as color in guinea pigs." These traits were disproportionately associated, scientists insisted, with the "lesser races." Groups like the Anglo-Saxon League urged immigration restriction to limit the dilution of the Anglo-Saxon race by inferior Asian, African, and eastern European bloodlines, arguing that "the idea of the great American melting pot, into which one can put the refuse of three continents and draw out good, sound American citizens . . . is simply and perilously false."

Middle-class whites had been sounding alarms about "race suicide" since Theodore Roosevelt's day, when it was first argued that the "wrong" people were having too many babies and the "right" sort were having too few. In addition to immigration restriction, eugenicists in the 1920s advocated selective breeding for human improvement. "Fitter Families" and "Better Babies" contests sprang up across the country (in Kansas, the competition was held in the "human stock" section of the state fair). Eugenicists spanned the political spectrum from white supremacists to socialists like Margaret Sanger. More often than not they were political and social progressives who saw the quest for a better gene pool as consistent with their broader dream of human advancement through public policy grounded in scientific methods.

Eugenicists' chief interest was to protect and improve the white race through state action. Buttressed by such works of "scientific racism" as Madison Grant's *The Passing of the Great Race* (1916) and Lothrop Stoddard's *The Rising Tide of Color against White World-Supremacy* (1920), American eugenicists disputed the conclusions of cultural anthropologists and sociologists, who denied the existence of a fixed spectrum of racial hierarchy or societies running from "primitive" to "civilized."

Eugenicists warned that people with unwholesome genes were rapidly proliferating and urged policymakers to take steps to limit their procreation. By 1929, 30 states had passed compulsory sterilization laws for individuals whose sterilization was considered to be "in the interest of the mental, moral, or physical improvement of the patient or inmate or for the public good." By the mid-1930s, approximately 20,000 individuals had been sterilized under the laws. Eugenicists argued that there was a high correlation between "feeblemindedness" and "sexual delinquents" such as prostitutes, peeping Toms, homosexuals, and sexually active unmarried women. In California, which led the nation in forced sterilization, three out of four sterilized women had been judged "sexually delinquent" prior to their institutional commitment.

In 1927, the Supreme Court upheld mandatory sterilization laws in *Buck v. Bell*, a case that originated in Virginia. Justice Oliver Wendell Holmes Jr., who wrote the opinion of the court, followed conventional eugenic thought when he explained, "It is better for all the world, if instead of waiting to execute degenerate offspring for crime, or to let them starve for their imbecility, society can prevent those who are manifestly unfit from continuing their kind." Referring to the family of the plaintiff, Carrie Buck, Holmes pronounced, "The principle that sustains compulsory vaccination is broad enough to cover cutting the Fallopian tubes. Three generations of imbeciles are enough."

PROHIBITION

Prohibition's champions hoped that passage of the Eighteenth Amendment would change people's behavior. It did—but in ways unanticipated by the anti-liquor crusaders.

The campaign to repeal the Eighteenth Amendment began almost as soon as it was passed. Ratification inspired the creation of Anti-Prohibition Leagues and triggered mass protests against the Volstead Act. Ethnic working-class communities understood the law as a disciplinary measure aimed at their leisure and personal habits, and they turned to familiar American language of liberty to protest the new alcohol-free universe. "We are citizens, not inmates, which are you?" read a banner at a 1921 protest in New York City.

Making drinking illicit made it even more fun for those so inclined, and led to widespread flouting of the law. The effort to halt the trade in alcoholic beverages created a thriving black market. Speakeasies (undercover bars), bootlegging, and criminal distribution syndicates proliferated. Prohibition opened the door to epic civic corruption, as speakeasies and bootleggers bribed the police and other public officials to look the other way. The war on alcohol severed the previously tight linkage between saloons and municipal politics, but that link was replaced with far worse ties between politicians and organized crime.

Corrupt public officials engaged in selective enforcement of the prohibition laws. Small producers of alcohol such as beer and wine ended up in jail while large suppliers, protected by their bribes to judges and the police, remained immune from prosecution. Racial and ethnic minorities were prime targets for the prohibition agents. In Los Angeles in 1924, 25 percent of those charged for liquor law violations were Mexican American—despite the fact that they accounted for only 10 percent of the population. Small-scale distributors were easier to find than small-scale producers. To find the mom-and-pop distilleries, federal agents invaded private homes on an unprecedented scale. The *Pittsburgh Courier*, a black newspaper, complained that "colored citizens here have suffered indignities from policemen and prohibition agents who crash into their homes unlawfully and make liquor searches and arrests in violation of the search and seizure provisions of the law on the pretext of quelling disorder."

Selective enforcement of the prohibition laws contributed to the growth of a libertarian "don't tread on me" identity among bootleggers that at times turned violent. Open warfare broke out between federal revenue agents and backcountry distillers in Appalachia. In Chicago and New York, rival gangs armed with pistols and machine guns battled over distribution networks. In 1927, Congress banned the sale of pistols through the mail, and the National Firearms Act of 1934 imposed a heavy tax on the transfer of machine guns and sawed-off shotguns.

A final unintended consequence of prohibition was the way it freed women to drink in public. Large numbers of "unaccompanied women" began to frequent night spots, jazz clubs, and speakeasies, both as guests and as employees. Drinking by young women and men became "an adventure," recalled one observer, "a gesture of daring, a sign of revolt." Another chronicler of New York's nightlife wrote, "Soon after 1920 great, raving hordes of women began to discover what their less respectable sisters had known for years—that it was a lot of fun, if you liked it, to get soused." By pushing alcohol underground, prohibition created a subculture not bound to middle-class rules of decorum, where gender norms and racial boundaries were also often transgressed. The gay communities in New York, Chicago, New Orleans, Baltimore, and San Francisco held enormous drag balls, where men in flowing gowns and feathered headdresses and women in tuxedoes paraded.

"AMERICANIZING" AMERICA

The WWI spirit of "100% Americanism," with its emphasis on conformity and the suppression of dissent, had long-term implications for American politics and society. It crushed radicalism, crippled the labor movement, set limits on freedom of speech and the press, and empowered repressive social movements that did not end with the war.

The largest and most important of these movements was the Ku Klux Klan, which burst on the scene in the early 1920s in defense of traditional social hierarchies. The Klan's social vision was holistic, meaning that everything was linked: family, church, republic, race, capitalism. Tampering with any of these elements would unhinge the others, with disastrous consequences for the nation. The Klan's causes—racial segregation, nativism, anti-Communism, free enterprise, patriarchy, anti-Catholicism, anti-Semitism, prohibition, and law and order—reflected its sense that everything was coming unglued.

Rooted in wartime vigilance committees, the Klan frequently resorted to extralegal violence to enforce its vision of proper moral behavior. Scofflaws, especially those who scoffed at prohibition and segregation, were common targets. So were young people who challenged traditional family structure or authority. Klansmen harassed couples "parking" in cars, broke up dances, and exposed adulterers. They stripped "fallen" women naked and whipped them.

Klansmen were especially concerned about the erosion of male privilege and power. The Klan vehemently opposed birth control. As the Imperial Wizard explained, "Citizenship for our young American women includes the essential duty of motherhood." Female independence set Klansmen's teeth on edge, even—perhaps especially—within their own organization. The men defined the Women of the Ku Klux Klan (WKKK) as a mere "auxiliary," to the consternation of the women, who insisted on organizational autonomy.

At its peak in 1925, the Klan boasted a membership of more than five million, nearly all native white Protestants, most of whom were considered respectable members of their communities. Joining the Klan was good for business, particularly since Klansmen often engaged in well-executed boycotts against Catholic and Jewish establishments. Ministers were heavily represented among Klansmen, in part because the Klan generously waived their dues.

The Second Klan was a national phenomenon. It was especially strong in the South, Southwest, and Midwest, although Oregon elected a Klansman governor in 1922. The Klan dominated politics in Texas, Indiana, Oklahoma, and Colorado, and was a significant political force in many cities, including Los Angeles, Chicago, Denver, Atlanta, and Dallas. Klansmen resisted African American "incursion" into white neighborhoods and clamored for racial segregation in the North. A Klan write-in candidate for mayor of Detroit, a city with a large African American population and a hub of organized labor, attracted more than one-third of the vote in 1924. Klan-backed candidates were elected to the US Senate in six states. Edwin Stephenson's lawyer Hugo Black was one of them.

Catholics and Jews were special targets of the Second Klan, which considered patriotism and Protestantism to be synonymous. As the Georgia Grand Dragon elaborated, "The Constitution of the United States is based upon the Holy Bible and the Christian religion, and an attack upon one is an attack upon the other." Worried about the rising generation, the Klan attacked parochial schools as Catholic cradles of un-American clannishness. Klan supporters in Oregon made *public* school attendance mandatory for children between ages 8 and 18. Elsewhere, Klan leaders took over local school boards, often dismissing Catholic principals and teachers and ensuring that Protestant religious values were part of the curriculum.

AMERICA FOR AMERICANS

Although many Americans rolled their eyes at the spectacle of the Klan's hooded marchers (40,000 strong outside the White House in 1926), the organization's demand that control of the nation be returned to "old stock" Americans reflected widespread sentiment in the 1920s. In 1924, political streams of nativism, racism, and religious bigotry merged to produce changes in American immigration policy that were designed to ensure that descendants of early immigrants would forever outnumber the children of the new. "America must be kept American," President Calvin Coolidge declared when signing the National Origins Act of 1924.

Massive postwar immigration spurred congressional champions of immigration restriction. The National Origins Act of 1924, passed at the height of post-WWI nativist agitation, set national immigration quotas for each country at 2 percent of its existing total US population based on the 1890 census: the last count before the mass influx of immigrants from southern and eastern Europe. The new law reduced Italian and Polish immigration dramatically, and barred the entry of anyone from Asia, which was defined expansively to include India. No limitation was placed on immigration from the Western Hemisphere, largely because of the reliance of much of the West and Southwest on Mexican migrant labor.

Immigration restriction and the upsurge in anti-Catholicism in the 1920s were both partly responses to the political power of urban Catholics in predominantly Democratic cities like New York and Chicago. The Democratic Party, an unwieldy combination of rural and small-town Protestants of the South and West and urban immigrant Catholics and Jews from the North, divided over prohibition and then all but ruptured in the 1924 presidential election. The Democrats' two leading candidates for the presidency, New York governor Alfred E. Smith and William Gibbs McAdoo, perfectly epitomized the party's urban-rural, religious, and sectional divisions. Smith, the working-class son of Roman Catholic immigrants, was a graduate of the Tammany Hall machine, spoke in a grating New York accent, and was known to take the occasional drink. The Georgia-born McAdoo, who was Woodrow Wilson's son-in-law, was described, fairly, as "the personification of strait-laced rectitude and sanctimonious moral judgment."

The Democrats convened in July at Madison Square Garden in New York City. The battle between the forces of Smith and McAdoo deadlocked the convention for nine days. On the 103rd ballot, the convention finally chose corporation lawyer John W. Davis as its candidate for president and William Jennings Bryan's brother Charles for vice president. A debate over whether to denounce the Ku Klux Klan devolved into fistfights and split the convention, leading humorist Will Rogers to quip, "I belong to no organized party; I'm a Democrat."

With the Democrats in tatters and the Republicans reborn as the party of big business, progressives coalesced to field their own ticket. Headed by legendary Wisconsin senator Robert F. La Follette, the Progressive Party garnered 17 percent of the national vote. The Republicans ignored Davis and concentrated their fire on La Follette, whom they depicted as a Bolshevik. The issue in 1924, declared Calvin Coolidge somberly, was "whether America will allow itself to be degraded into a communistic or socialistic state or whether it will remain American." The Republican slogan "Coolidge or Chaos" carried the day in November. Coolidge received more votes than Davis and La Follette combined.

Teach Your Children Well

Controversies over the definition of "Americanness" and majority rule that arose in prohibition, electoral politics, and eugenics campaigns figured in public education as well. If schools were incubators of citizenship, what happened when fundamental American ideals clashed with parents' belief systems? Did the state that could vaccinate public schoolchildren against infectious diseases have the right to expose children to ideas their parents found noxious? Was it true, as the American Legion insisted, that "for the good of us all, some of us must exercise authority over the rest of us, and . . . the rest of us, for the good of all, are bound in honor to obey them?"

STANDARDIZED CHILDREN

Oregon's Klan-backed 1922 mandatory public school attendance law was declared unconstitutional by the Supreme Court in 1925. In *Pierce v. Society of Sisters*, the court held that parents have a constitutional right to send their children to private, including religious, schools. The court explained that "the fundamental theory of liberty upon which all governments in this Union repose excludes any general power of the State to standardize its children by forcing them to accept instruction from public teachers only," and that the Oregon law "unreasonably [interfered] with the liberty of parents and guardians to direct the upbringing and education of [their] children."

Despite the circumstances in which the case arose, *Pierce* was not decided under the First Amendment's religion clauses. *Pierce* was, instead, based on the Fourteenth Amendment's guarantee of "fundamental liberty," and later became an important stepping-stone to other domestic privacy-based rights such as procreation, contraception, abortion, family relationships, and marriage. The animating issue in *Pierce* was parental control—the right to raise one's children according to one's own lights. *Pierce* gave parents a way to promote their own beliefs by removing their children from the influence of public school teachers.

Outside of the Northeast, public schools had relatively shallow roots. In many states, especially in the South, children spent more time in fields and factories than they did in classrooms. Few teenagers attended high school in the nineteenth century, and almost none did so in the rural South. This situation changed dramatically during the first quarter of the twentieth century, when progressives passed mandatory school laws and promoted spending on education. In 1900, only one child in ten attended high school. By 1931, that number was one in two.

Controversy over what would be taught in public schools was a predictable result of the expansion of public education. Who would define the curriculum? Teachers? Parent associations? Taxpayers? Popularly elected school boards? What role, if any, would religion play? Could parents insist that public schools tailor their teaching to their students' religious precepts?

The First Amendment to the Constitution prohibits the establishment of any official religion and guarantees the right of individuals to practice their religion free from government interference. In theory, the religion clauses create space for all faiths. In practice, until the mid-twentieth century they protected a "first among equals" status for Protestantism. Prayer and Bible reading were common in public schools. Did this practice constitute official approval of one religion, and therefore violate the establishment clause? Could parents control not only what was taught to their own children but also what was taught to the children of others? From the moment public schools became common across the nation, they became a site of persistent struggle between individuals and their community, and between communities and government.

SCIENCE, SCHOOLS, AND RELIGION

In line with recent trends in science education, America's growing public school systems included Darwinian concepts in their biology classes. By 1900, it was widely accepted that the earth had a very long geologic history punctuated into distinct epochs by natural catastrophes such as ice ages and massive floods, and marked by the progressive appearance of new life-forms. This scholarship clashed with the biblical account in Genesis, in which God created the heavens and earth and all creatures in six days, culminating in the creation of Adam and Eve, the forbears of all humans. Nineteenth-century Christians reconciled this clash by interpreting the biblical days of creation as symbolizing geologic ages. Few considered evolutionary claims a challenge to their faith because God's purpose could still be discerned.

By 1900, however, biologists increasingly accepted random, inborn variation as the driving force of evolutionary change. The theory of natural selection provided a mechanism that could explain evolutionary change independent of divine purpose. Many Americans associated the theory with the survival-of-the-fittest mentality that justified rapacious capitalism, imperialism, and militarism. Rather than originating in the divine love of a beneficent God, natural selection posited a world in which death was the agent of change. Natural selection was cruel and ruled a world in which justice and mercy were irrelevant.

Natural selection challenged belief in the supernatural power of God. For many Protestants, this was not problematic. So-called Modernist Protestants applied the techniques of German "higher criticism" to read the Bible like any other text written by people, and interpreted its stories in historical context. Miracles were metaphors for Modernists, who did not consider their faith challenged by not believing that Jesus walked on water or multiplied loaves and fishes.

Critics of Modernism asserted that the whole point of Christianity—Christ's power to redeem mankind from damnation—was lost with the Modernist interpretation of the Bible. These Fundamentalists argued that the fundamentals of Christian faith included the unquestionable accuracy and divine authorship of scripture and unearthly events such as the virgin birth, Jesus's miracles, his resurrection, and his second coming. Fundamentalists insisted that the Modernist Christianity that was invading mainstream seminaries and divinity schools was not a new interpretation of the faith but a new religion entirely.

Fundamentalists made teaching evolution controversial. But William Jennings Bryan turned anti-evolutionism into a cause. Now in his mid-60s, Bryan had remade himself as an evangelist after resigning as secretary of state in 1917. He cared less about Fundamentalist principles, including the literal truth of the Bible, than he cared about denial of the supernatural. "I object to the Darwinian theory," Bryan explained, "because I fear we shall lose the consciousness of God's presence in our daily life." In 1921, he began advertising the dangers of Darwinism. In 1923, the *Chicago Tribune* complained that Bryan had "half the country debating whether the universe was created in six days." During debate on an anti-evolution law in Tennessee, one lawmaker blamed the entire controversy on "that greatest of all disturbers of the political and public life from the last twenty-eight or thirty years, I mean William Jennings Bryan."

FREEDOM FROM SCIENCE

The clash between Fundamentalists and Modernists, and between Fundamentalism and Darwinism, moved from the sociocultural sphere into politics when state legislatures began outlawing the teaching of evolution in public schools. Five states, all predominantly Fundamentalist in religious outlook, passed anti-evolution statutes in the 1920s. As with prohibition, anti-evolution efforts were strong in the South and weak in the North. Oklahoma's bill to prohibit the teaching of Darwinism passed by a single vote in 1923, thanks to the influence of the Klan. In other regions, such efforts met stiff resistance and were defeated.

In 1925, William Jennings Bryan volunteered to defend Tennessee's anti-evolution law when the American Civil Liberties Union (ACLU) brought a test case involving John Scopes in tiny Dayton, Tennessee. Tennessee's Butler Act forbade teaching "any theory that denies the story of the divine creation of man as taught in the Bible, and teaches instead that man has descended from a lower order of animals." When Scopes violated that law, he was fined $100.

The ACLU was founded in 1919. It was the direct descendant of the National Civil Liberties Bureau, which was organized in 1917 by the Harvard-educated radical Roger Baldwin to defend conscientious objectors and antiwar protesters. The ACLU forged a sharp anti-majoritarian defense of individual liberties that influenced its response to the Fundamentalist anti-evolution crusade.

The *Scopes* case was straightforward. The 24-year-old biology teacher had taught evolution in violation of the law. The three ACLU attorneys who represented the young teacher were sent to attack the statute itself. They were led by Clarence Darrow, the most renowned trial attorney of his day and a committed agnostic. Bryan and Darrow, old colleagues-in-arms from the Populist era, went at each other mercilessly. To Darrow's charge that "you insult every man of science and learning with your fool religion," Bryan responded, "I am trying to protect the Word of God against the greatest agnostic in the United States." Although the trial, which became a media circus, is often remembered as a debate between Bryan and Darrow about the theory of evolution, in fact the case turned on a different axis: was it an unconstitutional establishment of religion for the state to prohibit the teaching of evolution in the public schools because it conflicted with Christian beliefs about the origins of the world?

Bryan's defense of the law was unabashedly majoritarian. "Teachers in public schools must teach what the taxpayers desire taught," he argued. "The hand that writes the pay check rules the school." The issue for Bryan was "whether the people . . . have the right to control the educational system which they have created and which they tax themselves to support." The case uncovered, Bryan charged, "a concerted attack upon revealed religion that is being made by a minority made up of atheists, agnostics, and unbelievers." Local opponents of laws prohibiting the teaching of evolution invoked individual freedom and the separation of church and state. "It isn't a question of whether you believe in the Book of Genesis, but whether you think the church and state should be kept separate," asserted a state senator who opposed enactment of the Tennessee law.

FREEDOM FROM RELIGION

Darrow's tactic was to pit the right of the government (in this case, the state legislature) to prescribe the course of study in the public schools against the state's own constitution, which followed the federal Constitution in guaranteeing religious freedom. "We have been informed," he said, "that the legislature has the right to prescribe the course of study in the public schools. Within reason, they no doubt have, no doubt." But, he continued, "the people of Tennessee adopted a constitution, and they made it broad and plain, and said that the people of Tennessee should always enjoy religious freedom in its broadest terms, so I assume that no legislature could fix a course of study which violated that." The anti-evolution statute was illegal, Darrow charged, because it established a particular religious viewpoint in the public schools.

To drive home this argument, Darrow objected to public prayer in the courtroom. "When it is claimed by the state that there is no conflict between science and religion," he argued, "there should be no . . . attempt by means of prayer . . . to influence the deliberations. . . . I object to the turning of this courtroom into a meeting house." The prayer was heard, and Darrow was cited for contempt of court. The judge later accepted Darrow's apology in the name of Christ, and the trial continued.

Darrow's arguments were losing ones. Scopes was found guilty, and the law was upheld. Darrow's grueling cross-examination of William Jennings Bryan, who volunteered to serve as an expert witness on the Bible, on the veracity of biblical miracles and contradictions and silences in Genesis (Which of the two creation stories did Bryan prefer? Where did Cain's wife come from?), has endured as the takeaway of the *Scopes* trial, although no one at the time saw the episode as decisive for the defense. Certainly Bryan did not. He revised his closing argument into a fiery stump speech he intended to take on tour. He never got the chance: he died in his sleep a few days after the trial's end.

The ACLU appealed the *Scopes* decision, but the Tennessee Supreme Court concluded that "we are not able to see how the prohibition . . . gives preference to any religious establishment." Expanding

Bryan's argument, the state rejected the plea for academic freedom and recognized no limits on majority rule: "What the public believes is for the common welfare must be accepted as tending to promote the common welfare, whether it does in fact or not."

The *Scopes* trial encouraged both sides of the curriculum debate. By the end of the decade, most states or localities where Fundamentalists held sway—across the South and in some of the West—had imposed anti-evolution restrictions by law, administrative ruling, or school board resolution. Although such laws were repulsed in the North, Fundamentalist-inspired restrictions influenced the content of high school biology textbooks everywhere. A 1941 survey of high school teachers found that one in three feared teaching evolution.

In 1968, the United States Supreme Court finally ruled unconstitutional an anti-evolution law passed in 1928. In *Epperson v. Arkansas*, the court described the statute as "a product of the upsurge of 'fundamentalist' religious fervor of the twenties" designed to correspond with a particular religious doctrine. In an opinion written by Justice Abe Fortas, who was a Tennessee high school student during the *Scopes* trial, the court declared that "the First Amendment does not permit the State to require that teaching and learning must be tailored to the principles or prohibitions of any religious sect or dogma," despite the "State's undoubted right to prescribe the curriculum for its public schools."

Division

According to the venerable *Black's Law Dictionary*, the rule of law is "the supremacy of regular power as opposed to arbitrary power." In the United States, it is embodied in such soaring constitutional phrases as "no person shall be deprived of life, liberty or property without due process of law," "no state shall deny any person the equal protection of the law," and no person shall be subjected to "cruel and unusual punishment." Holding these ideals is one thing. Living up to them is another. In the 1920s, the United States struggled, often unsuccessfully, to live up to its own aspirations.

THE JIM CROW NORTH

The African American migration sparked by wartime labor shortages in the North continued at a high rate through the 1920s and transformed cities across the country. By 1918, this great migration north

had become a mass social movement of entire families and communities that pulled up stakes and headed for "the promised land" north of
the Mason-Dixon line. By 1920, seven cities—Philadelphia, New York,
Chicago, Detroit, Pittsburgh, Indianapolis, and Cleveland—contained
40 percent of the North's black population. More than 80 percent of
black Chicagoans had been born in some other state, almost half in
either Tennessee or Mississippi.

Swollen black populations created a housing crisis and stimulated
white determination to enforce racial barriers. White neighborhood
associations formed to restrict black access to all but the most undesirable urban areas, enclosing African American communities within
"invisible walls of steel." Things got ugly fast in Detroit, where the
breathtaking growth of the auto industry fueled a massive migration
of workers, including many black southerners, whose numbers grew
tenfold in a single decade. By 1925, the NAACP reported a pattern
of black homes bombed, attacked, and threatened in cities across the
country.

On September 11, 1925, Dr. Ossian Sweet, who had bought a bun-
galow with his wife, Gladys, in a white working-class neighborhood
of Detroit, was arrested on charges of homicide after defending his
home against a mob of white men with the aid of his brother Henry.
NAACP leader Walter White hastened to Detroit from New York to
secure the best defense he could for the brothers. "The case was bigger than Detroit," White wrote later. "[It] was the dramatic climax of
the nationwide fight to enforce residential segregation." When no local
white attorney would take the case, Clarence Darrow, just back from
Tennessee, volunteered.

A first trial ended in a hung jury, but the Sweets were exonerated on
grounds of self-defense in a second trial marked by a soaring six-hour
closing argument by Darrow, who asked the all-white jury, "Who are
we, anyway?" before reducing the room to tears by unrolling "a complete panorama of the experience . . . of the American Negro, beginning with his African background, down to the present—a panorama
of his sufferings, his struggles, his achievements, his aspirations."

Ossian and Henry Sweet were free, but residential segregation
spread, accelerating the trend toward segregated education in the
North. Even when residential segregation did not produce segregated
schools, northern cities found other ways to construct dual school
systems. "Tracking" students by academic ability enabled school ad-
ministrators to channel black students into effectively segregated and

second-rate classes. Chicago gerrymandered school district lines and allowed white children to transfer out of predominantly black schools while denying that privilege to black students. In 1929, black sociologist Kelly Miller reported, "The color line in public education is vigorously asserting itself across the continent from Atlantic City to Los Angeles."

Although the NAACP rejected segregated schools as an affront to democracy, many African Americans supported them as black-controlled oases in a racist world. Black teachers incorporated African American history and literature into their classes and encouraged racial pride. Moreover, teaching remained a chief avenue to the middle class for educated African Americans. Indeed, even as the Philadelphia NAACP petitioned the school board to stop the advance of segregated schools, the Pennsylvania Association of Teachers of Colored Children endorsed separate—but equal—schools.

THE SHAME OF AMERICA

Although the vast majority of lynchings occurred south of the Mason-Dixon Line, the North was not immune to the disease. In Duluth, Minnesota, where US Steel imported southern blacks as cheap labor during WWI, a white mob numbering in the thousands hung from lampposts three young black circus workers accused of raping a white woman. Antilynching activist Ida Wells-Barnett could assert that "nobody. . . . believes that old threadbare lie that Negro men rape white women," but many whites either believed it or used it to justify their own violence against black men.

In 1921, the NAACP mounted an all-out effort to pass a federal antilynching law that would punish state and local officials who failed to protect individuals from lynch mobs. In 1920, more than half the victims of that year's 55 recorded lynchings had been taken from officers of the law, lending credence to the NAACP's argument that local and state governments were implicated in mob violence.

In 1921, the US House of Representatives passed the Dyer Antilynching Bill (after Missouri congressman Leonidas Dyer), which targeted local sheriffs who refused to stop mob action. Southerners howled about federal usurpation of state authority and denounced the proposed law as a "bill to encourage rape." The Dyer Bill squeaked through the Republican-dominated House but was filibustered by Democrats in the Senate. While the bill languished, three black men were burned alive in the town square of Kirvin, Texas, and 15-year old

Charlie Atkins was tortured and roasted "over a slow fire" before a mob of 2,000 in Davisboro, Georgia.

Some white southerners who opposed federal action on lynching were nonetheless determined to end southern lawlessness by pressuring local sheriffs to do their duty. In 1930, a group of 26 white women formed the Association of Southern Women for the Prevention of Lynching (ASWPL). Led by Texan Jesse Daniel Ames, the ASWPL insisted that lynching discredited the legal process and undermined respect for officers of the law, which made it harder for the authorities to maintain social control. Combined with the NAACP's drive to make lynching a federal crime, the ASWPL's campaign helped lower the number of lynchings dramatically.

Why a *women's* antilynching association? Historian Jacquelyn Dowd Hall argues that Ames attacked the story white men told themselves about lynching—that it was necessary to protect vulnerable white women from black rapists. The ASWPL rejected any responsibility for the barbarism of white men. As the *Macon Evening News* reported, women had "announced to their red-handed 'protectors' that they want no more of this rope-and-faggot courtesy." Lillian Smith, a trenchant critic of southern racial and sexual hierarchies, described the movement this way: "The lady insurrectionists . . . said calmly that they were not afraid of being raped; as for their sacredness, they could take care of it themselves; they did not need the chivalry of lynching to protect them and did not want it." It was, Smith concluded, "a truly subversive affair." Mobilizing traditional female networks to assert civic influence outside official, male-dominated channels, the ASWPL replaced the image of the delicate white lady with that of the woman citizen, requiring not the protection of men but the equal protection of the law.

"WE STAND DEFEATED AMERICA"

In July 1921, two Italian immigrants, Nicola Sacco and Bartolomeo Vanzetti, were convicted and sentenced to death for the murder of two men during a payroll robbery in South Braintree, Massachusetts. Neither had a criminal record, but both were well-known to federal authorities as militant anarchists with ties to the suspected Wall Street bombers of 1920. The verdict marked the beginning of a six-year worldwide effort to save the men's lives. The Sacco and Vanzetti Defense Committee agitated for a new trial, and presented petitions to the governor of Massachusetts signed by many leading intellectuals of diverse political opinion, including physicist Albert Einstein and playwright George Bernard Shaw. They were unsuccessful. When Sacco and Vanzetti were executed by electrocution on August 23, 1927, riots broke out around the world.

What was at stake in the Sacco and Vanzetti saga? Why did it ignite the passion of usually dispassionate law professors like Harvard's Felix Frankfurter as well as reliable radicals like novelist John Dos Passos, who chaired the defense committee? There was more to it than claims of innocence, although there were those. The contention that fired six years of protest was that Sacco and Vanzetti had been martyred to anti-immigrant and antiradical sentiment at the height of the Red Scare in a place — Boston — that was unusually agitated over leftist Italians. Their trial had been marked by serious prosecutorial misconduct and flagrant abuse of judicial discretion by a judge who openly appealed to the nativist passions and prejudices of the jury. The integrity of the American criminal justice system stood accused before the world, and with it the commitment of the United States to the rule of law.

In an increasingly unstable global political world, the commitment of the United States to immigration, political freedom, and equality before the law mattered to people far beyond the nation's borders. While American Klansmen disciplined wayward women and bootleggers, hundreds of anti-Semitic societies and nationalist militias cropped up across central Europe. French governments spanning the political spectrum toppled one after another. In Germany, roving corps of disgruntled ex-soldiers lashed out at the terms of the Versailles Treaty. One of them, Corporal Adolf Hitler, was briefly imprisoned after leading a failed coup in Munich in 1923. In 1922, Benito Mussolini, the leader of Italy's National Fascist Party, came to power in a coup in Rome. "The world is turning to the right," he declared.

To many leftists, at home and abroad, postwar America was unrecognizable. Americans prided themselves on being "the land of the free," wrote British novelist D. H. Lawrence in 1923, but "the free mob" had destroyed the right to dissent. "I have never been in any country where the individual has such an abject fear of his fellow countrymen." Many authors and artists abandoned the United States in the 1920s for Paris or Berlin. Dos Passos's 1927 plea for justice for Sacco and Vanzetti trumpeted his bitterness at the capture of the American ideal by the defenders of unity and cultural conformity. The chasm was too broad to be spanned. "All right we are two nations," Dos Passos concluded, and one — the nation of "the immigrant haters" — had defeated the other. "We stand defeated America."

THE 1928 PRESIDENTIAL ELECTION

The tensions between rural and urban America, between "old stock" Americans and newcomers, between Protestants and Catholics and "others," between wets and drys, between those worried about Anglo-Saxon supremacy and those who dismissed the notion as fantastical, converged in the presidential election of 1928 when four-time New York Governor Al Smith was chosen as the Democratic nominee. "For the first time," wrote the *New Republic*, "a representative of the un-pedigreed, foreign-born, city-bred, many-tongued recent arrivals on the American scene has knocked on the door and aspired seriously" to be president of the United States. "Al Smith," wrote another keen observer of American politics, "must rise or fall in our national life . . . as our first urbanite."

Opposing him was Republican Herbert Hoover, a self-made financier educated as an engineer who first came to public notice as the supremely organized and self-confident administrator of Belgian relief and the Food Administration during the war years. Impatient and ambitious, Hoover served as secretary of commerce under Presidents Harding and Coolidge—and, it was said, "Under-Secretary of all other departments." In 1927, Hoover headed the relief effort during the great Mississippi River flood, in which 15 inches of rain fell in New Orleans in 18 hours, producing the most devastating river flood in American history. When President Coolidge announced that he did not wish to run for reelection, Hoover was a natural choice.

After their dreadful showing in 1924, the Democrats were determined to compete as friends of business rather than, in the words of 1924 candidate John W. Davis, "a mere gathering of the unsuccessful." Smith's campaign manager was John J. Raskob, a Republican executive with General Motors who listed his employment as "capitalist." The Democratic platform was practically an identical copy of the GOP's.

The Democrats' decision to run as conservatives allowed the campaign to focus on cultural issues, chiefly religion and prohibition. Smith was no less Catholic in 1928 than he had been in 1924. Protestant ministers denounced Smith as a "cocktail President," charging that his election would open the floodgates of immigration and "turn this country over to the domination of a foreign religious sect." A wry Will Rogers noted the explosion of clergy in public life and observed, "A Preacher just can't save anybody nowadays. He is too busy saving the Nation."

The 1928 election stands out for many reasons, including the exceptionally high turnout (67.5 percent of eligible voters, compared to 51 percent in 1924), which reflected in part an outpouring of Catholic women. The Catholic vote in 1928 was strong enough to move both Rhode Island and Massachusetts into the Democratic camp. Smith polled 41 percent of the vote, more than any Democratic nominee since Woodrow Wilson, but he lost six traditionally Democratic states in the South. Hoover's popular-vote margin was only five million, but he won decisively in the Electoral College (444 to 87), and became the first president born west of the Mississippi.

Smith's religion, his ethnicity, and his identity as a New Yorker all combined to make him the personification of strangeness, of difference, to white Protestant America. As the *New Republic's* Walter Lippmann observed, "Quite apart even from the severe opposition of the prohibitionists, the objection to [machine politics], the sectional objection to New York, there is an opposition to Smith which is as authentic, and, it seems to me, as poignant as his support. It is inspired by the feeling that the clamorous life of the city should not be acknowledged as the American ideal." Intolerance remained integral to the definition of "100% Americanism."

*

In a 1928 speech in New York, Al Smith's home base, Herbert Hoover stated that the distinctive American "concept of self-government" was founded on the belief "that only through ordered liberty, freedom and equal opportunity to the individual will his initiative and enterprise spur on the march of progress." He warned, though, that the Democrats had "revived in this campaign . . . a series of proposals which, if adopted, would be a long step toward the abandonment of our American system." Greater government regulation of the economy, he declared, "would destroy political equality" and "stifle initiative and invention." Although denying that he was celebrating a "free-for-all and devil-take-hind-most" philosophy of governance, Hoover insisted that by withholding government regulation of economic liberty America was "nearer today to the idea of the abolition of poverty and fear from the lives of men and women than ever before in any land." America, he promised, was on the verge of lasting prosperity. Democracy might totter in Europe, but Americans had nothing to fear.

FIGURE 5. "Work Promotes Confidence," poster from the Works Progress Admin-istration, ca. 1936–1941. Posters: WPA Posters, Prints and Photographs Division, Library of Congress, Washington, DC, http://www.loc.gov/pictures/item/9851 8393/.

CHAPTER 5

Depression, 1928–1938

In 1932, Angelo Herndon, a young black Communist organizer in Atlanta, was prosecuted under a Reconstruction-era anti-insurrection act that carried the death penalty. Herndon's ostensible crime was possession of membership blanks for the Communist Party. The more serious crime, in the eyes of Georgia officials, was his organization of the unemployed through speeches, literature, and protests. Herndon boasted of his membership in the Communist Party, and received Communist literature. Worse, the charismatic Herndon held meetings that were interracial and also frequently included white women workers.

During the trial, the local prosecutor, John Hudson, defended Herndon's arrest and insisted, "If we wait until they seize the Capitol and the courts before we consider it an overt act, there will be no government left to punish insurrection." Hudson demanded the jury to find Herndon guilty and sentence him to death. The jury complied with the first demand, but not the second. Herndon was sentenced to 28 years in prison. He was 19 years old.

At the nadir of the Great Depression, insurrection was not outside the realm of the possible. In Atlanta, the Communist Party competed with the protofascist Black Shirts, whose members believed in saving jobs for working-class white men. Two days after Franklin D. Roosevelt's election on November 8, 1932, his aide Adolf Berle sketched a tentative legislative program for the new administration. But he cautioned, "It must be remembered that by March 4 next we may have anything on our hands from a recovery to a revolution. The odds are about even either way."

From his perch in Cambridge, Harvard law professor Zachariah Chafee ridiculed Georgia authorities and their supposed fear of violent insurrection. White Georgians, he insisted, "were afraid not that the United States Constitution would be overthrown, but that it might be enforced." Yet, Chafee continued, "you cannot indict a man for seeking to put the Fifteenth Amendment into wider effect." What Herndon and other African American Communists wanted was to participate in government. If that government was Communist, all the better: the Communist Party was officially committed to full equality for all people, including black people.

Chaffee acknowledged that a genuine attempt to overthrow the government by force could of course be punished. But, he concluded, that did not mean that the advocacy of "anything the community dislikes" could be considered an attempted revolt, even if its advocacy resulted in violence. Georgia prosecutors had not been worried about any plotted subversion of the lawful authority of the state of Georgia in 1932, said Chaffee. What worried them was Herndon's demand for equal rights for Negroes. "If he got going with that," Chaffee explained, "there was a clear and present danger of racial friction and isolated acts of violence by individuals on both sides."

When it overturned Angelo Herndon's conviction in 1937, the Supreme Court differentiated between seditious acts and political advocacy up to and including revolution, which the justices considered political speech and therefore protected by the First Amendment to the Constitution. States were not free to criminalize ideas and prevent people from criticizing the law or advocating a different outcome.

When faced with the possibility of Communist revolution in 1919, the German government organized the Freikorps, a militia composed of WWI combat veterans. During the 1920s, the remnants of this group evolved into the Sturmabteilung (SA, or Stormtroopers), the paramilitary arm of the Nazi Party. There were those in the Roosevelt administration who thought something similar might be required in the United States. A draft of a radio address from March 5, 1933, to the American Legion ended with the president suggesting a possible need to mobilize the veterans under his personal command. "As new commander-in-chief under the oath to which you are still bound I reserve to myself the right to command you in any phase of the situation which now confronts us. That is the highest compliment within my power."

FDR cut these sentences and replaced them with language asking for veterans to support his legislative program. He did so with the knowledge that it might be necessary to call on the army to put down an insurrection, whether promoted by Georgia Communists or Minnesota farmers. The main thing at the moment was to keep Americans' minds on Congress and the legislative process.

Meltdown, 1928–1933

When Republican Herbert Hoover was inaugurated as president on March 4, 1929, the United States was the richest nation on earth. Indeed, it was the richest nation the world had ever seen. Perennial Secretary of the Treasury Andrew Mellon proclaimed majestically that "the high tide of prosperity will continue," but the president had his doubts. Almost alone, he warned against the "speculative frenzy" of the stock market, and urged state governments to put aside resources for a rainy day. Delighted that "the modern technical mind was for the first time at the head of a government," Americans waited for the show to begin.

THE PREMIER BUREAUCRAT OF THE DECADE

Herbert Hoover liked to feed people. As chairman of the Commission for Relief in Belgium in WWI, he famously fed millions in the middle of a war zone. In postwar Austria, he once swapped two locomotives for two million eggs. As secretary of commerce in 1921, Hoover worked with private organizations to feed millions of starving Russians, saving as many as 10 million lives. Late in his career, after World War II, he had a hand in creating the United Nations International Children's Emergency Fund (UNICEF). Hoover traced his emphasis on food to the poverty of his upbringing. Orphaned by age 10, Hoover was shunted among Quaker families in Iowa before being sent to live with an uncle in Oregon. "You see," he explained in 1928, "I was always hungry then."

Hoover's insecure boyhood left him reclusive and wary, without a sense of humor and incapable of communicating effectively. He knew what he knew and was impervious to persuasion by anyone other than his beloved wife, Lou, a fellow Stanford geology graduate. Hoover was touchy and bridled at even modest criticism. On the other hand, he could be a ferocious critic of others, often alienating people for life. Hoover was a fearsomely effective business executive, taskmaster, and administrator, but he was an inept politician. As the ever-astute progressive journalist William Allen White observed, Hoover's "frigid desire to live a virtuous life" rendered him a singularly ineffective leader.

Hoover's Quaker upbringing instilled in him a deep faith in the power of voluntary cooperation and local community action that led him to favor private relief efforts over government action in times of crisis. Renowned for his constant drive to expand his portfolio as secretary of commerce, Hoover seemed oblivious to the fact that he was, ironically, both "the premier bureaucrat of the decade" and "the man most responsible for swollen government agencies."

Herbert Hoover assumed the presidency in March 1929 intending to fulfill his campaign declaration that "government must be a constructive force." His Republican predecessors, Warren Harding and Calvin Coolidge, had accomplished little in the way of domestic reform. Hoover hoped to pick up where Theodore Roosevelt and Woodrow Wilson had left off. "We want to see a nation built of home owners and farm owners," he announced. "We want to see their savings protected. We want to see them in steady jobs. We want to see more and more of them insured against death and accident, unemployment and old age. We want them all secure."

Hoover believed that government policies could help establish and maintain that sense of security. Throughout the 1920s, Hoover argued for a minimum wage, the 48-hour workweek, the eradication of child labor, improved housing for workers, and equal pay for men and women. He favored a graduated income tax and steep inheritance and gift taxes for the express purpose of "disintegrating large fortunes," which, in line with Theodore Roosevelt, he considered "a menace to true liberty" by encouraging inherited privilege. In 1928, he urged a gathering of governors to create a $3 billion reserve fund for public works "to ward off unemployment in lean years." With unemployment at 3 percent in early 1929, Treasury Secretary Andrew Mellon brushed off such concerns, pronouncing that "the high tide of prosperity will continue."

INTERNATIONAL ECONOMIC COMPLICATIONS

Under the terms of the Versailles Treaty, Germany was obliged to pay some $33 billion in reparations to Britain and France. The Germans defaulted on this debt repeatedly in the 1920s, resulting in French occupation of the Ruhr, Germany's industrial heartland, in 1923, and repeated renegotiations of the terms of the debt. In recognition of the

United States' new position as the world's leading creditor, these negotiations were brokered by Americans: Chicago banker and vice president of the United States Charles G. Dawes in 1924 and industrialist Owen D. Young in 1929.

Contrary to conventional wisdom, the reparations payments did not unduly tax the German economy (as forecast by economist John Maynard Keynes in 1919) and were not directly responsible for its breakdown in 1923. The extraordinary hyperinflation that led to the German economic collapse in 1923 was in fact orchestrated by the German government, which preferred short-term economic chaos to politically unpalatable reparation payments and gambled, correctly, that chaos would lead to renegotiation.

The United States received only nominal reparations from Germany. But the Allied governments owed the US Treasury some $10 billion for loans made during and immediately after the war. Britain and France objected to paying these debts, arguing that 90 percent of the money they borrowed had been spent in the United States on war supplies, sparking a domestic economic boom. French Prime Minister Georges Clemenceau argued that the Americans should count their blessings that their primary contribution to defeating the Germans had been in coin rather than blood, and challenged President Coolidge to "come see the endless lists of dead in our villages." Britain and France offered to ease their demands on Germany if the Americans would forgive the Allied loans, but the US government rejected any connection between German reparations and Allied debts, and Republican determination to lower domestic tax rates ruled out Allied debt forgiveness. In the end, Germany borrowed money from private American banks to help pay reparations to France and Britain, which in turn used those funds to repay their debts to the United States.

The isolationist and tightfisted Republican administrations of the 1920s refused to admit any link between German reparations and debts owed the US Treasury by the Allied governments. Americans considered efforts to scale back the Allied debts transparent schemes to shift the burden of the war's cost from European to American shoulders. Popular opinion on this issue was only hardened by Wall Street's support for war-debt cancellation, a move that would make the banks' own private loans more secure. Weary of European diplomatic intrigue at Versailles, disillusioned with the fate of the Wilsonian vision of a democratic Europe, disgusted by financiers' willingness to sacrifice taxpayer dollars to secure their own profits, Americans withdrew into their own world, cocooned, they thought, from the catastrophes Europeans brought on themselves.

By 1929, the national income of the United States surpassed those of Great Britain, Germany, France, Canada, Japan, and 17 other major nations combined. America was unquestionably the world's dominant economic power. This represented a shift of historic proportions. For 300 years, the United States had been a debtor nation, dependent on European capital to finance industrial expansion. For the first time, the economic balance of the world depended on the willingness of private bankers in America to lend money abroad.

SMASH-UP

In September 1929, the frenzied bull market faltered. Stock prices slid suddenly, recovered, and assumed a precarious balance. But on October 23, the market plunged; some $4 billion was lost in a matter of hours. The next day, Black Thursday, the floor of the New York Stock Exchange dissolved into pandemonium as stocks plummeted in record-breaking heavy trading. The following Tuesday, October 29, was even worse. By mid-November, industrial stocks were worth half what they had been worth only 10 weeks earlier.

As dramatic as the crash was, it directly affected only a relatively narrow slice of Americans. Less than 3 percent of Americans owned securities in 1929. The president believed that the nation was entering a short-term recession similar to that of 1921. Even so, he took action. Hoover convinced the Federal Reserve to ease credit and extracted a pledge from business leaders not to cut wages or jobs. Until the end of 1930, Americans believed that they were in the midst of a normal business downswing and that their president was intervening on their behalf in an appropriately aggressive and unprecedented manner.

Then the banks began to fail. As historian David Kennedy has noted bluntly, "American banks were rotten even in good times." There were too many banks, and a great number of them were dangerously undercapitalized. The rest of the developed world used branch banking, in which sound metropolitan institutions served outlying communities through branches. But centralized branch banking had been demonized in the United States by populist attacks on "the money power." The overwhelming majority of the approximately 30,000 American banks in 1929 were "unitary" banks that could look only to their own resources in the event of a panic.

The saying "If you see a line outside a bank, join it" gives a sense of the improvised volatility of a run on a bank. The 1930 run began in Louisville, Kentucky. Mobs of depositors pushed their way to tellers' windows demanding to withdraw their savings. Banks scrambled to meet this demand by calling in loans and selling assets, thereby driving down the value of assets in otherwise sound institutions and imperiling the entire banking system in an expanding ripple effect.

What the banks needed most was cash. But the desperate effort of thousands of individual banks to meet the demands of their depositors contracted the money supply, tightened credit, and strangled the system as a whole. In 1907, when a similar collapse threatened the economy, the House of Morgan had taken charge of the panic and used its own massive reserves to sort things out. Theoretically, the Federal Reserve was supposed to prevent such a crisis now, but it was not up to the job.

A liquidity crisis in America meant an investment crisis abroad. Because American banks now had no money to lend Europeans, German and Austrian banks failed. Hoover managed to ram through Congress a one-year moratorium on the repayment of "intergovernmental debts, reparations, and relief debts," which gave the Europeans some breathing room. But skeptical holders of European currencies began to demand payment in gold. On September 21, 1931, Great Britain defaulted on its gold payments to foreign investors. At this point, foreign investors, panicked by the European crisis, began withdrawing their gold and capital from American banks. Domestic depositors followed suit, triggering a liquidity crisis that dwarfed the one in 1930. By the end of 1931, 2,294 American banks had failed, and the economy was grinding to a halt.

COPING WITH CRISIS

It matters who is at the helm when a hurricane strikes. Americans had faith that Herbert Hoover, who had orchestrated massive relief efforts on two continents, would pilot them safely through the storm. Hoover, in turn, had faith that Americans would rise to the occasion, and that local government institutions and private charity would tide the nation over until the worst had passed. He had a "passionate, almost bigoted, belief in America," concluded William Allen White.

Hoover's faith in the power of volunteerism ignored the facts of his own experience. As head of the relief effort during the 1927 Mississippi River flood, Hoover never acknowledged that two-thirds of the relief funds came from the government or that he depended on federal agencies like the Department of Agriculture and the National Guard to carry out the rescue operation. Nor did he acknowledge that of the $12 million required monthly to feed the Belgians during WWI, $10 million came directly from the British and French treasuries.

Hoover's inclination to be selective with facts served him poorly as the depression worsened. In May 1930, he insisted that the worst was over. Not until a year after the crash, in October 1930, did he finally establish the President's Emergency Committee for Employment (PECE). When the Census Bureau estimated in April 1931 that between three and four million Americans were out of work, Hoover disagreed, insisting that fewer than two million were out of work, and asserted erroneously that "employment has been steadily increasing."

This approach played poorly at the polls in the 1930 midterm elections, by which time factory payrolls had plunged 35 percent and more than 25,000 businesses had failed. Democrats gained control of the House of Representatives for the first time since 1919, and picked up six seats in the Senate, reducing the GOP majority to a one-seat advantage. Growing calls for government relief elicited only presidential lectures. "Prosperity," Hoover intoned in his December 1930 State of the Union address, "cannot be restored by raids upon the public Treasury." He seemed to view the Depression (the word had become capitalized) as akin to a natural disaster. Congress, he thought, could no more speed recovery than it could "exorcise a Caribbean hurricane by statutory law." Rather than call an extra session of Congress to contend with the crisis, Hoover allowed it to recess from March 4 to December 7, 1931.

Hoover stood steadfast against direct federal relief, declaring that the dole was demoralizing. While millions of Americans huddled in miserable shantytowns dubbed "Hoovervilles" and suffered from hunger and exposure to the elements, the president proclaimed inaccurately that local governments "are providing against distress" and that "nobody actually starved." In truth, local governments and private philanthropy had collapsed beneath the accumulated weight of the destitute. The head of the PECE resigned as unemployment hit eight million. Alarmed that the federal government was running a historic deficit of nearly one billion dollars, the president convinced Congress to raise taxes and cut government spending. *Fortune* magazine estimated that 34 million Americans were "without any income whatever." This figure omitted 11 million farm families crushed under the double burden of the depression and a devastating drought.

FROM BAD TO WORSE

By early 1932, a presidential election year, more than 10 million people were out of work, nearly 20 percent of the labor force. In cities like Detroit and Chicago, which were home to hard-hit industries such as steel and automobiles, the unemployment rate was a staggering 40 percent. Local relief didn't begin to make up for lost wages. New York City provided relief to the unemployed equaling approximately 8 percent of a worker's lost wages; in Chicago, relief covered only 5 percent. In effect, a worker who had earned $2,000 per year received $100 per year in relief. *Business Week* wrote of a "complete breakdown." Chicago mayor Anton Cermak told Congress that if it refused to send federal funds for relief, it should send troops to keep the peace.

Recognizing the need to stabilize the banking system and generate liquidity, Hoover reluctantly agreed to intervene. In February 1932 the Glass-Steagall Act broadened the category of acceptable credit for Federal Reserve System loans, and in July the Federal Home Loan Bank Act helped families refinance their homes and thawed millions of dollars in frozen assets. Working at cross-purposes, however, the Revenue Act of 1932 raised taxes across the board.

Most significantly, the new Reconstruction Finance Corporation (RFC) was authorized to lend some $500 million to financial institutions. The money was expected to "trickle down" to the public through private loans, mortgages, and job creation. *Business Week* and the *New Republic* for once agreed, and praised the policy decision. Columbia University economist Rexford Tugwell was less complimentary. "Bank relief," he said, was like fertilizing the branches of a tree instead of its roots. Will Rogers was even more pointed. Bankers, he announced, had "the honor of being the first group to go on the 'dole' in America." Still the president resisted both direct federal relief for the poor and enhanced aid for the states.

New York senator Robert Wagner was incredulous: "We shall help the financial institutions; and I agree that we should. But is there any reason why we should not likewise extend a helping hand to that forlorn American, in every village and every city of the United States, who has been without wages since 1929? Must he alone carry the cross of individual responsibility?" Noting the eagerness of the government to help the banks, Wagner added, "We did not preach to them rugged individualism. We did not sanctimoniously roll out sentences rich with synonyms of self-reliance. We were not carried away with apprehension over what would happen to their independence if we extended them a helping hand."

Hoover still stubbornly resisted aid for the unemployed. He vetoed a relief bill in July 1932, but reluctantly signed the Relief and Reconstruction Act, which authorized the RFC to finance up to $1.5 billion in "self-liquidating" short-term public works projects and to loan up to $300 million to the states for relief. Hoover's image as callous was reinforced that same month when General Douglas MacArthur expelled from the District of Columbia the Bonus Army, tens of thousands of out-of-work WWI veterans who marched on Washington and demanded early payment of a war "bonus" due them in 1945. Federal troops were called in after a violent confrontation between veterans and police on Pennsylvania Avenue on July 28. Exceeding his authority, General MacArthur descended on the camp with six cannons, a column of infantry with fixed bayonets, and a detachment of cavalry. They drove out the unarmed marchers and set their tents ablaze. "Well, this elects me," concluded Hoover's Democratic opponent for president, New York governor Franklin Delano Roosevelt.

"Strong Medicine," 1933–1935

In 1928, Herbert Hoover carried 40 states; in 1932, he carried 6. The election was a referendum on Republican policies that failed to stem the economic bloodletting and eroded faith in the market's capacity to self-adjust. Franklin Roosevelt, who promised, vaguely, a "new deal" for Americans, won by default.

By 1932, the relationship of the state to the economy, and of the government to the people, had been a principal topic of debate for half a century. These issues were central to the crisis that Franklin Roosevelt faced. Crises do not necessarily lead to innovative solutions, but they do alter the conditions of the politically possible. At such a moment, new people and new ideas—or new people with old ideas—can slip through openings. In the depths of the Depression, many Americans' faith in the nation's political institutions to cope with the economic crisis had nearly dissolved. Some looked to more "modern" solutions.

ROOSEVELT REDUX

Franklin D. Roosevelt grew up roaming a bucolic estate overlooking the Hudson River in Hyde Park, New York. The only child of indulgent parents, he was a bright but uninspired student at Groton and Harvard. A year of Columbia Law School convinced Roosevelt that he did not want to practice law. In 1905, Franklin married his distant cousin Eleanor Roosevelt, who was escorted down the aisle by her uncle Theodore. The couple had four children in four years, one of whom died as an infant, and then another two during WWI. Franklin's affair with Eleanor's secretary, Lucy Mercer, nearly ended both the marriage and Roosevelt's political career. In the end, Eleanor remained in the marriage but not in the bedroom.

After a stint as a state representative in New York, Roosevelt was appointed assistant secretary of the Navy in 1913. He resigned in 1920 to serve as the vice presidential candidate for the doomed Democrats. The following year, Roosevelt contracted polio, which left him permanently paralyzed from the waist down. Despite months of therapy in Warm Springs, Georgia, Roosevelt failed to improve. Yet he was determined to walk again. Outfitted in steel braces and a cane, FDR was able to move a short distance by swiveling his torso and hips to propel his legs. In public, Roosevelt was always seen either seated or standing, with the assistance of an aide or one of his sons. In private, he was carried or used a wheelchair. Thanks to an obliging press, there are only two known photographs of FDR in a wheelchair and less than a minute of film of his excruciating, exhausting "walk." Not until the 1960s did the American public have any idea of how severely disabled he was.

To the very marrow in his bones, Franklin Roosevelt was what Herbert Hoover was *not*: a politician. Hoover was frank to the point of rudeness, alienating even those who agreed with him. Roosevelt was charmingly evasive, baffling his supporters and opponents alike. He was a master of conversation, listening attentively to everyone, punctuating talk with penetrating questions. He was a superb storyteller. Whether standing by leaning on his cane or continuing his relationship with Lucy Mercer, FDR could be duplicitous, and he enjoyed secrecy when it served his interests. These attributes served him well during his unprecedented 12-year presidency.

Roosevelt spent the 1920s learning to cope with the consequences of polio, avoiding the internecine Democratic Party struggle between the urban-north-Catholic-wet wing and the rural-western/southern-Protestant-dry faction. In 1928, when Al Smith lost the presidency to Herbert Hoover, Roosevelt was elected governor of New York.

Like the previous President Roosevelt, FDR considered government the active agent of the public interest. While President Hoover resisted government aid to the unemployed, Governor Roosevelt created a Temporary Emergency Relief Administration in New York. "What is the state?" he asked the New York legislature in 1931. "It is the duly constituted representative of an organized society of human beings—created by them for their mutual protection and well-being." Government extends relief, Roosevelt explained, "not as a matter of charity, but as a matter of social duty; the State accepts that task cheerfully because it believes that it will help restore that close relationship with its people which is necessary to preserve our democratic form of government."

DO WE NEED A DICTATOR?

Every industrialized nation was affected by the Great Depression, but none was hit as hard as the United States. Four years after the crash of 1929, gross national product (GNP) was half what it had been. At least a quarter, but more likely one-third, of American workers were unemployed. Millions more had lost their investments, their life savings, their homes, their land. Three-quarters of the value of stockholder assets had evaporated since 1929. More than 5,000 bank failures had wiped out some $7 billion worth of depositors' savings. Farm losses were staggering. By early 1933, banks were foreclosing on 20,000 farms a month.

Despite FDR's election, Hoover's term as president did not end until March 4, 1933. The timing could not have been worse. The social fabric, already badly frayed, began to dissolve as the economy hit rock bottom. An assassination attempt on the president-elect killed Chicago mayor Anton Cermak instead. A double line of rifle-bearing policemen on the Capitol steps separated Congress from 2,500 hunger marchers. Iowa farmers dragged a judge from his chambers and strung him up from a tree to protest farm foreclosure auctions. The president of the Farm Bureau Foundation warned the Senate in January 1933, "Unless something is done for the American farmer we will have revolution in the countryside within twelve months."

The crisis of capitalism was more than an economic disaster: it produced a global loss of confidence in democratic governance. Legislative bodies, with their partisan divisions, cumbersome rules, and internal conflicts of interest, suddenly seemed hopelessly outdated and incapable of coping with the crisis. One after another, European nations abandoned representative government and the rule of law and adopted single-party dictatorships, in the hope that they could more efficiently manage the Depression. With the exceptions of Britain, Scandinavia, and France before 1940, all of interwar Europe embraced authoritarianism, dictatorship, and/or fascism between 1925 and 1938. The new governments usually maintained neutered parliaments that were frequently overridden by "extraordinary measures" that concentrated power in the now-dictatorial executive.

The United States was not immune to this crisis of democratic confidence. In the same week that FDR was inaugurated, the cover of the *Nation* asked, "Do We Need a Dictator?" The magazine answered in the negative, writing that "however stupid and frightened" Congress might be, "if we muzzle Congress, muzzles for the rest of us will come as a matter of course." Other influential voices came to the opposite conclusion. *Barron's* magazine agreed that "even semi-dictatorships in peace time are quite contrary to the spirit of American institutions," but conceded that "a genial and lighthearted dictator might be a relief from the pompous futility" of Congress. The *New Republic*'s Walter Lippmann advocated "strong medicine," by which he meant a grant of "extraordinary powers" to the incoming president to form a temporary "soft dictatorship." Visiting the president-elect in Georgia in February, Lippmann argued that "the situation is critical, Franklin. You may have no alternative but to assume dictatorial powers."

Such was the conclusion of Germany's new leader. Soon after his installation as chancellor in January 1933, National Socialist Party leader Adolf Hitler eliminated all opposition. Following the burning of the Reichstag (parliament) in February, which was orchestrated by the Nazis but blamed on the Communists, Hitler's government issued emergency decrees suppressing freedom of speech and assembly. During the spring, the Nazis passed the Enabling Act, which placed all legislative power in Hitler's hands, dissolved the trade unions, and Nazified the universities and press. After the Nazi seizure of power, American novelist Thomas Wolfe wrote, "Here was an entire nation—infested with the contagion of an ever-present fear. It was a kind of creeping paralysis which twisted and blighted all human relations."

NOTHING TO FEAR

It was precisely this "unjustified terror" that FDR hoped to banish as he assumed office. What the nation needed was *action*. He knew, as he had said in May 1932, that the country needed "bold, persistent experimentation. It is common sense to take a method and try it: If it fails, admit it frankly and try another. But above all, try something." The United States, he insisted in his inaugural address, "had nothing to fear but fear itself."

The causes and consequences of the Great Depression remain topics of energetic debate to this day. There is, however, general agreement on two important points. First, despite the close sequence of events, the Depression was *not* caused by the collapse of the stock market in 1929. Second, there was a fundamental maldistribution of income in the United States, which constrained consumer purchasing power and limited economic growth during a moment of transition from an industrial economy to a broader consumer economy. Whereas profits leapt annually by 9 percent during the 1920s, wages rose only 1 percent. Agricultural regions remained poorer than urban areas. Whether the metric was average income or indoor plumbing, the South trailed the rest of the nation by a considerable margin.

Franklin Roosevelt understood that vast discrepancies in wealth among citizens and regions could undermine democracy. Like his cousin Theodore, FDR believed that government should play an active role as agent of the public interest. His speechwriter Raymond Moley, who wrote most of the president's first inaugural address, recalled that FDR had "a profound feeling for the underdog, a real sense of the critical imbalance of economic life, a very keen awareness that political democracy could not exist side by side with economic plutocracy." As Roosevelt himself explained, "Our civilization cannot endure unless we, as individuals, realize our responsibility to and dependence on the rest of the world. . . . Without the help of thousands of others, any one of us would die, naked and starved." In the final analysis, he concluded, "The progress of our civilization will be retarded if any large body of citizens falls behind."

Two types of citizens had fallen far behind by 1933: farmers and industrial workers. The president promised in his inaugural address to focus on both groups. The greatest task facing the country, he said, was "to put people to work," hinting that government employment programs were in the offing. He promised to "raise the value of agricultural products and with this the power to purchase the output of our cities." He called for "strict supervision of all banking and credits and investments," regulation of key industries, and cuts in government spending. He announced that he was calling a special session of Congress to address these issues.

The speech ended on a rather ominous note that produced the most sustained applause of the day. Should Congress prove unequal to the task, Roosevelt said to cheers, "I shall ask the Congress for the one remaining instrument to meet the crisis—broad Executive power to wage a war against the emergency, as great as the power that would be given to me if we were in fact invaded by a foreign foe." He would ask for the executive authority that Woodrow Wilson had exercised to manage the economy some 15 years earlier. Americans who were skeptical that Congress could meet the challenge seemed willing to empower the president to make decisions on their behalf. An astute journalist concluded, "America today literally asks for orders. Nobody is much disturbed by the idea of dictatorship."

100 DAYS: MONEY AND CROPS

Roosevelt issued two proclamations on March 5, the first full day of his presidency. One called Congress into special session, and the other invoked the WWI-era Trading with the Enemies Act to halt transactions in gold and declared a four-day national bank "holiday."

The banking system was in full free fall by March 1933: 297 banks had failed in the final months of 1932. As weak banks ran into trouble, frightened depositors, anxious to protect whatever assets they had left, withdrew holdings from other banks as well. One after another, state governors called a halt to banking operations to prevent complete collapse. The crisis accelerated in early 1933. By the first week of March, 16 states had declared bank holidays. On the morning of the inauguration, Illinois and New York, both financial hubs, shut their banks. The Chicago Board of Trade shut its doors for the first time since 1848.

Working around the clock, a group of new Roosevelt appointees (led by the so-called Brain Trust, professors poached from leading universities) worked with Hoover holdovers in the Treasury Department to craft new banking legislation. The House passed the Emergency Banking Act unanimously, sight unseen; the Senate followed suit with but seven dissenters. The president signed the law that evening, March 9, 1933.

Would Americans have enough confidence in the revised banking system to leave their money in it? The night before the banks were to reopen, tens of millions of Americans listened on the radio to Roosevelt's first "fireside chat," in which the president explained the state of the banks in everyday language and assured his listeners that "it is safer to keep your money in a reopened bank than it is to keep it under the mattress." Only a year earlier, Hoover had made a spectacularly unsuccessful appeal to depositors not to hoard their cash. But on March 11, 1933, banks reopened quietly across the country, with deposits far outnumbering withdrawals. Over the rest of 1933, only 221 banks failed.

The Glass-Steagall Banking Act of 1933 separated commercial banks (those that take deposits and invest them) from investment banks (those that raise capital for investors by issuing and selling securities, or stock), and created the Federal Deposit Insurance Corporation to guarantee deposits. A new securities law empowered the Federal Trade Commission (FTC) to supervise issues of new securities, required each new stock to release a statement of relevant financial information, and made company directors civilly and criminally responsible for misrepresentation.

Having stabilized the banking system, the administration turned to federal finances. The Economy Act cut the wages of federal employees and reduced veterans' benefits to balance the budget, a conservative move that raised howls from congressional Democrats. Capitalizing on Congress's repeal of the prohibition amendment, a new revenue act generated additional federal funds by taxing the sale of beer and wine. Already inclined toward lifting the economy through inflation, the president took the United States off the gold standard, which allowed the federal government to adjust the amount of money in circulation by raising or lowering interest rates.

Convinced that raising farm purchasing power was essential to restoring general prosperity and recognizing that FDR owed both his Democratic Party nomination and his general election victory to rural western and southern voters, the administration crafted the Agricultural Adjustment Act (AAA). At the heart of the law lay the Voluntary Domestic Allotment Plan, which offered financial incentives for farmers to cut acreage and reduce output, thereby raising prices. The program would be funded through a tax paid by the processors of agricultural goods (such as those who milled grain and turned it into flour). Although Secretary of Agriculture Henry A. Wallace and others were pained by limiting production while people went hungry, the plan worked as designed. Gross farm income rose 50 percent during Roosevelt's first term, crop prices climbed, and rural debts were reduced.

100 DAYS: MARKETS AND WORKERS

On May 12, 1933, for the first time in American history, Congress authorized $500 million in direct federal relief for the unemployed.

The Federal Emergency Relief Administration (FERA) was designed to distribute the aid through the agencies of the states. At its helm was Harry Hopkins, an experienced social worker and shrewd politician who would be at Roosevelt's side throughout the New Deal and WWII. Hopkins also set up the Civil Works Administration (CWA), a federal program that provided work at minimum wages. At its height, the CWA employed over four million people, including 50,000 teachers. CWA workers built or improved some 500,000 miles of roads and 40,000 schools, playgrounds, and athletic fields. The CWA pumped one billion dollars of purchasing power into the flaccid economy, and got the nation through the winter.

Near the end of the emergency session of Congress, the administration introduced its primary legislation to revive the economy: the National Industrial Recovery Act (NIRA). Designed to stimulate production of industrial and consumer goods and raise prices, the law allowed representatives of the nation's diverse industries to devise codes of fair competition and permitted them to set prices—more or less what antitrust laws had been devised to prevent. As a safeguard against monopoly, the codes had to be approved by the National Recovery Administration (NRA), which transferred a great deal of power over the economy from private to public hands.

NIRA regulated maximum hours and minimum wages, and affirmed the right of workers to form unions and engage in collective bargaining. To jump-start the economy, Congress provided $3 billion to develop the Public Works Administration (PWA) that would continue the work of FERA. From 1933 to 1939, the PWA helped construct 70 percent of America's new schools; 65 percent of its courthouses, city halls, and sewage plants; and 35 percent of the nation's hospitals. It helped build the Lincoln Tunnel in New York, linked Key West to the Florida mainland, and underwrote new planes, submarines, and ships for the army and navy.

In 1933, the Roosevelt administration used a WWI-era electric power plant on the Tennessee River to create the Tennessee Valley Authority (TVA) as a public corporation to generate cheap, abundant hydroelectric power. The TVA transformed the region and brought its residents at long last into the contemporary world of radios, electric lights, and household appliances. In 1935, the Rural Electrification Administration (REA) extended the TVA's agenda to the rest of rural America. These dramatic examples of state-promoted economic development were sharply criticized as un-American, but their beneficiaries were unconcerned about allegations of creeping socialism.

The emergency legislation of the 100 Days was drafted almost entirely by the executive branch and passed virtually unchanged by Congress. The laws themselves expanded dramatically the number and authority of federal agencies, thereby effectively transferring some power from the legislative to the executive branch. But as historian Ira Katznelson concluded, in the end "constitutional democracy was sustained, if bruised." In his second fireside chat on May 7, 1933, FDR reassured the public that there had been "no actual surrender of power. Congress still retained its constitutional authority and no one has the slightest desire to change the balance of these powers." In a moment of national crisis, the ultimate sovereignty of the people as represented by Congress was upheld.

A Government of Humanity

Although financially secure, Franklin Roosevelt knew what it was to be afraid and dependent. When he wasn't in a wheelchair, FDR relied on those who carried him. He felt particularly vulnerable in bed, and worried that fire would break out while he was sleeping and he would be unable to escape. He refused to lock his bedroom door, and practiced dropping from his bed to the floor and crawling to the threshold.

Roosevelt knew he could not banish fear or dependence. But he was determined to provide a sense of safety, of predictability, of security, for as many Americans as possible. FDR's social vision was always in plain view. "We are going to make a country," he said to Secretary of Labor Frances Perkins, "in which no one is left out." A few days after taking office, one New Deal administrator wrote in his diary: "This should be a Gov't of humanity." This phrase does not describe an economic recovery program: it describes structural reform of the government. Reform, not relief, was the New Deal's lasting legacy.

FORGING AN ECONOMIC CONSTITUTIONAL ORDER

Anyone looking for coherence in the New Deal is doomed to disappointment. Like the president, the New Deal was ideologically inconsistent. As historian Daniel T. Rodgers remarked, it was "less a program than a free-for-all of competing ideas and interests." Claims about the New Deal's legacy are similarly contradictory: It was an assault on economic liberty; it saved capitalism by limiting it. It was a triumph for labor; it co-opted labor. It showed compassion for the poor and unemployed; it perpetuated the class and racial prejudices of the white southerners who dominated the Democratic Party. The New Deal remains a topic of hot debate and is arguably the defining moment of modern American politics.

The New Deal was not a response to the Depression, which was already three years old by the time Roosevelt assumed office. It was, rather, a response to the failed Republican recovery programs. How, in the midst of chaos and confusion, did the New Dealers come up with so many new policy proposals so quickly? The answer is, they didn't. Much of the New Deal agenda and policy proposals arose out of the progressive past. Collective bargaining between labor and management, minimum wage and maximum hours standards, old-age and unemployment insurance, emergency work relief, rural electrification, banking and securities regulation, and, especially, agricultural reform all had roots in the Progressive Era. Furthermore, the Emergency Banking Act was effectively the work of the Hoover administration.

Rather than reflecting innovation, the New Deal was the culmination of a generation of progressive proposals and ideas that had been sidelined by WWI and the postwar conservative reaction. Remarking on the United States' status as a "welfare laggard" among industrialized nations, one informed observer concluded in 1934 that Roosevelt "sought with a passionate suddenness, to do, as it were overnight, something akin to what the Liberal Government in England had sought to do" before WWI. The president agreed. "In five years I think we have caught up twenty years," Roosevelt remarked in 1938, with his mind on British social policy. "If liberal government continues over another ten years we ought to be contemporary somewhere in the late Nineteen Forties."

It was never the goal of New Dealers to destroy capitalism. Like late nineteenth-century reformers, their aim was to devolatilize capitalism and to distribute its benefits more evenly across the population. The federal initiatives of the 100 Days were designed, observed NRA director Donald Richberg, "to promote a more stable and more evenly distributed prosperity," to create, writes historian Ira Katznelson, "a more vibrant and less unequal capitalism in a manner that would be consistent with democratic values."

What did this mean? What America needed, Roosevelt explained in a major policy speech in 1932, was to rebalance the relationship between the economic rights of the individual and those of the collective. What was needed, Roosevelt declared, was a new "economic constitutional order" in which property rights did not trump the rights of "personal competency" guaranteed by the Bill of Rights. In the view of the New Dealers, it was the responsibility of government to maintain the balance between individual and collective good, and that rather than violating individual rights of liberty and property, government regulation of the economy was the only way to protect them.

CHASING SECURITY

Hitler and Mussolini did not pose the only threat to American democracy during the Depression. There were internal dangers as well. At the top of that list was severe economic inequality and poverty, which undermined democracy by eroding popular faith that the government was by and for *all* the people. Noting the "well-nigh universal lack of security" for millions of Americans, the sociologist Howard Odum warned in 1935 that American democracy was at risk from the nation's "multiplied inequalities of opportunity for the majority of the people." Boston financier Joseph P. Kennedy warned in 1936 that "democracy will not be safe for this country unless we constructively deal with causes of dictatorships. . . . If our democracy is to survive the attacks of dictatorship, whether open or veiled, we must solve the problem of security."

The president elaborated on this theme in a fireside chat in September 1934. Individual workers and citizens were impotent against the organized power of "great aggregations of capital in enormous industrial establishments," with their outsized influence on the economy and politics. Such circumstances called for "the intervention of that organized control we call government." It was in great measure a question of balance. The federal government, he concluded, was established "to promote the general welfare," and it is government's "plain duty to provide that security upon which welfare depends."

There was no shortage of suggestions about how to achieve greater security. Most came from people and parties to the political left of Roosevelt. Although small in numbers, American Communists were well organized and adept in street politics. Communist-organized antihunger marches attracted large numbers of non-Communists, as did the Communist Party's national network of Unemployed Councils, which bargained with local governments for relief and helped people fight evictions. As one worker in Chicago put it, "Even if they are Communists, they are trying to help us help ourselves, and no one else is doing that."

African Americans appreciated the Communists' outspoken stand against racism and the party's defense of the Scottsboro Boys, nine young black men falsely accused of raping two white women in Alabama. While the party of Lincoln segregated black delegates to the GOP convention behind chicken wire in 1928, the CPUSA ran a black man, James Ford, for vice president. Always a presence but rarely a player, Communists' efforts won the party more gratitude than votes.

Of greater concern than the Communists to FDR was Huey P. Long, the flamboyant senator from Louisiana, whose "Share Our Wealth" movement went much further than any New Deal policy to constrain business and redistribute wealth. Long's plan called for confiscatory taxes on fortunes worth more than one million dollars and guaranteed every family an income of $5,000 per year. By 1935, there were thousands of "Share Our Wealth" clubs across the country. Long's presidential ambitions were apparent from the first but ended suddenly when he was assassinated by a political opponent. "The country," remarked Secretary of the Interior Harold Ickes, "is much more radical than the Administration."

This radicalism was reflected in the 1934 congressional elections. Normally, the party of the president loses seats in midterm elections. But in 1934, the Democrats picked up 13 seats in the House and won more than a two-thirds majority in the Senate. With only seven governorships, less than one-third of Congress, and no popular leader, the Republican Party for the moment was effectively eliminated from national politics.

SOCIAL SECURITY

Before the New Deal, Americans did not look to the state to help them out in hard times. Their social needs were met, if at all, by private organizations: churches, charities, ethnic associations, local branches of political machines, and, occasionally, company unions. The Depression pushed millions of Americans already perched on the edge of poverty into a state of catastrophic need. Addressing the needs of these desperately vulnerable citizens was at the top of the Democrats' agenda.

Flanked on one side by such conservative organizations as the National Association of Manufacturers (NAM), which rejected government subsidies to the poor and prescribed individual "thrift and denial" as the answer to need, and on the other side by radical organizations like EPIC (End Poverty in California) and the Communist Party, which called for confiscatory taxation and government-guaranteed employment, the Roosevelt administration steered a course through a narrow middle channel. Legend has it that Labor Secretary Frances Perkins locked the President's Committee on Economic Security in her dining room with a bottle of whiskey and refused to let them out until they had drafted social insurance legislation.

The Social Security Act, signed by FDR in August 1935, offered government-sponsored security to workers for the first time in American history. This landmark measure established a permanent system of compulsory insurance that included unemployment compensation, old-age pensions, disability, and aid for disabled and dependent children. Although the American Medical Association killed a proposed individual health insurance provision, modest sums for public health services survived. All these provisions had inspired but eluded progressives for a generation. This combined federal/state program came to emblematize the essence of the New Deal, and has proved to be its most enduring reform.

Because Social Security was financed through a regressive payroll tax that capped both contributions and benefits, the program was only minimally redistributive. Edwin Witte, the main architect of the law, explained, "Only to a very minor degree does it modify the distribution of wealth and it does not alter at all the fundamentals of our capitalist and individualistic economy." Nonetheless, Social Security promised both a stable retirement to people who worked all their lives and at least subsistence support in bad times.

At the same time, the law excluded many of the people who needed help the most. At the insistence of southern congressmen, it denied benefits to agricultural workers and domestic laborers, the very people whose chronically low wages and irregular employment left them among the poorest in the land. Because of this exclusion, almost a third of all workingwomen and a majority of African American women and Latinas were ineligible for both unemployment and pension benefits. Likewise, instead of establishing a minimum national unemployment benefit, the system again bowed to the South and authorized the states to set the dollar level of unemployment benefits. The exclusion of agricultural and domestic workers and the state control of unemployment benefits protected what white southerners considered the "greatest natural asset" of their region — the low-wage, low-tax regime that kept the South competitive in the world of agriculture, manufacturing, and industry — and the Jim Crow environment of state-sponsored racial discrimination and inequality.

LABOR RISING

Workers already frustrated by the unreliability of welfare capitalism in the 1920s felt abandoned by their employers in the crisis of the Great Depression as jobs disappeared, benefits were slashed, and the security of families was undercut. Workers in industries that remained profitable in the 1930s were particularly bitter. Between 1930 and 1933, for example, Chicago's Armour & Co. made a profit of over $51 million and paid dividends of $23 million to stockholders—while cutting meat-packers' wages and benefits. Industrial workers blamed the Great Depression on a capitalist system that had been manipulated and corrupted by big businessmen until it was dangerously tilted in their favor. Workers did not want to uproot capitalism so much as distribute its fruits more evenly and constrain its unpredictability.

Section 7(a) of the 1933 National Industrial Recovery Act (NIRA) ostensibly guaranteed labor's right to collective bargaining and energized workers to address grievances accumulated over decades of unbridled industrialization exacerbated by four years of economic collapse: low wages, arbitrary work rules, no job security, and no union to address these problems. But if they honored 7(a) at all, most employers established company unions, which were reliably pro-management. When workers tried to establish their own unions, employers resisted, sometimes savagely—encouraged, in part, by the government's indecisive enforcement of the law.

What can only be called open class warfare erupted across the country in 1933 and 1934. In Toledo, Ohio, in May 1934, skittish national guardsmen fired into union ranks. After police killed two striking longshoremen in San Francisco in July, the leader of the International Longshoremen's Association, Australian Harry Bridges, called a general strike that turned the city into a ghost town for four days. In Minneapolis, where "old stock" Yankees controlled the giant flourmills and the railroads, a rabidly antilabor Citizens Alliance created a private army to keep immigrant workers in place. When weary truckers struck there, police fired on a crowd, killing 2 and wounding 67. Even greater violence swept the textile industry that fall, from New England to South Carolina, when the United Textile Workers struck to force mill operators to honor the provisions of the Cotton Textile Code, adopted under the NRA in July 1933. Beset by the police, the UTW called off the strike in October, saying, "We won't have our people going up against machine guns."

Events like these convinced a reluctant Roosevelt that labor needed more robust support from the state. In 1932, the Norris-LaGuardia Act limited the authority of federal courts to issue injunctions against strikers in labor disputes. More important, the Wagner National Labor Relations Act of 1935 guaranteed labor's right to organize in unions, required employers to bargain with union representatives, and created the National Labor Relations Board (NLRB) to supervise union elections and resolve disputes. The act prohibited a range of "unfair labor practices" such as discrimination against union members, refusal to bargain, and management sponsorship of company unions. When the American Liberty League, an antilabor organization, insisted that the Supreme Court would declare the act unconstitutional, many employers announced their intention to defy the new law.

TRIUMPH OF THE WILL

Along with a favorable political environment and an upturn in the economy after 1935 that rendered employers vulnerable to strikes and slowdowns, the Wagner Act invigorated the labor movement. As one union organizer recalled, before the New Deal, laboring people "thought of the government as somebody else's. Part of the rich world's affairs." The notion that government could do something for them was "a sensational revelation. The sense of empowerment that came with the Wagner Act was absolutely stunning."

On the eve of the Wagner Act, 12 percent of nonagricultural workers belonged to trade unions. By 1939, that number more than doubled, from four million to eight million. Most striking was the remarkable growth of the Congress of Industrial Organizations (CIO). Formed in 1935 to organize the industrial workers excluded by the AFL, the CIO quickly became a major force in politics and in labor. Led by the flamboyant head of the United Mine Workers (UMW), John L. Lewis, the CIO threw itself into organizing workers and reelecting FDR in 1936. CIO unions contributed more than $750,000 to the president's campaign—an enormous sum that helped replace the donations of wealthy Democrats put off by the tenor of the New Deal.

The CIO's first organizing target was steel, a historic bastion of antiunionism. In 1892, a strike over recognition of the Amalgamated Association of Iron and Steel Workers was broken in a legendary confrontation at Homestead, Pennsylvania, in which 10 steelworkers died. For the next 40 years, the "Steel Barons" defied labor organizers and even federal authorities. Labor Secretary Frances Perkins was prevented from speaking in Homestead's public park in 1934.

Already trending toward labor during the Depression, public opinion stacked up higher behind workers after June 1936, when a Senate Civil Liberties Committee led by Wisconsin's Robert La Follette Jr. exposed the criminal underside of corporate labor policies, including infiltrating unions and spying on workers, personal intimidation, and "armed thuggery." When Michigan governor Frank Murphy refused to send troops to break a CIO sit-down strike in Flint, General Motors reluctantly recognized the United Auto Workers (UAW) as the lawful collective bargaining representative of its workers. Caught up in an organizing campaign by its workers, US Steel, the largest steel manufacturer in the world, announced that it would recognize the Steel Workers Organizing Committee (SWOC), a CIO-organized union.

Not everyone capitulated. On Memorial Day 1937, Republic Steel, backed up by Chicago police, shot unarmed picketers, including women and children, in the back. Caught on film, the Memorial Day Massacre shocked everyone, including Chicago mayor Edward Kelly, who promptly facilitated the unionization of the meat-packing industry by threatening to shut off the water supply to Union Stockyards if it failed to respect an NLRB election. By mid-1941, the NLRB had supervised some 6,000 elections involving nearly two million workers.

Industrial unionism proceeded with stunning speed. UAW membership exploded from 88,000 at the end of the sit-down strike to 166,000 a month later and over 200,000 by the end of 1937. Within two months of US Steel's capitulation, 300,000 men joined the SWOC. By August 1937, the 3.4 million members of the CIO outnumbered the ranks of the AFL.

Workers who joined the New Deal coalition were incorporated into American politics through the CIO and the Democratic Party. Rather than turning workers against the political system, the Depression tied workers more tightly to the state as they became voters and beneficiaries of government programs. Unlike in Germany, where mass politics helped destroy democracy, mass political participation in America preserved democracy.

Balance

"The word that appears most frequently in the writings of New Deal theorists is 'balance,'" writes William E. Leuchtenburg, the premier historian of the era. "They believed that the best society was one in which no important element held preponderant power." Much of the New Deal was designed to right an economic system that had listed

so far to one side that it finally tipped over, and to curb the disproportionate power wielded by business and augment that of farmers and
industrial labor.

Addressing the national dimensions of the economic catastrophe
raised questions about another kind of balance: that among the various
branches of government, and between the federal government and the
states. The constitutionally prescribed boundaries of each were tested
by New Deal legislation and practices, with lasting and sometimes surprising results.

THE SUPREME COURT AND THE NEW DEAL

Much of the New Deal legislation passed by Congress raised three distinct constitutional questions. First, to what extent can government,
state or federal, regulate private economic transactions? This was the
old "liberty of contract" issue of the *Lochner* era, when the court invalidated a broad range of progressive legislation. Is it constitutional,
for example, for government to demand that employers pay their
workers a minimum wage?

Second, to what extent can the *federal* government constitutionally
regulate commercial activity? Under the Constitution, the national
government is a government of limited and specified powers. The
commerce clause of the Constitution empowers the federal government to regulate "commerce among the several states." Presumably,
the national government can prohibit certain goods (for example, lot-
tery tickets, which were then illegal in most states) from being shipped
across state lines. But can the national government regulate prices for
legal products *within* a state because those prices might affect prices
in other states? What is the limit of Congress's power under the commerce clause?

Third, to what extent can Congress delegate its lawmaking authority
to the president? Can Congress constitutionally pass a law granting
the president or other executive agencies the power to make laws? Or
is that an unconstitutional abdication of congressional authority?

All three of these issues played an important role in the Supreme
Court's initial assessment of the constitutionality of New Deal legislation. In a 5–4 vote in June 1934, the court held the Railroad Retirement
Act of 1934 unconstitutional on the grounds that whereas Congress
had power under the commerce clause to regulate the safety of railroads that crossed state lines, it lacked authority to establish a compul-

sory retirement and pension plan. Such a plan, the majority reasoned, was too "remote from any regulation of commerce as such."

The court's unanimous decision in *Schechter Poultry Corp. v. United States* (1935) invalidated the National Industrial Recovery Act (NIRA), the conceptual centerpiece of the New Deal recovery programs, and endangered NIRA's implementation agency, the National Recovery Administration (NRA). The NRA's Live Poultry Code established a 40-hour workweek and a minimum wage of 50 cents per hour, prohibited child labor, established the right of employees to organize and bargain collectively, and regulated a variety of trade practices. One issue in *Schechter* was whether Congress had exceeded its power to regulate interstate commerce and encroached on the authority of the states.

Chief Justice Charles Evans Hughes acknowledged the dilemma posed by the grave national crisis of the Depression and supported, in principle, federal efforts to respond to the emergency. But, he wrote, "extraordinary conditions do not create or enlarge constitutional power." Although Congress could constitutionally regulate *intra*state commerce when it *directly affected* interstate commerce (a doctrine that had been established at the end of the nineteenth century in disputes involving railroad rates, safety regulations, and monopoly control), he held that Congress could not constitutionally regulate intrastate activity merely because it had an *indirect* effect on interstate commerce. The government argued that federal wage and hour restrictions were necessary to prevent local businesses from undermining price structures across the nation, but the court rejected this argument in *Schechter*, explaining that "it is not the province of the Court to consider the economic advantages or disadvantages of a centralized [commercial economic] system. It is sufficient to say that the Federal Constitution does not provide for it."

JUDOCRACY

Although sharply divided, the court took a firm stand against government efforts to regulate the economy. As Chief Justice Hughes had explained in *Schechter*, "If the commerce clause were construed to reach all enterprises and transactions which could be said to have an indirect effect upon interstate commerce, the federal authority would embrace practically all the activities of the people and the authority of the State . . . would exist only by sufferance of the federal government." Such an interpretation of the commerce clause, the court concluded, would undermine if not obliterate the federal system of government. The court also held that the industrial "codes of fair competition" negotiated by the NRA violated the constitutional separation of powers by delegating legislative power to the executive branch—further undermining the ability of the administration to address the national economic crisis. By the middle of the Depression, the court had struck down hundreds of state and federal statutes designed to help manage the economy.

The court continued its invalidation of New Deal legislation in 1936, holding the Agricultural Adjustment Act unconstitutional on the grounds that the tax on processors that funded the crop limitation program exceeded Congress's taxing and spending authority. In dissent, Justice Harlan Fisk Stone accused the majority of rampant judicial activism, objecting that "courts are not the only agency of government that must be assumed to have capacity to govern." In this moment of economic desperation, the Supreme Court replayed Progressive Era arguments about the relationship of the courts to legislatures and the executive branch.

Shortly thereafter, in *Morehead v. New York ex rel. Tipaldo*, the court, in a 5–4 decision, invalidated a New York state minimum wage law as an unconstitutional infringement on the liberty of contract. Justice Stone exploded: "There is a grim irony in speaking of the freedom to contract of those who, because of their economic necessities, give their services for less than is needed to keep body and soul together." The court's other 1936 decisions had invalidated federal power in the name of states' rights. *Tipaldo* attacked the regulatory powers of the states themselves. The president observed that the court had for all purposes marked off a "no-man's land where no Government—State or Federal—can function."

By 1936, battle lines had been drawn: Would the conservative justices of the Supreme Court, applying a controversial and highly activist judicial philosophy, continue to thwart governmental efforts to fight the Depression? Supporters of the New Deal accused the court's conservatives of overreaching their constitutional authority. Alabama Senator Hugo Black blasted the court's conservatives for assuming the right "to determine the reasonableness of State and Federal laws. The Constitution never gave that majority any such power." More than 100 laws were introduced in Congress to rebalance relations between the legislative and judicial branches of government. Even Herbert Hoover joined the cause, calling for a constitutional amendment to restore to the state and federal governments "the power they thought they already had."

To describe Franklin Roosevelt's reelection on November 2, 1936, as a triumph is an understatement. Running against Republican Alf Landon, FDR took 61 percent of the popular vote and won the Electoral College by a lopsided margin of 523 to 8. The Democrats increased their majority in Congress, piling up 331 members of the House as opposed to the GOP's 89. In the Senate, 12 freshmen Democrats had to sit with the Republicans because there was not room for all 75 Democrats on their side of the chamber.

Correctly viewing his smashing victory as popular ratification of the New Deal, Roosevelt took on the one remaining obstacle to his program: the Supreme Court. He proposed a judiciary reorganization bill that would add a new judge to any federal court, including the Supreme Court, whenever a judge on that court reached the age of 70 and failed to retire. At the time, six justices of the current court were over the age of 70. What came to be called the "court-packing plan" was a transparent effort to discipline and transform a conservative activist court into one more sympathetic to government regulation of the economy.

Developed in secrecy and sprung on an unsuspecting Congress, FDR's court reorganization plan was denounced by nearly everyone. Even Roosevelt's supporters accused him of aggrandizing the executive branch at the expense of the judiciary. The president who in 1933 had spurned dictatorial powers when urged to accept them now opened himself to charges of lawless despotism. The court-packing plan was a public relations nightmare.

Meanwhile, the Supreme Court was considering the constitutionality of another rash of progressive laws, including the Social Security Act and the NLRA. To everyone's surprise, in *West Coast Hotel v. Parrish*, the justices, in a 5–4 vote, upheld a Washington state minimum wage law that was effectively identical to the New York statute they had overturned only a year earlier in *Tipaldo*. The shift of a single vote, that of Justice Owen Roberts, had produced "the greatest constitutional somersault in history."

Soon after, in *NLRB v. Jones and Laughlin*, the same 5–4 majority upheld the constitutionality of the federal Wagner Act and the National Labor Relations Board (NLRB). The turnaround was stunning. "The Court," wrote one constitutional scholar shortly afterward, "has discarded the idea that the laissez-faire, noninterventionist conception of governmental action offers a feasible approach to the problem of adapting the Constitution to the needs of the Twentieth Century," and come around to the view that *the National Government is entitled to employ any and all of its powers to forward any and all of the objectives of good government.*"

As if this were not victory enough, within three years of the failed court-packing plan, there was a wholesale turnover in the makeup of the court. Roosevelt had the opportunity to appoint five new justices of his own, starting with Hugo Black. The newly constituted court took a much more restrained approach to its exercise of judicial review and upheld a broad range of regulations of the economy by narrowing the notion of liberty of contract, abandoning the prior court's aggressive prohibition on congressional delegation of authority to regulatory agencies, and expanding the court's understanding of Congress's authority under the commerce clause. It was, for Roosevelt and his band of New Dealers, a vindication.

DEFENDING DIXIE

Many Americans, including solid New Dealers, were unsettled by the court-packing plan. Among this group were powerful congressional Democrats from the South, who worried about their own diminished influence on the federal judiciary, which had thus far upheld Jim Crow. The solidly Democratic South had been the bulwark of the Democratic Party since the disenfranchisement of black men in the 1890s. But as growing numbers of voters in the North and West clambered onto the Roosevelt bandwagon, they formed a "New Deal coalition" that challenged the influence of the Solid South within the party. The fastest-growing population groups in the United States, Catholic and Jewish immigrants and their second-generation children, moved en masse into the Democratic Party, as did African Americans in northern and western cities. In 1934, Chicagoan Arthur W. Mitchell became the first African American Democrat ever elected to Congress. The African American migration from the party of Lincoln to that of FDR was complete by 1938, when a *Fortune* poll revealed that 84.7 percent of black respondents self-identified as pro-Roosevelt.

Southern Democrats held extraordinary power in Congress. The

South's restricted, disproportionately small, white electorate reelected its Democratic representatives over and over, allowing them to amass uncommon seniority, which gave them control over the most influential congressional committees and outsized influence in national affairs. Practically speaking, southern Democrats held veto power over the New Deal. No legislation on either economic affairs or race relations that was uncongenial to southerners could make it through Congress.

This explains the exclusion of agricultural and domestic workers—two-thirds of southern black workers—from Social Security and the Wagner Act, as well as the local administration of national policies such as the AAA, which allowed white landowners to pocket government checks while driving black tenants and sharecroppers from the land. It also explains the inability of northern Democrats to pass an antilynching bill, or indeed any piece of civil rights legislation. Always ready to repel federal assaults on "local institutions" such as segregation, disenfranchisement, and a racially discriminatory economic system, southern Democrats rallied around the flag of "states' rights." Despite NAACP protests and behind-the-scenes efforts by First Lady Eleanor Roosevelt, a firm supporter of equal rights, the president considered his hands tied. If he alienated southern Democrats by supporting federal efforts to challenge Jim Crow, he explained, "they will block every bill I ask Congress to pass to keep America from collapsing."

The fight over a federal wages and hours law, the Fair Labor Standards Act of 1938, revealed the sectional schism within the Democratic Party and marked the end of the New Deal. Following a sharp economic downturn in 1937, the Roosevelt administration pushed for new legislation to regulate the conditions of labor. The FSLA prohibited child labor and required industrial employers to adopt a 40-cent hourly minimum wage and a maximum 40-hour workweek.

Southern Democrats objected to two aspects of the FLSA: its inclusion of agricultural laborers, and its refusal to differentiate between black and white workers. Insisting that a black man should not be paid the same wages as a white man, southern congressmen succeeded in having agricultural workers and domestic laborers once again written out of a federal labor law. Even this was not enough for the South, whose representatives in Congress voted overwhelmingly against the law. The Democratic coalition was shattered. With the aid of the GOP, the FLSA was the last piece of New Deal legislation passed.

ISOLATIONIST-IN-CHIEF

In his first inaugural address, Franklin Roosevelt announced that he would "dedicate the Nation to the policy of the good neighbor." Intended to apply worldwide, the Good Neighbor policy came to be associated primarily with the United States' approach to Latin America. Building on Hoover's presumption of nonintervention, Roosevelt agreed at the Seventh International Conference of American States that no state had the right to intervene in another's "internal or external affairs." He also endorsed liberalization of trade policy in the Americas, although many New Deal measures, such as the NRA's wage and price-setting rules and the AAA's efforts to raise agricultural prices, depended on insulating the American economy from foreign competition. Roosevelt's commitment to hemispheric self-determination was tested when a conservative government in Cuba overthrew a junta that had itself unseated the dictator Gerardo Machado. Rather than send the Marine Corps, the United States sent economic aid.

Achieving balance in an era of tumultuous international relations proved an elusive goal. As Germany violated the terms of the Versailles Treaty through rearmament, civil war broke out in Spain between constitutionalists and fascists, and Italy invaded Ethiopia, Americans turned their backs on international affairs. In 1935, the Senate rejected FDR's proposal that the United States join the World Court. That same year, Congress passed a series of neutrality acts that prohibited American arms sales, loans, and credits to nations at war. In 1936, reflecting the opinion of a diverse and powerful peace movement centered in the Midwest, Roosevelt announced that his primary foreign policy goal was to "isolate" America from war. That same year, Germany reoccupied the Rhineland in violation of the Versailles Treaty, and France did nothing.

By July 1937 everything was unraveling. Having occupied Manchuria in 1931, a vast area that included modern Korea (North and South), Japan now struck south and captured the key cities of Beijing, Tianjin, Shanghai, and Hangzhou, as well as the national capital, Nanjing (Nanking). In what came to be known as the Rape of Nanking, Japanese troops rampaged through the city and its countryside, raping thousands of women and beheading, bayonetting, and gunning down as many as 200,000 Chinese civilians. When Japan bombed and sank the American gunboat *Panay* in the Yangtze River outside Nanking and strafed escaping survivors, the American response was avoidance, not engagement. "We should learn that it is about time for us to mind our own business," declared Texas Democrat Maury Maverick in the House.

The *Panay* incident so incited pressure for American isolation that 73 percent of Americans supported Indiana Democrat Lewis Ludlow's campaign for a constitutional amendment that would require a national referendum before Congress could vote a declaration of war. Resisted forcefully by the Roosevelt administration, the Ludlow Amendment was defeated by a narrow margin of 209 to 188 in the House. But it, like the Neutrality Acts, reinforced the reality of the political and legal framework within which the president could conduct foreign policy. Close observers got the message. "Because of its neutrality laws, America is not dangerous to us," announced Hitler in April 1939.

∗

By 1939, American capitalism had been recast through a wave of statutes, and American government had demonstrated the capacity of democracy to cope with momentous challenges without resorting to dictatorship. Moreover, although southern blacks were still uniformly disenfranchised, their brethren in the North and West, along with industrial laborers throughout the nation, had been incorporated into the American polity. Nowhere else in the world during the Great Depression did political participation expand rather than contract.

Not without reason did Franklin Roosevelt, running for an unprecedented third term as president, conclude with satisfaction in October 1940, "We have behind us eight terrible years of a crisis we have shared with all countries. Here we are, and our basic institutions are still intact, our people relatively prosperous, and most important of all, our society relatively affectionate."

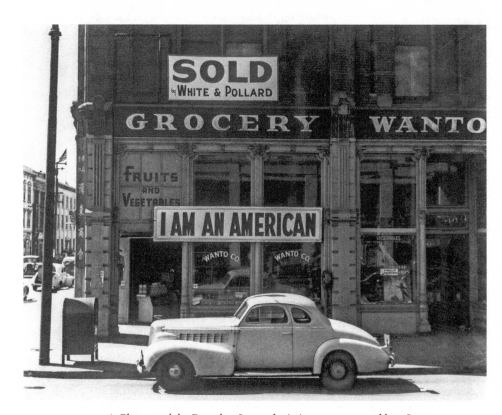

FIGURE 6. Photograph by Dorothea Lange depicting a store owned by a Japanese American in Oakland, California, March 1942. This "I am an American" sign appeared on December 8, 1941, one day after Pearl Harbor was bombed by the Japanese. Prints and Photographs Division, Library of Congress, Washington, DC, http://www.loc.gov/pictures/item/2004665381.

CHAPTER 6

Assertion, 1938–1946

On the night of November 9, 1938, state-sanctioned anti-Jewish riots broke out across Germany in retaliation for the murder of a German diplomat in Paris by a Polish Jewish teenager. Over the course of a few hours, 267 synagogues were burned or destroyed, 7,500 Jewish businesses were vandalized or looted, and 91 people were killed. The riots—dubbed Kristallnacht (Night of Broken Glass) in reference to the window glass that littered the streets the next morning—marked an intensification of Germany's already brutal anti-Jewish policies. Jews were arrested on a mass level and sent to concentration camps such as Buchenwald, Dachau, and Sachsenhausen. Those with the resources to leave suddenly did so. The combined German-Austrian immigration quota to the United States (27,370) was filled in 1939 for the first time since the Nazis came to power. Tens of thousands more German Jews fled to western Europe, Palestine, and Shanghai.

The following night in Rome, Italian physicist Enrico Fermi and his wife, Laura, sat in their spacious apartment awaiting a phone call from Stockholm. Over the radio they heard a new set of anti-Semitic "racial laws" read that limited the civil status of Italian Jews. Jewish children could not attend public school. Jewish teachers, including university professors, were dismissed. Jewish lawyers, physicians, and other professionals could practice their trades only with other Jews. Italian Jews' passports would be confiscated. The danger for people like Laura Fermi was suddenly magnified, and she knew it.

When the call from Stockholm finally came, it was, as the Fermis expected, to announce that Enrico had been honored with a Nobel Prize for his groundbreaking work in nuclear and particle physics, in particular his discovery of "slow neutrons" and their role in nuclear fission (splitting atoms). In December, the entire Fermi family journeyed to Stockholm for the award ceremony. They packed no more than was necessary for a brief vacation, although a close observer might have noticed that Enrico had a new, very expensive watch and that Laura Fermi wore rather more jewelry than was tasteful, as well as a brand-new beaver coat. Before leaving Rome, they had outfitted themselves with the "émigré's trousseau": everything could be pawned for cash if necessary. A more obvious signal that the Fermis did not intend to return to Rome was Enrico's refusal to give the Fascist salute to the King of Sweden. From Stockholm, the Fermis continued on to New York, where Enrico joined fellow émigré physicist Leo Szilard, a Hungarian Jew who had fled Germany in 1933, at Columbia University.

While still in Germany, Szilard had theorized a nuclear chain reaction in which fission could be controlled, producing a steady stream of energy typified by today's nuclear power reactors, and in which it could not be controlled—in which case it would explode. In 1939, Danish physicist Niels Bohr traveled to Princeton to discuss with Albert Einstein German scientists' success in splitting uranium and, in the process, transforming mass into energy in precisely the way Einstein had theorized it might be done in 1905 ($e = mc^2$). Alarmed by the possibility that the Nazis might succeed in building an atom bomb, Einstein and Szilard wrote a letter to Franklin Roosevelt describing the race to split the atom and the uses to which atomic fission could be put. In the summer of 1942, the Manhattan Project was formed, and Fermi and Szilard moved to the University of Chicago. There, on December 2, 1942, Fermi and his team succeeded in taming atomic power through a self-sustaining nuclear chain reaction. University of Chicago physicist Arthur Compton placed a long-distance call to his colleague James B. Conant at Harvard, chairman of the National Defense Research Committee. "The Italian navigator has landed in the New World," he said "How were the natives?" asked Conant. "Very friendly," replied Compton.

Not everyone was received so warmly as Fermi by the New World—whether that new world was atomic or simply American. Not long after Fermi left Italy, for example, more than 900 German Jewish refugees refused entry by Cuba were left stranded on the SS *St. Louis* and returned to Europe after American officials refused to receive them. But for many, America *was* a haven from terror. Many of these newcomers would contribute enormously to the war effort; some of these contributions, like Fermi's, would catapult the United States to a position of global dominance utterly unimaginable in 1938 even as they forced reconsideration of the nation's core values.

Entangling Alliances

America's fundamental foreign policy position was one of distance and diplomacy. This worked well enough until another nation called the bluff, which Japan did in 1931 when it occupied Manchuria. A string of Japanese incursions into Chinese territory followed, and six years later, on July 7, 1937, Japanese and Chinese troops clashed at the Marco Polo Bridge near Beijing. What Japan called "the China Incident" devolved into full-scale war and was, in fact, the beginning of World War II in Asia—a full two years before the German invasion of Poland ignited the war in Europe.

None of the WWI Allies could stomach war. This aversion to military force was not simply a failure of the leadership class: it reflected popular opinion. A 1937 Gallup poll in the United States found that 94 percent of respondents favored efforts to *avoid* war to efforts to *prevent* war. "What the majority of the American people want," wrote the *Nation* magazine, "is to be as un-neutral as possible without getting into the war."

NOT OUR PROBLEM

In the fall of 1938, Hitler, fresh from his forced annexation of Austria that spring, turned on Czechoslovakia. One of the small nations formed out of the remnants of the Habsburg Empire at the end of WWI, multiethnic Czechoslovakia was home to three million German-speakers, housed mostly in the prosperous western region known in German as the Sudetenland. Czechoslovakia was, theoretically, shielded by a treaty of protection with France.

Hitler was determined to destroy the country he called "a French aircraft-carrier in the middle of Europe." In two meetings in Munich in September 1938, the leaders of Britain, France, and Italy acquiesced to Germany's demand for the Sudetenland. British prime minister Neville Chamberlain's announcement that the Munich accords had guaranteed "peace in our time" was received skeptically by Franklin Roosevelt, who was hamstrung by an isolationist Congress and excluded from negotiations. As historian Robert Divine concluded in 1965, "American isolation had become the handmaiden of European appeasement."

American indifference to the growing Nazi menace was matched by anti-immigrant sentiment that prevented German Jews from entering the United States. The restrictive 1924 National Origins Act had no category for refugees or mechanism to offer asylum to victims of political or religious persecution. There was no incentive for Congress to tamper with this law. More than 80 percent of American Christians and an astonishing 25 percent of American Jews opposed the admission of more European refugees in mid-1939—after Kristallnacht, after Vienna's Jews had been set to work cleaning the streets on their hands and knees, after the acquisition by force of all of Czechoslovakia in March 1939.

Such attitudes were explained at the time by fear of unemployment and were later excused by invoking ignorance and blaming the press. Determined not to offend the German regime, both the United States government and leading American newspapers and magazines adopted a circumspect stance toward Nazi racism. Venues owned and operated by whites like the *New York Times* and *Life* magazine were disengaged and skeptical about Nazi anti-Jewish policies.

African American papers, on the other hand, reported early and often on Nazi racism. Papers like the *Chicago Defender* and the *Baltimore Afro-American* (each of which had a national readership) saw an opportunity to make fascism synonymous with racism and to tie democracy to nondiscrimination. Establishing the first half of this equation was increasingly easy, particularly after passage of the 1935 Nuremburg Laws regulating and restricting German Jewish life, which leading Nazis and the African American press both pointed out were modeled on Jim Crow statutes. The argument that the defense of democracy demanded the demise of racism became, in time, a powerful justification for the war and the conditions under which it was fought.

As 1939 advanced, war seemed irresistible. On April 9, a few days after Italy invaded Albania, Britain introduced conscription. France and England sent out feelers to the Soviets, to no avail. On August 23, Germany and the Soviet Union announced that they had signed a mutual nonaggression pact. For the Germans, the Nazi-Soviet pact eliminated the danger of a two-front war (until they were ready to invade the Soviet Union, as intended). In a secret protocol, the Soviets gained half of Poland, the Baltic states, and part of Finland and Bessarabia (Moldova). More importantly, they gained time to prepare themselves for the expected German invasion. The last days of August, wrote Assistant Secretary of State Adolph Berle, "produced almost exactly the sensation you might have waiting for a jury to bring in a verdict on the life or death of about ten million people." Berle turned out to be off by a factor of seven—but he could not have foreseen the global conflagration set in motion by Germany's invasion of Poland on September 1, 1939.

BLITZKRIEG, SITZKRIEG, AND SITTING ON HANDS

The awesome *Blitzkrieg*, or "lightening war," of mechanized tanks and precision bombers waged by the Germans against the Poles gave way, in late September, to a six-month long *Sitzkrieg*, or "sitting war," in which the Wehrmacht lay idle rather than turn its guns west. All remained quiet on the western front, as the British and French allowed Germany to destroy Poland without having to defend its western borders. American isolationists sneered at the "phony war" declared by England and France on September 3, and made it politically impossible for the president to take any actions inconsistent with his pronouncement that "the United States will keep out of this war."

The *Sitzkrieg* ended abruptly in April 1940. With breathtaking speed, German troops occupied Denmark and Norway. In England, Neville Chamberlain was replaced by Winston Churchill as prime minister on May 10, the same day that German bombers flattened the core of Rotterdam and airborne troops descended on Holland, Belgium, and Luxembourg. Four days later, 1,800 German tanks catapulted through the dense Ardennes forest, north of the fortified Maginot Line that was supposed to protect France. Within a matter of weeks, the Wehrmacht stormed across the border, swept the French Army and the British Expeditionary Force into the sea at Dunkirk, imposed an armistice on France, and welcomed Hitler in a triumphant parade in Paris.

Thanks to the combined effort of the British navy and seagoing civilians, more than 300,000 troops were rescued from Dunkirk. But "the whole equipment of the Army," lamented Churchill, including 120,000 vehicles and 90,000 rifles, was abandoned. Provisioning the British became a top priority for Roosevelt, particularly after the Battle of Britain, the first major military campaign to be fought entirely by air forces, began in June 1940. The Neutrality Act of 1939 finally lifted an arms embargo, but the "cash and carry" provision from the Neutrality Act of 1937 remained: England had to pay cash for whatever it needed, and transport it from the United States via its own ships. (Theoretically, Germany could also have bought US goods under the provisions of "cash and carry," but as in WWI, Britain controlled the Atlantic.)

Slowly, the United States inched out from under its isolationist hood of the 1930s. The Neutrality Acts of 1935 and 1937 were repealed, and American citizens and ships were barred from entering war zones.

As the Luftwaffe shifted from attacking airfields to terror bombing civilians in London, Roosevelt—who was then campaigning for an unprecedented third term as president—stretched his executive authority to the maximum and authorized the transfer of 50 destroyers to Britain. The ultra-isolationist *Chicago Tribune* denounced the transfer as an act of war. Churchill agreed cheerfully that it was "a decidedly unneutral Act."

Just as the French had hoped the Belgians would bear the brunt of any war with Germany, and England had hoped to shield itself behind France, so the United States expected Britain to repel the Nazis while Americans remained secure on their side of the Atlantic. From the fall of 1940 through December 7, 1941, Britain did everything it could to draw the Americans into the fray, and the United States did all it could to keep the British fighting without joining the war itself.

SELF-PRESERVATION

As Britain ran short of dollars in late 1940, FDR questioned the wisdom of "cash and carry." In a memorable news conference on December 17, Roosevelt argued that the best defense of America was to help Britain defend itself, and posited that it would be counterproductive to refuse to sell arms to Britain if it could not muster the cash. Suppose, he put it to the reporters gathered at the White House, that your neighbor's house caught fire, and you had a garden hose on hand. Would you say to your neighbor that you spent $15 on that hose, and he'd have to pay you before he could use it? Of course not! The flames endangered your home, too. You would lend him the hose. If it came through the fire all right, he would give it back to you; if it were ruined, he'd buy you another. Either way, the fire would be out, both houses would be saved, and you'd have your hose at the end of the day.

Two weeks later, the president embroidered on this homely message in a fireside chat. "If Great Britain goes down," he explained, "the Axis powers will control the continents of Europe, Asia, Africa, Australasia, and the high seas—and they will be in a position to bring enormous military and naval resources against this hemisphere." To prevent this, America had to have "more ships, more guns, more planes—more of everything. . . . We must be the great arsenal of democracy."

Given the persistent isolationism of congressional Republicans, revving up the armament industry was the best Roosevelt could do at this time. To get the ships and guns and planes to the Allies, the president proposed a lend-lease bill in his annual message to Congress in January 1941. Formally titled An Act to Promote the Defense of the United States, the bill allowed for the transfer of war materiel without payment. The president presented lend-lease as vital to the defense of the "four essential human freedoms" he pledged to secure: freedom of speech and of religion, and freedom from want and from fear.

What quickly became known as the Four Freedoms tied America's war aims to the New Deal and became the basis of Anglo-American cooperation. In August 1941, FDR and Churchill announced their common "hopes for a better future" and issued the Atlantic Charter. Disclaiming territorial ambitions, the two leaders highlighted their belief in "the right of all peoples to choose the form of government under which they will live," declared their support for "improved labor standards, economic advancement, and social security" in all nations, expressed their desire for people everywhere to "live out their lives in freedom from want and fear," and supported "a wider and permanent system of general security" for the world. On New Year's Day 1942 the United States, along with the Soviet Union (which had switched sides in June after the Germans finally invaded), Britain, China, Canada, and 21 other nations pledged to uphold the Atlantic Charter principles and to "preserve human rights and justice in their own lands as well as in other lands" by signing the Declaration of the United Nations.

RISING SUN

Dependent on others for oil and other raw materials and foodstuffs, the island nation of Japan saw no reason why it should not join the ranks of imperial nations and establish colonies to supply necessities and provide a market for Japanese manufactures. France had Indochina (Vietnam, Cambodia, and Laos), did it not? America had the Philippines. England had Burma and India. Why should not Japan have part of China? Why not make good on the Japanese slogan "Asia for the Asians"? The southern Pacific was a place where 800,000 Dutch, English, and French controlled 450 million Asians in Indonesia, the Philippines, Malaysia, and India. Japan wanted to replace these colonial overlords with its own people.

In 1937, Japan invaded the Chinese province of Manchuria and settled it with a half million Japanese colonists. The United States re-fused to recognize the new Japanese government, and Chinese resis-tance remained strong enough to embarrass and annoy Tokyo. In the summer of 1940, Japanese troops landed in southern Indochina. On September 27, 1940, Japan signed the Tripartite Pact with Germany and Italy; each pledged to declare war on any nation that attacked any of them. By the summer of 1941, Japan had established a protector-ate over all of French Indochina. Certain that Japan intended to use Indochina as a springboard for further conquests, President Roosevelt froze Japanese assets in the United States and restricted oil exports. He also merged the armed forces of the Philippines with the Army of the United States, and put its commander, General Douglas MacArthur, in charge of American forces in East Asia.

Sunday, December 7, 1941, dawned beautiful and still on the Hawai'ian island of Oahu. After weeks of unsuccessful diplomatic efforts to convince the United States to allow Japan a free hand in China, the new Japanese premier Hideki Tojo determined to attack the American naval installation at Pearl Harbor. The Americans were caught entirely off guard. While officers who had dashed off for a relax-ing round of polo struggled to return to their men, Japanese bomb-ers pummeled the Pacific Fleet. Of the eight battleships anchored in Pearl Harbor, three were sunk, one was grounded, another capsized, and the rest were damaged severely. At nearby Hickam Field, close to 200 American planes, parked wing to wing and unable to become airborne, were picked off by Japanese fliers like fish in a barrel. By the time it was over, 2,403 men were dead, including 1,103 entombed in the USS *Arizona*, which sank immediately when hit in its forward magazine. Another 1,178 soldiers and civilians were wounded.

For all its power, the Japanese attack at Pearl Harbor was not an un-varnished success. First, they chose not to return later that day to at-tack the oil tanks and machine shops that supported the Pacific Fleet. More consequentially, by providence or kind fortune, the American aircraft carriers normally docked at Pearl Harbor were out to sea that morning, and so survived to fight another day. This fact would prove decisive in May 1942, when American planes routed the Imperial Japa-nese Navy at the Battle of Midway Island and initiated the Yanks' slow progress west toward Japan. But this lay in the future as Pearl Har-bor smoldered. On December 8, President Roosevelt signed the con-gressional declaration of war on Japan. That same day, Japanese forces spread through the South Pacific. Within days, Hong Kong, Guam, and Wake Island fell. On December 11, Germany and Italy (playing, as usual, "the role of jackal to Hitler's lion") brought things full circle by declaring war against the United States.

Mobilizing for War

Once it had joined the battle, the United States threw all its considerable might behind the war effort. A generation that had been unemployed its entire working life was anxious to get the war effort rolling. Draft-age men suddenly found themselves inducted or employed. Women exchanged aprons for overalls and went to work in shipyards and airplane factories. Through the creation of war industries and an overnight military buildup, the federal government ignited the smoldering Depression economy and put the country back to work.

THE GROSS NATIONAL PRODUCT WAR

There are two ways for governments to pay for anything: they can increase revenue or they can borrow money. The president preferred to raise taxes; Congress preferred to take on debt. They compromised in the Revenue Act of 1942, which raised only a modest amount of money but universalized the federal tax structure by making everyone a taxpayer for the first time. Most of the war was paid for through loans to the federal government that were repackaged and sold to citizens as war bonds. Bond sales increased the national debt, but also soaked up purchasing power, which helped keep inflation in check. Government spending on the military began, at last, to lift the American economy out of the depression that had plagued it for a decade. All in all, wartime manufacturing and government spending more than doubled the gross national product between 1940 and 1945, from $100 billion to $214 billion.

War industries clustered on the peripheries—along the East and West Coasts, the Gulf Coast, and the Great Lakes. The greatest internal migration in American history took place between 1940 and 1950, as roughly eight million people moved to that portion of the country soon to be known as the Sunbelt. By 1943, Los Angeles was second only to Detroit in industrial activity.

One result of the mass migration of war workers was the expansion of African American communities in cities that had negligible numbers of blacks before Pearl Harbor. The black populations of Oakland, Los Angeles, and San Diego tripled. Seattle's black population expanded tenfold, from 4,000 to 40,000. The Hispanic population swelled as well, as the Bracero Program, created by the federal government in 1942, imported Mexican farm workers to fill the agricultural jobs vacated by the new war workers.

Over six million women entered the workforce during the war. For the first time, married women outnumbered single women in the workforce. They were not secretaries, either: they were plumbers, toolmakers, machinists, welders, blacksmiths, even lumberjacks. By 1944, women made up 14 percent of all workers in shipbuilding and 40 percent in aircraft plants. Women served in the military as well: 240,000 women served in the Women's Army Corps (WAC) and the US Navy's Women Accepted for Volunteer Emergency Service (WAVES), 23,000 served in the Marine Corps Women's Reserve (MCWR), and 13,000 enlisted in SPARS (Coast Guard Women's Reserve). Crucially, another 76,000 served as army or navy nurses in all the major theaters of the war.

The American "production miracle" that produced 40 percent of all the world's arms by 1944 was the result of a national talent for mass production combined with a preference for quantity over quality. While the Germans focused on improving the quality and variety of weapons, and refused to allow women to work in war industries, the Americans called on all hands and focused on production organization and economies of scale. Once revved, the engines of war production sent forth a dizzying number of ships, trucks, tanks, rifles, and bullets.

The United States was the only nation that managed to build a war economy on top of a consumer economy. A few goods were rationed—coffee, sugar, meat, tires, gasoline—but overall Americans had never had it so good. This home front experience was in marked contrast to that in Britain or the Soviet Union. In Britain, personal consumption shrank by nearly a quarter. Rationing did not end there until 1954. After the German invasion, the Russians were forced to fight from a diminishing economic base; every step west taken by the Red Army was underwritten by calamitous civilian sacrifices.

Americans sacrificed at home, too, but on a completely incommensurate scale. With beef rationed, enterprising housewives searched for alternative sources of protein. "Peanut butter carrot loaf" was one mother's nutritious if much-maligned invention. Urged to supplement his diet with game, one food writer turned poetic: "Although it isn't / Our usual habit, / This year we're eating / The Easter Rabbit."

WHY WE FIGHT

It was not immediately apparent to many African Americans why they should risk their lives fighting for a nation seemingly indifferent to its own core principles. Harry Carpenter of Philadelphia was arrested for treason when he remarked in public that the war was "a white man's war and it's no damn good." Why should black Americans support the war while Jim Crow reigned at home?

This was a question that had been asked and answered during the First World War. Now, as then, black Americans agreed to fight for their country because they saw the war as part of their own struggle to gain access to democracy. Determined not to let the opportunity of wartime change slip away, America's leading civil rights organizations exhorted, "Now is the time *not* to be silent about the breaches in democracy in our own land." To this end, African Americans added a fifth freedom—freedom from segregation—to the Four Freedoms already denominated by Roosevelt. The *Pittsburgh Courier* dubbed this binding of local and national interests the "Double V" campaign—for victory at home and abroad.

Victory abroad was more easily defined than victory at home. In the long run, African Americans wanted what they had demanded since emancipation: equal rights before the law. In immediate, concrete terms, black leaders wanted an end to segregation in the government, including the military, and equal access to employment in war industries. The army managed somehow not to call a single African American in the first selective service requisition after Pearl Harbor. Black volunteers were assigned to segregated noncombatant units. The navy accepted a handful of blacks as cooks and stewards. The elite air and marine corps were entirely off-limits to nonwhites. This did not satisfy the NAACP, whose journal the *Crisis* lectured that "a jim crow army cannot fight for a free world."

The war industries were, if anything, worse than the armed forces. Not one of the booming shipyards on the Gulf Coast employed even a single black welder; black workers wielded brooms, but not drills, in Detroit's aircraft factories. A. Philip Randolph, the leader of the most influential African American union, the Brotherhood of Sleeping Car Porters, had spent the Depression years arguing in favor of black unity and organization. In the spring of 1941, he denounced the national defense as corrupted by "race prejudice, hatred, and discrimination," and called on black America to "march 10,000 strong on Washington, D.C." to demand the "Right to Work and Fight for Our Country." After a face-off with Randolph at the White House, the president finally relented, and issued Executive Order 8802, which stipulated equal hiring practices in defense industries but did not desegregate the armed forces. To administer the order, Roosevelt created the Fair Employment Practices Committee (FEPC).

Endowed with investigatory but not enforcement power, the FEPC illuminated but was unable to alter the racially stratified war economy. FEPC hearings on wartime industrial practices crystallized white opposition to the African American war agenda in the South, where war industry and military bases clustered. For white southerners, the FEPC represented a clear federal response to black political power—which was reason enough to despise it. No other federal agency, either during the war or after it, elicited such passionate support, on the one hand, and loathing, on the other.

DOMESTIC VIOLENCE

Military bases and defense factories became sites for the reassertion of white supremacy. In January 1942, white MPs and civilian police wounded 21 black soldiers and killed 10 in a riot in Alexandria, Louisiana. In Mobile, Alabama, white workers rioted when a shipbuilder promoted a handful of black welders. All in all, wartime America saw 6 civilian race riots, more than 20 military riots and mutinies, and between 40 and 75 lynchings. As Howard Donovan Queen, a black officer in the Regular Army who eventually rose to the rank of colonel, recalled years later, "The Negro soldier's first taste of warfare in World War II was on army posts right here in his own country."

The most exceptional and the most common violent outbursts concerned control over public space. Detroit (known as the "Arsenal of Democracy" for its massive war industry) witnessed both the mundane and the spectacular. In April 1943, more than a hundred Detroit teenagers of both races duked it out on a municipal playground. Three months later, a hot summer day's worth of individual fights on Belle Isle touched off four days of rioting in which Detroit's white police officers killed 17 of the 25 African American victims.

Not every black soldier was jolted into militant opposition to Jim Crow by WWII, but many became determined to assert their political, as well as their economic, rights. They were aided by the Supreme Court, which ruled in 1944 in *Smith v. Allwright* that the South's system of racially restrictive primary elections violated the Fifteenth Amendment.

Smith v. Allwright posed a clear threat to the South's segregated society. As the *New York Times* editorialized approvingly, *Smith* put America "a little closer to a more perfect democracy, in which there will be but one class of citizens." Thurgood Marshall, who argued the school desegregation cases before the court a decade later, considered the white primary decision his most important victory. *Smith v. Allwright* did not herald the dawn of African American enfranchisement: it would be another 20 years before a majority of black southerners were able to exercise the right to vote without fearing for their lives and livelihoods. But in a context of heightened African American activism and a wartime ideological environment in which racism was increasingly suspect, the court's decision endorsed and enhanced black power in a moment of national political transition. By the end of the war, a majority of white Americans agreed with the sentiment that "men who faced bullets overseas deserve ballots at home," and that black disenfranchisement reflected "the hateful ideologies" that the nation opposed in WWII.

World War II changed the course of American race politics, as the fight against fascism shifted the terms of the debate about segregation in America, and racial minorities challenged white supremacist assumptions and institutions. Progress on this front was halting, however, and marked by wholesale retreats: as when the government interned 120,000 of its own citizens, thereby falling, in the words of Supreme Court Justice Frank Murphy, into "the ugly abyss of racism."

"ILL-ADVISED, UNNECESSARY, AND CRUEL": JAPANESE AMERICAN INTERNMENT

As America pivoted onto a war footing, Attorney General Francis Biddle was determined to avoid the excesses of WWI, when nearly 12,000 legal aliens and naturalized citizens were deported under the Alien Act of 1918. The attorney general's calm was eroded at the end of January 1942 by a report suggesting that Hawai'i-based espionage agents had assisted the Japanese at Pearl Harbor. Rumors began to fly: of ship-to-shore radio communications (denied by the FBI), of submarine attacks along the coast.

In February, General John L. DeWitt, chief of the US Army's Western Defense Command, demanded complete evacuation of Japanese

Americans from the West Coast. Secretary of War Henry Stimson supported DeWitt, but worried that singling out Japanese Americans on the basis of "racial characteristics" while ignoring Germans and Italians would "make a tremendous hole in our constitutional system." DeWitt was unburdened by such concerns. "A Jap's a Jap," he announced. "It makes no difference whether he is an American citizen or not."

On February 19, 1942, President Roosevelt signed Executive Order 9066, which authorized the War Department to exclude "any and all" persons from prescribed military areas. Attorney General Biddle protested that the order was "ill-advised, unnecessary and unnecessarily cruel," but the president ignored him. Under the order, 120,000 Japanese Americans—two-thirds of them citizens, one-third under the age of 19—were removed from their homes on the Pacific coast and transferred to camps east of the Sierra Nevada mountains. The first evacuees arrived at Manzanar, a dried-up lake bed in east-central California, in June 1942. The camp was enclosed by barbed wire fencing punctuated by guard towers, machine-gun installations, and searchlights.

Since it was admitted by the government that none of the internees had committed a crime, the War Relocation Authority had to devise some other reason for the camps. The answer arrived at was assimilation. In the circular logic of the WRA, cultural assimilation was both a measure of Japanese American loyalty and productive of it. WRA officials discouraged the use of the Japanese language, the practice of non-Christian religion, and (nondemocratic) kinship structures of community leadership. Photographer Ansel Adams, famous for his black-and-white pictures of Yosemite National Park, captured high school students at Manzanar dressed in all-American bobby socks and saddle shoes. "Manzanar is only a detour on the road to American citizenship," Adams intoned—forgetting, apparently, that the young people at Manzanar had been born in the United States and were already citizens.

The decision to intern Japanese Americans was the president's, but responsibility for the nullification of citizenship rights for some 70,000 Japanese Americans lay ultimately with their fellow citizens and the courts. Unwilling to challenge the state in wartime, even groups founded to fight discrimination such as the NAACP remained silent about this grave violation of civil liberties. The courts did not distinguish themselves either. In *Hirabayashi v. United States* (1943) and *Korematsu v. United States* (1944), the Supreme Court upheld a curfew on enemy aliens and citizens of Japanese descent, and the exclusion and evacuation of Japanese Americans from the Western Command of the US Army. Yet *Korematsu* enunciated a limiting principle that would guide civil rights legislation for a generation: that classification and discrimination based on race *may* be legitimate (particularly in wartime), but was "immediately suspect" and should be subject to "the most rigid scrutiny" by the court. If it were true, as Justice Frank Murphy charged in dissent, that *Korematsu* allowed for the "legalization of racism," then the concept of "heightened scrutiny," if strenuously applied, could work as a powerful check in the future against racially discriminatory laws.

War without Mercy

In the Second World War, the most destructive and far-reaching conflict in history, 400,000 Americans lost their lives. Those lives were lost on two battlefronts separated by 10,000 miles—an ironic conclusion to the isolationist insistence on hemispheric independence. After 1942, America inched its way into the war in Europe, testing the waters of the Mediterranean before launching a massive assault across the English Channel in June 1944. Attacked head-on by the Japanese in the Pacific, however, the United States threw everything it had at the Imperial Japanese Army. The knockout punch to that fight set the world spinning, and established the United States, already the political and economic front-runner, as a principal global power.

THE WAR IN EUROPE

America's oceanic blanket insulated the nation from an invasion, but it was a severe handicap when it came to moving men and material to the fields of battle. To fight the Nazis, the United States had to ship everything from oil and food to airplanes and men across the Atlantic. In order to do *that*, ships had to get past the German U-boats (submarines) that patrolled the ocean highways of the Atlantic. Outside of Pearl Harbor, Americans' first taste of war came in their own eastern coastal waters, where the Nazis picked off tankers in New York Harbor and, in broad daylight on June 15, 1942, torpedoed two freighters within full view of thousands of vacationers at Virginia Beach, Virginia. By destroying precious cargo on its way to support the British and the Russians, Chief of Staff General George C. Marshall warned, losses to German submarines off the Atlantic seaboard and in the

Caribbean threatened the entire war effort. As General Dwight D. Eisenhower put it in July, *"We should not forget that the prize we seek is to keep 8,000,000 Russians in the war."*

Winston Churchill would have agreed—and perhaps added a prayer that those eight million might be reduced by half. This, certainly, was the suspicion of the Soviets, who were adamant on the absolute necessity of opening a second front against the Germans in western Europe as soon as possible. The Russians had shouldered the burden of fighting the Nazis for nearly two years, and Stalin was increasingly impatient with the prevarications of the Brits and, to a lesser degree, the Americans. "We've lost millions of people, and they want us to crawl on our knees because they send us Spam," complained one Russian.

In late 1942 and early 1943, the English had the upper hand in Allied strategic planning for the simple reason that the Americans were not yet in Europe in full force. That would change, but for the moment Churchill got his way, and his way did not include a cross-Channel invasion. Rather, the Allies targeted North Africa during the winter of 1943, while the Red Army confronted more than 200 divisions and killed more than 200,000 German soldiers in the Battle of Stalingrad. In late January 1943, Churchill and Roosevelt met in Casablanca to discuss Allied war aims and strategy. While General Marshall fretted about the British propensity for "periphery-pecking," Churchill was still the senior partner in the Atlantic alliance. Rather than invade France, the Allies would build on their victory in North Africa and attack Sicily. The threat this posed to Germany may be judged by the response of the Wehrmacht, which transferred 36 fresh divisions to the *eastern* front. While fewer than 20 German divisions inflicted 300,000 casualties on the Allies in Italy, the Red Army destroyed the Wehrmacht's offensive capability in the Battle of Kursk, an epic clash of 4,000 aircraft, 6,000 tanks, and 2 million men.

By November 1943, when FDR flew halfway around the world to Tehran to meet Josef Stalin and discuss a cross-Channel invasion, the Americans worried that the Soviets, currently rolling toward the Polish frontier, were no longer interested in a second front. They were, but they made clear the price the Allies would pay for having left the Red Army to fight the Nazis alone for nearly three years: neither Britain nor America would interfere with Soviet control over eastern Europe and the Baltic states.

THE WAR IN THE PACIFIC

By May 6, 1942, when 13,000 American troops surrendered on Corregidor Island in the Philippines, Japan controlled everything between itself and Australia. Rather than consolidate their wins, the Japanese pressed on, sending their naval air force — the largest in the world, consisting of six large carriers and some 500 high-performance aircraft — ever southward. In the Battle of the Coral Sea (May 3–8, 1942), planes launched from American aircraft carriers prevented the Japanese from reaching Australia.

Less than a month later, Japanese naval commander Admiral Isoruku Yamamoto turned toward Midway Island, the northwestern end of the Hawai'ian archipelago. Like Pearl Harbor, this attack was meant to be a surprise. But thanks to American cryptologists, who cracked the Japanese naval code, US Admiral Chester Nimitz was forewarned. As at Coral Sea, the Battle of Midway (June 4, 1942) was fought entirely by aircraft taking off from ships that never came within eyesight of each other. Within five minutes, American dive bombers from the carriers *Enterprise* and *Yorktown* turned the tide of the Pacific war by mortally wounding three Japanese aircraft carriers (a fourth sank the next morning). In a single blow, Japan had lost four of the six carriers that had attacked Pearl Harbor only six months earlier, as well as the aircraft and many of their crack fliers.

Japan needed to win at Midway for the same reason it had to attack Pearl Harbor: it needed to cripple a much larger enemy before it was prepared to fight. After Midway, the war in the Pacific became as much a battle of production as of fleets, a war of resources rather than grand strategy. Japan was unlikely ever to win such a contest. In the two years after Midway, Japanese shipyards built only 6 additional carriers, while the United States produced 17.

In addition to carriers, a naval war was a war of landing strips, petrol, and transportation routes. On August 7, 1942, the marines embarked on the first of a series of brutal amphibious invasions, this time on Guadalcanal, where the Japanese were building an airstrip from which to attack ships on their way to Australia. It would take seven months, but superior American manpower and munitions eventually forced a Japanese evacuation, at the cost of thousands of seasoned troops. Equally significant was Admiral Nimitz's invasion of the Marshall Islands in the western North Pacific Ocean at the end of January 1944. By June, the Americans had taken the Marianas as well.

In April 1944, the Japanese had captured crucial American airfields in south China. American troops, under the direction of General Mac-Arthur, invaded the Philippines in response. In the Battle of Leyte Gulf (October 25, 1944), still the largest naval engagement in history, the Japanese lost most of their remaining sea power and resorted to an extreme air tactic. Suicide attacks by kamikaze units sank one US carrier and damaged others severely. Like the Japanese troops who had refused to surrender on Tarawa Island in 1943, where 1,000 Americans lost their lives rooting out 4,000 entrenched Japanese soldiers, kamikaze attacks reinforced a growing belief among American GIs that the Japanese did not value life the way Americans did.

ENDGAME IN EUROPE

General Dwight Eisenhower had studied war his entire adult life but never tasted it until the North Africa campaign. His new assignment — the cross-Channel invasion codenamed Operation Overlord — had a fifty-fifty chance of success. To invade Normandy, an armada of thousands of ships would have to ferry 150,000 soldiers across the treacherous waters of the English Channel. Those soldiers would have to storm fortified beaches.

Two factors tipped the balance in the Allies' favor. A disinformation campaign convinced the Germans that the attack would be at Calais, 200 miles to the north. Second, Eisenhower decided to go forward on the night of June 6, 1944, despite a serious storm over the Channel. While surprised German commanders debated whether this was the real cross-Channel invasion or a diversion from Calais, Allied troops struggled ashore. On Utah Beach the Americans faced only faint opposition, but four miles to the east on Omaha Beach soldiers were caught in heavily mined water facing German guns. When the second wave landed on that afternoon's low tide, they encountered a watery hell of beached ships and floating bodies.

But the Yanks — and they were mainly Yanks — kept on coming. By the end of June, the Allies had landed a million troops, 170,000 vehicles, and a half million tons of supplies. Paris was liberated on August 25. As the Allies barreled east toward Germany, they stretched their supply lines to the breaking point and sputtered to a stop between the Meuse and Rhine Rivers.

While the Allies approached Germany from the west, the Soviets made their way through Poland. Expecting Soviet support, the Polish

Home Army mounted a revolt in Warsaw. Rather than come to the aid of their nominal allies, the Soviets paused outside the city and watched while the Germans crushed the revolt. As had been agreed in Tehran, eastern Europe would pay the price for the late arrival of Allied troops in Europe.

In the west, the Allies dug in for the winter in the Ardennes forest. On December 16, 1944, German tanks caught Allied troops by surprise when they came crashing through the woods. Some 10,000 American soldiers surrendered at once—the largest Allied surrender in the war in Europe. Advancing almost without opposition, the Germans pushed out from their original battle line along a 50-mile wide "bulge." General George Patton's three divisions finally pushed them back, but at enormous cost to both sides. With more than 70,000 Allied casualties, the Battle of the Bulge was a decisive defeat for Germany, whose dead and wounded topped more than 100,000.

As British and American troops raced deep into Germany, the ailing American president retired to his cottage in Warm Springs, Georgia, to rest for the upcoming Charter Conference of the United Nations in San Francisco. Franklin Roosevelt's health was in decline well before he won an astonishing fourth term as president in November 1944. Bowing to the concerns of party conservatives, Vice President Henry Wallace had been replaced with Missouri senator Harry Truman. On April 12, 1945, the president awoke with a headache. He died that afternoon of a cerebral hemorrhage, attended by Lucy Mercer, his beloved companion of three decades.

On April 30, in a bunker below central Berlin, Adolf Hitler denied the Russians the honor of capturing him. Propaganda Minister Joseph Goebbels also committed suicide in the bunker, as did his wife, Magda—after first killing all six of their children. Berlin fell on May 2, and the Germans signed an unconditional surrender on May 8, 1945. Massive victory celebrations in Allied capitals were tempered by mourning for Roosevelt, and by the shocking discovery of Nazi death camps in the eastern reaches of the Reich.

RACE WAR

While fighting continued in the Philippines, in February 1945 the US Marines invaded Iwo Jima, a five-square-mile bit of volcanic rock 750 miles from Tokyo needed to provide a landing strip for bombers and their escorts. Japanese defenders in underground caves cost 20,000

American casualties, including nearly 7,000 dead. The battle for Oki-
nawa, a southern Japanese island large enough to stage an invasion
of the nation's four main islands, was even costlier. The United States
suffered 50,000 casualties with over 12,000 killed in battle; some
140,000 Japanese and an additional 42,000 Okinawans also died.
Many of these civilian deaths were suicides, committed at the urg-
ing of the Japanese soldiers who provided hand grenades to local men
and women and warned that American troops would murder and rape
them as the Japanese had done.

American troops were not beyond such acts. "What kind of war do
civilians suppose we fought, anyway?" asked one correspondent afterward. "We shot prisoners in cold blood, wiped out hospitals, strafed
lifeboats, killed or mistreated enemy civilians, finished off the enemy
wounded, tossed the dying into a hole with the dead, and in the Pacific
boiled the flesh off enemy skulls to make table ornaments for sweet-
hearts, or carved their bones into letter openers."

Such brutality was in good measure a response to the Imperial Japanese Army, whose soldiers massacred civilian populations, worked
thousands to death in forced labor camps, maltreated and starved prisoners of war, and murdered men in uniform in violation of the Geneva
Conventions. Such tactics were not the last resort of a defeated military: the Bataan Death March, in which thousands of Filipino and
American POWs perished, was in April 1942, at the height of Japanese
power. Of Japan's Anglo-American prisoners, 27 percent died in the
hands of their captors, as opposed to 4 percent held by the Germans.

There was an undeniable racial subtext to the war in the Pacific.
Most white Americans harbored a set of racist assumptions about
Asians: they were treacherous; they were sneaky (Pearl Harbor did
nothing to diminish this belief); they were automatons with no will
of their own; they were bestial, brutal, and subhuman. The Japanese,
for their part, considered themselves genetically pure, the uncontaminated Yamato race, inherently superior to decadent, lazy whites,
especially to white Americans mongrelized through breeding with
Europe's castoffs. As racist as their Anglo-American counterparts, the
Japanese obliterated white supremacist myths about Asians and shattered beyond repair the European and American colonial structure in
the Greater East Asia Co-Prosperity Sphere. At the same time, myths
about them—that they were, in President Harry Truman's words, "sav-
ages, ruthless, merciless, and fanatic," survived.

VICTORY IN ASIA

The only way to deal with such an enemy, Americans believed, was to demand its unconditional surrender. By the fall of 1944, it was clear to leaders on both sides of the war that Japan was doomed, its economy crippled, its fleet destroyed, its diplomats sending peace feelers to the Soviets. Yet the Imperial Japanese Army fought on. The only way to end the war, Allied leaders believed, was to follow Churchill's advice offered to Congress in 1943: lay Japan's cities in ashes. Between March and July 1945, American bombers attacked 66 Japanese cities, killing 900,000, injuring up to 1.3 million more, and leaving more than 8 million people homeless. Only the army's desire to have virgin targets for the atomic bombs dubbed "Little Boy" and "Fat Man" left Hiroshima and Nagasaki untouched through August 1945.

Since December 1942, when Enrico Fermi initiated the controlled release of nuclear energy in a laboratory beneath the football stadium at the University of Chicago, scores of scientists had labored to harness that power for a weapon. Led by University of California physicist Robert J. Oppenheimer, the Manhattan Project employed 130,000 people in three main sites and cost over $2 billion before bearing fruit in July 1945, when the first atomic bomb was tested successfully in the desert outside Los Alamos, New Mexico. Those who had dedicated themselves to achieving this feat were struck by the awful beauty of the mushroom cloud produced by the explosion (the equivalent of 20 kilotons of TNT), and sobered by its awesome destructive power. There was some debate among the scientists and military officials about the feasibility of a demonstration to Japanese officials to convince them of the unimaginable power of the new weapon, but leaders in Washington did not hesitate for a moment. As President Truman—who had not, as vice president, been informed of the existence of the Manhattan Project—put it later, "I regarded the bomb as a military weapon and never had any doubt that it should be used."

The first atomic weapon was dropped on Hiroshima on August 6, 1945. Approximately 70,000 people died instantly. Double that number had died by the end of the year as the result of radiation poisoning and other injuries. On August 9, the United States exploded a second bomb over Nagasaki, killing 70,000 there. The death toll in Hiroshima and Nagasaki was horrific but not unprecedented: the Allied firebombing of Dresden in Germany killed 100,000 women, children, and elderly men. The ease with which the atom bomb accomplished the effects of a prolonged bombing campaign signaled the dawn of a new era of terrifying weapons of mass destruction, but the willingness of governments to target populations rather than armies preceded the atomic era and did not depend on it. Of those who died in the First World War, 90 percent were military personnel, but of the estimated 50 million persons who perished during WWII, 40 percent were civilians. The Germans had targeted lesser "races" and bombed London and Canterbury; the Allies had flattened Hamburg and Tokyo. When Japan bombed Chinese cities in 1937, the League of Nations protested. By 1945, the league was no more, and the world was inured to civilian deaths.

At the Summit of the World

Franklin Roosevelt had promised Americans freedom from fear if they all pulled together in the war effort. But could there be freedom from fear in a world where civilians were the target of exterminationist politics and weapons of mass destruction? Preventing the horrors of the war from reoccurring required vigilance, coordination, and a commitment to the rights of individuals and minorities as well as to nation-states. In April 1945, delegates from 46 nations gathered in San Francisco to draft a charter for a new international agency dedicated to the maintenance of peace and security and the recognition of equal human rights. At the helm was the nation that had resisted the pull of world leadership so fervently only a few years earlier.

BEYOND BELIEF: THE HOLOCAUST

In the summer of 1943, Supreme Court Justice Felix Frankfurter met with Polish socialist Jan Karski at the Polish embassy in Washington. A passionate Zionist, Frankfurter was concerned about rumors of Nazi atrocities against the Jews of eastern and central Europe. Karski reported that in Belzec, a death camp in southeastern Poland, upwards of 500,000 Jewish men, women, and children had been systematically exterminated in gas chambers over the course of 10 months. When Karski finished speaking, Frankfurter was incredulous. "I am unable to believe you," he announced, and left.

Frankfurter was not alone in his skepticism. Assistant Secretary of War John J. McCloy was equally dubious, and declined to bomb the notorious labor camp at Auschwitz despite the recommendation of the War Refugee Board.

Six million European Jews were murdered by the Nazis and their collaborators during World War II. Much has been made of the American decision not to bomb Auschwitz or its rail line in the winter of 1945, but the truth is that the vast majority of the work of the Shoah (Hebrew for "calamity") had been accomplished already. Two-thirds of the six million were already dead by the end of 1942, the victims of mass executions over pits at gunpoint or by carbon monoxide channeled into mobile killing vans or pumped into gas chambers at Treblinka, Belzec, and Sobibor in occupied Poland.

Of the Jews in occupied Europe, 78 percent were killed in the Holocaust; 70 percent of these were either Polish or Soviet Jews. To recognize this fact is not to discount the suffering of western European and Mediterranean Jews deported from Italy, France, Greece, Belgium, and the Netherlands to death camps in Poland, Austria, and eastern Germany. Nor is it to exculpate the French and Dutch who arrested and deported their fellow citizens. It is to emphasize that Hitler's original expansionist aim of *Lebensraum*, or living space for Germans, was directed east.

What Frankfurter and McCloy could not believe was documented scrupulously by the state that killed with such ruthless efficiency. Indeed, those in charge bragged of their deeds and complained that their fellow citizens would never comprehend the true magnitude of their accomplishment. Others worked ceaselessly to get the story out to the Allies. In his *Axis Rule in Occupied Europe*, published in November 1944, jurist Raphael Lemkin, a Polish Jewish émigré, included a term he had coined in late 1943 to describe the Nazis' acts in the east: "genocide," the deliberate, systematic destruction, in whole or in part, of an ethnic, racial, religious, or national group. Many of those who participated in genocide between 1941 and 1945 were later tried at Nuremburg for offenses so enormous they could only be described as "crimes against humanity." But most Nazi executioners slipped through the cracks. Karl Höcker, the deputy to the final commandant at Auschwitz, worked for a bank in his hometown of Engershausen until 1963, when he was tried in Frankfurt and found guilty of causing the deaths of 1,000 Jews. He served five years in prison. The bank held his job for him.

THE UNITED NATIONS

One of the lessons of the Paris Peace Conference of 1919 had been the necessity to plan for peace well in advance of an armistice. In August 1941, FDR and Winston Churchill had issued the Atlantic Charter, which called for a "wider and permanent system of general security" to replace the defunct League of Nations, and offered suggestions to shape the postwar world. The peace envisioned by the charter was one "which will afford assurance that all the men in all the lands may live out their lives in freedom from fear and want." To speak in 1941 of individuals rather than states ("all the men in all the lands") was revolutionary. The idea that the dignity of the individual was an appropriate topic of international affairs was embraced immediately by groups already committed to fighting racism and colonialism as well as Nazism.

The "system of general security" that became the United Nations was sketched out by delegates of the four chief Allies (Britain, the United States, the USSR, and China) at Dumbarton Oaks, a mansion outside of Washington, DC, in late 1944. There, an exclusive group of diplomats and policy experts drafted the charter for an inclusive international organization. There were moments of rancor, especially when discussing veto power in the Security Council and the Soviets' idea to count each of its recently acquired satellite states as an independent nation for voting purposes. But in the end, the delegates' work was rooted clearly in the Atlantic Charter, with one exception: there was no statement on the universal rights of the individual or disavowal of racial discrimination.

Insulted by their exclusion from Dumbarton Oaks and angry that the draft charter neither protected individual rights nor condemned racial discrimination, representatives of Latin American and Asian states, backed by organizations like the Council of Christians and Jews and the NAACP, pressed for an unequivocal statement of racial equality in the charter. Having outlined a world organization they thought they could control, the Great Powers were about to discover the reality highlighted by W. E. B. Du Bois in his famous essay "Human Rights for All Minorities": that the world's minorities "*together form a majority.*" In San Francisco, this majority succeeded in defining the United Nations as dedicated to the goal of achieving human rights and fundamental freedoms "for all without distinction as to race, sex, language, or religion" (Article 1 and Article 13) and of promoting respect "for the principle of equal rights and self-determination of peoples" (Articles 55, 62, and 68).

Respecting human rights was one thing; enforcing that respect was another. Even the nations that supported the elevation of human rights in the charter balked at the abridgement of national sovereignty required to protect them. Worried about the social and economic rights being read into an ever-expanding definition of human rights,

America's senior foreign policy advisor in San Francisco, John Foster Dulles, insisted on an escape clause as the price of American support for the treaty. Under the leadership of the American and British delegations, with the enthusiastic support of the Soviets, Article 2, paragraph 7, was inserted into the charter, which read: "Nothing contained in the present Charter shall authorize the United Nations to intervene in matters which are essentially within the domestic jurisdiction of any state or shall require the Members to submit such matters to settlement." Responsibility for human and civil equality remained lodged in the individual states that made up the United Nations.

A NEW WORLD AT HOME

Beginning in 1932, with his speech to the Commonwealth Club of San Francisco, Franklin Roosevelt had argued for a principled balance between private liberty and public good, between the economic and political rights of the individual and those of the collective. In his State of the Union Address in 1944, broadcast live to millions over the radio, Roosevelt called for "a Second Bill of Rights . . . an economic bill of rights" that would guarantee every citizen a job, a living wage, education, decent housing, adequate medical care, and "protection from the economic fears of old age, sickness, accident, and unemployment." Together, these rights spelled "security," which was a legitimate expectation of every citizen and the responsibility of the nation. If the original Bill of Rights to the Constitution was a list of "thou shalt nots" designed to limit the reach of the federal government, Roosevelt's "second Bill of Rights" was an affirmation of government's capacity and obligation to balance and regulate the economic and political rights of the individual against those of the collective, and vice versa.

Roosevelt's vision of an "economic constitutional order" didn't go very far. But it did inspire another bill of rights, the Servicemen's Readjustment Act of 1944, known popularly as the GI Bill of Rights. Designed to reintegrate millions of returning soldiers, the GI Bill reached eight out of ten men born in the 1920s. Between 1944 and 1971, federal spending for former soldiers totaled over $95 billion. With the help of the GI Bill, millions attended college, bought homes with federally guaranteed low-interest mortgages, started business ventures with small-business loans, and found jobs via the United States Employment Service (USES). No group of Americans, before or since, has been given such a leg up by American taxpayers.

African American veterans, predictably, benefited less from this burst of federal largesse than whites did. With the options for black veterans limited by the pre-*Brown* world of segregated higher education, the gap in educational attainment between blacks and whites widened, rather than closed, after 1945. Of arguably even greater lasting significance, African American veterans were systematically discriminated against by the lending institutions created by the bill, which made it very difficult, often impossible, for blacks to qualify for mortgages.

Women, too, benefited less than their brothers did from the GI Bill. Only about 2 percent of military personnel in the Second World War were women, which means that 98 percent of American women were by definition excluded from such benefits as the bill's new college subsidy plan. Female veterans did not receive the same benefits as men did (women had to prove their independence from a male breadwinner, for instance, before receiving unemployment aid). Colleges that had filled their classrooms with women during the war scaled back in order to accommodate as many men as possible. Professional schools that had resigned themselves to teaching women during the war now reverted to their previous men-only policies. The tens of thousands of men and women dismissed from the military with a "blue discharge" for being homosexual were also denied rights under the GI Bill.

Even so, no other piece of legislation was more influential in creating the broad American middle class of the postwar era than the Servicemen's Readjustment Act. And no other piece of legislation illustrated so obviously the capacity of the federal government to act creatively, efficiently, and effectively on behalf of those citizens who had offered their lives on behalf of the Republic.

CIVIL RIGHTS AND HUMAN RIGHTS

The distance between universalistic American goals and discriminatory American practice, between "All men are created equal" and the nation's intricate system of racial discrimination, left the United States vulnerable to charges of hypocrisy. In the new postwar world, America's internal race problem became entangled in foreign policy, and vice versa. The goodwill that accrued to the United States by virtue of its Declaration of Independence and its robust constitutional democracy was eroded in many places by reports of domestic racial violence, disenfranchisement, segregated housing and schools, and restrictive marriage laws. A 1947 State Department report titled

"Problems of Discrimination and Minority Status in the United States" stated forthrightly that Jim Crow practices were "obviously in conflict with the American creed of democracy and equality of opportunity for all."

Groups inside the United States also exploited the fact that the "leader of the free world" tolerated racial discrimination. In October 1947, the NAACP presented to the United Nations a 155-page petition titled "An Appeal to the World: A Statement on the Denial of Human Rights to Minorities in the Case of Citizens of Negro Descent in the United States of America and an Appeal to the United Nations for Redress." Drafted by a committee of black academics and lawyers under the supervision of W. E. B. Du Bois, the appeal demanded "elemental Justice against the treatment which the United States has visited upon us for three centuries."

Whereas a significant cadre of foreign policy analysts considered American race politics dangerous for the nation's role in global politics, the guardians of Jim Crow considered American participation in international organizations such as the United Nations a threat to the established social order. Petitions aside, the danger to the sovereign status quo lay in the interpretive possibilities of the UN Charter and its relationship to American law. In a 1946 challenge to segregated interstate transportation, Howard Law School dean William H. Hastie argued that when the United States had ratified the UN Charter, America had "embedded in its national policy a prohibition against racism and pledged itself to respect fundamental freedoms for all without distinction as to race, sex, language or religion."

This position was reinforced in 1948, when four justices of the US Supreme Court included references to the UN Charter in their opinion in *Oyama v. California*, a challenge to a law restricting landownership by noncitizen Japanese. Noting that the United States had recently pledged to "promote . . . universal respect for, and observance of, human rights and fundamental freedoms for all without distinction as to race, sex, language, or religion," Justice Hugo Black asked, "How can this nation be faithful to this international pledge if state laws which bar land ownership and occupancy by aliens on account of race are permitted to be enforced?"

Caught between the determination of white southerners to reestablish the antebellum racial status quo and the deepening commitment of African Americans to press for full equality, the federal government adopted positions inconceivable before 1945 and became, for the first time since Reconstruction, an ally of the black freedom struggle. If it is too much to say that Hitler "gave racism a bad name," it is nonetheless true that many Americans reevaluated the harsh realities of white supremacy at home during the years they fought fascism abroad.

*

If it didn't happen to kill you, one of George Orwell's characters once remarked, war was bound to start you thinking. The Second World War started all sorts of people thinking. Those who fought thought about what they had fought for. Some—most—fought principally to preserve and protect their homeland and secondarily to defeat tyranny in Europe and Asia. Some—many—fought to change their homeland and their own place in it. Others, like Enrico Fermi and the scientists of the Manhattan Project, thought about all they had achieved, and worried for the future. Still others wondered how to steer the great ship of the Republic through the uncharted seas of world dominance. Above all, the desire for full citizenship animated the politics of American minorities. The coming generation was not inclined to patience. "We want and are entitled to the basic rights and opportunities of American citizens," 17-year-old M. L. King Jr. wrote of African Americans in a letter to the editor of the *Atlanta Constitution* in 1946. It was, indeed, a new world.

CHAPTER 7

Containment, 1946–1953

In August 1946, filmmaker Orson Welles—who had a weekly Sunday afternoon radio program—devoted his time to a discussion of the race problem in America and its connection to the nation's new role in the world: "I have met Southerners who expect and fear a Negro insurrection. I see no purpose in withholding this from general discussion. There may be those within that outcast 10 per cent of the American people who some day will strike back at their oppressors. To put down the mob, a mob would rise. Who will put down that mob?"

Not another mob, Welles was quick to explain. Americans were going to have to take care of the mob, but in a different way: through the rule of law. Warning that "there is no room in the American century for Jim Crow," Welles insisted that "what was excused in us before is no longer excusable," and reminded Americans that the eyes of the world were upon them. "Our [r]epublican splendor in this new age will shine by its own virtues, not by virtue of contrasting tyranny," he intoned. It was not enough to be better than the Nazis. Americans had a duty to defend their values wherever they were besieged, whether at home or abroad.

Challenged from without by the Soviets, American values, particularly the rule of law, were also under attack by Americans. During the summer of 1946, southern whites blinded, castrated, and killed 56 African Americans. Many of these were veterans. Arguing that there was a "need today for a dramatic reminder to our people of the American heritage which they enjoy," President Truman announced in May 1947 a moving exhibit of America's key democratic documents, including original copies of the Declaration of Independence and the Emancipation Proclamation. Dubbed the Freedom Train, the red, white, and blue streamliner visited each of the 48 contiguous states. Towns

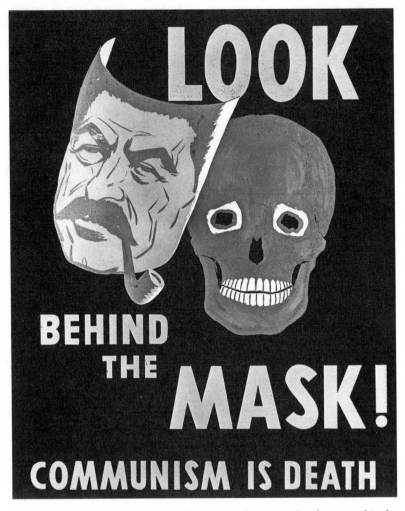

FIGURE 7. Anti-Communist poster depicting Stalin. From the photos used in the 1984 Truman Centennial Exhibit. Library of Congress photo no. LC-USZ62-80757. Courtesy of the Harry S. Truman Library & Museum.

and cities were encouraged to hold "Rededication Weeks," coinciding with the arrival of the traveling exhibit, in which citizens would pledge to uphold the democratic principles of the nation. Drawing conflict out into the open, the Freedom Train forbade segregated viewing of the exhibit. Memphis and Birmingham let it pass them by.

In addition to indoctrinating Americans in democracy, as Attorney General Tom Clark put it, the Freedom Train had another mission, which was to demonstrate to the world the virtues of the American way of life. That way of life was suddenly center stage, as the United States assumed its new role as global leader. By 1946, the world was dividing in two: on one side, the "free societies" of North America and Western Europe; on the other, the Soviet Union and the one-party regimes it established in the Eastern European countries occupied by the Red Army in 1945. The Soviets could not be pushed back from Eastern Europe. But their future influence could be "contained," if countered by the partisans of democratic politics and free enterprise.

"Containment" became the centerpiece of US foreign policy during what was eventually dubbed the Cold War. Like a game of chess, the United States and the USSR checked and counterchecked each other across the globe for 40 years. Had containment been merely a foreign policy, it could be regarded as a strategic success: at the very least, the two great powers of the atomic age avoided nuclear war. But containment was also a domestic policy to silence critics of the government, of capitalism, of segregation, of foreign policy—of nearly anything.

Containing Communism abroad was costly. Before the decade was out, it would cost the United States nearly 120,000 dead and wounded in Korea. The price to contain it at home was also high, although paid in a different coin. Dissent became un-American. Rather than court danger, people censored themselves. Millions of Americans may have viewed the Bill of Rights aboard the Freedom Train, but those rights would be contained and compromised over the course of the coming decade.

Postwar/Cold War

The United States' competition with the USSR was conducted on multiple fronts—in the realm of ideas (ideology), politics, economic planning (especially government regulation), foreign cooperation, scientific research, and military action.

There were many ways to win the hearts and minds of the world for capitalism, democracy, and free enterprise. With the help of the Marshall Plan, which was designed to provision the people of Western Europe with military protection, credit, and consumer goods, the United States constructed sturdy ties among its allies and lessened the allure of the USSR. Just as Europe was stabilized, however, the Cold War went east and turned hot in 1950, when the United States went to war in Korea in defense of containment, making clear in the process that the Cold War knew no geographical boundaries.

NEW DIVISIONS

The Cold War was the product of the particular postwar moment, but its roots lay in a more remote past. The confrontation between Western Europe and the United States and Soviet Russia dated to 1918, when England and America intervened militarily in the Russian Civil War on the side of the anti-Bolsheviks. The ideological and political competition between democracy and Communism raged through the 1920s and 1930s. In 1935, after Italy invaded Ethiopia, the international Communist governing body, the Comintern, announced the Popular Front to unite socialists, liberals, and Communists in opposition to fascism. The membership of the Communist Party of the United States (CPUSA) tripled between 1934 and 1939, from 26,000 to 85,000.

The 1945 Yalta agreement had called for democratic elections in Eastern Europe, but it was clear immediately after the fall of Berlin that this would not happen. On May 12, 1945, Winston Churchill warned Truman in a telegram about the Soviets, "An iron curtain is drawn down upon their front. We do not know what is going on behind." What was going on was a consolidation of power. With Soviet troops to back them up, local Communists purged the opposition. The Allies watched helplessly as Communist-dominated governments sprouted in Poland, Czechoslovakia, East Germany, and Hungary.

Nothing could be done about what would soon be known as the Eastern Bloc. But there had to be a way to keep the Soviets from expanding their political sphere infinitely. In 1947, George F. Kennan, a midlevel career diplomat with expertise in Russian history and politics, analyzed the situation and counseled patience: "The main element of any United States policy toward the Soviet Union must be that of a long-term, patient but firm and vigilant *containment* of Russian expansive tendencies." *Containment*: the word has a nice feel to it, firm without being aggressive, reasonable. But how, exactly, could this notion be applied to foreign policy? To contain something is to confine it within a boundary. Could Communism be confined within Eastern and Central Europe? What would be required if that were the goal?

In 1946, the USSR began to pressure Turkey to allow Soviet naval bases on the Bosporus, a key portal between the Mediterranean and the Black Sea. At roughly the same time, civil war broke out in Greece between a government backed by the British and a Communist opposition. In 1947, the British informed the Americans that they could not afford to support the anti-Communist government in Greece. On

March 12, President Truman requested an unprecedented $400 million for economic aid to both Greece and Turkey and for authority to send American military personnel to train their soldiers. In his speech to Congress, the president articulated the Truman Doctrine, which was substantially more proactive that the containment policy. "I believe," Truman announced, "that it must be the policy of the United States to support free peoples who are resisting attempted subjugation by armed minorities or by outside pressures." Congress approved, and by 1950 Turkey had been stabilized and the Communist insurrection in Greece defeated.

THE MARSHALL PLAN

In June 1947, General George C. Marshall, now serving as secretary of state, applied the principles of the Truman Doctrine to Europe and announced that the United States would fund a massive economic recovery program there. "Our policy," he declared, "is directed not against country or doctrine, but against hunger, poverty, desperation, and chaos." Millions of Europeans were still at risk of starvation in 1947. Perhaps more to the point, millions of Europeans were at risk of voting Communist. During the 1930s, the New Deal had stabilized American politics as it stabilized the economy. Could a New Deal for Europe do the same?

Between 1948 and 1951, the United States provided a staggering $12.5 billion in economic aid to Europe. As a result of Marshall Plan policies, Europe embarked on an unprecedented two decades of economic growth that saw a marked rise in the standard of living. The Marshall Plan also underwrote political stability in postwar Europe. Thanks to American aid, governments were able to suspend austerity programs that had contributed to discontent and political unrest. This is not to say that America's motives were all altruistic. Kindling economic recovery in Europe was good for American manufacturers who needed a European market capable of purchasing American goods. The vast majority of Marshall Plan funds were used to purchase goods from the United States, leading to resentment from other nations reliant on exports to Europe such as Canada and Argentina. Congress took pity on its neighbor and ally, and passed legislation allowing aid money to be used in Canadian purchases. Canada's economy boomed. Argentina, which was officially neutral during the war but harbored a number of Nazi war criminals afterward, got nothing.

In its optimism, its faith in the capacity of public institutions to solve big problems, and its acceptance of government regulation of economic and fiscal policy, the Marshall Plan was a natural successor to the New Deal and the most successful planned economy of the twentieth century. Its progressive genealogy was spotted at the time; critics labeled the plan "a bold Socialist blueprint" and muttered about central planning. Congressional commitment to ideology faded, however, in the face of Soviet aggression. In February 1948, Communists staged a coup in Czechoslovakia and overthrew a democratically elected coalition government. Two weeks later, the popular and longtime Czech foreign minister Jan Masaryk, who had been educated in the United States, was found dead. Any hope that the USSR would allow free elections in the Iron Curtain countries dissolved. Congress voted overwhelmingly in favor of the "bold Socialist blueprint" for reconstructing Europe.

The Marshall Plan *was* bold. It was also provocative. Although all the countries of Europe were invited to participate in the plan, including Russia and the nations now in the Soviet sphere of influence, America's intention to shape the European economy and political system in its own image was obvious. The Russians, predictably, declined the American overture for itself and Eastern Europe. For all its virtues, the Marshall Plan accelerated rather than slowed the long slide into acrimony and distrust that marked US-Soviet relations between 1945 and 1950.

NEW ALLIANCES AND NEW STATES

As the Marshall Plan was formulated, the Allies prepared to unite their zones of occupation in western Germany, preparatory to the creation of a new federal republic. Eastern Germany remained under the control of the Soviets, with one glaring exception: Berlin, the former capital of the Reich, which lay some 100 miles inside the Soviet occupation zone, was itself still divided into French, British, American, and Soviet quadrants. The Kremlin tried repeatedly to gain control of all Berlin. The most serious attempt was the first, in the summer of 1948.

On June 23, 1948, Stalin ordered all roads and railroads closed to traffic from the west. The next day he cut electricity to the western sector, and the day after that he halted all food deliveries to West Berlin. The Soviets wanted the Allies out, in part because they wanted to make Berlin the capital of East Germany, and in part because this outpost of capitalism and democracy was an irritant to the new Communist German state that surrounded it.

With Berlin blockaded, the question became how to stymie the Soviets without starting a war. With sea and land routes blocked, the only alternative was the skies. On June 26 Operation Vittles went into gear. US and British military flights came through Berlin's Templehof Airport on a schedule as precise as a Swiss watch. Jeeps bearing pretty German hostesses tore around the tarmac refueling the pilots while their planes were unloaded and refueled. The airlift improved efficiency month by month, until by April 1949 more than 12,000 tons of supplies were delivered daily. The Soviets finally threw in the towel, and the airlift ended officially on September 30, 1948, after delivering 2,326,406 tons of supplies at a cost of $224 million.

Rather than dislodge the Allies from Berlin, the blockade cemented a fractious alliance dominated by the United States. The North Atlantic Treaty Organization (NATO), formed in April 1949, committed its members to collective security in general and the United States to the military defense of Europe in particular. The original 12 signatories included all the major Western European nations besides neutral Sweden and Switzerland, and Spain, which was still a right-wing dictatorship. Greece and Turkey joined in 1952, and West Germany in 1955. France, emboldened by its acquisition of a nuclear bomb, withdrew from the alliance in 1966, only to rejoin some 40 years later.

The one foreign policy issue Stalin and Truman agreed on was the creation of a Jewish homeland in the Middle East. The animating issue was less a Jewish territorial claim to the Holy Land than a practical problem about refugees, especially after Holocaust survivors returning home were greeted with violence (1,000 were killed in one anti-Jewish riot alone in Poland in 1946). Such events created a stream of migrants to Palestine, which was not an independent nation but under British colonial control. Britain intercepted the refugees and warehoused them in camps on Cyprus. Pressed by Zionists (those who supported Jewish sovereignty in the Holy Land) and by American congressmen outraged by the incarceration of Holocaust survivors, the British handed the problem to the United Nations.

Despite Arab pledges to destroy any Jewish state, the UN divided the land into two states, Israel and Palestine, in late 1947. Both the United States and the USSR recognized the new Jewish state when it declared independence on May 14, 1948. True to their word, Egypt, Transjordan, Syria, Lebanon, and Iraq invaded immediately. Saudi Arabia sent troops. Britain withheld recognition until the Israelis won the war in 1949, by which time the Israelis had added significantly to the territory originally allotted them by the UN.

KOREA

Occupied by Japan in 1905 and annexed in 1910, the Korean Peninsula was divided at the Potsdam Conference (July–August 1945) at the 38th Parallel, with Americans occupying the South and the Red Army the North. The South became the haven of anti-Communist nationalists under the leadership of Syngman Rhee, a Princeton-educated member of the anti-Japanese provisional government. The North was the stronghold of the Communists, who had provided most of the soldiers for wartime anticolonial assaults against the Japanese occupiers.

On June 25, 1950, with Stalin's ostensible blessing but no promise of support, North Korean leader Kim Il-sung sent 80,000 troops, backed by artillery, tanks, and aircraft, across the 38th Parallel into South Korea. President Truman was caught by surprise, and underestimated the importance of Korea's indigenous Communists. In the president's mind, the North Koreans were Stalin's puppets, testing America's commitment to contain Communism everywhere. "Korea is the Greece of the Far East," the president explained. "There is no telling what [the Communists] will do if we don't put up a fight now." When the United Nations Security Council agreed to stop the North Korean aggression using troops mainly from the United States, Truman ordered two American divisions into action under the direction of Far East commander Douglas MacArthur.

After a string of roller coaster victories, UN troops were pushed by the North Koreans to Pusan, at the southern tip of the peninsula. In September 1950, MacArthur launched a daring amphibious invasion and pushed the North Korean troops back across the border. Then, ignoring repeated warnings by the Chinese that they would consider an American advance into North Korea aggression against China, MacArthur marched through the North until his troops reached the Yalu River, the border between China and Korea. In November 1950, 300,000 Chinese troops, many of them battle-hardened veterans, descended on the UN troops. In some of the bloodiest hand-to-hand fighting of the twentieth century, wave after wave of Chinese troops attacked and drove the Americans back to the 38th Parallel. The conflict ended with a negotiated peace in 1953 in which each side occupied the territory it had held when the war began. MacArthur was relieved from duty for his strategic miscalculation and his subsequent decision to complain to Congress about the commander in chief's conduct of the war.

Even though the war ended in a stalemate, the lesson seemed to be that containment was the only way to keep the Soviets from spreading Communism throughout the world. The cost in lives of learning this lesson was high: 36,000 American dead and 100,000 wounded, in addition to the roughly 1 million South Korean troops killed and wounded and 1.5 million enemy troops, of whom 900,000 were Chinese. The cost in terms of treasure—and the things money can support, such as infrastructure and social programs—was also high.

The Korean War had two important consequences. The first was a noteworthy reallocation of resources toward the military. The $53 billion defense budget of 1953 quadrupled that of 1949, and represented 60 percent of government expenditures (versus 33 percent in 1950) and 12 percent of GNP (gross national product) (versus 5 percent in 1950). Second, because the war was waged through the United Nations, President Truman was able to bypass Congress, which has the power to declare war, and commit US troops on his own executive authority. This was a significant expansion of executive power in a moment when Cold War foreign policy and national security were already merging in the White House.

To Secure These Rights

In January 1947, announcing a new program to expose Communists and Communist sympathizers in the federal government, the House Un-American Activities Committee (HUAC) pledged that Congress would "ferret out" everyone opposed to the "American way of life." "Opposition" to the "American way of life" could take many forms, from an African American veteran challenging white supremacy to a librarian promoting books critical of US foreign policy to a government employee passing sensitive information to the Soviets. Containing subversion could take many forms as well, from a lynch mob led by officers of the law to a hearing before a congressional committee to the addition of the phrase "under God" to the Pledge of Allegiance. In the name of containing Communism, the federal government launched a host of new programs to protect national security and mounted an unprecedented peacetime military buildup. To protect itself from a totalitarian state, America expanded its own state massively.

CREATING THE PERMANENT WAR STATE

In 1940, Franklin Roosevelt had to resort to sophism to justify supporting the British through the lend-lease program. Seven years later,

Roosevelt's successor convinced Congress to spend $400 million supporting Turkey and Greece and launched a massive program to rebuild shattered Europe. How did the United States move from isolationism to interventionism in less than a decade?

In good measure, it was the war and its outcome that pushed America toward an internationalist posture. But there is another answer: fear. When President Truman asked Michigan senator Arthur Vandenberg, the chairman of the Senate Foreign Relations Committee, how to sell his Turkish aid package to Congress, Vandenberg recommended that the president give a speech and "scare [the] hell out of the country." Truman complied, and warned his fellow Americans that "at the present moment in world history nearly every nation must choose between alternative ways of life"—between democratic self-government and free institutions and minority rule based on terror and the suppression of personal freedoms. The president's approval rating jumped 10 points.

In the late 1940s, the architects of American internationalism created the conditions for the growth of a permanent war economy and for a war executive. The war economy depended on defense appropriations that supported scientific research and development in universities as well as corporations such as IBM, Boeing, and General Electric. By 1960, the government supplied 64 percent of the country's funding for basic research.

The research and development (R&D) underwritten by the government helped create a "knowledge revolution" that transformed the American occupational structure. In 1940, not quite three million people were engaged in technical and scientific work. By 1964, that figure had more than doubled. There were 370% more engineers in 1964 than there had been in 1930, and a staggering 930% more scientists. In addition to stimulating the economy by creating jobs, government funding underwrote corporate prosperity through the application of defense-related research to consumer products. Young Bill Hewlett and Dave Packard had already founded Hewlett-Packard in 1939, but the first real computers were the product of WWII-stimulated research.

The war executive was anchored in the creation of new agencies that reported to the president. In 1947, Congress passed the National Security Act, which centralized power in the White House, established the Department of Defense to oversee all branches of the armed services, formed the Joint Chiefs of Staff, and created the National Security Council (NSC), a cabinet-level body overseen by the president and charged with coordinating military and foreign policy. Also formed was the Central Intelligence Agency (CIA), the espionage arm of the NSC. The war in Korea put teeth into these bureaucratic innovations.

The creation of the war executive relied on Congress and the people ceding to the federal government some of their own sovereignty. In this respect, the Cold War may be seen as a way of overcoming the populist antistatism—the impulse to ask much of the federal government while simultaneously denouncing its programs as corrosive of state sovereignty and individual liberty—so prominent in American politics. In April 1950, faced with the challenges of a nuclear-armed USSR and a war in Korea, the NSC issued National Security Council Memorandum 68 (NSC-68), which called for a nearly fourfold increase in the defense budget, from $13 billion to $50 billion a year. This concentration of resources and influence in the executive was necessary, NSC-68 explained, to contain a Soviet system driven by "a new fanatic faith" bent on world domination. In the name of defending democratic "freedom" against totalitarian "slavery," NSC-68 mandated a massive transfer of resources from those parts of government that maintained the basic building blocks of democracy—education, employment, the health and welfare of the people—to the military charged with protecting those things.

POSTWAR CIVIL RIGHTS

In June 1947, Harry Truman became the first president to address the NAACP's annual convention. He understood that he spoke not only to African Americans, but also to the millions of Africans and Asians determined to free themselves of colonial overlords. In a live radio address broadcast around the world, the American president proclaimed that "there is no justifiable reason for discrimination because of ancestry, or religion, or race, or color," and carefully dissected what he called "new concepts of civil rights" from the broader category of human rights. "Every man should have the right to a decent home, the right to an education, the right to adequate medical care, the right to a worthwhile job, the right to an equal share in making the public decisions through the ballot, and the right to a fair trial in court," he enumerated. He announced the formation of the President's Commission on Civil Rights (PCCR).

These were radical words from an American president, and they signaled a profound shift in the struggle for equal rights in the United States. For the first time since the 1870s, the executive branch of the federal government was in alignment with the fight against Jim Crow. This meant that the attorney general's office was now free to side with the plaintiffs in civil rights cases before the Supreme Court, which it did in 1948 when it joined an NAACP challenge to racially restrictive housing covenants. In its decision in *Shelley v. Kramer*, the court ruled that judicial enforcement of private agreements forbidding the sale of homes to African Americans (and, frequently, Jews, Asians, and Catholics as well) was enough "state action" to bring such laws under the umbrella of the Fourteenth Amendment, which forbade racial discrimination by the state, but not by individuals.

Truman elaborated on his decision to use the power of the executive in the cause of civil rights in a special message to Congress in February 1948. There he laid out a 10-point legislative agenda based on the recommendations outlined in the report of the PCCR, "To Secure These Rights," which called for desegregation of the armed forces and federal employment as well as a federal antilynching law, creation of a permanent commission on fair employment, and abolition of state poll taxes. Although he did not adopt the committee's general condemnation of segregation, Truman did pledge at this time to issue executive orders against discrimination in federal employment and to end segregation in the armed forces "as rapidly as possible."

Congress approved none of Truman's civil rights initiatives in 1948. In July, Truman issued Executive Order 9981, which initiated the desegregation of the armed forces. This action pleased the liberal wing of the Democratic Party but alienated segregationists. Tempers flared at the 1948 Democratic National Convention in Philadelphia. Led by Minnesotan Hubert Humphrey, who was running for the US Senate, the liberals succeeded in passing their own, stronger civil rights plank. When Humphrey challenged the delegates "to walk out of the shadow of states' rights and into the sunlight of human rights," 35 delegates from Alabama and Mississippi stalked out of the convention hall instead.

CHALLENGES FROM THE RIGHT AND THE LEFT

The Dixiecrats, as they were dubbed by the press, formed the National States' Rights Party and nominated South Carolina governor J. Strom Thurmond for president. Although he advocated "complete segregation of the races" in order to protect the "racial integrity" of each race, Thurmond insisted that the real issue at stake in the 1948 election was one of sovereignty: "the right of people to govern themselves." The president's plan to enforce civil rights through federal power would "convert America into a Hitler state," warned Thurmond. Or it might result in Communism, since the expansion of federal power had its "origin in communist ideology." Either way, the future was totalitarian.

Challenged on the right by Thurmond, Truman was also vulnerable to his left. As the candidate of the new Progressive Party of America, former vice president Henry Wallace challenged Truman's confrontational foreign policy stance toward the Soviet Union, denounced segregation everywhere he went, and promised the people expanded social services.

Dismissed by many conventional politicians of both parties as impractical and idealistic, Wallace was a stalwart defender of the downtrodden and a consistent exponent of civil equality. He was an early supporter of the black press's wartime Double V campaign, and identified black suffrage as key to the domestic war against bigotry and discrimination. Campaigning for the Democrats in 1940, Wallace argued that the United States "cannot plead for equality of opportunity for people everywhere and overlook the denial of the right to vote for millions of our own people."

In addition to his unqualified support for civil rights, Wallace was a steady backer of the United Nations. ("If the United Nations is untested, let us test it. If the United Nations lacks support, let us support it. If the United Nations is weak, let us strengthen it.") He was also an uncensored critic of the president's loyalty program, which he denounced for engendering suspicion and intolerance, and which he predicted would target supporters of civil rights and the UN such as himself.

Throughout 1948, Wallace traveled the nation, speaking exclusively to nonsegregated audiences. His open defiance of Jim Crow enraged white supremacists, who shouted down the candidate, manhandled his team, and disrupted rallies with violence. No hotel would admit the Wallace entourage, so they slept, for the most part, in the homes of black supporters, and ate out of picnic baskets on the side of the road. He and his running mate, Idaho senator Glen Taylor, made it out of the South alive, but were catcalled, pelted with rotten eggs, and interrupted with cries of "Communist!" and "Nigger lover!" (Roughly synonymous terms in the South.) Both he and the Progressive Party, Wallace declared, "are fighting to end racial discrimination." A defiant Taylor scuffled with police and was arrested in Birmingham after entering a building through the "Negroes Only" entrance.

The odds of a fractured Democratic Party beating a unified GOP seemed slim until the Republicans nominated New York governor Thomas E. Dewey. Able and efficient, Dewey was also uninspiring and overconfident. He was criticized for campaigning too little, but that might have been clever—the *Louisville Courier Journal* reduced Dewey's stump speeches to four sentences: "Agriculture is important. Our rivers are full of fish. You cannot have freedom without liberty. The future lies ahead."

THE 1948 PRESIDENTIAL ELECTION

The 1948 election was the last before television transported political debate from union halls and stadiums to private living rooms. Taking to the rails, as Truman did, would be obsolete by 1952. In a breathtaking demonstration of an old-fashioned whistle-stop campaign, Truman gave 351 speeches before an estimated 12 million Americans. He reminded America's farmers and workers who had brought them prosperity and won the war, and blamed the GOP-dominated "do-nothing" 80th Congress for high utility rates, a shortage of public housing, and the lack of public health insurance. He railed against "Republican gluttons of privilege." When crowds chanted, "Give 'em hell, Harry!" the president responded, "I don't give 'em hell. I just tell the truth and they think it's hell."

As election day neared, however, Truman was lagging in the polls. In October, 50 top political journalists predicted Dewey's victory. On election night, after the polls had closed but before the votes had been counted, the *Chicago Tribune*, a reliably Republican paper, ran as its headline, "DEWEY DEFEATS TRUMAN." The photograph of a beaming president Truman holding up that paper the next day told it all: in the most dramatic upset victory in presidential history, Truman beat Dewey by 2.1 million popular votes, which translated to a 303 to 189 victory in the Electoral College. In California, Illinois, and Ohio, states rich in electoral votes, black voters carried Truman across the finish line. Thurmond carried four Deep South states with 39 electoral votes; Wallace came in a distant fourth. The success of the National States' Rights Party with white southern voters signaled the beginning of a massive shift in partisan allegiance in that region, from the Democrats to, eventually, the Republicans. For the moment, however, Truman's victory brought with it Democratic majorities in Congress. The new group of senators included Hubert Humphrey and "Landslide Lyndon" Johnson of Texas, who squeaked into office by 87 disputed votes.

Truman's reelection demonstrated the continuing appeal of Roosevelt's New Deal reforms. Americans liked their newfound security, and they wanted it to continue. Economic planners, political scientists, and anti-Communist liberal organizations like the Americans for Democratic Action (ADA) still centered their thought on FDR's Four Freedoms and his Economic Bill of Rights. President Truman's "Fair Deal" had all the earmarks of the era of New Deal economic rights. "Every segment of our population and every individual has a right to expect from our Government a fair deal," he declared in his 1949 State of the Union address.

The 81st Congress was responsive to Truman's agenda. In the most energetic effort at reform since 1935, Congress increased the minimum wage, passed the National Housing Act of 1949 (which provided for low-income housing units in rural and urban areas and for slum clearance), increased Social Security benefits, and extended rent controls. But Congress rejected Truman's proposal for federal aid to education as well as his plan for a national health insurance system—which was denounced by the American Medical Association (AMA), in a massive advertising campaign, as "socialized medicine" likely to "lead to socialization of other phases of American life." The president's civil rights initiatives also languished.

Anti-Communist Crusades at Home

Harry Truman's decision to scare the electorate into supporting anti-Communism was a political choice that had lasting implications for domestic life. In the name of constraining Communism abroad, Americans constrained their Constitution at home. At the same time that they ceded unprecedented power to the federal government, Americans worried about the relationship between citizens and the state in a democratic system. The efforts of Americans at every level of society to extinguish anything hinting of "Communist subversion" had a profound impact on American life for decades.

SEEING RED

Unlike the Socialist Party, which drew hundreds of thousands of votes in the early twentieth century, the CPUSA as a *political* entity was never all that important. More important was the influence of Communists in a variety of industries and institutions. Midcentury American Communists played important roles in industrial unions, in the motion picture industry, in the world of literature and the arts, and in progressive organizations such as the National Lawyers Guild, founded in 1937 to provide a counterweight to the American Bar Association, which limited its membership to white Christian men. Government agencies were crosscut with people who had rubbed shoulders, and sometimes more than that, with Communists. But the vast majority of American Communists were regular Joes, veterans, skilled workers whose kids went to the local public school and who dreamed at night not of insurrection but of full employment and summer vacations.

In March 1947, President Truman established a loyalty program for all civilian government employees. Under its terms, no individual could work for the federal government if "reasonable grounds exist for belief" that he or she was "disloyal to the Government of the United States." Evidence of "disloyalty" included membership in "any foreign or domestic organization . . . designated by the Attorney General as totalitarian, fascist, Communist, or subversive." As during WWI, no definition of "subversive" was ever offered.

The federal government was not the only organization worried about disloyalty in its ranks. In 1946, Walter Reuther, the powerful head of the United Auto Workers (UAW), purged Communists from his organization. The Congress of Industrial Organizations (CIO) followed his lead in 1949, and expelled nine unions, representing 900,000 workers, for refusing to purge themselves of Communist leaders. In between, Congress passed the Taft-Hartley Act of 1947, which required union leaders to sign oaths that they were not members of the Communist Party. It also banned the closed shop (in which nonunion workers could not be hired), and supported state "right to work" laws that outlawed even a union shop (in which joining the union was required of new workers). Truman vetoed Taft-Hartley, gaining the applause of labor, but Congress overrode his veto.

Hollywood was another prominent location for Communists, many of them refugees from Nazism. In 1947, the House Un-American Activities Committee (HUAC) held hearings to determine the degree of "Communist influence" in the motion picture industry. When ten "unfriendly witnesses" refused to answer questions about their political beliefs or to identify individual Communists, they were charged with contempt of Congress and served jail terms of six months to one year. They were then blacklisted by studio executives along with another 200 tight-lipped writers, actors, and directors.

There *were* internal threats to American security. Former State Department officer Alger Hiss, who was convicted of perjury but not espionage, *did* pass government documents to the Soviets. Julius Rosenberg, who was arrested with his wife, Ethel, on charges of espionage in 1950, *did* recruit a circle of spies who provided Moscow with technical information. But Julius did not have access to the atomic secrets he was charged with passing to the Soviets. Those who did (and who later confessed, including David Greenglass, Ethel Rosenberg's brother) served brief sentences in prison.

Julius Rosenberg was tried, justifiably, for espionage. Although also convicted of espionage, Ethel Rosenberg was, effectively, tried for her association with Julius, and for her long affiliation with Communist organizations (Ethel and Julius met in 1936 at the Young Communist League). Electrocuted on June 19, 1953, Ethel and Julius Rosenberg remain the only civilians ever executed for conspiracy to commit espionage.

SCARED

By 1950, if it was not a crime to *be* a Communist, it was dangerous to *associate* with them. The 1950 Internal Security Act (better known as the McCarran Act, for its sponsor, Nevada senator Patrick A. McCarran) required that Communist organizations, including so-called Communist front organizations, register with the attorney general and produce membership lists. The act barred all members of registered organizations from government employment or private defense industry work, and authorized the president to preemptively detain all persons likely to participate "in acts of espionage or sabotage" in the event of war or insurrection.

Harry Truman compared the McCarran Act with the Alien and Sedition Acts of 1798, and he vetoed the bill. The president's veto was overridden by the same Congress he had fear-mongered into sending aid to Turkey and Greece, with roughly the same rationale: Communist success abroad threatened democracy at home. The victory of Chinese Communists in their civil war in 1949 had brought further evidence of the Communist menace, and the Russians' detonation of an atomic weapon in September 1949 triggered a new round of nightmares.

By focusing on associations rather than actions, the McCarran Act stifled political debate and opened the door to persecution on the basis of belief, thus blurring the boundary between a free society and a police state. Its goal was to contain the possibility of unorthodox thought. If the American government was not quite telling people what to think, it was telling them what *not* to think, and whom to avoid in the process of not thinking these things. In the dissent in *Dennis v. United States* (1951), in which 11 members of the CPUSA were convicted of conspiring to advocate the overthrow of government, that is, of talking about talking about overthrowing the government, Supreme Court justices Hugo Black and William O. Douglas were lonely defenders of the right of free speech. In the margin of another justice's concurring opinion, Black wrote despairingly, "1st Amendment presumes that free speech will *preserve*, not destroy, the nation."

This assumption did not guide federal policy in the 1950s. The defendants in *Dennis* were prosecuted under the Smith Act of 1940, which made it a crime to "advocate" or "abet" the overthrow of the government by violence, or to "organize any association which . . . encourages such an overthrow," or to be a member of such an association. There were only two prosecutions brought under the Smith Act during WWII, because FDR's attorneys general opposed the law. But it remained on the books, ready to support the McCarran Act and to smooth the way for the *Dennis* decision, which gave the green light to the FBI. Two weeks after the decision, in June 1951, the FBI arrested 17 Communist leaders in New York. More arrests followed. Between 1951 and 1957, 145 members and leaders of the CPUSA were arrested and prosecuted under the Smith Act.

In 1957—after major personnel changes on the Supreme Court and a negotiated end to the fighting in Korea—the justices reversed themselves, and ruled that mere belief in the need for violent overthrow of the government was not punishable under the Smith Act. Even advocacy of revolution was "too remote from concrete action" to warrant restriction of First Amendment rights. As Justice John Marshall Harlan explained in *Yates v. United States*, "Those to whom the advocacy is addressed must be urged to *do* something, now or in the future, rather than merely to *believe* in something."

ASSAULTS ON LIBERTY

Taken together, the federal loyalty program, the McCarran Act, and prosecutions under the Smith Act had a profound "chilling effect" on political expression in the United States. The loyalty program, in particular, all but demanded self-censorship. Explained one government employee, "If Communists like apple pie and I do, I see no reason why I should stop eating it. But I would." During the Truman presidency (1945-1953), more than 4.7 million government employees were investigated. Approximately 20 percent (ca. 8,000) of these investigations led to formal investigation by a department or agency loyalty board. Of these individuals, 90 percent were cleared. Of the 500 or so people actually fired, the Civil Service Commission's Loyalty Review Board overturned about a third of the disloyal verdicts. Thus, approximately 350 federal employees—roughly 1 for every 13,000 investigated—were discharged because of doubts about their loyalty during the Truman years.

If 90 percent of people quarantined during a smallpox epidemic failed to develop the disease, doctors would blame the diagnostic. In their investigations of more than 4 million federal civilian employees, government loyalty boards failed to uncover a *single* instance of espionage or subversive malfeasance. This failure did not discourage either Truman or his successor, Dwight D. Eisenhower, from pursuing investigations. Perhaps hoping for an actual conviction, President Eisenhower in May 1953 expanded the definition of disloyalty to include "any behavior, activities or associations which *tend to show* that the individual is not reliable or trustworthy" (emphasis added). The following October, Eisenhower added a new basis for automatic dismissal—invocation of the Fifth Amendment privilege against compelled self-incrimination in an inquiry involving alleged disloyalty. Between 1947 and 1956, about 2,700 federal employees lost their jobs and another 12,000 resigned "voluntarily" as a result of the government's loyalty program.

Many of these "voluntary" resignations were likely people who were gay or homosexual. By 1950, the definition of government "subversives" had broadened beyond political beliefs to include sexual behavior. Because homosexual conduct was illegal in every state, homosexuals were at risk of blackmail as well as arrest, and thus, theoretically, could endanger national security. The chairman of the Republican National Committee wrote in a letter that "the sexual perverts who have infiltrated our Government" were as dangerous as Communists. Tabloid journalist Arthur Guy Mathews warned, "Communists are now converting American youth to homosexuality to defeat us from within." In 1950, a Senate Committee demanded "strict and careful screening" to keep homosexuals "off the Government payroll."

Loyalty investigations destroyed individual lives and pulled at the threads of the social fabric. What associations tended to show unreliability? Belief in racial equality and involvement in civil rights activities was enough for some loyalty boards, because until 1948 the CPUSA was the only political party to endorse equal rights for all. "The fact that a person believes in racial equality doesn't *prove* that he's a Communist," admitted the chairman of one loyalty board. "But it certainly makes you look twice, doesn't it? You can't get away from the fact that racial equality is part of the Communist line."

The loyalty program undermined core American values of free speech and due process. Defendants had no chance to confront or cross-examine their accusers, who were often anonymous and unreliable, and the meaning of "disloyalty" itself was so fluid that it could easily become synonymous with "critical." University of Chicago President Robert Maynard Hutchins made this point in 1949. "It is now fashionable to call anybody with whom we disagree a Communist or a fellow-traveler," he complained. "One who criticizes the foreign policy of the United States, or the draft, . . . or who believes that our military establishment is too expensive, can be called a fellow-traveler, for the Russians are of the same opinion. One who thinks that there are too many slums and too much lynching in America can be called a fellow-traveler, for the Russians claim that they ought to be opposed." By limiting the capacity of Americans to think and speak critically about their government, the loyalty program and anti-Communist legislation overturned the wisdom of the Founders that in a democratic society the government is the servant, and not the master, of the people.

FIGHTIN' JOE

This was the state of American politics when Joseph R. McCarthy entered the conversation on Communism and loyalty. McCarthy's past was as imaginary as most of his charges of treason would turn out to be. He campaigned as a war hero, but in fact had worked as an intelligence officer; his limp was caused not by "ten pounds of shrapnel" in his leg but by slipping and falling while running a gauntlet of paddle-wielding sailors during a navy hazing ceremony. In 1946, he was elected to the Senate from Wisconsin. Looking for a way to make his name, McCarthy took up the "Communists in government" theme. In an infamous speech in Wheeling, West Virginia, in February 1950, he waved a piece of paper and claimed to have a list of 205 Communists working in the State Department. Only a year after the "loss" of China to Communism, McCarthy decried the "egg-sucking liberals" whose "pitiful squealing . . . would hold sacrosanct those Communists and queers" in the State Department who had sold China into "atheistic slavery."

Republicans supported McCarthy as long as he targeted Democrats. McCarthy's political tastes became more nonpartisan after his reelection in 1952, however. In 1953, he was named chairman of the Senate Committee on Government Operations, which included the Senate Permanent Subcommittee on Investigations. McCarthy appointed two lawyers, Roy Cohn and 27-year old Robert F. Kennedy, as counsel to the subcommittee. The subcommittee investigated allegations of Communist influence in the Voice of America (VOA) radio network, which was administered by the State Department's United States Information Agency (USIA). Questioned on live television, before packed galleries, VOA personnel were subjected to false accusations and hostile innuendo by McCarthy and his lawyers. Roy Cohn toured the overseas libraries sponsored by the USIA, looking for subversive books written by Communists, fellow-travelers, or "controversial persons."

In the fall of 1953, the committee opened an investigation into the United States Army. Republican president Dwight Eisenhower, who had come to his position directly from his seat as first supreme commander of NATO, was unsympathetic to McCarthy's latest witch-hunt, particularly after the committee mistreated Brigadier General Ralph W. Zwicker, a WWII battlefield hero. The hearings, broadcast on live television for 36 days, culminated in a dramatic confrontation between McCarthy and Joseph Welch, the chief lawyer for the army, after McCarthy attacked a young lawyer in Welch's Boston firm for his membership in the National Lawyers Guild, which Attorney General Herbert Brownell Jr. had called "the legal mouthpiece of the Communist Party." "Have you no decency, sir, at long last?" shouted Welch. "Have you left no sense of decency?" It was as if a fever broke. The gallery erupted in applause and a recess was called. The hearings were inconclusive, and in December 1954 the Senate voted to censure their colleague from Wisconsin.

Joseph McCarthy was not the only person to practice "McCarthyism" during these Cold War years. Most Americans did the job for themselves, every time they paused before reading a book, or going to a meeting (of, say, the National Lawyers Guild), or signing a petition. Edward R. Murrow, a pioneer in broadcast journalism and a clear-headed observer of politics, summarized McCarthy this way:

His primary achievement has been in confusing the public mind, as between the internal and the external threats of Communism. We must not confuse dissent with disloyalty. We must remember always that accusation is not proof and that conviction depends upon evidence and due process of law. . . . We cannot defend freedom abroad by deserting it at home. The actions of the junior Senator from Wisconsin have caused alarm and dismay amongst our allies abroad, and given considerable comfort to our enemies. And whose fault is that? Not really his. He didn't create this situation of fear; he merely exploited it—and rather successfully.

The American Way of Life

The 1950s are often portrayed as orderly and smooth, a world where fathers ruled benignly, women spent their energy on their family, and children—and racial minorities—knew their place. But it was not so simple. Keeping track of the generations helps clarify things. Men who were between the ages of 20 and 45 in 1955 had likely seen service in either WWII or Korea. The 20-year-old antiwar activists of 1968 spent their school days learning how to "duck and cover" in case of atomic attack. Events like the polio "plague season" of 1952, during which a record 21,000 people suffered permanent paralysis and 3,000 died, and the explosion that same year of the first hydrogen bomb, which was far more powerful than the bombs dropped on Hiroshima and Nagasaki, contributed to a growing sense of dread. Essayist James Thurber thought America had become a "jumpy" nation, "afflicted with night terrors," perched not on the brink of war but on "the Brink of Was"—of extinction.

THE CONSUMERS' REPUBLIC

Americans linked their roles as consumers and citizens repeatedly in the first half of the twentieth century by putting the market power of the buyer to work politically. Sometimes these citizen-consumers fought for consumer and worker safety through government regulation and inspection; sometimes they used their collective buying power to advance political goals, as in African Americans' antisegregation "don't buy where you can't work" boycotts in the 1930s. After WWII, a new ideal emerged of the purchaser as citizen. As *Life* magazine put it, mass consumption was a civic responsibility designed to provide "full employment and improved living standards for the rest of the nation." The integration of citizenship and consumption in the new Consumers' Republic left its mark on many aspects of postwar American life, including its class structure, its race politics, its gender dynamics, and the ways people related to the government.

Between 1945 and 1960, the gross national product (GNP) nearly doubled, the median family income rose from $3,083 to $5,657, and real wages rose by almost 30 percent. This remarkable prosperity was fueled by a dramatic increase in consumer spending. The purchasing frenzy was not simply the result of pent-up desire, or a response to the "baby boom" that began as soon as the first wave of GIs came home. Spending money was good for America, and it was government policy. In 1950, President Truman insisted that "the uses of the powers of Government to achieve a higher living standard and a fair deal for all the people is not statism and it is not socialism. It is part of the American tradition." In 1958, the editor of *Fortune* magazine drew the obvious conclusion using the familiar Cold War vocabulary. "Thrift is now un-American," he proclaimed.

Before the 1950s, most Americans saved up for major purchases or bought them through installment plans. Before the war, there were gas and retail store charge cards, but third-party universal cards were an innovation of the 1950s. The first was Diner's Club in 1949. American Express, Bank of America, and Chase Manhattan followed in 1958. This "democratization of credit" made it much easier for middle-class Americans to accumulate both consumer goods and debt. Total private debt more than doubled during the 1950s, from $104.8 billion to $263.3 billion, facilitating the purchase of, among other things, 56 million automobiles, 50 million televisions, and 143 million radios.

In addition to credit expansion, government spending fueled economic growth. Apart from military spending, the most important federal investment in the economy took place via the GI Bill, which helped 16 million servicemen and women restart their lives through three key benefits: unemployment insurance, which expanded purchasing power even in a moment of high unemployment; tuition for further education or training, which injected capital into higher education; and loans to purchase land or homes or to start a business, which supported both banks and the housing industry. One-fifth of all single-family residences built between 1945 and 1960 were financed by GI Bill mortgages. Most of these homes were built in the new suburbs sprouting up on the edge of cities.

FLUSHING TOGETHER

Architectural conformism and social like-mindedness were intrinsic to the new planned communities, with their single-family homes, lawns, and driveways. So was racial homogeneity. After *Shelley v. Kramer* in 1948, municipal governments could not enforce residential covenants forbidding home sales to racial and religious minorities. No worries: realtors did the job for them. The ethics code of the National Association of Real Estate Boards, which did not allow black members, specified that a realtor "should never be instrumental in introducing to a neighborhood . . . any individual whose presence will be clearly detrimental to property values. . . . No matter what the motive or character of the would-be purchaser." By 1970, America's suburban population was 95 percent white.

In addition to being white, suburbanites were mostly Protestant, young, and married with children. After a post-1945 spike in which hasty wartime marriages were dissolved, the divorce rate ebbed before surging in the 1960s. Reversing a trend of a hundred years, Americans married younger in the postwar years. Between 1940 and 1955, the United States' population grew 27 percent, from 130 million to 165 million. *Life* magazine called children the "Built-in Recession Cure," concluding that this massive generation soon tagged the "baby boomers" would drive consumer design, production, and advertisement, and constantly renew postwar prosperity.

During WWII, American women had helped build battleships and aircraft carriers. Now they were told by *Life* magazine that "of all the accomplishments of the American woman, the one she brings off with the most spectacular success is having babies." The rigidity of middle-class gender norms of the mid-1950s left little wiggle room for enterprising women, who found themselves contained in the home. Wives were advised to forget their own preferences. In 1950, a trustee of Barnard College—the women's arm of Columbia University—called on educated women to announce "that no job is more exacting, more necessary, or more rewarding than that of housewife and mother."

What did all these stay-at-home suburban mothers do with their time? In addition to caring for the children and the house, mothers joined and ran clubs, served on the school PTA, led Girl Scout troops, played bridge, gardened, joined local political movements, and sometimes started their own. And they drove. They drove to the new suburban malls that lured shoppers away from downtown department stores with one-stop shopping and massive parking lots (why parallel park a 207-inch-long Buick Roadmaster sedan when there was an attractive alternative?). Women drove from suburb to city, from suburb to suburb, on the new roads created by the Highways Act of 1956, whose 41,000 miles of highway connected the new communities and also, not incidentally, connected the East Coast with the remote locations in the hinterland where atomic weapons were stockpiled.

If the 1950s were conformist, it is in part because television set a common standard for Americans north, south, east, and west to observe and emulate. Radio languished after 1950. Who wanted to listen to a baseball game when the World Series was on live TV? The minority of Americans who did not own a television set by 1960 could always cluster around the windows of the nearest appliance store. Attendance at movies and nightclubs plummeted. Not only did television influence political beliefs and expose millions of people to the same joke at the same time; it shaped their personal habits. Millions of toilets flushed simultaneously during the commercial breaks of the most popular live TV shows. *E pluribus unum*, indeed!

"HORROR IN THE NURSERY"

In 1952, between 80 and 100 million comic books were sold every week in the United States, and the average issue was passed along to six or more readers. A third of those comic books were horror comics with titles like *Chamber of Chills* and *Tales from the Crypt*. Most of the rest were crime comics, or romance, plus *Donald Duck* and *Archie*. In the early 1950s, comic books reached more people than magazines, radio, or television did. Most of those people were children.

In April 1954, a subcommittee of the Senate Judiciary Committee charged with investigating the causes of juvenile delinquency put comic books on the stand. The star witness for the prosecution was Dr. Fredric Wertham, a psychiatrist whose best-selling book, *Seduction of the Innocents*, argued that comic books taught children racism and sadism. Comic books, intoned Dr. Wertham, were "definitely harmful to impressionable people," and who could be more impressionable than children? He condemned *Wonder Woman* as sadomasochistic and *Batman* as homoerotic, and linked violent comics with rising levels of juvenile crime. William Gaines, the publisher of a number of horror comics and, later, *Mad* magazine, defended the industry as being in good taste. Gaines was skewered by Tennessee senator Estes Kefauver, the grandstanding committee chairman, who questioned Gaines about an issue of *Crime SuspenStories*:

> KEFAUVER: Here is your May 22 issue. This seems to be a man with a bloody axe holding a woman's head up which has been severed from her body. Do you think that is in good taste?
>
> GAINES: Yes, sir, I do, for the cover of a horror comic. A cover in bad taste, for example, might be defined as holding the head a little higher so that the neck could be seen dripping blood from it, and moving the body over a little further so that the neck of the body could be seen to be bloody.
>
> KEFAUVER: You have blood coming out of her mouth.
>
> GAINES: A little.

By November 1954, 70 percent of Americans believed that comic books were a cause of juvenile crime. A dozen states passed laws restricting the sale of comic books. There were public comic book burnings. Rather than give comics the equivalent of a motion picture R rating, the Comics Magazine Association of America imposed an extremely restrictive code of standards that put most comic books out of business. When comics came back in the 1960s, they featured superheroes—Spider Man, the Green Lantern, the Incredible Hulk. "It was a bad time to be weird," one artist recalled later. "You were either a Communist or a juvenile delinquent."

The line dividing the comics' advocates and opponents was generational, not geographic. This was not the heartland rising up against the coastal cultural elites. When William Gaines defended gory comics as being in good taste, he offended not only parents but also the presumed custodians of good taste. Rather than protect the young from the wider culture, comics' critics sought to protect the wider culture *from* the young—to contain the influence of youth-based commercial culture.

The culture wars of the 1950s and 1960s are usually seen as rooted in rock and roll music, but this is not quite true. There *was* something subversive to comic books, with their gangsters and their supersexy (if headless) women. Rock and roll did not provide its own opening act. Chuck Berry and Elvis Presley added the soundtrack to a scene drawn in comic books. And then they turned up the volume.

GOOD ROCKIN' TONIGHT

In 1950 Americans purchased 189 million records. By the end of the decade that number hit 600 million. Teenagers accounted for nearly 70 percent of all record sales. Parents could complain about the "jungle rhythms" of the new music, the creeping Negrophilia of rock and roll, but record producers knew who their audience was: the largest generation of teenagers ever seen, with the greatest purchasing power of American adolescents in history.

In August 1953, one of those teenagers walked into the offices of Sun Records in Memphis, Tennessee, and asked to buy enough minutes of studio time to make a recording. Born in Tupelo, Mississippi, in 1935, Elvis Aaron Presley moved with his parents to Memphis when he was 13 years old. Neither prosperous nor ever quite respectable, Elvis's family straddled the margins of the color line in the postwar South. Elvis lived in a middle-class neighborhood in Memphis, but in a *black* middle-class neighborhood. There he listened to "race music" and hung out on Beale Street, the hub of Memphis's thriving blues scene. By his senior year in high school, Elvis dressed in the flashy clothes sold by Lansky Brothers, a Beale Street store that catered to black clientele. There were other fashion peculiarities: Elvis grew out his sideburns and styled his hair with rose oil and Vaseline. He wore mascara and eyeliner.

Sun Records was owned by a white native Alabaman, Sam Phillips, who was smitten with the blues. Phillips was one of the few southern whites who would record African American musicians, and he recorded some of the very best: B. B. King, Howlin' Wolf, Junior Parker. When 18-year-old Elvis Presley showed up wanting to sing, Phillips was intrigued. It was another year before Presley recorded his rockabilly hits "That's All Right, Mama" and "Blue Moon of Kentucky," and a bit longer still before the radio stations would play him: he sounded too black for the white stations, and the black stations thought he sounded too much like a hillbilly.

Having bled comics dry in the early 1950s, the national press concerned with juvenile delinquency and morality feasted on Elvis Presley in the late 1950s. Reporters' critique had less to do with the songs Elvis sang than with his onstage performance, and his effect on his audiences. Cultural critics denounced his act as "strip-tease with clothes on" that left youngsters convulsive. Suddenly everything was blamed on "Elvis the Pelvis," as he was nicknamed for his habit of leading with his crotch when he danced. Juvenile delinquency, the breakdown of morality and cultural values, race mixing, irreligion: all were blamed on the mild-mannered and unfailingly polite young man from Memphis.

Raised smack-dab on the color line, Elvis Presley embodied the cultural hybridity that characterized many parts of the South. Like many white southerners, Elvis spent his youth surrounded by African Americans: at the Assembly of God church he attended in Mississippi, where he learned to love gospel music; in his neighborhood in Memphis; on Beale Street and on the radio he listened to at night. If he had closed himself to the black culture all around him, Elvis would never have made the music he did. Years later, Sam Phillips was still amazed by Elvis's openness to the world. "The lack of [racial] prejudice on the part of Elvis Presley had to be one of the biggest things that ever could have happened to us. . . . It was almost subversive, sneaking around through the music—but we hit things a little bit, don't you think? I went out into this no-man's land, and I knocked the shit out of the color line."

*

The immediate postwar years in the United States were prosperous economically but politically tumultuous. The period 1946 to 1953 was characterized by boundary marking: Communist versus non-Communist, "loyal" versus "disloyal," conformist versus contrarian. In 1949, University of Chicago president Robert Maynard Hutchins, an outspoken defender of freedom of thought and expression, addressed the question of ideological conformity and government censorship in an early test of government assaults on the First Amendment. Testifying before a committee of the Illinois state legislature, Hutchins's exchange with committee counsel J. B. Matthews demonstrated the danger of employing totalitarian techniques in the interest of protecting a democracy:

MATTHEWS: Do you recall the manner in which President Truman characterized Communist Party members when he was asked about it?
HUTCHINS: I do.
MATTHEWS: His statement was that they are all traitors.
HUTCHINS: I recall his statement.

MATTHEWS: Do you concur with the President?
HUTCHINS: Am I required to?

Hutchins's sarcastic question went to the heart of early Cold War America. The question of whether individuals or groups or even states had an obligation to concur with the executive branch would be raised over and over again in the coming years. Did the South have to abide by Supreme Court decisions on civil rights? With whom did war powers reside—Congress or the president? Were young people obliged to agree with their elders, or was it their responsibility to question authority? Were the agencies created by NSC-68, especially the CIA, answerable to anyone beyond themselves? Were private citizens required to obey segregations laws? By 1953, when Sam Phillips recorded Elvis Presley, the war had been over for eight years—but it seemed like the world just got scarier and scarier.

FIGURE 8. Members of the Congress of Racial Equality participate in a protest at Woolworth's lunch counter on September 9, 1960. *Left to right*: Jerome Smith, Ruth Despenza, Joyce Taylor, Hugh Murray Jr., Archie Alen, and William Harrell. Photo by Ralph Uribe. Courtesy of The Times-Picayune Archive and Barcroft Media.

CHAPTER 8

At Odds, 1954–1965

Earl Warren was no stranger to racial discrimination. As attorney general of California, he presided in 1942 over the forced relocation of thousands of Japanese Americans considered a wartime security risk on the coast. As governor, he saw the Ku Klux Klan blossom in areas newly populated by African American war workers. But he was also well-acquainted with arguments against racism, many of which were articulated most forcefully in his home state. Following a successful lawsuit brought by the League of United Latin American Citizens (LULAC) in 1947, Warren oversaw the desegregation of California public schools. In 1948, the Republican governor observed that the sky did not fall when the California Supreme Court declared that racially restrictive marriage laws, which in California and 30 other states prohibited marriages between "whites" and "nonwhites," served no public good and were an unconstitutional infringement on the fundamental rights of citizens.

After coming within inches of the vice presidential mansion as Thomas Dewey's running mate in 1948, Warren was serving an unprecedented third term as governor of the nation's most racially heterogeneous state when President Dwight Eisenhower appointed him chief justice of the Supreme Court in October 1953. The new chief justice was confronted immediately with the most incendiary question in American politics: the race question. Five separate NAACP-sponsored school desegregation cases from four states and the District of Columbia were already on the court's docket when Warren arrived in Washington.

The Supreme Court had not ruled on a racial discrimination case since 1948, but a 20-year string of NAACP antidiscrimination victories marked a clear legal trajectory. Fractured along personal and political lines, the court was divided between those who considered segregation "Hitler's creed" (in the words of Justice Robert Jackson, who had prosecuted leading Nazis at the Nuremberg trials after World War II) and those who were unprepared to impose a social revolution on the South. Patient, polite, and aware of popular support for racial segregation in public life, Warren worked assiduously to find the judicial common ground in which to root a unanimous opinion.

The opinion in *Brown v. Board of Education of Topeka, Kansas* (after 10-year-old Linda Brown, the plaintiff whose name came first alphabetically) was written by Warren and delivered by him on behalf of a unanimous court on May 17, 1954. The ruling itself was short and to the point. It was the opinion of the court "that in the field of public education the [*Plessy*] doctrine of 'separate but equal' has no place. Separate educational facilities are inherently unequal." Sidestepping the implementation question entirely, the chief justice explained that the court would consult with southern state attorneys general about compliance. These consultations informed the court's vague implementation decision a year later, known as *Brown II*, which directed local authorities to move with "all deliberate speed" toward the goal of desegregated public schools.

The *Brown* decision did not override *Plessy v. Ferguson* or herald the downfall of Jim Crow. It did not destroy the legal basis for racial segregation: that would not happen until 1967, when the Supreme Court, still led by Earl Warren, declared racially restrictive marriage laws unconstitutional. It did not mark the beginning of a mass movement for civil rights—that movement's roots went back to the interracial organizations of the 1930s and the voting rights challenges of the 1940s. The decision did, however, highlight the potentially revolutionary role of the judiciary in setting the boundaries of public life, and it revived old debates about the proper relation of federal power to state power. Responses to the ruling spanned the spectrum from violent resistance to prayerful compliance, and revealed deep divisions among Americans about the definition of equal citizenship, the capacity and will of the nation to live up to its core principles, and the role of the judiciary in a republic of laws. Taunted by the Soviet Union and its allies for the deep inequities that continued to mar the American republic and challenged by civil rights activists to overcome them, Americans were forced to confront their own conflicting values and desires.

A Nation of Men or of Laws? Responses to *Brown*

Announcing the *Brown* decision was one thing. Enforcing it was another. Both the court and the NAACP underestimated the cost that white southerners would pay to maintain segregation. Rather than concede the sovereignty of the Supreme Court in matters relating to the Constitution, some white southerners declared war on the court. Others, however, spotted the flexibility of the court's ruling in *Brown II* and worked to resist desegregation legally. The tokenism and foot-dragging achieved via "minimum compliance" with the court's implementation decree in *Brown II* ultimately proved a more viable way to protect white supremacy than violent resistance.

MASSIVE RESISTANCE

White southerners did not all react to *Brown* the same way. Just two weeks after *Brown*'s announcement, the 10,000 messengers of the Southern Baptist Convention endorsed the Supreme Court's decision, proclaiming it "in harmony with the constitutional guarantee of equal freedom to all citizens, and with the Christian principles of equal justice and love for all men." The Presbyterians, Methodists, and Catholics quickly followed suit. In Baltimore, officials implemented a desegregation plan they had drawn up in advance. The city's Catholic archdiocese, whose privately funded schools were unaffected by *Brown*, took a preemptive stance against white flight to parochial schools by announcing its intention to follow the ruling.

Desegregation proceeded largely without incident in the North and the West, although the number of nonwhite children to enter previously all-white schools remained miniscule until the mid-1960s. The Upper South (Delaware, Maryland, West Virginia, Tennessee, and Arkansas) followed a similar trajectory, particularly in cities. Most of west Texas desegregated peacefully after 1955, as did North Carolina and southern Missouri.

Had all the public officials sworn to uphold the law actually done so, this pattern might have held true across the entire nation. But they did not, and the resigned submission of law-abiding white southerners proved no match for the organized passion of their more combustive neighbors. Many southern politicians and journalists denounced what they called the "activism" of the Supreme Court. Mississippi senator James Eastland, who chaired the Senate Judiciary Committee's subcommittee on civil rights, warned that the South would not "abide by or obey this legislative decision by a political court." The court's vague directive in *Brown II* (1955) mollified no one.

In the spring of 1956, 82 of 106 southern congressmen and every southern senator except Lyndon B. Johnson of Texas and Albert Gore and Estes Kefauver of Tennessee (all three of whom had national political ambitions) signed what its Senate sponsors Strom Thurmond and Richard Russell called the "Southern Manifesto." The manifesto denounced the *Brown* decision as a "clear abuse of judicial power" and called for white southerners to resist by "any lawful means" what it labeled "forced integration."

Southerners responded enthusiastically to this invitation to what Virginia Democrat Harry Byrd dubbed "massive resistance." In the Mississippi Delta, where the first White Citizens' Council organizations were formed to forestall implementation of the *Brown* decision, whites waged an economic war of attrition against African American parents who had filed desegregation petitions with local school boards by boycotting black-owned businesses and firing employees who dared assert their rights. The Mississippi legislature created the State Sovereignty Commission, a secret police force designed to "prevent encroachment upon the rights of this and other states by the Federal Government." In a deliberate effort to tie up the NAACP in court, Mississippi and other states abolished mandatory school attendance laws.

Given a green light by Congress, other states refused to enforce *Brown*. Alienating almost as many white parents as black ones, Virginia closed any public school ordered to desegregate (the state bought off the white parents by offering to pay their children's tuition at segregated private schools). Playing to the masses, South Carolina and Alabama adorned their state capitols with the Confederate battle flag, which had not flown atop a government building for 90 years. Georgia incorporated the stars and bars into its state flag. Vacillating, white southern self-denominated "moderates" stood by helplessly through it all, prompting journalist Carl Rowan to ask, "For what are the 'moderates'? Are they moderately *for* or *against* compliance with the United States Supreme Court's decision?"

VIOLENCE

The Eisenhower administration's reluctance to intervene as southern state governments encouraged defiance of federal law emboldened more extreme defenders of racial hierarchy and oppression in the South. Reviving tactics used against black voter registration drives in the late 1940s, white supremacists in the Deep South turned to violence to protect their privileged way of life. Between May and August 1955, three black political leaders were gunned down in the Mississippi Delta. Two, the Reverend George Lee, an NAACP activist, and Lamar Smith, a farmer and WWII veteran active in voter registration efforts, were killed; a third, Gus Courts, a grocer and NAACP member, recovered from his wounds and fled the state.

Mississippi's reign of terror might have passed unnoticed by the rest of America had half brothers Roy Bryant and J. W. Milam not decided to punish 14-year-old Emmett Till after he offended Bryant's 22-year-old wife, Carolyn. A summer visitor from Chicago, Till was unfamiliar with the elaborate social rules of Jim Crow Mississippi. Bryant and Milam did not intend to kill Emmett when they carried him away in the back of their pickup truck from the home of his great-uncle, sharecropper Moses Wright. But Till's defiance sealed his fate. Enraged, Bryant and Milam beat the teenager brutally before executing him with a shot to the head. Then they tied a fan from an old cotton gin to Till's body and threw him into the Tallahatchie River. His decomposing body surfaced three days later.

Emmett's mother, Mamie Till, was determined to impart meaning to her only son's death. Insisting that Emmett's body be sent by train to Chicago rather than buried in Mississippi, Mamie staged an open-casket funeral attended by 50,000 grim-faced black Chicagoans. In September, *Jet*, a leading African American magazine, brought southern violence before the eyes of the entire country when it published sickening photographs of Till's mutilated corpse.

Milam and Bryant's trial put tiny Sumner, Mississippi, on the world stage, as nearly 100 newspaper reporters and television crews crowded into the courtroom. The determination of Mississippi's political establishment to protect the reputation of their state by providing a fair trial was undermined by the claim of the local sheriff that the killing was an NAACP plot and by the defense lawyer's challenge to the jury to summon their Anglo-Saxon courage and acquit the defendants. They did. Free men and immune from further prosecution, Milam and Bryant sold their story to *Look* magazine in early 1956 and admitted that they had, in fact, killed Emmett Till.

Of all the causes offered for the blossoming of civil rights activism after 1955, one—rage—is often overlooked. After the *Brown* decision, angry and defensive white southerners reacted more decisively to black behavior that challenged racial norms. Rather than intimidating black southerners, however, white aggression convinced many people who had never before participated in civil rights protest to push back against white oppression and discrimination. People were frightened, but they were also galvanized. Young African Americans as diverse as Mississippian Anne Moody, who was horrified by the murder of someone her own age in her home state, and Black Panthers leader Eldridge Cleaver, who was enraged by the lynching of black males for perceived violation of white womanhood, found themselves propelled toward activism by the murder of Emmett Till and the acquittal of his killers by an all-white, all-male Mississippi jury. As Till's great-uncle Moses Wright concluded in 1956, "What happened down there last year is going to help us all."

THE MONTGOMERY BUS BOYCOTT

Rosa Parks's refusal to surrender a bus seat to a white rider on Thursday, December 1, 1955, marked the culmination, not the beginning, of her civil rights activism. In the 1930s, the seamstress and her husband, Raymond, hosted Voters League meetings and raised money for the defense of the Scottsboro Boys, nine young men accused falsely of rape in Alabama. In 1944, Parks organized the Committee for Equal Justice, which brought attention to the rape of black women by white men and demanded their arrest and prosecution. By 1955, Parks had been Secretary of the Montgomery branch of the NAACP for more than a decade, where she worked alongside E. D. Nixon, who was president of the Alabama NAACP and head of the local Brotherhood of Sleeping Car Porters. Parks's later explanation of her action on the bus—"I felt it was just something I had to do"—obscured, perhaps intentionally, the organization that both preceded and transformed her one-woman sit-down strike into something larger.

While Parks waited to be bailed out of jail, her colleagues in the Montgomery Women's Political Council (WPC) called for a one-day boycott of city busses by African American patrons to protest Parks's arrest. The following Monday, the busses ran empty, their usual occupants packed into private automobiles or walking purposefully down the sidewalk. The hastily organized Montgomery Improvement Association (MIA) called a mass meeting that evening to test community support for a continued boycott. An overflow crowd at Holt Street

Baptist Church sang, prayed, and listened spellbound to the speech of a 26-year-old newcomer to town, the Reverend Martin Luther King Jr.

King cast the boycott as both patriotic and Christian. Observing that "we couldn't do this" in a Communist dictatorship, he declared the constitutional right to protest "the great glory of American democracy" and exhorted his listeners to "keep God in the forefront. Let us be Christian in all of our actions." King affirmed the crowd's primary identity as American citizens "determined to apply our citizenship to the fullness of its meaning," and he called on the nation to live up to its democratic promise. Tying the boycott to the *Brown* decision, King then connected both to divine authority. "If we are wrong," he thundered, "then the Supreme Court of this nation is wrong. If we are wrong, the Constitution of the United States is wrong. If we are wrong, God Almighty is wrong."

In the beginning, the MIA's goals were modest: black riders wanted to be treated courteously by bus drivers, have black drivers on routes through black neighborhoods, and have seats distributed on a "first come, first served" basis, with blacks filling the bus from rear to front and whites from front to rear. The city refused. With the backing of the NAACP, the MIA challenged the segregated bus laws. In June 1956, a three-judge federal court ruled in *Browder v. Gayle* that city and state bus segregation statutes were unconstitutional. The Supreme Court upheld the decision in November. Montgomery's African Americans returned to the buses in December and sat where they liked.

If Montgomery's buses were integrated by court order and not as a result of the boycott, did the boycott really matter? It did, for organizational and tactical reasons. Rather than being led by the NAACP, the boycott was organized by Montgomery's black workingwomen and their ministers. Shortly after the boycott, King and other preacher-politicians founded the Southern Christian Leadership Conference, which combined basic Christian tenets like the "beloved community" of believers with a commitment to social and political equality. Rooted in the South, the SCLC nevertheless benefited tremendously from the advice and support of northern-based campaigners for social justice such as Ella Baker and Bayard Rustin, whose institutional memory included the CIO's dramatic sit-down strikes of the 1930s, the mass media campaign for the Scottsboro Boys, and the March on Washington Movement during WWII. When it came time to roll, the SCLC would not have to reinvent the wheel.

TROUBLE IN LITTLE ROCK

The "Southern Manifesto," which damned the Supreme Court school decisions as encroachments on "the reserved rights of the States and the people," complicated the lives of southern governors, who had to bring their states into compliance with federal law. If Congress could defy the court, why couldn't governors? Was it not true, as states' rights advocates argued, that "a sovereign state is immune to federal court orders?"

The Upper South city of Little Rock, Arkansas, was an unexpected location for the first showdown between the federal government and a southern governor over desegregation. Governor Orval E. Faubus was prepared to stand by while Little Rock implemented its school desegregation plan, which called for "the least amount of integration over the longest period." However, under pressure from parents and anti-integration civic associations emboldened by the defiance of many southern lawmakers, Faubus capitulated.

Nine African American students had been chosen to integrate Central High School on September 4, 1957. The six girls and three boys were prevented from entering the school by a threatening mob of white Arkansans on one side and the Arkansas National Guard on the other. Had the guardsmen let the black students inside the school, there would have been no constitutional crisis. But when the National Guard turned away the Little Rock Nine, it preserved the peace while maintaining segregation, in defiance of federal authority.

Republican president Dwight D. Eisenhower, elected in 1952, refused to exert pressure on southern elected officials to enforce the *Brown* decision. Eisenhower's disclaimer "I don't believe you can change the hearts of men with laws or decisions" encouraged segregationists and enraged southern moderates like Faubus, who were responsible for enforcing the new, deeply unpopular law. The president was also frustrated. What was he supposed to do? Send in the army to enforce the orders of a federal court?

On September 24, 1957, Eisenhower authorized the army to subdue a mob and dispatched the 101st Airborne Division to Little Rock. That evening, the president addressed the nation on television. When local government refuses to uphold the rule of law, Eisenhower explained, "the President's responsibility is inescapable." Distancing himself from the court, Eisenhower explained, "Our personal opinions about the decision have no bearing on the matter of enforcement; the responsibility and authority of the Supreme Court to interpret the Constitution are very clear." It was the duty of Americans to set aside personal distaste and obey the law not only for its own sake, but to demonstrate "to the world that we are a nation in which laws, not men, are supreme."

Far from being a local issue, what happened in Little Rock concerned the entire nation and was of interest to the world. America's long-brewing domestic civil rights problem had become a foreign policy liability. "Our enemies are gloating over this incident and using it everywhere to misrepresent our whole nation," Eisenhower lamented. In addition to violating the nation's own principles of equality before the law, the United States was also revealing itself as "a violator of those standards of conduct which the peoples of the world united to proclaim in the Charter of the United Nations." Commanded once again by the general who had led the way to Berlin, the army now cleared the path for nine young Americans to claim their rights as guaranteed by the Constitution. Escorted into Central High on September 25, 1957, Minnijean Brown, one of the nine, said, "For the first time in my life I feel like an American citizen."

A Divided America in the Cold War Years

The distance between America's rhetoric about equality and the nation's intricate system of legal discrimination by race had long left the United States vulnerable to charges of hypocrisy by its own citizens and outsiders alike. For a nation that styled itself "the leader of the free world," it was no longer possible to ignore these charges. Increasingly, America's credibility as a world leader was tied to its treatment of its most vulnerable citizens at home. Although not an enthusiastic supporter of the Civil Rights Movement, President Eisenhower understood the connection between civil disturbance at home and America's image abroad. As he noted in his Little Rock speech in 1957, white southern disrespect for the law had damaged "the nation in the eyes of the world."

THE DANGERS OF A BIPOLAR WORLD

The domestic gap between democratic rhetoric and reality visible in places like Little Rock was matched and underscored by a parallel tendency in American foreign policy. In their efforts to uproot Communism, policymakers often had trouble separating political questions from economic questions. A totalitarian political system was clearly incompatible with democracy. In a bipolar political universe, it was easy to conceptualize economic systems as similarly opposed. Democratically elected regimes that favored protectionist or nationalizing economic policies were seen (rightly) as threats to American economic interests and thus (wrongly, or at least not necessarily) as threats to American foreign policy interests.

Political leaders could be enthusiastic about democracy and still resist market forms that favored European or American economic interests over their own national ones and support policies common in European social democracies, such as national health insurance. But such regimes were branded "Communist" by American intelligence agencies and conservative members of Congress.

Neither Guatemala's Jacobo Árbenz Guzmán nor Iran's Mohammad Mosaddegh were Communist dupes of Moscow. Both, however, had been elected after promising to reduce the control of foreign corporations over their nations' economies. Mosaddegh nationalized the British-controlled Anglo-Iranian Oil Company. Árbenz proposed a land-reform policy and seized more than 200,000 acres controlled by the American-owned United Fruit Company, the most profitable business in Guatemala. Branding Árbenz and Mosaddegh Communists, the newly created Central Intelligence Agency (CIA) organized military coups against both leaders in 1953 and 1954. In Iran, the United States installed the pro-western Shah Mohammad Reza Pahlavi. Árbenz was replaced in Guatemala by a right-wing military dictatorship that inaugurated a bloody campaign to annihilate the political Left. The relative ease with which the CIA engineered "regime change" in these early days of the Cold War encouraged a false sense of invincibility among American foreign policymakers while alienating nations that might have been allies.

During WWII, Franklin Roosevelt had been sympathetic to the calls of Vietnamese nationalists for an end to French colonial rule in Indochina (Vietnam). After the "fall" of China to Mao Zedong's Communists in 1949, however, the United States began to worry that the slightest push would cause the rest of Southeast Asia to topple like dominoes into the Communist camp. In 1954, the French, defeated by Vietnamese forces at the jungle fortress of Dien Bien Phu, signed the Geneva Accords, which called for popular elections in 1956. Refusing to reconcile itself to the possibility that Communists would win the day, the United States supported Ngo Dinh Diem, a corrupt but staunchly anti-Communist leader in the south of the country who refused to participate in the elections. This was not the first time the United States strapped itself to an unsavory leader whose only redeeming characteristic was an aversion to property redistribution, and it would not be the last; but in the case of Vietnam, the cost of first alliance and then intervention would be higher than anyone dreamed at the time.

The propensity of top American foreign policy analysts to see left-leaning nationalist movements in Asia, Africa, Latin America, and the Middle East as Soviet pawns severely limited US relations with much of the world in the 1950s and left a bitter aftertaste that persists. Both the USSR and the United States supported unsavory Third World surrogates in pursuit of superpower interests. But whereas the Soviets straightforwardly incorporated their satellites into an empire directed from Moscow, the United States promised its allies freedom and democracy—which is why the Americans, more than the Russians, were vulnerable to charges of hypocrisy when right-wing allies in Spain or Portugal or Chile crushed popular movements upholding democratic ideals.

BRINKSMANSHIP

Dwight Eisenhower, the former supreme commander of the Allied forces and NATO, came to the presidency well-equipped to manage foreign policy. Convinced of the superiority of American ideals of democracy and free enterprise and determined to counter Soviet expansion with American military might, Eisenhower was also a fiscal conservative determined to balance the budget. In pursuit of both agendas, he lowered defense spending by increasing the nuclear arsenal and cutting conventional troops and weapons. A new strategy of massive retaliation promised that any Soviet attack on an American ally would trigger a nuclear assault on the USSR.

Termed "brinksmanship" by its critics, after Secretary of State John Foster Dulles's apparent willingness to bring the world to the brink of nuclear war before settling differences diplomatically, Eisenhower's foreign policy did not comfort a nation already spooked by the addition of the hydrogen bomb (in 1952) to the arsenal of apocalyptic weapons. Educational films taught young Americans to "duck and cover" at the first sight of the blinding flash of a nuclear explosion, and school districts issued military-style necklaces, or dog tags, to identify their students' remains after a nuclear blast.

When the Soviet Union's team of WWII German rocket scientists beat America's team of WWII German rocket scientists and launched the first satellite in October 1957, Americans were shaken—so much so that the federal government poured money into higher education, and the gentlemen's agreement that had kept Jewish engineers out of high technology firms was ended. Sputnik reminded complacent Americans that the USSR was capable of producing more than vodka and bad chocolate. When asked what the USA would find on the moon should its rockets ever reach it, Edward Teller, the father of the hydrogen bomb, replied testily, "Russians."

One of the ways Americans differentiated their republic from the Union of Soviet Socialist Republics was by comparing the relationship between the government and the economy in each. In the USSR, the state and the economy were one. The United States, by contrast, was a land of free enterprise—free from coercive government regulation and planning. After peaking in World War II, the American government's presence in the economy increased as the Cold War got hotter. At the height of the New Deal, federal spending had reached 10.5 percent of the gross national product (GNP). For the period 1947-1960, it averaged 17.3 percent.

This worried President Eisenhower for two reasons. First, he was concerned that a permanent war economy based on an arms race would bankrupt the nation. He also feared that what he dubbed the "military-industrial-congressional complex" would erode free enterprise and make the USA more like the USSR by making American economic growth reliant on state spending for defense. Eisenhower's solution was to base America's defense on atomic weapons and limit government defense contracts. He scuttled NASA's expensive Apollo manned moon expeditions.

Eisenhower's successor John F. Kennedy reversed course in 1961. In the largest peacetime military buildup in the nation's history, Kennedy replaced Eisenhower's fiscally conservative defense strategy with $17 billion of military appropriations. This money supported universities as well as private businesses and resurrected the infant space program. This was all to the good for scientists, engineers, and entrepreneurs, but the existence of a battery of sophisticated new weapons begged for an opportunity to test them somewhere other than a laboratory.

SUPERPOWER CONFRONTATIONS IN
EUROPE AND THE MIDDLE EAST

Although he had something of a tin ear when it came to differentiating between Third World anticolonial nationalist movements and Communist conspiracies, Secretary of State John Foster Dulles was not wrong about the desire of Europeans living in "one-party peoples' states" to escape their new postwar Communist regimes. So many East Germans melted into West Berlin in the 1950s that their government threw up a wall to stop them in 1961. Radio Free Europe, broadcasting from Munich, encouraged the people to rise against the hated Soviets and promised Western help if they did. In 1956, Hungary tested America's capacity to live up to its own democratic rhetoric.

In late October 1956, rebellious Hungarians turned on their Soviet puppet government. The Kremlin sent in the Red Army to "restore order." This was a miscalculation: however much various factions of Hungarians hated each other, they were united in their loathing of the Soviets, who had occupied their country after WWII and effectively run it from Moscow ever since. Young Hungarian "freedom fighters" (as they called themselves), mainly students and workers but also some soldiers, were fearless and adept at blowing up tanks with Molotov cocktails. Amazingly, they ran the Soviets out of town. The new prime minister, Imre Nagy, told Soviet ambassador Yuri Andropov that Hungary would withdraw from the Warsaw Pact and sent a cable to the United Nations declaring his nation's new neutrality.

This was the moment American anti-Communists had been waiting for since 1945: an indigenous uprising against Soviet occupation. Surely the United States, backed by its NATO allies, would intervene, if not on the ground (for this was unlikely) then at the diplomatic level.

They might have done so had not England and France, with the aid of Israel, chosen exactly this moment to "liberate" the British-owned Suez Canal in Egypt from President Gamal Abdel Nasser, who had nationalized it some months previously. On October 29, 1956, Israeli forces invaded the Gaza Strip and the Sinai Peninsula, ostensibly to ferret out terrorists. At the same time, the British and French began bombing Egyptian air bases.

President Eisenhower was livid and came down on Nasser's side. Attention shifted from Budapest to Cairo. The USSR denounced the Western imperialist aggression and hinted that it might send troops to Egypt or use tactical nuclear weapons on its behalf. Rather than offend the Soviets by bringing up their conduct in Hungary, the United Nations hammered away at the British, French, and Israelis. No one came to the aid of the Hungarians when the Soviets returned on November 4, this time 500,000 strong, to reclaim their buffer zone against Germany. While the Americans voted, reelecting Eisenhower by a large majority, Budapest became a battleground. More than 100,000 Hungarians fled into the woods of Austria and Germany.

Other than providing regular doses of anti-Communist propaganda via Radio Free Europe, the United States played no role in bringing on the Hungarian Revolution, but America's inaction doomed it to failure. Confronted by two major crises involving the Soviets at once, Eisenhower capitulated, reversing British, French, and Israeli gains in Egypt, and making it clear that the United States would respect the Iron Curtain boundary line. Had there been no Suez crisis, the Soviet victory in Hungary might have been more limited. As it was, the United States upheld the sovereignty of "nonaligned" Egypt, whose army carried Soviet arms, and sacrificed a genuine anti-Communist revolt in the interest of maintaining the East-West balance of power in Europe.

The New Frontier

In his inauguration speech on January 20, 1961, President John F. Kennedy vowed to "pick up the torch of the American Revolution" and lead the nation into a "New Frontier" of international prominence and domestic prosperity. Over the course of the three years of Kennedy's presidency, which was cut short on November 22, 1963, by an assassin's bullet in Dallas, the assumptions and agenda of the president and his New Frontiersmen would be tested on all sides—by Cubans and their Soviet allies, by the need to provide for the common defense while still seeing to the day-to-day concerns of citizens at home, and by civil rights activists in hot pursuit of civic equality determined to enlist the power of the federal government for their cause.

JFK

Calm, composed, at ease in white tie and tails, John Fitzgerald Kennedy was the very definition of grace under pressure. Like the young president himself—the first born in the twentieth century—most of Kennedy's advisors came from privileged backgrounds, had elite edu-cations, and had served in World War II. (An accomplished sailor, Kennedy was a captain in the navy.) Both the war and the New Deal were living history for them and affected their approach to the future. "We were activists," one recalled. "We thought the world could be changed. We thought one man could make a difference."

When Kennedy entered the White House in January 1961, he was focused on external dangers to America, not internal challenges. His vision of the future was surprisingly bleak. America, he believed, was locked in a death grip with totalitarianism. His inaugural address, recalled for its soaring rhetoric of patriotic selflessness ("Ask not what your country can do for you; ask what you can do for your country"), was understood at the time as a battle cry against Communism. The "revolutionary beliefs" of liberty and freedom were threatened around the globe. "Let every nation know," declared the president, "that we shall pay *any* price, bear *any* burden, meet *any* hardship, support *any* friend, oppose *any* foe, in order to assure the survival and the success of liberty." Kennedy was even blunter in his first State of the Union address. "Each day we draw nearer to the hour of maximum danger," he told Congress. "The news will be worse before it is better."

The news was already bad. In January 1961, Soviet premier Nikita Khrushchev challenged America's bid for world leadership, announcing Soviet support for "wars of national liberation" across the globe. The poster child of Soviet success was Cuba, where Fidel Castro's Communist-led popular insurgency first overturned the rule of dictator Fulgencio Batista in 1959 and then embarrassed the United States by allying with the USSR. Despite his proximity to the United States, Castro posed little threat. The Cuba question was one of honor: Castro had to go.

The ensuing fiasco at the Bay of Pigs on April 17, 1961, where an uprising led by 1,400 CIA-trained Cuban exile troops was put down in two days, humiliated Kennedy, who had approved an invasion strategy that his own Joint Chiefs of Staff, who were not involved in the planning, thought had only a 30 percent chance of success. This was not the way to export democracy, or to encourage strategic alliances in the Southern Hemisphere, as Kennedy hoped to do through his Latin American Alliance for Progress initiative. The United States "looked like fools to our friends, rascals to our enemies, and incompetents to the rest," pronounced the *New York Times*.

Kennedy was embarrassed in Cuba when there was no spontaneous popular uprising in celebration of American ideals, as the invasion's promoters promised. This was nothing, however, compared to the massive numbers of people fleeing the new Soviet bloc nations. Between 1945 and 1950, 15 million people emigrated from Soviet-occupied Eastern Europe to the West. The 4.5 million East Germans who had left by 1961 represented 20 percent of that nation's population. The brain and labor drain damaged the economic viability of the state and the political credibility of East Germany's Communist rulers.

Two months before the Bay of Pigs debacle, Kennedy had suggested a diplomatic summit with Soviet premier Khrushchev. The two leaders met on June 1, 1961, in Vienna. At the top of the agenda was Berlin.

BERLIN AND CUBA

West Berlin held outsized symbolic importance for both sides in the Cold War. For America, Berlin represented Western determination not to capitulate further to Soviet territorial demands in Europe. For the Soviets, West Berlin was a magnet for miserable East Berliners and an enemy outpost in the espionage capital of the world.

In 1958, Khrushchev tried, and failed, to "normalize" divided Berlin by incorporating it completely into East Germany. In 1959, the Soviet leader raised the geopolitical temperature when he thundered that the USSR was "determined to liquidate" America's rights in West Berlin. "What good does it do you to have eleven thousand troops in Berlin?" he asked. "If it came to war, we would swallow them in one gulp. . . . West Germany knows that we could destroy it in ten minutes."

Kennedy was alarmed by Soviet threats to cut off access to West Berlin. When he returned home from Vienna, he called up US Army Reserve units and asked for an increase in military appropriations. In a speech in July, the president reaffirmed America's commitment to defend West Berlin. No fan of Eisenhower's position that he would rather be atomized than Communized, Kennedy encouraged his fellow Americans to build nuclear fallout shelters. (The Peace-O-Mind Shelter Company was happy to assist.) The Soviets backed off, but not before their East German satellite erected, within the space of 24 hours, a 100-mile concrete barrier topped with barbed wire that divided Berlin down the middle, and shut down the east–west migratory path. The Berlin Wall became the most visible landmark of the Cold War.

The most dangerous foreign policy crisis of the Kennedy administration, and arguably of the entire Cold War, occurred a year after the Vienna meeting, over the course of 13 days in October 1962. The Cuban missile crisis began when US intelligence reported that the Soviets had installed in Cuba offensive intermediate-range ballistic missiles (IRBMs) armed with nuclear warheads. Kennedy was convinced that this, too, was about Berlin—"What's basic to them is Berlin," the president said in a White House meeting—meaning that if the United States acted rashly in Cuba, Moscow would retaliate by taking Berlin. Resisting advice to attack before the missiles became operative, Kennedy instead announced a naval "quarantine" of Cuba to prevent the arrival of more weaponry. (A naval "blockade" would have been an act of war.) This "quarantine" brought the nuclear superpowers to the brink of war, where they teetered for several tense days until Khrushchev announced he would withdraw the missiles in exchange for an American vow not to invade Cuba. Kennedy agreed, and secretly promised as well to remove American missiles from Turkey, which bordered the Soviet Union.

The Cuban missile crisis brought home to all who lived through it, including the president, the heart-stopping danger of nuclear diplomacy. Cold warrior though he was, Kennedy was sobered by the callousness of military leaders who spoke of "winning" a nuclear exchange that would have killed millions of Russians and Americans. After the crisis, he changed his tone when speaking of the Eastern Bloc. Announcing that "no government or social system is so evil that its people must be considered as lacking in virtue," Kennedy began to explore ways to reduce tension with the USSR. In the summer of 1963, the two nations signed a treaty that banned testing nuclear weapons in the atmosphere, outer space, and underwater. Reflecting that "a journey of a thousand miles begins with a single step," the man who had warned Americans in 1960 that "to be an American in the next decade will be a hazardous experience" took the first step toward the relaxation of Cold War tensions.

ECONOMIC GROWTH AND ECONOMIC EQUITY

Flanked by a growing rebellion against Jim Crow and the still-smoking remains of the anti-Communist crusades of the 1950s, the Kennedy administration walked a narrow path in the center by avoiding conversations about fundamental beliefs and by concentrating on economic growth. Most of America's problems, said Kennedy, "are technical problems, are administrative problems. They are very sophisticated judgments which do not lend themselves to the great sort of 'passionate movements' which have stirred this country so often in the past." The New Frontiersmen saw no need to question their assumption that, as their seagoing president put it, "a rising tide lifts all boats": that economic expansion would create shared prosperity and, it followed, lessen economic inequality, which would, in turn, reduce social tension.

Economic growth was also an essential component of Cold War foreign policy. While suburban Americans worried about keeping up with their neighbors, the Kennedy administration worried about keeping up with the Soviets, who understood the connection between economic growth and geopolitical influence. Soviet leader Nikita Khrushchev had clarified the matter for any doubters in 1959: "Growth of industrial and agricultural production is the battering ram with which we shall smash the capitalist system, enhance the influence of the ideas of Marxism-Leninism, strengthen the Socialist camp and contribute to the victory of the cause of peace throughout the world."

The economic growth of the postwar years slowed noticeably and unemployment rose during the final years of Eisenhower's presidency. The Kennedy administration's first job was to rev up the economy, which it achieved by means of a variety of policy initiatives. The New Frontiersmen expanded demand through a massive tax cut, and stimulated investment via a tax credit for capital outlays on new machinery. They developed wage-price guidelines, talked business and labor into cooperating, and attacked unemployment by instituting programs to educate and retrain workers. They convinced Congress to raise the minimum wage. The results were little less than spectacular: between 1961 and 1965, gross national product, which had stalled under Eisenhower at 2 percent, increased at a rate above 5 percent per year. Employment grew by 2.5 percent per year, and the percentage of Americans living below the poverty line dropped from 22.4 percent in 1960 to 14.7 percent in 1966. Inflation hovered below 2 percent per year.

The Kennedy administration, and that of Kennedy's successor Lyndon B. Johnson, believed that economic growth would result in greater economic equity. It did, moderately. But income equality remained skewed. As economist Paul Samuelson described the disparities of wealth in America in 1970, "If we made an income pyramid out of a child's blocks, with each layer portraying $1000 of income, the peak would be far higher than the Eiffel Tower, but almost all of us would be within a yard of the ground." Many Americans, especially blacks, Native Americans, Hispanics, and the elderly, could have jumped off the pyramid without hurting themselves at all. Economic growth alone—expanding the pie—did not result in a more economically equitable society. That goal required tax reform as well as tax reductions, and government spending in the areas of education, health, housing, and urban renewal programs. Congress enacted some of Kennedy's domestic agenda—it approved the Area Redevelopment Act, which provided federal aid for impoverished regions such as Appalachia, and dedicated $4 billion for federally financed housing. But it declined to provide federal aid to education or finance an ambitious health care plan for the elderly, and it refused to use federal taxes as a way to redistribute income away from the wealthy and toward the poor.

THE WOMAN QUESTION

Racial minorities were not the only Americans who suffered from discrimination in politics, education, and the workplace. Women were excluded from nearly all elite colleges and universities. The best law and medical schools admitted a few but discouraged most from applying. Major corporations rarely hired female executives. Even the civil rights organizations relegated all but the most assertive women to the rear. A 1959 study of female academics explained that because women scholars remained "outside the prestige system," they could not succeed professionally, and concluded that "in the world of ideas, women simply do not count."

Undervalued in academe, educated women played an increasingly large role in the economy. Between 1940 and 1960, the percentage of women working outside the home doubled, from 15 percent to 30 percent. College-educated women were more likely to work than women who had not advanced in education beyond high school. The income brought home by workingwomen was crucial to achieving the middle-class lifestyle that was the goal of so many American families. It was often Mom's check that paid for that summer vacation and the children's college tuition.

At the same time that more women than ever were entering the paid workforce, the gap between men's and women's wages in America remained the highest in the industrial world. Median wages for women were less than half those for men. Prodded by Esther Peterson, the head of the Women's Bureau (a division of the US Labor Bureau), President Kennedy established the President's Commission on the

Status of Women (PCSW) in 1961. Chaired by Eleanor Roosevelt, the commission's charge was to develop recommendations for overcoming discrimination in employment on the basis of sex and to propose services that would make it easier for working mothers to do both their jobs well.

The PCSW's final report, published in 1963, proposed childcare tax benefits for lower-income women and improved maternity benefits for all. It mandated equal pay for equal work, demanded "equal opportunities" for hiring in private as well as in federal employment, and proposed expanding Social Security benefits to include female domestic and agricultural workers still uncovered by the Fair Labor Standards Act of 1938. The PCSW also called on states to repeal outdated laws that constricted women's citizenship rights by keeping them off juries or that limited their ability to control their own property. (This was no idle errand: various states continued to consider married women lacking in "legally recognized feelings or rights" through the 1970s, and as late as the 1980s, a Louisiana statute gave husbands exclusive control over joint property.)

In response to the PCSW, Congress passed the Equal Pay Act in 1963, which applied to women working in identical jobs as men. Title VII of the Civil Rights Act of 1964 prohibited employment discrimination based on sex as well as race, national origin, and religion. When the Equal Employment Opportunity Commission (EEOC), the federal agency charged with enforcing Title VII, failed to attend to women's complaints, a group of 16 delegates to the 1966 Third Annual Conference on the Status of Women formed the National Organization of Women (NOW). Modeled on the NAACP, NOW demanded "action to bring American women into full participation in the mainstream of American society now" and heralded a resurgence of feminism that would redefine the role of women in the Republic.

Civil Rights: The Next Generation

Ten months before John Kennedy's election, four college students launched a campaign of mass civil disobedience by sitting at a whites-only lunch counter in Greensboro, North Carolina. The sit-ins, which spread rapidly across the South, were both more spontaneous and more aggressive than the Montgomery bus boycott. Rather than *not* do something, the students *acted*: they took over public spaces from which they had been excluded. In the process they courted the ire of segregationists, some of whom spat on the protesters, poured ketchup on them, and ground out cigarettes on their backs. They also exposed themselves to the police, who arrested them for trespassing. Given what was still to come, this was mild abuse, but it indicated that the Civil Rights Movement had moved into a new phase of direct confrontation.

THE SIT-INS

On February 1, 1960, four students from North Carolina A&T, the state's leading African American college, sat down at the lunch counter of Woolworth's department store in Greensboro. Woolworth's counter, with its high swiveling stools, was a prominent site of white privilege, a place for white shoppers to relax and refuel in a store that accepted the dollars of black patrons but refused to serve them a cup of coffee. Informed by a black waitress that they could not be served, the students remained in their seats until the store closed, and they came back the next day. Soon other students joined them, including a few whites.

Activists elsewhere followed the Greensboro example; at least 70,000 people participated in sit-ins in over 100 cities in the winter and spring of 1960. Several thousand protesters were arrested, and violent counterdemonstrations—often pitting, in the words of the *Richmond News Leader*'s James Kilpatrick, himself no fan of black rights, "a ragtail rabble" of "slack-jawed, black-jacketed, grinning" white boys against colored students wearing suits and ties—made headlines around the world.

Like Montgomery's Rosa Parks, the young men who began the sit-in movement in Greensboro had deep roots in their local African American community. Two of the students belonged to an NAACP youth group started in 1943 by Ella Baker, who in 1960 was the national director of the association's youth wing. Some of their parents were members of the NAACP; others belonged to churches with an activist bent. All four had attended all-black Dudley High School, where civil rights was a daily topic of conversation.

Reluctant to endorse civil disobedience (it was a lawyer's job to get clients *out* of jail, not put them in, Thurgood Marshall remarked), the NAACP nonetheless provided bail money and legal advice and urged its members to support the sit-ins through consumer boycotts and picketing. White southerners, as ever, were divided. Many who had supported desegregation because it was the law of the land were troubled by violation of the law in the name of social justice. The SCLC was more concerned by what it interpreted, accurately, as a challenge to civil rights leadership by the rising generation. In April 1960, students meeting at Shaw University in Raleigh, North Carolina, formed the independent Student Non-Violent Coordinating Committee (SNCC, pronounced "Snick"). Like the SCLC, SNCC was southern and largely, although not exclusively, black. Unlike the SCLC (which the students criticized for its King-centered "cult of leadership"), SNCC developed a "group-centered leadership" grounded in democratic process and lack of hierarchy.

Most unlike the SCLC, SNCC's leadership cadre included women, among them Nashville's Diane Nash, an articulate and courageous opponent of Jim Crow. With the NAACP still manning the legal front, the SCLC and SNCC would together take the movement for equal rights for all to a new level of militant confrontation with proponents of racial hierarchy. Their confrontational tactics and their capacity to both attract and generate media attention would ultimately succeed in forcing the Kennedy administration to enter the fray on the side of the activists.

FREEDOM RIDERS AND OTHER DISTURBERS OF THE PEACE

The men and women who spent the 1960s working to achieve equal citizenship for all were motivated by many different impulses. Some, particularly older people who had served in or lived through World War II, were repulsed by the distance between the conditions of life in the South and America's professed democratic values. Others believed deeply in the human right of self-determination and brought to the American crusade lessons learned observing national liberation movements in colonial Africa and Asia. Still others were drawn to the movement by a sense of social justice that was often anchored in a profound commitment to the basic tenets of Christianity. All were convinced of the utility of direct action protests, as well as legal action, to challenge Jim Crow and his keepers.

Before the *Brown* decision and reactions to it stimulated a mass movement for racial equality in the South, civil rights activity was concentrated in northern and western cities that had significant African American populations. Campaigns to end racial discrimination in the 1940s and 1950s attracted a wide variety of Americans committed to the notion of equal citizenship for all. Quaker pacifists and followers of

Gandhi such as Bayard Rustin rubbed elbows with Christian socialists, labor activists, and Communists. Ideologically diverse, these activists shared a commitment to nonviolent direct action tactics such as boycotts, picketing, marches, and sit-ins. The most important of these organizations was the Congress of Racial Equality (CORE), founded in Chicago in 1942.

In May 1961, an integrated group of CORE workers embarked on a "freedom ride" through the South. Their aim was to draw a reluctant federal government into the civil rights struggle by testing a recent Supreme Court decision that barred segregation in facilities involved in interstate transit and, it was expected, by exposing southern noncompliance with federal law. The Freedom Riders were mauled by segregationists in Anniston, Alabama, and in Birmingham, where the commissioner of public safety Eugene "Bull" Connor allowed an armed mob to attack the riders free from police interference for precisely 15 minutes. They were further assaulted in Montgomery, where a Justice Department official sent to monitor the proceedings was knocked unconscious by a mob armed with clubs, chains, and iron bars.

Alabama's one-two punch on the rule of law and its federal representatives drew a reluctant Robert Kennedy into the fray, as CORE had intended. The attorney general instructed the Interstate Commerce Commission (ICC) to ban segregation and discrimination in interstate travel. At the same time, Kennedy implored civil rights leaders to back away from direct action tactics, which generated a public relations nightmare for JFK and American diplomats. Why not focus on something less confrontational, he asked, like voter registration? SNCC was glad to comply.

In the summer of 1961, Robert Parris Moses, a former high school mathematics teacher from New York, journeyed to Mississippi, where only 5 percent of eligible African American voters were registered. Moses was convinced by local civil rights leaders of three things: first, that white supremacy rested on disenfranchisement and only voters could break the back of Jim Crow; second, that a voter registration drive in the Deep South was as direct a challenge to white power as any sit-in; and third, that it would provoke an even more dramatic response from local whites than the Freedom Rides had in Alabama. As one rights worker put it, "If you went into Mississippi and talked about voter registration, they [were] going to hit you on the side of the head and that's about as direct as you can get."

This final assessment proved tragically accurate. Violence followed the SNCC workers as they fanned out across southwest Georgia and the Delta counties of Mississippi and Alabama. After only a few weeks of activity, four black churches in Georgia used as voter registration centers were firebombed. SNCC workers in Mississippi were arrested and beaten. Robert Zellner, a white Alabaman, nearly lost an eye when an assailant gouged it from its socket. Fannie Lou Hamer, a black Mississippian, suffered for the rest of her life from a brutal beating she received while in police custody. In a calculated warning to local blacks with civic ambition, E. H. Hurst, a member of the Mississippi state legislature, shot and killed local civil rights activist Herbert Lee, a farmer and WWII veteran.

President Kennedy was hesitant to bring the full power of the federal government to bear on Mississippi and elsewhere in the South. Influenced by white southern histories of Reconstruction that emphasized the futility of any attempt to enforce racial equality through federal imposition, the Kennedy administration insisted that southern state governments were responsible for keeping the peace and enforcing the law within their domain. In September 1962, JFK finally capitulated, like Eisenhower before him, to the necessity of backing up federal authority with military power when he called in the army after the integration of the University of Mississippi had degenerated into a riot that resulted in the deaths of two people.

BIRMINGHAM AND THE MARCH ON WASHINGTON

Even those dedicated to nonviolent direct action understood the power of photographic and television images of white mobs assaulting stoic young black people trying to ride a bus or register to vote or attend a state institution of higher learning. In the spring of 1963, Martin Luther King led a group to Birmingham, Alabama, to force a showdown against segregation in one of the most violently racist cities in America. The subsequent images of police chief "Bull" Connor's officers attacking young black men and women with batons, snarling police dogs, and high-pressure fire hoses shocked the world and embarrassed the United States. Criticized for pushing his agenda beyond the social breaking point, King's "Letter from Birmingham Jail," composed in April 1963 while serving a sentence for violating a state ban on protest marches, blasted the complacency of "whites of goodwill" and capitalized on the violence in the Deep South by declaring that the only alternative to civil disobedience was revolution.

This message was heard clearly in Washington, where both Kennedy brothers were increasingly involved in negotiating the civil rights struggle. While Robert Kennedy worked behind the scenes with Birmingham businessmen to defuse the local crisis and initiate a process of gradual desegregation, John Kennedy tried to convince Alabama governor George C. Wallace to allow the peaceful integration of the University of Alabama. When Wallace refused, and furthermore declared his undying commitment to upholding segregation now and forever, Kennedy came down finally and decisively on the side of the movement.

Faced with open defiance in Little Rock in 1957, President Eisenhower defined civil rights in terms of the law. In a televised speech on June 11, 1963, John Kennedy presented the civil rights struggle as a moral issue "as old as the scriptures and . . . as clear as the American Constitution." America had been founded "on the principle that all men are created equal, and that the rights of every man are diminished when the rights of one man are threatened." At the height of the Cold War, JFK said, "We preach freedom around the world, and we mean it, and we cherish it here at home, but are we to say to the world, and much more importantly, to each other that this is the land of the free except for the Negroes; that we have no second class citizens except Negroes; that we have no class or caste system, no ghettoes, no master race except with respect to Negroes?" The time had come, declared the president, for the nation to "fulfill its promise. . . . A great change is at hand, and our task, our obligation, is to make that revolution, that change, peaceful and constructive for all." As Kennedy's historic broadcast ended, Mississippi NAACP leader Medgar Evers was gunned down in the driveway of his house in Jackson.

The following week, Kennedy called on Congress to draft laws in support of voting rights, to help school districts trying to desegregate, to ban segregation in public facilities, and to empower the attorney general to initiate legal proceedings against school districts that failed to comply with federal law, and to draft a general civil rights nondiscrimination act. He also gave his proposed tax cut a civil rights spin by pointing out that unemployment was three times higher for black men as for whites and that average black income relative to whites had barely advanced since 1947, remaining roughly half of the median family income of whites. Meanwhile, building on growing national disgust with the defense of Jim Crow, the SCLC announced a massive march on Washington for August 1963. The August 28 civil rights demonstration at the Lincoln Memorial, which drew some 250,000 people, remains a symbolic landmark in the struggle for equal citizenship rights. Martin Luther King's impassioned "I Have a Dream" speech, in which he imagined an America where people were judged by their characters and not by the color of their skin, elevated him to the status of international icon for liberation movements everywhere.

CIVIL RIGHTS AND VOTING RIGHTS LAWS

The assassination of John F. Kennedy in Texas on November 22, 1963, spurred passage of the slain president's proposed civil rights act. Lyndon B. Johnson propelled the 1964 Civil Rights Act through Congress. Understanding that black economic inequality was as severe as black political inequality, Johnson launched the social welfare programs he called the "Great Society." Voting rights still remained at the top of civil rights organizations' agenda, however, and for good reason: in 1964, only two million of the South's five million blacks of voting age were registered to vote. That summer a coalition of civil rights organizations, led by SNCC's Bob Moses, launched a massive voter registration drive in Mississippi staffed by local blacks and white college students from across the nation. The interracial Freedom Summer group was greeted by an unprecedented campaign of violence and intimidation. A thousand people were arrested in Mississippi; many of them were brutalized by the police. To the consternation of Mississippi authorities trying to keep the feds out of their state, the Ku Klux Klan launched what it considered a counteroffensive. Thirty-five churches (common sites for civil rights meetings) were burned to the ground that summer, and six people were murdered. Three of them — James Chaney, a black Mississippian, and white volunteers Andrew Goodman and Michael Schwerner — were killed together and buried in an earthen dam. News of their deaths, broadcast by a riveted media, clarified for white Americans outside the region the degree of violent resistance to black equality in the South.

The extent of that resistance was demonstrated once again in Selma, Alabama, where King and the SCLC chose to mount their own voter registration campaign in 1965. In February, police attacked a night march in a small town near Selma and fatally shot 26-year-old Jimmie Lee Jackson, who was shielding his mother and grandmother from the police. Jackson's death prompted black leaders to organize a 54-mile march from Selma to the governor's mansion in Montgomery to demand protection for those registering to vote. Defying an order forbidding the march, on March 7 more than 600 protesters followed SCLC and SNCC leader John Lewis onto the Edmund Pettus Bridge. There they were attacked by bullwhip-wielding mounted state troopers, whose gas masks protected them from the noxious fumes unleashed on the demonstrators.

Vowing to continue the march, the Alabama protesters were joined by Americans from all over the country who had seen television coverage of the assault on the bridge. Especially prominent were clergy of all faiths, whose appearance at Rev. King's side added credence to civil rights activists' longtime claim that God was on their side. White supremacists could grumble about the influence of "outside agitators," but their presence, and the nationwide rallies organized in support of the Selma marchers, demonstrated conclusively that civil rights was a national issue. On Capitol Hill, President Johnson declared that "it is not just Negroes, but really all of us who must overcome the crippling legacy of bigotry and injustice," and asked Congress to craft a powerful new voting bill, the Voting Rights Act of 1965, which banned literacy tests and allowed the federal government to oversee elections in counties in which less than 50 percent of the population had voted in the 1964 presidential election.

THE WARREN COURT AND CIVIL LIBERTIES

As civil rights activists called for equal voting rights, the Supreme Court scrutinized the ways state and local governments drew boundaries around legislative districts. In many places, particularly in the South, local leaders limited the influence of urban, frequently African American, voters by apportioning legislative seats based on outdated population data that favored rural areas at the expense of cities. *Baker v. Carr* (1962) forced states to redistribute offices according to current population, and not by "lands or trees or pastures." Two years later, in a split decision, the court made "one person, one vote" the general rule for apportioning all representative bodies, including upper houses, in state legislatures.

The court also revolutionized criminal procedure at the local level, provoking outraged responses from law enforcement officers and middle-class Americans worried about rising crime rates. In *Gideon v. Wainwright* (1963), the justices upheld the Sixth Amendment's right of indigent criminal defendants to legal representation, and in *Esco-*

bedo v. Illinois (1964), a bare majority held that people in police custody had to be informed of their right to remain silent until a defense lawyer was present.

Miranda v. Arizona (1966) explained how to enforce *Escobedo*. Any accused person, Chief Justice Warren wrote, "must be warned that he has a right to remain silent, that any statement he does make may be used in evidence against him, and that he has the right to the presence of an attorney, either retained or appointed." Warren had strong feelings about crime—his father was killed in an unsolved murder. But he also felt that when the police neglected fairness, they became "a menace to society," particularly to the poor and uneducated.

The Supreme Court's criminal procedure decisions caused lasting controversy, but it was religion that really moved the court to center stage in national politics. In *Engel v. Vitale* (1962), the justices came down strongly in favor of the separation of church and state, ruling that mandatory prayer and Bible reading in public schools violated the First Amendment of the Constitution.

The separation of church and state, Justice Hugo Black explained, was premised on two assumptions: first, "that a union of government and religion tends to destroy government and to degrade religion," and second, "that governmentally established religions and religious persecutions go hand in hand." This was, Black recalled, precisely what caused many of America's early colonists to seek religious freedom in the New World.

The Supreme Court's decision in *Engel v. Vitale* was almost universally decried. Former presidents Truman and Eisenhower denounced the decision; 80 percent of Americans agreed with them. A Methodist bishop announced that the *Engel* decision "makes secularism the national religion." Southern whites quipped that the court "had put Negroes in the schools, and now they have driven God out." Liberal Protestants accepted the decision reluctantly; Catholics and conservative Protestants rejected it. About the only people who approved of the court's action were American Jews, who resented the openly Christian atmosphere of public schools.

Banished from the schools, God went into politics. The *Engel* decision inaugurated the formation of new political alliances rooted in religious belief. Conservative Protestants and Catholics—previously at odds—united against those they considered the agents of secularism: liberal Protestants and Jews. They were aided by the court's 1965 decision in *Griswold v. Connecticut*, in which the justices ruled that a state ban on the sale and use of contraceptives by married couples violated a "right to marital privacy." This decision helped religious conservatives link the battle for prayer in the schools with broader questions of family life and sexual behavior. Derided by many, the right to privacy would become the center of a legal whirlwind in 1973, when the court used that concept to justify its decision in *Roe v. Wade* that women had a constitutional right to terminate an unwanted pregnancy.

*

The decade following the *Brown* decision, which is often referred to as "the rights revolution," saw the rights of individuals as against the state vastly expanded in response to a mass movement of citizens. As the Supreme Court intervened decisively in areas of governance that many Americans considered the business of Congress and state legislatures, it provoked a storm of protest that the justices had departed from their role as the chief interpreters of the law and had embarked on a new career as legislators. The court itself, and particularly the chief justice, became a lightning rod for critics of the assertive federal presence in public life. Billboards alongside the nation's new interstate highway system implored America to "Save Our Republic! Impeach Earl Warren!"

The actions of the Warren Court and of its detractors were both grounded in readings of the Constitution. The victory of one vision over another was not about recovering some fundamental truth of the Constitution, but reflected a shifting consensus about what the Constitution meant. That consensus was neither permanent nor stable, as the coming decades would reveal.

FIGURE 9. Photograph of President Lyndon B. Johnson on July 31, 1968, as he listens to a tape sent by Captain Charles Robb from Vietnam. Captain Robb was Johnson's son-in-law and a Marine Corps company commander in Vietnam. Jack E. Kightlinger, photographer. Collection LBJ-WHPO: White House Photo Office Collection, 11/22/1963–01/20/1969, Lyndon Baines Johnson Library, National Archives and Records Administration, 192617.

CHAPTER 9

Riven, 1965–1968

On October 21, 1967, more than 50,000 anti–Vietnam War demonstrators gathered at the Lincoln Memorial and then marched across the Potomac River toward the Pentagon. There they encountered 6,000 federal marshals and paratroopers. Describing the ensuing confrontation, novelist and journalist Norman Mailer observed that there was "terror on each side" as each came "face to face with its own conception of the devil." The demonstrators were "prepared (or altogether unprepared) for any conceivable brutality." The troops, who had heard for years about "the venality, criminality, filth, corruption, perversion, addiction, and unbridled appetites" of the "hippie" protesters, did not know "whether to expect a hairy kiss on their lips or a bomb between their knees."

Some marchers urged the troops to join them. Others put flowers in the soldiers' rifle barrels. Still others urinated on the Pentagon, threw rocks at the windows, or taunted, insulted, and spat on the soldiers. Most simply stood vigil, letting their presence signify their opposition to the war. "This is the beginning of a new stage in the American peace movement in which the cutting edge becomes active resistance," declared the march's mastermind, 52-year-old pacifist David Dellinger. Going to jail to protest war, as Dellinger had during World War II, was an act of individual resistance. Occupying the grounds of the Pentagon was collective defiance.

Sometime after midnight, new columns of paratroopers relieved their comrades. Suddenly, the soldiers cut through the demonstrators and used tear gas, rifle butts, and cudgels to scatter the crowd. By the end of the night, 647 demonstrators had been arrested and 47 hospitalized.

One of the greatest tragedies of the American war in Vietnam was the way it made enemies out of allies. By 1967, 57 percent of Americans disapproved of the government's war policy, yet the reaction to the Pentagon demonstration was largely critical, as pundits and politicians rushed to demonize the protesters. *NBC Nightly News* commentator David Brinkley described the demonstrators as "coarse" and "vulgar." Barry Goldwater called them "hate-filled, anti-American, pro-Communist and violent." President Lyndon Johnson called the protesters "storm troopers" and suggested that the CIA had proof that the antiwar movement was run by Communists. The *Christian Century* observed that it was "difficult to think of a moment since the Civil War" so accurately described by the words "crisis" and "doom." The optimism that had ushered in the 1960s, the sense that anything was possible, such as sending a man to the moon or toppling Jim Crow, was shattered. By 1967, the United States was in the midst of the worst civil violence since the end of the First World War.

The violence in this era stemmed from two sources that were independent of one another but merged so often it was hard to tell them apart: the African American freedom movement and opposition to the war in Vietnam. Inner-city blacks battled the police; white homeowners torched the houses of unwelcome African American neighbors; political leaders were murdered one after another. "Stop the Draft" protests erupted across the country, as did prayer vigils and "teach-ins" at colleges and universities. Thousands of young men refused to submit to the draft. More than 3,000 of them went to prison for their failure to serve. Both causes sundered families, divided houses of worship, and polarized politics. The president elected by a colossal margin in US history in 1964 was so reviled by 1968 that he barely dared to leave the White House. It is hard to think of another period in American history when the Republic was under pressure from so many directions at once. If it seemed to many Americans that the country was "coming apart," that is because it was.

Lyndon Johnson's America

Born in the Texas Hill Country in 1908, Lyndon Baines Johnson's first job was teaching school in Cotulla, a small town near the border between Texas and Mexico. Already he was thinking big, planning how to bring the American dream within the grasp of those living on the edge: "I shall never forget the faces of the boys and the girls in that little Welhausen Mexican School, and I remember even yet the pain of realizing and knowing then that college was closed to practically every one of those children because they were too poor. And I think it was then that I made up my mind that this nation could never rest while the door to knowledge remained closed to any American." When he got the chance to open that door and others for his fellow citizens, he threw himself into the job, sending federal money down the line to communities across the nation in the largest expansion of government services since the New Deal.

THE GREAT SOCIETY

The phrase "larger than life" does not even begin to do justice to the outsized personality of Lyndon Baines Johnson, who became the nation's 36th president when John F. Kennedy was assassinated in Dallas on November 22, 1963. A large, physically imposing man, the veteran Texas congressman and Democratic House majority leader was perhaps the greatest American politician of all time. Rooms seemed to contract when Johnson entered them. Stories about his fabled powers of persuasion abound. Strong men shrank when they saw LBJ striding purposefully toward them.

Johnson's goals for the nation were as grandiose as his sense of self. In a May 1964 commencement speech at the University of Michigan, one of the land-grant universities established during the Civil War, he unveiled a breathtaking vision of the future Republic. The United States was the richest, most powerful nation on the globe. How would its citizens use that wealth and power? "Your imagination," he told his youthful (but voting-age) audience, "your initiative, and your indignation will determine whether we build a society where progress is the servant of our needs, or a society where old values and new visions are buried under unbridled growth." Could prosperity be harnessed to complete the social network begun a generation earlier in the midst of desperate want? Now was the moment, he said, to decide whether America would "move not only toward the rich society and the powerful society, but upward to the Great Society."

What was this Great Society? One, the president explained, that "rests on abundance and liberty for all. It demands an end to poverty and racial injustice, to which we are totally committed in our time. . . . The Great Society is a place where every child can find knowledge to enrich his mind and to enlarge his talents. . . . It is a place where the city of man serves not only the needs of the body and the demands of

commerce but the desire for beauty and the hunger for community."
Like the Republic itself, the Great Society was a work in progress, "a
challenge constantly renewed, beckoning us toward a destiny where
the meaning of our lives matches the marvelous product of our labor."
No single person—not even LBJ—could accomplish this goal: only
the collective could do this. "Will you join in the battle to give every
citizen an escape from the crushing weight of poverty? Will you join
in the battle to build the Great Society?"

THE WAR ON POVERTY

Elected in November 1964 with 61 percent of the popular vote, Johnson asked Congress to translate his vision into public policy. Pass legislation to renew America's neglected cities, urged the president. Guard
our air and water from industrial pollution. Protect consumers. Outlaw discriminatory voting practices, subsidize scholarship and the arts,
provide medical care for the elderly and the poor, and fund the schools.
Lift as we climb, exhorted the president, sounding like a life member
of the National Association of Colored Women. Do everything!

There could be no Great Society, Johnson knew, without first addressing the paradox of poverty in the richest nation on earth. The
Kennedy administration had been contemplating a federal anti-
poverty program at the time of JFK's assassination. In his first State of
the Union speech on January 8, 1964, Johnson announced a "war on
poverty." Like his hero Franklin Delano Roosevelt, LBJ believed that
democracy could not flourish in a society characterized by vast discrepancies in the distribution of wealth and power. When he declared
"unconditional war on poverty," the president intended to clear the
ground upon which he would then build the Great Society.

Congress did not enact every item on the president's Great Society
list, but it passed a great deal of legislation that bettered the lives of
untold numbers of Americans, especially the most vulnerable: the very
young and the very old, the sick, the unemployed, and the destitute.
Medicaid did for the poor what Medicare had done for the elderly. Social Security benefits were expanded, the federal minimum wage was
increased, and an additional 9.1 million workers were brought under
the umbrella of the Fair Labor Standards Act.

The centerpiece of the War on Poverty was the Economic Opportunity Act of 1964, which created the Office of Economic Opportunity
(OEO) to administer a wide array of new programs designed to help

people develop job skills and attend to other needs. The Community Action Program nurtured local leaders and political aptitude among underrepresented populations. Legal Services helped the poor navigate the criminal justice system, and the Neighborhood Youth Corps tried to limit the number of young people in need of legal advice. The Revenue Act of 1964 cut taxes to stimulate economic growth and job creation, and the Food Stamp Act of 1964 made sure that people living below the poverty threshold had enough to eat.

The government also invested in education at every level. Alluding to FDR's 1941 "Four Freedoms" speech, the former rural Texas schoolteacher called freedom from ignorance "the Fifth Freedom." The Higher Education Act provided students access to low-interest federal loans. The Elementary and Secondary Education Act pumped federal money (and federal antidiscrimination policies) into the local public schools. Head Start prepared the children of the poor for kindergarten and, incidentally, provided safe, cost-free childcare for working mothers. Adult Basic Education provided exactly that to thousands of Americans.

As long as it was funded, the War on Poverty succeeded in its goals. In 1960, 40 million Americans (roughly 20 percent of the population) were classified officially as poor. By 1969, that number had fallen to 24 million, or 12 percent of the population. The percentage of African Americans living below the poverty line dropped from 55 percent in 1960 to 27 percent in 1968. Thanks in great measure to Medicaid and food stamps, infant mortality among the poor, which had barely declined during the booming 1950s, was cut by a third after 1965.

PURSUING EQUALITY

On June 4, 1965, President Lyndon Johnson delivered the commencement address at Howard University, the alma mater of so many civil rights leaders. The world had changed dramatically during the graduates' four years in college. The 1963 March on Washington for Jobs and Freedom had broadened the southern assault on segregation, the Civil Rights Act of 1964 prohibited racial discrimination in employment and in public facilities and accommodations, and the jewel in the crown—the Voting Rights Act of 1965—was expected to reach Johnson's desk in a matter of days.

The president celebrated these achievements. But he wanted more. "Freedom is not enough," he stated flatly. "You do not wipe away the scars of centuries by saying: Now you are free to go where you want, and do as you desire, and choose the leaders you please. You do not take a person who, for years, has been hobbled by chains and liberate him, bring him up to the starting line of a race and then say, 'You are free to compete with all the others,' and still justly believe that you have been completely fair." All Americans, Johnson said, "seek not just . . . equality as a right and a theory but equality as a fact and equality as a result. . . . Equal opportunity is essential, but not enough, not enough." Equal treatment in the present could not address the lingering effects of severe inequality in the past.

Title VII of the Civil Rights Act of 1964 prohibited employment discrimination for reasons of race, color, sex, religion, or national origin. An obvious and crucial problem with Title VII enforcement was proving discrimination. Were few police officers black or female because of discrimination, or because they lacked the "necessary" qualifications for the job? And who decides when a qualification is "necessary" or instead a cover for discrimination? If, as the president believed, equal opportunity was not sufficient to remedy decades of discrimination, disadvantage, and humiliation, what sort of action might be necessary to achieve a more just society? Following JFK's example, Johnson put the power of the purse behind antidiscrimination, and issued an executive order to mandate that federal contractors—private companies that did business with the federal government—take "affirmative action" to remedy possible employment discrimination.

Housing discrimination was even harder to address than employment discrimination. Neighborhoods in northern and western cities were effectively segregated along race lines. The all-white National Association of Real Estate Boards (NAREB) "steered" white and black buyers to their "correct" neighborhoods. African Americans who wanted to buy in "their" neighborhoods, meanwhile, were refused loans by banks that considered whole neighborhoods bad investment risks and removed them from consideration through redlining (outlining proscribed neighborhoods in red on maps).

To address the discriminatory housing market, some states passed open-housing laws that outlawed discrimination in advertising and lending practices. Realtors and landlords objected to these laws, claiming that they violated "freedom of association" by impairing the right of people to live and associate only with people they preferred. In 1964, in a campaign led by a coalition of realtors and landlords, Californians voted to repeal their state's fair-housing laws by a two-to-one ratio.

RACIAL INEQUALITY IN THE CITIES

The problems of the urban black poor were different from those of the rural South. Voting rights and desegregated public accommodations did not top the list of northern black demands: jobs and housing did. Young black men were unemployed at double the rate of whites, and four times as many African Americans lived in poverty as whites. Changing this would require more than antidiscrimination legislation. Many of the War on Poverty programs (such as the Job Corps) were designed with urban African Americans in mind. Several of the Great Society programs, such as Head Start, were designed explicitly to get whites and blacks to the starting line at the same time in order to even the odds of a fair race.

Concentrated in segregated neighborhoods in the inner cities, blacks in the North and West lived in substandard housing, attended segregated, inferior schools, and did the hardest, dirtiest work for the lowest wages—if they had jobs at all. Black neighborhoods like New York's Harlem, Chicago's South Side, and Los Angeles's Watts expanded in population but not in territory after WWII. Urban ghettos were crowded, dangerous, expensive, and unhealthy. Residents paid high rents for apartments with no heat, leaky roofs, and plugged toilets. Because chain businesses such as department and grocery stores refused to open outposts in ghettos, the people who lived there bought food and other essentials at local stores that charged high prices for poor products. Milk was frequently sour; vegetables were rotten; clothing was shoddy. As James Baldwin tried to explain to the high-brow readership of *Esquire* magazine in 1960, "Anyone who has ever struggled with poverty knows how extremely expensive it is to be poor."

Whites whose racial consciences had been pricked by televised images of police dogs attacking black schoolchildren almost never paused to consider the conditions of life for blacks in their own backyards. They had no idea of the pent-up rage in the urban ghettos of Chicago, Cleveland, Detroit, Los Angeles, Newark, and hundreds of smaller cities in between. When the leading black neighborhood in Los Angeles, Watts, exploded on August 11, 1965, whites were at a loss to explain this frightening turn of events. Between 1964 and 1968, there were 329 major riots in 257 northern and western cities; 52,629 people were arrested, 8,371 were injured, and 220 were killed: mostly African American civilians. Although the most spectacular scenes occurred in large cities, 45 percent of the uprisings of the summer of 1967 took place in cities with fewer than 50,000 residents.

Nearly all the major urban riots of the mid-1960s began as an altercation between ghetto residents and white police officers. In Watts, California Highway Patrol officers pulled over Marquette Frye on August 11, 1965, for driving under the influence of alcohol. It was a warm evening and the streets were crowded—it was cooler outside than inside the un-air-conditioned homes. By the time Los Angeles Police Department officers arrived on the scene, bottles were flying at the police. The disorder spread and intensified, despite the efforts of black leaders to contain the violence. (LAPD chief William Parker's description of the rioters as "monkeys in the zoo" did not help matters.) After five days, 3,000 national guardsmen finally managed to restore the peace. By the time it was over, nearly 300 buildings had burned in Watts, upwards of $40 million in property was destroyed, and 34 lives were lost. An investigatory commission appointed by Governor Pat Brown listed unemployment and police brutality at the top of a long list of causes contributing to the violence.

RAGE

Blacks in the North and West could vote. They had access to restaurants and theaters and public transportation. Why would they burn down their own neighborhoods? The perennial American question came once again to the fore: *What does the Negro want?* "Anything worth having" was Harlem resident Hannah Nelson's answer.

This was more or less the conclusion arrived at by the Kerner Commission (named after its chair, Illinois governor Otto Kerner) in 1967, after two summers of urban uprisings culminated in catastrophic violence in Newark and Detroit. Charged by President Johnson with investigating the riots, the commission found that African Americans were united by specific grievances and aspirations that were clearly visible in their targets: local police, who represented white authority and/or racism, and businesses owned by nonblacks, whom ghetto residents believed cheated them. Rioters rarely ventured into white neighborhoods, and left white or integrated institutions alone for the most part. They did not pillage factories or torch sports arenas. They left university buildings and hospitals intact.

Although spontaneous and unorganized, the urban uprisings were not meaningless. "What the rioters appeared to be seeking," concluded the Kerner Commission, "was fuller participation in the social order and the material benefits enjoyed by the majority of American citizens. Rather than rejecting the American system, they were anxious to obtain a place for themselves in it." These were not Communist agitators trying to destroy the government. These were people demanding to be let in. In 1967, the proportion of African Americans in local government was still substantially smaller than their proportion of the population. Only 3 of the 20 cities studied by the commission had more than one African American legislator; none had ever had a black mayor or city manager. Police departments remained white bastions. Only 3.5 percent of the LAPD was black in a city whose population was 16.5 percent black in 1965. The report condemned "indiscriminate use of force against wholly innocent elements of the Negro community" during the riots.

Warning that racial discrimination and segregation now threatened the future of every American, the commission voiced concern about the "continuing polarization of the American community." America, it said, was rapidly becoming "two nations, separate and unequal." The report did not exonerate the rioters, but it did try to explain them to a white audience (in the White House as well as on Main Street). "What white Americans have never fully understood but what the Negro can never forget," the commission concluded, "is that white society is deeply implicated in the ghetto. White institutions created it, white institutions maintain it, and white society condones it." The resources of "the richest and most powerful nation on this earth" needed to be poured into the quest for a solution to the race problem.

Rather than embrace the report, Johnson criticized it for (like the rioters themselves) underestimating the achievements of the Great Society. But as he admitted later, he had failed to do much for African Americans. "As I see it," he mused after leaving office, "I've moved the Negro"—Johnson's ego was still intact, if not his dreams—"from D+ to C−. He's still nowhere. He knows it. And that's why he's out in the streets. Hell, I'd be there too." There was no lack of understanding the grievances of the urban poor. There was no lack of solutions. The real issue, the president admitted, was funding. "That was the problem," he wrote later. "Money." He didn't want to admit it at the time, but the world's richest country was going broke.

Johnson's Dilemma

LBJ always knew that he could fight a war or he could create a Great Society, but he could not do both. "If I left the woman I really loved—

the Great Society—in order to get involved with that bitch of a war on the other side of the world, then I would lose everything at home," Johnson explained to historian Doris Kearns Goodwin shortly before his death. "All my programs. All my hopes to feed the hungry and shelter the homeless. All my dreams to provide education and medical care. . . . But if I left that war and let the Communists take over South Vietnam, then I would be seen as a coward and my nation would be seen as an appeaser, and we would both find it impossible to accomplish anything for anybody anywhere on the entire globe. Oh, I could see it coming all right."

In addition to costing 58,000 American lives, as well as those of 3-4 million Vietnamese, and $100 billion, the conflict in Vietnam permanently divided a generation and shaped American politics for the next 40 years. Lyndon Johnson was a visionary, but even he could not have foreseen the total tragedy of America's war in Vietnam.

ENGAGEMENT

Lyndon Johnson inherited the war in Vietnam from John Kennedy, who had inherited it from Dwight Eisenhower. It was an undesirable legacy. American policy in Vietnam was based on two premises. The first was that, given the influence of China in Asia, if Vietnam "fell" to Communists, then the rest of Southeast Asia would follow like a row of dominoes. The second was the belief that American intervention in Vietnam could prevent one side in a civil war—the Communist North—from winning. Neither turned out to be true.

Like Eisenhower, President Kennedy considered Vietnam critical to Cold War efforts by the United States to contain and combat Communism. Concerned about Communist military advances in southern Vietnam, Kennedy increased the number of US military advisors there from 3,200 in late 1961 to more than 23,000 in 1963. These advisors worked with South Vietnam's Army of the Republic of Vietnam (ARVN) on strategy and tactics, but were prohibited from carrying out those strategies themselves. As the months passed, Washington's confidence in ARVN's future and in South Vietnamese president Ngo Dingh Diem eroded precipitously. When Diem was overthrown by a military coup on November 1, 1963, American policymakers hoped that the regime change would produce a period of political stability.

It did not. Between 1963 and 1965, there were a dozen different governments. The North Vietnamese National Liberation Front (NLF, also known as the Vietcong) capitalized on political instability in the South, gaining both territory and popular support. ARVN's monthly losses tripled between January and December 1963 (not counting the legions of deserters). President Johnson resisted calls to increase military aid to ARVN, fearing for the future of his Great Society dreams. Pressed on one side by foreign policy advisors chosen exclusively by John Kennedy—the men who, in other words, had guided US policy in Vietnam to this point—and harassed by Republicans as irresolute, Johnson approved a series of covert operations in northern Vietnam that included coastal commando raids by South Vietnamese forces with the assistance of American advisors and ships. American ships thus became targets for North Vietnam.

On August 2, 1964, a cluster of North Vietnamese torpedo boats approached the destroyer USS *Maddox* in the Gulf of Tonkin. The *Maddox* opened fire and the Vietnamese boats launched torpedoes before retreating. Two days later, the *Maddox* and a second destroyer, the USS *Turner Joy*, reported being under attack 60 miles off the coast of North Vietnam. Evidence of the attack was inconclusive at the time, and it was later determined that it never occurred. But LBJ leapt at the opportunity to demonstrate his spine to the North Vietnamese and to GOP presidential candidate Barry Goldwater, whose eagerness to use nuclear weapons in Vietnam thrilled his supporters and terrified everyone else. Framing the attacks as "open aggression on the high seas," Johnson authorized retaliatory air strikes against North Vietnamese naval bases and had congressional allies draft a resolution authorizing the president to employ "all necessary measures to repel any armed attack against the forces of the United States and to prevent further aggression" in Southeast Asia. The Tonkin Gulf Resolution effectively gave the president a blank check with which to wage the war in Vietnam.

ESCALATION

On November 3, 1964, Lyndon Johnson was awarded a presidential term in his own right, winning the largest share of the popular vote in American history. If ever there was a moment to disengage from Vietnam, this was it. If it is true that Johnson anticipated the war devouring the Great Society—that he was able to "see it all coming"—then why did he stay the course?

There are three main reasons. First, Johnson believed that a Communist victory in Vietnam would be bad for the United States and disastrous for the Vietnamese people, who would sink into a life of totalitarian repression. Second, he—like the leaders of the armed forces, his own foreign policy experts, and the vast bulk of the American people—believed in the domino theory, which meant that abandoning South Vietnam was tantamount to handing all of Southeast Asia over to the Chinese. Third, Johnson expected the United States to win the war, and quickly.

In early February 1965, Vietcong forces attacked US soldiers at a military base in Pleiku. Johnson demanded action; the Pentagon responded by launching Operation Rolling Thunder, a full-scale bombing campaign against the North. The escalation in the air was matched by a parallel course on the ground. By late April, nearly 50,000 American combat troops had joined the US advisors in Vietnam.

The decision to deploy ground troops represented a fundamental shift in US policy and was implemented only after fierce debates among Johnson's advisors—although it later became clear that the president had already made up his mind in advance. General William Westmoreland, the top-ranking US Army officer in Vietnam, advocated escalating the war by sending thousands more troops. Secretary of Defense Robert S. McNamara sided with Westmoreland at the time but changed his mind later. Under Secretary of State George Ball disagreed strenuously and insisted that the war in Vietnam was impossible to win. America could not count on the support of the South Vietnamese; politically, Ball argued, Vietnam was "a lost cause." The more US forces deployed in Vietnam, he concluded, "the harder we shall find it to extricate ourselves without unacceptable costs as the war goes badly."

When Secretary of Defense McNamara recommended a substantial increase in American troop strength in Vietnam, he insisted on two simultaneous actions: a call-up of 100,000 reservists and National Guard troops to fill the gap in America's forces created by the deployment of troops to Vietnam, and a substantial increase in federal taxes to underwrite the war. These steps had practical benefits. The tax increase was designed to forestall deficit spending or deep cuts in domestic programs. But they also had instructional value: they would inform Congress and the American people of the enormity of the decisions being made in the summer of 1965.

Had the president requested a tax increase from Congress, he would have ignited a national debate about the nation's involvement in Vietnam and imperiled funding for his Great Society domestic programs, the most important of which were still under deliberation. Thus, when Johnson announced an increase of American troops in Vietnam from 75,000 to 125,000, he assured the nation that this new commitment would *not* entail any new taxes or call-up of reserve or National Guard troops. By the end of the year, approximately 184,300 US ground troops were in southern Vietnam; within two years, that total ballooned to almost half a million.

Because bombing was cheaper in both American treasure and lives, the air war grew massively (from 25,000 sorties in 1965 to 108,000 in 1967). Bombing was, however, imprecise and indiscriminate in its victims. American bombs hit approximately 70 percent of the rural north and killed an estimated 100,000 North Vietnamese civilians, and yet still failed to sever the flow of supplies and soldiers from north to south.

ON THE GROUND

The ground war was no easier. The enemy proved elusive, disappearing into the forest as Americans arrived. No matter how hard the American military machine hit the Vietcong, they bounced right back again. "It was like a sledge hammer on a floating cork," recalled one American journalist.

The American soldiers charged with submerging the cork and keeping it there were, comparatively speaking, kids. The average soldier in World War II had been 26 years old. When William Westmoreland captured and held the last remaining bridge crossing the Rhine in March 1945—a daring feat that helped hasten the end of the war in Europe—he was 31 years old. The average American soldier in Vietnam was 19. Sent on search-and-destroy missions in furtherance of General Westmoreland's war of attrition against the North, these soldiers did not fight on battlefields; they fought in villages and in rice paddies and in dense tropical forests. "It was the land that resisted us," Marine Lieutenant Philip Caputo recalled. "The land, the jungle, the sun." There were no battle lines and no decisive battles. Body counts therefore became the crucial marker of success. The army's enemy body counts were wildly exaggerated and included civilians. As time went by, first the media and then the American public came to doubt the numbers they heard and General Westmoreland's optimistic interpretation of them. The credibility gap between the US government and the American people eventually grew so wide that it was impossible for either side to bridge.

It was difficult if not impossible to distinguish soldiers from civilians in a war in which the enemy wore no uniforms and included women, and it did not take long for American officers and soldiers to stop trying to tell the difference. The definition of the enemy went from the Vietcong to the Vietnamese; every village was potentially enemy territory. After fighting for hours to capture a village, US troops would arrive to find it populated exclusively by nursing mothers, small children, and the aged. Everyone else, including the Vietcong, had melted into the jungle. At first American soldiers were philosophical. Greeted in the spring of 1965 by an old woman and a mother cradling an infant whose head was covered in sores, the troops relaxed. "One of our corpsmen [treated] the infant with the skin ulcers, daubing salve on the sores while other marines entertained the baby to keep it from crying," recollected their leader. At the same time, he continued, their interpreter threatened to blow off the old woman's head. Soft hearts were soon hardened by seeing their buddies blown up by booby-trapped deserted villages, however. "We'd go through and that was it," one GI remembered. "We'd rip out the hedges and burn the hooches [huts] and blow all the wells and kill every chicken, pig and cow in the whole fucking village. I mean, if we can't shoot these people, what the fuck are we doing here?"

As the war dragged on, soldiers' morale and living conditions deteriorated. Drug use, especially heroin, became common, as did "fragging," the term soldiers used to describe the assassination of their own officers when they seemed too willing to put troops in harm's way. The military kept information about fragging and drug use under wraps, and also concealed some of the most heart-breaking details of the war—such as a commander's decision not to tell grieving parents that their terrified son had put his own M16 rifle to his head and killed himself in the heat of a losing battle.

1968: THE BEGINNING OF THE END

Despite constantly rising troop levels (from 184,300 in 1965 to 385,300 in 1966 to 485,600 in 1967 to a peak of 536,100 in 1968), the war in Vietnam remained a stalemate. Increasingly, political leaders and the media began to question the wisdom of the government's course. More and more people asked why Americans were laying down their lives to defend a government incapable of inspiring its own people. Even the South Vietnamese no longer believed in the likelihood of a decisive outcome. South Vietnamese families hedged their bets by sending one son to serve in the ARVN and another with the NLF.

Where the NLF was especially strong, the US Army and ARVN established free-fire zones in which artillery and air power, as well as napalm (an incendiary weapon featuring gelled gasoline) and toxic chemical defoliants (e.g., Agent Orange), were used. Villagers in central Vietnam saw some of the greatest atrocities of the war. Between May and November 1967, the US Army's "Tiger Force" traveled the central highlands, killing hundreds of unarmed civilians, in some cases torturing, mutilating, and raping them before they were shot. In March 1968, an American platoon that had suffered recent losses raped and murdered at least 347 unarmed Vietnamese civilians in My Lai before burning their village to the ground. The killing was halted when Hugh Thompson Jr., who witnessed the killing from the air, landed his helicopter in the line of fire between American troops and fleeing villagers with its guns facing the Americans. Platoon leader Lieutenant William L. Calley was tried and sentenced to life imprisonment for his role in the killings but was later pardoned by President Richard M. Nixon.

On January 30, 1968, North Vietnamese troops launched a general offensive in the South. Consciously repeating a tactic that the Vietnamese had used successfully against the Chinese in the late eighteenth century, Hanoi attacked on Tet, the Vietnamese lunar New Year, the most important holiday in Vietnam. Since the start of the war, both sides had honored a cease-fire during Tet. The South Vietnamese and the Americans were caught off guard, but they recovered quickly. A small suicide detachment of Vietcong permeated the American embassy in Saigon but was dispatched eventually. "What the hell is going on?" CBS news anchor Walter Cronkite demanded. "I thought we were winning!" The most famous photograph of the Tet Offensive, of the chief of South Vietnam's national police pulling the trigger of a gun held to the head of a Vietcong suspect in the middle of a Saigon street, circulated widely in the United States and made many Americans wonder if their nation had rallied round the wrong side.

The Tet Offensive was a major military defeat for the North and the NLF. The NLF lost 80 percent of its fighting force (as many as 50,000 casualties). But in the realm of unanticipated outcomes, Tet *did* succeed in altering fundamentally the nature of the American war. The psychological shock of the offensive throughout southern Vietnam undermined the optimistic insistence of General William Westmoreland that he could see "the light at the end of the tunnel." For the first time, a clear majority of Americans believed that the United States was not making progress in the war in Vietnam. This would affect America's policy in Vietnam, but indirectly, through a radical transformation of the domestic political scene in the presidential election year of 1968.

We Can Change the World: The Rising Generation

The generation of Americans born immediately after the Second World War — the so-called baby boomers — was the largest, most self-conscious generation in American history. Boomers at all levels of social class, from sharecroppers in Mississippi and Alabama to urban inhabitants of the ghetto to the sons and daughters of the expanding middle class, were unusually energetic, idealistic, and politically engaged. Boomers born into the middle class, expanding thanks to the GI Bill and the postwar economic boom, swelled college enrollments and turned universities into sites of social and political protest. In time, they carried their politics from the dorms into the streets.

QUESTION AUTHORITY

In 1940, 15 percent of Americans aged 18 to 22 went to college. By 1965, with a booming economy and changing expectations, 44 percent of young people — an unprecedented six million — did. Universities experienced correspondingly massive growth. They also changed in important ways. Responding to a Cold War atmosphere that rewarded the development of defense-related technology, universities entered into a new alliance with government and private industry. Academic research teams funded by government agencies worked with corporations such as Dow Chemical, which in addition to introducing Saran Wrap into American kitchens supplied the army with napalm and Agent Orange. Universities that had once considered themselves wholly independent of the state — and therefore free to criticize it at will — were now becoming arms of the state themselves.

At the same time, students became increasingly vocal in their criticism of government, universities, family life, gender roles, consumer culture: pretty much everything. What began as criticism of limited courses of study and burdensome restrictions on social life, such as curfews and single-sex dormitories, gradually became a broader critique of society. In 1962, Students for a Democratic Society (SDS), founded in 1960 at the University of Michigan, published the Port Huron Statement. Written primarily by SDS field secretary Tom Hayden, the manifesto argued that the United States was dominated by massive, impersonal organizational structures—governments, corporations, universities, and unions that suppressed individual freedom. Unless individual citizens organized and pushed back, the nation would be overwhelmed by "The System." Many of the statement's themes, such as the virtues of participatory democracy and the desire for work to feed the soul as well as the body, were rooted in past generations' critiques of America. Others, including the sense that "we may be the last generation in the experiment with living," derived from the fear of nuclear annihilation that marked this generation worldwide.

The Port Huron Statement's rejection of defeatism, its hopefulness, and its passionate pursuit of passion touched a generational nerve already stimulated by the charismatic young president who in 1961 challenged America's youth to serve their nation. An unprecedented number of college students volunteered in a broad spectrum of causes. Thousands joined the Peace Corps (established in 1961) and its domestic counterpart, VISTA (Volunteers in Service to America, founded in 1965). A smaller but more politically influential group joined "the Southern struggle" for civil rights, where they saw black college students use civil disobedience to challenge racial discrimination and put themselves in harm's way to fulfill the nation's highest aspirations.

Two branches of student activism merged in September 1964 at the University of California at Berkeley after several groups, including CORE, SNCC, and SDS, violated university policy forbidding the distribution of political materials on campus. When the university continued to deny what students considered their First Amendment right to freedom of speech, a thousand of them occupied the administration building to protest the university's policy. Rather than handle the matter internally, the university invited 600 regular police and California highway patrolmen to storm the building. This, along with the arrest of some 800 students, brought national attention to what was soon known as the Free Speech Movement (FSM).

Like the Civil Rights Movement, the Free Speech Movement championed participatory democracy in the name of reason and reform. Like the growing antiwar movement, the FSM was about the role of dissent in a self-governing society and the obligation of citizens to challenge authority when it exercised power in immoral, unjust, or simply undemocratic ways. Parents who had labored to give their children every possible advantage—suburban schools, summer camp, backyards, college—were bewildered and hurt when those children put aside "material things" in the interest of "making a difference" in the world. Indeed, so many families in the 1960s were divided along so many fronts that a new term was coined: "the generation gap."

BLACK POWER

"Black power" may be the most misunderstood phrase in American history. "Black folks took two innocent words, 'black power,' and everybody went crazy!" joked civil rights activist, pacifist, and comedian Dick Gregory. "Had we said 'brown strength,'" he continued, "oh, everybody would accept that! We wouldn't be able to walk down the street without white folks greeting us and saying, 'Brown strength, my brother, brown strength!'" The problem with black power, Gregory quipped in a 1967 interview, was that it "made whites think of 'white power,'" which meant "napalm, tanks, state police departments, high finance, overthrowing governments."

"Black Power" as a slogan came to national attention in 1966, when SNCC leader Stokely Carmichael invoked it at a civil rights demonstration in Mississippi. The words are often used as shorthand to differentiate between two phases of the African American freedom struggle—"civil rights" and "black power"—and to mark a generational, geographical, and ideological shift in leadership from black southerners committed to nonviolent civil disobedience to younger, militant, northern African Americans. This is true in part, but only in part.

The African American leader associated with the phrase "black power" had been dead for a year when Carmichael invoked it in 1966. Malcolm X—born Malcolm Little in Omaha, Nebraska, in 1925—does not, at first blush, fit the black power model. His generation fought in WWII, not Vietnam; his contemporaries were not the Young Turks of SNCC but rather Martin Luther King and the other middle-aged ministers of the SCLC. Malcolm hailed from the North, insofar as Nebraska was not part of the South; he spent his adolescent years in a series of foster homes in Boston and New York after his father died and his mother was institutionalized. Imprisoned in 1946 for burglary, Malcolm Little emerged a new man in 1952, having converted in prison to the Nation of Islam (NOI), a blend of traditional Islamic principles and pride in African American culture and achievements. Malcolm replaced his surname with the letter "X" to symbolize the unknowable "true African name" that whites had stripped from his slave forebears. Malcolm was 40 years old when he was murdered by a fellow black Muslim on February 21, 1965; Martin Luther King was 39 when he was assassinated by a white supremacist in Memphis three years later.

Malcolm and Martin are usually placed at opposite ends of the political spectrum: Malcolm, the herald of armed self-defense, versus Martin, the pacifist; Malcolm, the racial separatist and abuser of white "blue-eyed devils," with his list of grievances and demands for reparation, versus Martin, the conciliatory integrationist committed to overcoming the legacies of white supremacy. Their differences can be exaggerated. King was always a sharp critic of capitalist exploitation of African Americans. In his 1963 "Letter from Birmingham Jail," he denounced the smothering of 20 million Negroes "in an airtight cage of poverty in the midst of an affluent society." By 1968, he had become an outspoken opponent of the war in Vietnam.

Malcolm respected American political institutions and advocated working within the system rather than smashing it. His famous essay "The Ballot or the Bullet?" advocated the first but did not rule out the second ("I believe in action on all fronts by whatever means necessary"). Writing while southern Democrats were filibustering the Civil Rights Act in 1964, Malcolm urged African Americans to "take an uncompromising stand" and insist on civic equality. "I don't mean go out and get violent," he clarified. "But don't die alone. Let your dying be reciprocal. This is what is meant by equality."

BALLOTS AND BULLETS

Yet there were sharp differences between the men. King saw himself as an *American* who happened to be black, and who wanted the civil rights and privileges enjoyed by other Americans. Malcolm X presented himself as a black man, a person of African descent who happened to be a US citizen. Malcolm's message was black pride, self-respect, and autonomy. He urged his listeners to take pride in African Americans' past resistance to white domination and not allow their black culture to be "integrated out of existence."

Martin Luther King convinced white Americans that the goals of the Civil Rights Movement were identical with the hopes and dreams of the nation itself. Most whites outside the South found civil rights leaders' call for an end to racial discrimination and equal political rights unobjectionable and thought, erroneously, that federal legislation would have no concrete effect on their own lives. They were far less comfortable with Malcolm's argument that the oppressed had a natural right to armed self-defense, and that justice if not necessarily equality required action in realms beyond law and politics. Whereas King exhorted Americans to "overcome," Malcolm dwelt endlessly on exactly what needed overcoming. His narrative was one of transcending structural racism (discrimination built into the institutional fabric of the nation), from the transatlantic slave trade to the urban ghetto, not "discrimination."

Unlike King, who was unceasingly conciliatory toward whites, Malcolm did his best to make whites squirm. Impoverished urban African Americans loved him for it. Northern blacks admired Dr. King, but Malcolm spoke their language and had experienced first-hand the conditions of their lives: in foster homes, in prison, in unemployment lines, in depressing, dank apartments.

Between 1966 and 1968, civil rights organizations came apart at the seams and new groups tied only loosely to the earlier movement emerged. First SNCC and then CORE expelled its white members, explaining that black members needed to demonstrate to themselves their capacity to lead. Young whites who had dedicated themselves wholeheartedly to the cause of racial justice struggled to comprehend the rejection of their erstwhile comrades even as they recognized their own tendency to take charge. King declined to denounce SNCC as "reverse racists," but the integrationists were predictably disturbed by the direction of events.

More alarming than the turn to racial separatism by older African American organizations was the rejection of nonviolence by new ones. None captured the attention of the public, including the media, more completely than the Black Panther Party. Founded in Oakland, California, in late 1966 in response to the shooting of an unarmed black teenager by the San Francisco police, the Panthers blended street theater with a passionate commitment to civic equality. They were a study in contrasts: while Panther women provided free breakfasts in schools, Panther men cultivated an image of gun-toting black machismo.

Middle-aged civil rights advocates like CORE's Roy Innis and the National Urban League's Whitney Young could insist that Black Power was just a new name for "what a lot of people were already thinking," but whites were dubious. Everything ran together in white minds, especially after 1967: tanks in Detroit, Panther shootouts with police, swaggering armed black men in leather jackets and berets. A 1967 Detroit poll revealed that a majority of white respondents thought Black Power meant a violent "black takeover." Julius Lester's 1968 book *Look Out Whitey! Black Power's Gonna Get Your Mama* hardly reassured.

THE ANTIWAR MOVEMENT

Although many issues inspired activism by young Americans in the 1960s, including racial justice, poverty, workers' rights, and the environment, by 1965 the war in Vietnam eclipsed the other concerns. The escalation of the war and its ever-increasing need for manpower led to a dramatic expansion of both the military and the antiwar movement.

As more and more young people found themselves eligible for the draft, what had previously been political was suddenly very, very personal. At the same time, a concerted effort by older antiwar protesters to educate the young about Vietnam through campus "teach-ins" energized the student population. Before 1966, students did not have to worry about being drafted: they were allowed to postpone military service as long as they remained in school. In 1965, 98 percent of draftees were from either poor or working-class families, which meant that a disproportionate number of them were racial minorities, particularly African American. Recognizing the unfairness of a draft policy that protected the children of the privileged, and peeved by growing student protests against the war, President Johnson phased out the graduate student deferment after 1966.

The citizen apathy that had been decried by SDS was replaced after 1965 with growing dissent against both the war and the administration that could not seem to end it. Although plenty of people opposed the war on moral grounds before 1966, the antiwar movement exploded the minute white college graduates began to be drafted. Attendance at antiwar rallies swelled, and on April 15, 1967, the Spring Mobilization to End the War in Vietnam brought together upwards of 500,000 people in New York's Central Park. When Columbia University closed its doors temporarily as a result of student protests in April 1967, it joined a growing number of universities shut down by students opposed to the war in Vietnam.

By 1967, 57 percent of Americans disapproved of the government's war policy. Some wanted to win the war by any means, but most just wanted out of a war they no longer considered winnable. This latter group was itself divided by class, education, and moral standards. The broader critique of American society put forth by the New Left (as the various social/political movements—students, civil rights, antiwar— became lumped together) was not shared by blue-collar Americans whose sons still shouldered most of the weight of the war. These anti- antiwar Americans were repulsed by student antiwar activists, who mocked their patriotism, their fear of Communism, their defense of American democracy, their respect for authority, and, above all, their sacrifices. When the sons of auto workers and plumbers were drafted, they trudged to the nearest induction center, however grudgingly. Middle-class white boys, however, often found ways to evade service or to serve behind the lines, where they were unlikely to lose their lives, or their limbs, making their way through booby-trapped jungles. As one tradesman put it, "Here were these kids, rich kids, who could go to college, who didn't have to fight, they are telling you your son died in vain. It makes you feel your whole life is shit, just nothing."

1968

The year 1968 remains one of the most spectacularly momentous peri- ods in modern history. The Vietnam War, whose end seemed as distant as ever, had bled the nation dry, siphoning off resources from domestic programs designed to fight poverty and address persistent racial dis- crimination and inequality. The government's refusal to conduct a full and open discussion of the war in Vietnam had led to that conversation being held in the streets in an atmosphere of open confrontation be- tween the government and the people. Lyndon Johnson's secrecy and deception tarnished his own reputation and that of the office he ven- erated: the presidency. Popular faith in America's leaders and, more perilously, its institutions, hit a post-WWII low.

LYNDON'S FALL

While the politics of the Vietnam War played out on college cam- puses and courthouse steps, a revolt was brewing within the Demo- cratic Party. Allard Lowenstein, vice-chairman of the Americans for Democratic Action (ADA), fomented a "dump Johnson" movement on college campuses. By 1967, antiwar activists of all ages had found a champion in Minnesota senator Eugene McCarthy, who announced his intention to challenge LBJ for the Democratic nomination in 1968. Antiwar college students, activists, and housewives rushed to New Hampshire to volunteer for McCarthy in the first Democratic primary.

McCarthy lacked the usual senatorial attributes: he had no charisma, he did not seem to care what people thought of him, and he had no patience for the legislative process. But he was certain the war was wrong, and he was not afraid to risk his political career by saying so. He hoped, through his candidacy, to allow the young people demonstrating in the streets "entrance back into the political process." McCarthy attacked LBJ's Vietnam policy, proposing instead a cease-fire and a negotiated settlement.

With the nation already sundered along regional, generational, and political lines in their views on Vietnam, popular disillusionment with the war and the president was heightened dramatically by the Tet Offensive on January 31, 1968. Within weeks, support for the president's conduct of the war fell from 40 percent to 26 percent. The horrifying footage captured by intrepid reporters in Vietnam continued to contradict the administration's rosy predictions of victory. In February 1968, widely respected CBS news anchor Walter Cronkite reported, "It seems now more certain than ever that the bloody experience in Vietnam will end in stalemate . . . [and] that the only rational way out . . . will be to negotiate, not as victors, but as honorable people who lived up to their pledge to defend democracy and did the best they could." Instead, on March 10 the Joint Chiefs of Staff requested 200,000 more men and an increase in bombing. Two days later, Eugene McCarthy won 20 of the 24 Democratic delegates in the New Hampshire primary. Four days later, New York senator Robert Kennedy entered the race as a second antiwar candidate challenging the president within his own party.

On March 31, President Lyndon Johnson announced in a dramatic televised speech that he was taking steps to "de-escalate the conflict . . . unilaterally and at once." Adding to the surprise of that announcement, Johnson acknowledged the current "division in the American house," and then declared, "I shall not seek, and I will not accept, the nomination of my party for another term as your President."

The larger-than-life man who had rammed the Civil Rights Act through Congress, signed the Voting Rights Act, and initiated the landmark Great Society social welfare programs was quitting. LJB's dreams for America had been overwhelmed by the war in Vietnam, whose economic repercussions all but ensured that his domestic initiatives would not have the chance to grow and flourish. By the time he stepped down, the war in Vietnam had consumed 27,000 young American lives and was eating up almost 15 percent of the national budget annually.

SPRING: KILLING SEASON

Robert F. "Bobby" Kennedy was no left-wing radical. He began his political career at the side of Senator Joseph McCarthy, where he gained a reputation as a "ruthless" anti-Communist. As attorney general, he tolerated FBI infiltration of both the civil rights and the antiwar movements. A strict Catholic and father of ten children, Kennedy had no patience with the more hedonistic aspects of the youth movement. Devastated by his older brother John's assassination in November 1963, Bobby plunged into a deep depression. He emerged a more empathetic man, who came to identify with and to champion the interests of the disaffected, the impoverished, and the excluded.

Elected to the Senate in 1964 from New York State, he quickly became an outspoken opponent of the Vietnam War. Beseeched by antiwar Democrats to challenge LBJ for the presidential nomination in 1968, the freshman senator initially declined. But after McCarthy's stunning victory in the New Hampshire primary, Kennedy reconsidered and announced his candidacy.

Asked forthrightly why he was running, Kennedy's response indicated the distance he had traveled since 1963. "Because I found out something I never knew," he said. "I found out that my world was not the real world." The average American's world was not one of wealth, privilege, and access to power. In 1968, Kennedy took this knowledge with him when he visited American Indian reservations and spent time with people like César Chávez, the charismatic leader of the United Farm Workers.

Bettering Americans' lives would require a new kind of Democratic Party, Kennedy explained, one that united working-class whites and minorities and young people. "It's class, not color," that would bind Democrats together to end the war and promote the Great Society, he insisted. "What everyone wants is a job and some hope."

After three summers of violent urban riots sparked by confrontations between African Americans and white police officers, Kennedy was the last liberal politician who could keep white working-class America within the Democratic Party. "Working people trusted Kennedy," recalled one reporter. "They identified with his patriotism, his toughness, his Catholicism, his sense of loss, his law-and-order background, his devotion to family."

Kennedy was not the only American political leader who criticized the war while emphasizing economic justice. Martin Luther King linked the war and domestic unrest. "Flame throwers in Vietnam fan the flames in our cities," he explained. "I don't think the two can be separated." On April 4, 1968, King was shot and killed by James Earl Ray in Memphis, Tennessee, where King had traveled to lend support to a strike by municipal sanitation workers. King's murder sparked riots in 125 cities, as African Americans exploded in grief and rage. Whites who commented on the irony of marking the death of the "prince of peace" with violence were not calmed by CORE director Floyd Mc-Kissick's response: "Nonviolence is a dead philosophy, and it was not the black people that killed it." Campaigning in Indiana on that tragic spring day, Kennedy turned to the poet Aeschylus for language to inform a horrified crowd of King's murder. "Let us dedicate ourselves to what the Greeks wrote so many years ago," he pleaded. "'To tame the savageness of man and make gentle the life of this world.'"

This was not to be. Celebrating his critical victory in the California primary on June 4 at the Ambassador Hotel in Los Angeles, Robert Francis Kennedy was gunned down by Palestinian Sirhan Sirhan in protest of Kennedy's support of Israel. The man who moments earlier had flashed a peace sign and vowed to make his supporters' voices heard at the Democratic convention in Chicago in August was dead.

SUMMER IN CHICAGO

In 1968, 75 percent of Democratic delegates to the national party convention were chosen in local conventions and in the backroom meetings run by bosses such as Chicago's mayor Richard J. Daley (rather than in primaries). Although Lyndon Johnson had taken himself out of the race, his vice president, Hubert Humphrey, was seen as his stand-in and thus committed to Johnson's Vietnam policy. Two bitter fights were shaping up at the convention: one on the convention floor, where former Kennedy and McCarthy delegates pushed for a peace plank in the party platform, and the other on the streets outside, where two groups—the National Mobilization Committee to End the War in Vietnam (MOBE) and the Youth International Party (Yippies)— protested the proceedings within. The MOBE, led by David Dellinger and SDS leader Rennie Davis, was an umbrella group that aimed to forge consensus out of the cacophony emanating from the New Left. The Yippies were "led" by Abbie Hoffman and Jerry Rubin, both of whom were famous for their political street theater. In Chicago, they courted the media and baited the police by unleashing a greased, curly tailed presidential candidate, "Pigasus," in the Civic Center plaza. "Our candidate! Don't shoot our candidate!" cried Hoffman as police fingered their service revolvers.

Both the MOBE and the Yippies came to Chicago itching for confrontation with the establishment. The stage was set for disaster when the city refused to give the MOBE a permit to march or to allow the Yippies to sleep overnight in the parks. Undeterred, thousands of young antiwar protesters congregated in the parks.

As the Democrats wrangled in the convention hall, demonstrators clashed with police in the parks outside. Having obeyed the 11:00 p.m. municipal curfew the first few days of the convention, on Sunday, August 26, a 14-year-old boy defied the police and everyone else, crying "Onto the streets!" The Yippies followed; the MOBE begged them to stop. The young people taunted the police with their usual cry of "Pigs! Pigs!" The police charged, billy clubs swinging, tear gas canisters flying. Shotgun and rifle butts struck skulls randomly. In the Hilton parking lot, reporters watched policemen slash the tires of every car sporting a McCarthy bumper sticker. Pandemonium reigned. Abbie Hoffman was arrested for having "FUCK" written on his forehead.

Things only got worse over the next few days—which meant the story got juicier. The police beat reporters; they beat cameramen to prevent them from filming policemen beating up demonstrators. The cops teargassed the marchers. Order broke down on the floor of the convention, as thugs posing as Secret Service agents manhandled delegates and the police charged down the aisle with billy clubs. National guardsmen, bayonets drawn, patrolled the streets. Part of the central hallway of the Hilton was turned into a first aid station. Television cameras captured it all, as protesters chanted, "The whole world is watching! The whole world is watching!" Inside, New York senator Abe Ribicoff speechified for McGovern and then turned on Mayor Daley. "With George McGovern as president of the United States, we wouldn't have to have Gestapo tactics in the streets of Chicago!" No microphone captured Daley's emphatic response, but an expert lipreader later suggested that he was saying, "Fuck you, you Jew son of a bitch, you lousy motherfucker, go home."

The blame for what a federal investigatory commission labeled, officially, a "police riot" rests squarely on the shoulders of Mayor Daley. It was Daley who refused a permit for a peaceful antiwar demonstration, who encouraged the take-no-prisoners mentality of the cops, who ensured that Chicago would be the place where the unbridgeable gaps among Americans were revealed for all to see. "The war is destroying our country as we are destroying Vietnam," concluded leftist gadfly I. F. Stone. Veteran political correspondent Theodore White's verdict was more limited and more succinct. "The Democrats are finished," he scrawled in a notebook as he watched police chase hippies down Michigan Avenue.

AUTUMN: THE ELECTION

The twin legacies of the Chicago convention debacle and LBJ's aggressive Vietnam policy handicapped Hubert Humphrey's campaign from the start. If the Democrats could not control their own convention, how would they rule the country? The economy was booming, buoyed by government spending on the increasingly unpopular war in Vietnam. It was bad form for a vice president to criticize a sitting— if lame-duck—president. In September, Humphrey finally distanced himself from Johnson's foreign policy and declared that as president he would stop the bombing of North Vietnam and "move . . . towards de-Americanization of the war." With this, Humphrey became a plausible peace candidate. At the same time, an enormous AFL-CIO drive for Democratic votes began to show results.

This late surge helped create the impression that the election was closer than it actually was. Republican former vice president Richard Nixon took 43.4 percent of the popular vote; Humphrey 42.7 percent. The remaining 13.5 percent went to former Alabama governor and strict segregationist George C. Wallace, who ran as an independent Democrat and detached crucial Democratic constituencies from their traditional base. Urban, working-class whites, the sort who voted for Chicago's Democratic mayor Richard Daley, were attracted to Wallace. More than 10 percent of voters in Ohio, Michigan, Indiana, and Illinois cast their ballots for Wallace. Westerners liked him too, especially in Idaho and Nevada. Wallace split the white southern vote with Nixon; together, they took every state in the South except LBJ's Texas. The old New Deal coalition was no more.

The one issue that might have pushed Humphrey past Nixon was a viable path to ending the war in Vietnam. In October 1968, Henry Kissinger, a freelance Republican foreign policy advisor, advised Nixon that the Soviets had offered President Johnson a deal: if he would halt all bombing of North Vietnam, the Soviets would direct Hanoi to engage in peace talks. Nixon undercut Johnson's peace negotiations by reaching out to South Vietnamese president Nguyen Van Thieu through an intermediary, who urged the South Vietnamese to stay the course. When Johnson learned of Nixon's meddling, he called it a crime, and it likely was: the Logan Act (1799) forbids American citizens from undercutting US policy or interests by engaging with foreign governments.

During the campaign, Richard Nixon promised to end the Vietnam War, restore "law and order" to America, and "bring us [the nation] together." At the GOP convention, he pledged to speak for "the great majority of Americans, the forgotten Americans, the non-shouters, the non-demonstrators." This message appealed to Americans weary of riots and assassinations, exhausted by campus protests, and frankly terrified of black men with guns. George Wallace offered his own spin on the same problems, and said frankly, "We're gonna have a police state for folks who burn the cities down." Everyone knew the race of those "folks."

After the election, Nixon's running mate, former Maryland governor Spiro T. Agnew, who celebrated the "positive [political] polarization" of the 1960s, elaborated on the meaning of "bringing us together." "It is time to rip away the rhetoric and to divide on authentic lines," the new vice president declared. "When the President said 'bring us together,' he meant the functioning, contributing portions of the American citizenry." The president would have his job cut out for him: apparently distrustful of executive power, the same Americans who catapulted Nixon into the White House gave the Democrats both houses of Congress. The man who promised to bring at least some Americans together would be the first president since Zachary Taylor in 1849 to take office without a majority in either chamber.

*

The baby-boom generation was a global phenomenon; the struggles of 1968, whether against universities or political parties or repressive social systems, were a generational experience. Student movements challenged governments in Spain, France, Mexico, and, most memorably, Czechoslovakia. Journalist Hunter S. Thompson described it well: "Every now and then the energy of a whole generation comes to a head in a long fine flash, for reasons that nobody really understands at the time—and which never explain, in retrospect, what actually happened." There was, he reminisced, "a fantastic universal sense that whatever we were doing was right, that we were winning." It was this "sense of inevitable victory over the forces of Old and Evil. Not in any mean or military sense; we didn't need that. Our energy would simply prevail. . . . We had all the momentum; we were riding the crest of a high and beautiful wave." For Thompson and so many others, 1968 was the high-water mark of that wave: "that place where the wave finally broke and rolled back."

FIGURE 10. Grant Park, Chicago, 1968. Courtesy of Jeff Blankfort Photography.

CHAPTER 10

Breakdown, 1968–1974

Flying home from Vietnam in October 1966, Secretary of Defense Robert McNamara turned to his companion, Pentagon official Daniel Ellsberg, and said, "We've put more than a hundred thousand more troops into the country over the last year, and there's been no improvement." In fact, he confessed, "the underlying situation is really worse!" Ten minutes later, on the tarmac in Washington, DC, McNamara told reporters, "Gentlemen, I've just come back from Vietnam, and I'm glad to be able to tell you that we're showing great progress in every dimension of our effort."

A former marine, Daniel Ellsberg was an anti-Communist hawk. He worked for the Rand Corporation, a leading defense research center, where he specialized in developing strategies to deter a Soviet nuclear attack. In 1965, Ellsberg volunteered to serve in Vietnam as a State Department representative. What he saw there changed his views about the war and about American involvement in it. He grew especially concerned that the information Americans received about the war was frequently inaccurate and, worse, deceptive.

Ellsberg was not alone in his doubt. Even as he misled the public, Secretary McNamara was beginning to question American policy toward Vietnam. In 1967, McNamara commissioned a secret "history of U.S. decision-making process on Vietnam policy, 1945–1967." Two years and 7,000 pages later, the study documented how successive presidents knowingly misled the American people about the conduct and success of the war. Alaska senator Mike Gravel later observed that the report revealed "the purposeful withholding and distortion of facts" from the American people and a complete disregard "for the impact of our actions upon the Vietnamese people." McNamara was more blunt: "You know, they could hang people for what's in there."

Ellsberg read McNamara's study, known today as the Pentagon Papers, soon after its completion in 1969. He and an associate, Anthony Russo, secretly copied the entire report. In March 1971, Ellsberg—by then a professor at MIT—decided that the public should know what he knew. He passed a copy of the Pentagon Papers to the *New York Times*, which began to publish excerpts from the secret government report on June 11, 1971.

An enraged Nixon administration went to federal court to obtain an injunction forbidding any further revelations by the *Times*. Ellsberg then offered the Pentagon Papers to the *Washington Post*, which leapt at the chance to pick up where the *Times* left off. Ruling quickly, the Supreme Court held in a critically important freedom of speech case that the government could not constitutionally enjoin, or prevent by court order, the publication of such material, even though it might harm national security. "Security," wrote Justice Hugo Black, "is a broad, vague generality whose contours should not be invoked to abrogate the fundamental law embodied in the First Amendment."

The Pentagon Papers captivated the nation. After reviewing them, *Times* reporter Neil Sheehan, who had covered the war in Vietnam, came to the sobering conclusion that the government of the United States was not what he thought it was. It was as if there were a secret government within the government, Sheehan wrote, "far more powerful" than anyone could have imagined, that had "survived and perpetuated itself . . . using the issue of anti-Communism as a weapon against the other branches of government and the press." This internal government "[did] not function necessarily for the benefit of the Republic but rather for its own ends," using secrecy and deceit to protect itself from the people. Daniel Ellsberg took the argument one step further. "What these studies tell me," he told CBS news anchor Walter Cronkite, is that "we must remember this is a self-governing country. *We* are the government."

The Supreme Court decision in *New York Times Company v. United States* did not let Daniel Ellsberg off the hook: after surrendering to the authorities, he and Anthony Russo were indicted for stealing documents belonging to the government. The White House wanted a conviction. On September 3, 1971, the "plumbers," a secret White House group charged initially with plugging leaks, broke into the office of Ellsberg's psychiatrist looking for information that could help the government damn him in the press. When the judge presiding over Ellsberg's prosecution learned of the burglary, he dismissed all charges

because the "unprecedented" government misconduct "incurably infected the prosecution of this case." President Nixon was incredulous.
"The sonofabitching thief is made a national hero and is going to get
off on a mistrial. And the *New York Times* gets a Pulitzer Prize for stealing documents. . . . *What in the name of God have we come to?*" By the
middle of Nixon's second term, as layer after layer of government du-
plicity was revealed, the rest of America was asking the same question.

Bringing the Nation Together, 1968–1972

As he entered office in January 1969, President Nixon knew that he
had to soothe a nation that had fractured into multiple groups (whites,
African Americans, women, men, youth, old folks, workers, intellectuals) all at odds with each other. During the campaign, he had championed what he called "the silent majority" of Americans who paid
their taxes, sent their sons to war, and did not take to the streets in
protest. "Middle America," where presidential elections would be won
or lost for the next half century, did not exist as a popular term before
the mid-1960s and was more marsh than solid ground in 1969. Maintaining a majority formed by the merger of disgruntled white Democrats with an increasingly conservative Republican Party would be
tricky, but it was possible. Indeed, Nixon's election turned out to be a
bellwether: Democrats would win only one of the six presidential elections between 1968 and 1992. Nixon's campaign to bring "real" Americans together reflected the beginning of a profound shift in American
politics.

REALIGNMENT

Nixon realized that his future depended in part on his ability to woo
those Americans who had voted for George Wallace in 1968. He understood that Wallace voters were spooked by the rapid social changes
of the sixties. As a candidate in 1968, Nixon had challenged Wallace
for the "law and order" mantle, and he would continue to cast himself as the protector of Middle (white) America against the lawless
urban (black) element. This vision resonated strongly with urban
whites—traditional Democratic voters—whose neighborhoods bordered poor black areas. Black street crime soared in such places in the
1960s. When white Americans closed their eyes and imagined Afro-
America in 1969, they no longer saw John Lewis beaten by Alabama

state troopers on the Edmund Pettus Bridge. They saw angry blacks in Watts chanting "Burn, baby, burn!"

White support for black demands for justice and equality dropped precipitously after 1965. "Crime in the streets" leapfrogged to the top of the list of white domestic concerns and fused in white minds with ghetto riots, poor peoples' marches, hippies, student protests, and drugs, creating an opening for ostensibly race-neutral "law and order" rhetoric. Their eyes opened by black frustration and even rage in America, whites responded, unsurprisingly, with fear.

Aware of these shifts, Nixon undertook the difficult task of bringing Democratic defectors in the Northeast and Midwest—ethnic Catholics, blue-collar workers, union members, some lower-middle-class Jews—into a "New Majority" GOP dominated by social and economic conservatives. Disgruntled white Democrats felt unrepresented by their party (under the direction now, it seemed, of African Americans and well-off, white "limousine liberals"), but they remained stalwart defenders of the New Deal safety net that Republicans like Barry Goldwater wanted to remove.

Like Wallace, Nixon understood that "the race question" was inextricably bound up with issues of class. Americans wanted security. They wanted to feel secure in their homes, on their sidewalks, in their schools. They wanted to be secure in their employment and confident of their retirement. Wallace's American Independent Party called for increases in Social Security, national health care, and the right to collective bargaining. "Country and Western Marxism," as the leading conservative GOP magazine dubbed it, appealed strongly to working-class whites.

To romance New Majority workers, Nixon embraced key elements of Lyndon B. Johnson's Great Society vision, signing into law a bevy of bills passed by the Democratic-controlled Congress: the National Environmental Policy Act, which created the Environmental Protection Agency (EPA); the Clean Air Act; the Consumer Product Safety Act; the Federal Water Pollution Control Act; the Noise Pollution and Control Act; the Equal Employment Opportunity Act; the Federal Election Campaign Act of 1971; the Employment Retirement Income Security Act; and the Occupational Safety and Health Act (OSHA). Workers who were in dangerous occupations like coal mining, or who had been exposed to hazardous substances like asbestos, cheered, but GOP business interests held their applause. The Republican president, *Fortune* magazine moaned, was "putting cuffs on capitalism" through corporate regulation. Nixon's "baffling blend of Republicanism and radicalism" confused the editors of the *New York Times*, but it was congenial to the "Country and Western Marxist" heirs of Populism and the New Deal whom Nixon hoped to lure into the new GOP.

STANDARDS

Working-class prosperity had been considered synonymous with the national interest since WWII, when Franklin Roosevelt began to "lay the plans" for "the establishment of an American standard of living higher than ever known before." Speaking of human rather than constitutional rights, the president said in 1944 that every American had the right to a job, a living wage, a home, and an education. "We cannot be content," FDR added, "no matter how high that general standard of living may be, if some fraction of our people . . . is ill-fed, ill-clothed, ill-housed and insecure."

Americans found this vision appealing in 1944, and they still did 30 years later. According to a January 1973 Gallup poll, 91 percent of Americans believed that tax laws should be changed to "ease the burden on moderate and low income" citizens and to increase it for "high income people and corporations." When given the statement "The federal government has a responsibility to do away with poverty in this country," 72 percent of Americans agreed. Although 69 percent were skeptical about welfare, 62 percent felt more should be done to help the poor.

The key to prosperity in America since the New Deal was opportunity: namely, the opportunity to work. When FDR entered the White House in 1933, 25 percent of Americans could not find a job. Throughout the 1930s, unemployment never dipped below 14 percent. By the 1950s, unemployment had fallen to 4.6 percent. By 1969, when Nixon entered office, it stood at 3.9 percent. Between 1945 and 1970, Americans became richer overall and, at the same time, the gap between the rich and poor contracted. Full employment remained a goal of government, as did the eradication of poverty. These goals intersected and reinforced one another.

Policies designed to redress the effects of racial discrimination in employment and education through "affirmative [government] action" were not controversial when first formulated in the late 1960s. For example, the requirement that the workforce on federally funded construction projects reflect the local racial composition was a Nixon innovation in 1969. Neither a passionate supporter nor an opponent of black civil rights, Nixon called for "a middle course." This consisted of trying to block congressional renewal of the Voting Rights Act in 1970 (it was passed over the president's veto), acquiescing in Supreme Court decisions that chipped away at white privilege, and supporting affirmative action in circumstances where racial discrimination had clearly undermined black employment.

For the most part, Americans influenced by the Civil Rights Movement and the urban uprisings of the 1960s understood that improving the condition of "a whole people . . . marked as inferior by law" in the past (as LBJ put it) would require some sacrifice in the present. As long as America's rising economic tide was strong enough to lift all boats, most people were willing to accept government action designed to remedy past economic injustice. The future, however, was another story. Efforts to end racial discrimination in public schools turned out to be far more politically inflammatory than equal access to employment.

"it's not the bus, it's us"

Two separate but complementary issues characterized school desegregation efforts circa 1970: how to end discrimination resulting in segregated schools, which had been declared unconstitutional in *Brown*, and how to promote integration, which was not constitutionally mandated but commonly considered a beneficial effect of desegregation. Everyone agreed that *Brown* called for desegregation of public schools—but how?

Until 1969, everything the federal courts tried was stymied in the South by white resistance, including violence, the wholesale desertion of public schools for private all-white "segregation academies," and foot-dragging by state legislatures and municipal governments. In *Alexander v. Holmes County Board of Education* (1969), an exasperated and unanimous Supreme Court, led by Chief Justice Warren Burger, Nixon's first appointment to the court, ordered 33 school districts in Mississippi to desegregate their schools "now"—ending the delays occasioned by *Brown II*'s requirement of "all deliberate speed."

After *Alexander*, small towns had little choice but to desegregate. Bigger cities, though, managed to maintain what were effectively dual systems of neighborhood schools based on segregated residential patterns. Then, in *Swann v. Charlotte-Mecklenburg Board of Education* (1971), a unanimous Supreme Court endorsed the practice of assigning students to particular schools, even if they were not the closest to their homes, in order to desegregate school districts whose policies intentionally perpetuated segregated schools across district lines. This process came to be known as "busing."

These decisions, along with the 1964 Civil Rights Act, which authorized the Department of Health, Education, and Welfare (HEW) to withhold federal funds from segregated school districts, finally broke the back of school segregation in the South. Most white parents still balked at integration, but young people were increasingly calm. "If the parents would leave us alone, we'd make it," opined one white student in Yazoo City, Mississippi. By 1973, 46 percent of southern black children attended integrated schools—more than anywhere else in America.

As efforts to desegregate public schools moved into the North, white resistance was often as fierce as it had been 15 years earlier in the South. When a Detroit judge ordered busing in 1974, Mothers Alert Detroit (MAD) attacked the busing mandated by the decision, claiming to oppose busing rather than desegregation. SNCC founder and Georgia congressman Julian Bond was skeptical, commenting wryly, "It's not the bus, it's us."

When a court ordered busing between black and white Boston neighborhoods in 1974, enraged white mobs pelted school buses with bricks and bottles. Angry white mothers formed ROAR, an antibusing organization that pledged to "restore our alienated rights." When a black South Boston High School student stabbed a white antagonist, a thousand whites surrounded the school and fought off police efforts to free the 130 black students trapped inside.

White parents in Boston fought school integration tooth and nail. They were not necessarily more racist than other whites (although some of them certainly were). They were scared. They had seen what happened when neighborhoods desegregated. They had had realtors knock on their doors, whisper that the block was "turning," and warn against being the last family to sell before blacks moved in and property values nosedived. *Time* magazine declared busing "the most unpopular institution imposed on Americans since Prohibition." Before integration, whites constituted 60 percent of students in Boston's public schools. Fifteen years later, that number had fallen to 26 percent.

WHITE FLIGHT

It did not take whites long to figure out that the best way to liberate themselves from the stress of desegregation was to leave the cities entirely and move to the overwhelmingly white suburbs. As a consequence, cities like Memphis, Atlanta, and Richmond found that their recently desegregated school systems had resegregated overnight. This avenue of escape was cut off briefly in 1974, when a federal judge ruled that school district lines were "simply matters of political convenience" and ordered busing between Detroit and its suburbs, but this solution was short-lived. The Supreme Court rejected this approach in *Milliken v. Bradley* (1974), ruling 5–4 that busing was inappropriate if school segregation was "entirely" due to private residential choices.

After *Milliken*, whites could avoid urban school desegregation by abandoning the cities. White flight had devastating consequences for urban blacks, because as wealthier whites moved to the suburbs, urban schools were left with less money to spend per student. In a bitterly divided 5–4 decision in *San Antonio v. Rodriguez* (1973), the Supreme Court held that such disparities in school funding did not violate the Constitution for two reasons: because they were not *intended* to harm blacks and other racial minorities, and because, they said, there is no constitutional right to an equal education.

As even middle-class whites fled to the suburbs, those whites left behind despaired as their city (Detroit, Boston, Baltimore, Oakland, New York) struggled to maintain itself on a dramatically reduced tax base. Signs of urban decay and deterioration were everywhere: in the pothole-ridden streets, in the schools, in the crime statistics, in the empty storefronts on formerly vibrant commercial streets, in the garbage that piled up on corners.

In buying their modest homes in the 1950s and 1960s, working-class whites had invested in a package that included white neighbors and schools—community. Now, working-class, white neighborhoods were deteriorating, and residents could do nothing about it. They blamed liberal politicians and judges—Democrats—for effectively laying the entire burden of northern desegregation on white, working-class shoulders, abandoning them to live *like* black people, with no public services, as well as *with* them. In the presidential election of 1972, these traditional Democrats voted for a Democratic-controlled Congress that would protect the New Deal but split sharply from "their" party to reelect a president who stood for "law and order" and resisted busing. Charles Colson, the White House strategist responsible for the creation of the president's New Majority strategy, acknowledged that these resentful white Democrats "may not ever become Republicans," but, he proclaimed, "they're Nixon."

Americans Abroad

Ever since the US-Soviet face-off during the Cuban missile crisis in 1961, both the Soviets and the Americans had premised their foreign policy on the doctrine of mutually assured destruction (MAD). In a world of instantaneous and massive nuclear retaliation, neither side dared attack: to do so would have meant the total destruction of itself as well as the other. MAD really was mad: since each side held the other hostage, each was caught in a vicious cycle of arms escalation. MAD was a mainstay of the old Cold War policy of containment, which was in turn based on ideological rigidity, on an absolute, unbending opposition to Communism at home and abroad. Nixon was no ideologue, however, and neither was his brilliant, egomaniacal foreign policy architect, Henry Kissinger. Together, they worked to inject some 1970s "live and let live" spirit into American foreign policy.

VIETNAM

A brilliant statesman, President Nixon was desperate to disentangle the United States from Vietnam so he could pursue an ambitious new anti-Soviet agenda. Aided by National Security Advisor Henry Kissinger, who supplanted the secretary of state, William P. Rogers, in articulating American foreign policy, Nixon announced what came to be known as the Nixon Doctrine. Effectively a rejection of the containment policy that had shaped America's relationship to Communist nations since 1947, the Nixon Doctrine announced that although America would reward its friends with foreign aid and weapons sales, it was no longer willing to dedicate its own military resources to combat Communist growth in Asia, Africa, and Latin America.

At the same time, Nixon developed a three-pronged approach to end the war in Vietnam "honorably," which meant preserving an independent, pro-US government in South Vietnam. He sought to accomplish this by holding a series of secret meetings in Paris between Kissinger and the North Vietnamese, by replacing US troops with South Vietnamese soldiers (the Vietnamization of the war), and by expanding the air war in an effort to force North Vietnam to compromise. None of these tactics, including a massive bombing campaign in December 1972 known as the "Christmas bombings," succeeded.

As the war continued, the antiwar movement expanded. In November 1969, 750,000 people participated in the November Moratorium in Washington, DC—the largest antiwar demonstration in American history. The antiwar movement also split and turned violent. From the fall of 1969 to the spring of 1970, at least 250 bombings were directed at draft boards, induction centers, federal offices, the headquarters of certain corporations implicated in the war, and ROTC buildings on college campuses. The goal of these bombings was to "bring the war home," to force Americans to experience the violence endured on a far greater scale by the Vietnamese. As a member of the Weather Underground Organization (which split from SDS in 1969) explained, "We felt that doing nothing in a period of repressive violence is itself a form of violence. . . . If you sit in your house, live your white life, go to your white job, and allow the country that you live in to murder people and to commit genocide, and you sit there and you don't do anything about it, that's violence."

In March 1969, Nixon ramped up the bombing campaign against North Vietnam and secretly—without informing Congress—extended it to Viet Cong bases and supply routes in neighboring Cambodia and Laos. In April 1970, Nixon sent South Vietnamese and American troops across the Cambodian border. Not only did this strategy fail to dislodge the North Vietnamese from Cambodia; it prompted Hanoi to increase its support of local Communist insurgents fighting to overthrow the government there. The resulting Khmer Rouge victory was catastrophic for the Cambodian people, two million of whom fell victim to the Communists' genocidal rural relocation program.

The revelation of the president's Cambodian policy sparked immediate protests in Congress, in the media, and on college campuses nationwide. At Kent State University in Ohio, a public school with a largely working-class, white student body, students buried a copy of the Constitution and then burned down the campus ROTC building. Denouncing the students as "the worst type of people we harbor in America," Governor James Rhodes dispatched National Guard troops to quell the unrest. Unnerved by antiwar 19-year-olds throwing rocks, 19-year-old guardsmen fired on the demonstrators without warning. When the shooting ended, 4 students were dead and 13 were wounded—including some who had not participated in the protests at all, but found themselves within the two-mile range of the troop's M1 rifles.

BLOODLETTING

The response to the Kent State murders was fast and furious. Within a few days, 1.5 million students nationwide walked out of class, and a fifth of the nation's colleges and universities closed their doors temporarily. Eleven days after the Kent State killings, Mississippi highway patrolmen turned their guns on a dormitory at all-black Jackson State College during an antiwar protest there, killing two students.

Still the war dragged on. A year after Kent State, in April 1971, a half million people gathered in the nation's capital to demand America's immediate withdrawal from Vietnam. A week later, thousands of protesters assembled in Washington aiming to use massive nonviolent protests to paralyze the city. Before they had a chance to act, police and the military swept the downtown area: 7,000 people were arrested and incarcerated temporarily in Robert F. Kennedy Stadium. *Newsweek*, appalled, commented that the attack on the protesters "seemed more appropriate to Saigon in wartime than Washington." President Nixon was unperturbed. A few days later, he told his aide Charles Colson, "One day we'll get them—we'll get them on the ground where we want them. And we'll stick our heels in, step on them hard and twist—right, Chuck? Right?" Somewhere between 1967 and 1971, the war had ceased to be between North Vietnam and the United States and had become a vicious battle among Americans.

President Nixon finally achieved a negotiated settlement in Vietnam in January 1973. American bombing ended, as did the draft. The United States Armed Forces would henceforth be all volunteer. In November 1973, Congress passed the War Powers Act, which spelled out procedures to be followed when the introduction of American forces could lead to their involvement in combat. Passed over President Nixon's veto, the War Powers Act has been interpreted by every president since as an unconstitutional infringement on the power of the executive. The Paris Peace Accords negotiated by Kissinger spared the government of South Vietnam, but left North Vietnamese and Viet Cong troops in control of part of the South: thus failing to address the basic issue of the war—whether Vietnam would be one country or two. That question was answered definitively in the spring of 1975, when North Vietnam launched a military offensive against the South, and the United States failed to intervene. On April 30, 1975, Americans glued to their television sets watched as North Vietnamese tanks rolled into Saigon and US helicopters airlifted American embassy personnel to safety.

The final cost of the war in Vietnam may be measured in many ways: in the 58,000 American lives lost (20,000 of them, or 40 percent, on Nixon's watch) and the 3–4 million Vietnamese dead, in the 300,000 Americans and countless Vietnamese wounded, in the $100 billion price tag that all but guaranteed the failure of the Great Society, in the widespread violation of civil liberties, in the precipitous decline of respect for the military and the executive branch, and in the loss of American international prestige and power.

Finally, and perhaps most enduringly, the Vietnam War permanently divided a generation and shaped American politics for the next 40 years. Those who had fought a war now considered a mistake, those who were beaten by police in the streets, and those who saw their peers stomp on the flag and blow up buildings or shoot unarmed protesters had all burned the bridges that might have reconnected an exhausted and fragmented nation. Avoiding "another Vietnam" became an American foreign policy obsession, although it did not deter the nation from involving itself in the civil wars of others.

FURTHER FOREIGN FAULT LINES

When the Soviets crushed the Czechoslovakian reform movement in 1968, they alarmed more than the United States. They startled their ally China. Chinese and Soviet Communists had never been as close as American policymakers imagined they were. America had yet to formally recognize the People's Republic of China (PRC); since 1949, the United States had maintained that Taiwan, the island to which Chiang Kai-shek's nationalist government had fled after being ousted by the Communists, was the "real" China. By 1968, however, both the Chinese and the Americans wanted to find some way to reconcile. China was simply too powerful for the United States to ignore. At the same time, China could not play a meaningful role in the world if it continued to be seen as a Soviet pawn.

With wit and perception, the Chinese began with ping-pong. Beijing hosted a US team in April 1971. Ten months later, on February 21, 1972, Richard Nixon flew to China, the first sitting American president ever to visit the People's Republic. His goal was to "seek normalization of relations." Nixon's every move was captured by television and beamed into American living rooms: the president eating with chopsticks, the president at the Great Wall, the president toasting Premier Jou En-lai (Chou En-lai) in the Great Hall of the People. In Beijing,

Nixon agreed to the gradual withdrawal of American troops from Taiwan and accepted the PRC's claim that Taiwan remained part of China.

Nixon's China visit, orchestrated by Henry Kissinger without the knowledge of the State Department, opened the way to full diplomatic relations with China, which in turn opened the door to trade with this massive and enormously productive nation. The China gambit turned American relations with Communist nations into a complex three-dimensional game, with the Soviet Union and China paired off one against the other. It was a brilliant strategy. Only a diplomat willing to privilege practical political realities over moral or ideological positions could have engineered it, and only a president with the impeccable anti-Communist credentials of Richard Nixon could have pulled it off. Had any Democratic president attempted such a move, Nixon and his allies would have made mincemeat of him for selling out Taiwan and kowtowing to the Communists. Hence the saying "Only Nixon could have gone to China."

Although the domino theory had been discredited with regard to the spread of Communism in Asia, it *did* apply to the arms race. China detonated a nuclear bomb in 1964. In May 1972, Nixon became the first American president to visit the Soviet Union, where his strategy of détente—French for the easing of hostilities—bore fruit. He engaged in strategic arms limitation talks (SALT) and came home with a treaty regulating antiballistic missiles (ABM).

Even as he negotiated with the two leading Communist nations, Nixon continued to resist Communist regimes elsewhere, especially in "his" hemisphere. When Chile elected Socialist Salvador Allende as president in 1970, Kissinger, irked, declared, "I don't see why we need to stand by and watch a country go Communist due to the irresponsibility of its own people." In 1973, Allende committed suicide during a military coup in which the CIA played a shady role. Five days after the coup, the following exchange, captured on Nixon's secret tape recorder in the Oval Office, took place between Kissinger and President Nixon:

KISSINGER: The Chilean thing is getting consolidated and of course the newspapers are bleeding because a pro-Communist government has been overthrown.

NIXON: Isn't that something. Isn't that something.

KISSINGER: I mean instead of celebrating—in the Eisenhower period we would be heroes.

NIXON: Well we didn't—as you know—our hand doesn't show on this one though.

KISSINGER: We didn't do it. I mean we helped them. . . . [We] created the conditions as great as possible.

NIXON: That is right. And that is the way it is going to be played.

Allende was replaced by General Augusto Pinochet, who was condemned around the world for his use of political repression and torture. Pinochet's government was rewarded by the Nixon administration with economic aid that had been withheld from Allende.

In Africa, Nixon backed white supremacist regimes in Rhodesia and South Africa, while the CIA instigated a plan to murder Congolese president Patrice Lumumba. As in Vietnam, American support of repressive antidemocratic regimes in Africa and Latin America convinced many people around the world that the United States was a bulwark of authoritarianism rather than a beacon of freedom.

MIDDLE EASTERN COMPLICATIONS

In 1945, the United States pumped more oil than all other oil-producing countries combined. Domestic oil production peaked in 1970, but domestic oil *consumption* continued to rise. Americans' love affair with the automobile had a lot to do with it—the number of cars on the nation's roads doubled between 1950 and 1970. So did suburban sprawl: all those living rooms with plate-glass windows had to be heated.

In 1960, the leading North American oil producers outside North America joined forces in the Organization of Petroleum Exporting Countries (OPEC) to reduce competition, regulate production, and raise prices. In June 1967, after Israel repulsed a coordinated attack by its Arab neighbors in the Six-Day War, capturing strategic territory from Syria and Egypt in the process, the Arab oil states linked the politics of oil to the Israel question. The message was clear: oil-importing nations would pay for their support of Israel in high energy prices. It was a fair move—the United States did something similar every time it cut foreign aid to countries that elected leftist governments. But it spelled trouble for the United States and Western Europe.

On October 6, 1973, which was Yom Kippur (a sacred Jewish day of prayer and fasting), Egypt and Syria launched another full-scale attack against Israel. Caught off guard and outgunned by armies carrying Soviet arms, Israel appealed to the United States for help. Wanting to send a message to the Soviets as well as support Israel, President

Nixon responded with an airlift of arms that enabled the Israelis to fight their way back from the brink of disaster.

Saudi Arabian king Faisal bin Abdul-Aziz al Saud had threatened an oil embargo if the United States resupplied Israel during the war. On October 20, two days after Nixon announced $2.2 billion in military aid to Israel, Saudi Arabia ended oil shipments to the United States and the Netherlands, which alone among the European nations aided the Israelis. Together, the embargo and cutbacks in production sent the price of crude oil skyrocketing.

Overnight, the price of gasoline quadrupled (from 30 cents a gallon to $1.20). States instituted rationing—last seen during WWII. The oil crisis spurred the nation to think about conservation and the exploration of alternative energy sources, and to consider the links between smog, cars, gas, and their monthly budget. To conserve energy, Congress lowered the speed limit on interstate highways from 70 to 55 miles per hour. This assault on automotive liberty further annoyed Americans still griping about new state laws requiring seatbelt use.

The oil crisis of 1973–1974 delivered a strong punch to an economy already weakened by rising unemployment and inflation. Beginning in 1969, inflation rose at the same time as unemployment. In the most dramatic intervention in the economy since WWII, President Nixon introduced wage and price controls in 1971 (setting limits on each) in an effort to check inflation. The economy stabilized momentarily, but inflation came roaring back in the winter of 1973, hitting a record 11 percent, while unemployment rose to 8.5 percent. The 1970s became one of the few decades in American history in which Americans were poorer at the end than at the beginning.

A final effect of the 1973 oil embargo was to propel the Middle East to the forefront of American foreign policy. Negotiating peace between Israel and its neighbors became a matter of US national interest. With Britain and France suddenly receptive to Arab claims against Israel (whose continued occupation of territory gained in 1967 remained a flashpoint of controversy), various organizations claiming to speak for Palestinians stepped onto the world stage. The Palestine Liberation Organization (PLO), led by Yasser Arafat, gained a hearing at the United Nations.

Other associations turned to terrorism to get the attention of the West. Black September torpedoed Germany's triumphant 1972 Munich Olympics when its operatives massacred Israeli athletes in their dormitory. In 1976, the Popular Front for the Liberation of Palestine and the German Baader-Meinhof Gang commandeered an Air France jet carrying 258 passengers from Tel Aviv to Paris and forced it to land at Uganda's Entebbe Airport. The terrorists released non-Jewish and non-Israeli hostages but promised to execute the remaining 105 unless Israel acceded to their demands. In a made-for-the-movies gambit, Israeli Defense Forces (IDF) soldiers flew to Uganda, stormed the plane, and rescued all but three hostages. "This is what Americans used to do," former California governor Ronald Reagan remarked wistfully.

A Government of Laws or of Men?

Richard Nixon campaigned in 1968 as a healer and as a miracle worker: he vowed to end the war in Vietnam, bring the troops home, restore faith in the executive branch, and soothe a troubled nation. As president, Nixon had many successes. But restoring faith in government was not one of them. Instead, his cavalier violations of the law precipitated the greatest constitutional crisis since the Civil War.

REELECTION: THE "SILENT MAJORITY" SPEAKS

By 1972, Nixon's courting of Wallace voters was at risk of being undone by George Wallace himself, who again announced his candidacy for president, speaking for the "beauticians, the truck drivers, the office workers, the policemen and the small businessmen." Wallace was the only Democratic candidate openly opposed to "forced busing" of school children. Anxious to avoid antagonizing black voters, the other leading Democrats—Maine senator Edwin Muskie, liberal warhorse Hubert Humphrey, and South Dakota senator George McGovern— were paralyzed by Wallace, who taunted them as well as the president. "If I win in Florida, you just watch," Wallace told reporters. The White House would come down "both feet" against busing, and Nixon would be outside "taking the batteries out of the buses." Anxious to demonstrate his administration's opposition to "forcibly integrated education," the president still had to enforce the law. When Secretary of Health, Education, and Welfare Elliot Richardson enforced the federal courts' busing decrees, Nixon ordered his chief domestic advisor, John Ehrlichman, to "personally jump Richardson and [the Department of] Justice and tell them to *Knock off this Crap*. . . . Do what the law requires," Nixon instructed, "and not *one bit more.*"

Wallace won the Florida Democratic primary on March 15, 1972. Journalists wrote Wallace off as outdated, but Nixon recognized that he had just glimpsed the future. Less than 48 hours after Wallace's victory in Florida, the president appropriated language from the antiwar movement and called upon Congress to impose a "moratorium" on the federal courts to prevent them from issuing any new busing orders.

When Wallace finished second in Wisconsin, a traditionally liberal state, he confirmed Nixon's view that the "gut issues" in the election would be crime, busing, drugs, and welfare. By mid-May, Wallace was favored to win in Michigan and Maryland. The Democrats were doomed, Nixon concluded. Because there were far more delegates who were local officials and other party functionaries than delegates pledged through primary elections, McGovern was ahead in the delegate count and likely to receive the nomination. But Wallace voters, Nixon reckoned, would never go for liberal McGovern. If Wallace ran as an independent as he had in 1968, he would divide the Democratic vote; if he did not run, his voters would flock to the GOP. Either way, Nixon concluded, his reelection was in the bag.

On May 15, greeting the crowd at an event in Maryland, George Wallace was shot point-blank by Arthur Bremer, a mentally unstable white man from Milwaukee. Bremer's first target, it was revealed later, was Nixon, whom Bremer had stalked all spring but was unable to approach because of the tight security around the president. Wallace survived the shooting, but he was paralyzed from the waist down.

Informed of the shooting, Nixon's first impulse was to link the shooter with McGovern: "Wouldn't it be great if [Bremer] had left-wing propaganda in [his] apartment?" Nixon asked presidential advisor/professional yes-man Charles Colson. In a spur-of-the-moment scheme as audacious as it was illegal, Nixon had Colson send the same man who had broken into the office of Daniel Ellsberg's psychiatrist to Bremer's apartment to see if he could plant McGovern campaign materials there. It was too late—the press and the FBI were there already. Never mind, said the president.

THE NEW MAJORITY

The Democratic convention in Miami was less violent than the 1968 convention in Chicago had been, but the outcome was, if anything, more divisive. Nixon made sure Wallace made it to Miami, providing a C-147 hospital plane on "humanitarian" grounds. The Democrats had rewritten their party rules after 1968 to limit the power of organized labor and white ethnics in northeastern cities and to ensure the representation of women, African Americans, and the young. As rank-and-file white Democrats moved to the right, party activists and delegates moved to the left. George McGovern won the nomination, but the internal dissent his candidacy provoked augured poorly for the November election. Three times McGovern met with Wallace seeking his endorsement. Wallace refused, explaining, "The problem, George, is that our people, even if I was to endorse you, I couldn't get them to support you." The AFL-CIO had the same problem, and for the first time in its history declined to endorse a presidential candidate. Wallace delegates, many of whom were AFL-CIO members, remained passionately devoted to defeating McGovern, who supported busing, amnesty for draft dodgers, and abortion rights, and opposed the death penalty.

All the earnest antiwar college students who went door-to-door for McGovern could not change the white middling sorts' impression of the Democratic candidate as implacably opposed to their interests. Nixon captured the endorsement of the teamsters', longshoremen's, and construction workers' unions. Of Democratic voters who had voted for Wallace in 1968, 80 percent voted for Nixon in 1972. Almost 10 million Democrats voted for Nixon, including 70 percent of the white working class. The president defeated McGovern in a rout, winning every state except Massachusetts.

It is vital to be precise when drawing conclusions from the 1972 election. Richard Nixon's reelection did not signify a general desire to limit federal authority at home or American power abroad, or to limit the portfolio of the federal government. As in 1968, the same voters who flocked to Nixon also elected a Democratic-controlled Congress they expected to regulate the economy and protect Social Security and Medicare. Nixon's New Majority wanted the president to end the Vietnam War, but with honor and not on his hands and knees, as McGovern had promised to do if that was what it took to make peace with North Vietnam. It wanted to protect black civil rights, but cautiously. As polling analysts noted at the time, Nixon was the only candidate of the three whose supporters wanted to maintain black progress at its current levels rather than slow it down (Wallace) or speed it up (McGovern). The New Majority did not want to go back to the 1950s. But it did want a moment to catch its breath.

DIRTY TRICKS

If the White House had not sent operatives to break into the office of Daniel Ellberg's psychiatrist hoping to find compromising personal information, it is likely that Ellsberg would have gone to jail for stealing and copying the Pentagon Papers. But convicting Ellsberg was not enough for Nixon: he wanted Ellsberg destroyed. "Don't worry about the trial," the president explained to Kissinger and Attorney General John Mitchell, shortly after the leaks began in June 1971. "Just get everything out. Try him in the press. . . . Everything, John, that there is on the investigation, get it out, leak it out. We want to destroy him in the press. Press. Is that clear?" Convinced that there was a conspiracy behind Ellsberg, the president demanded repeatedly that the Brookings Institute (Ellsberg's former employer) be burgled, too. "I want the Brookings Institute's safe *cleaned out*," the president commanded. "Get it done."

Break into Ellsberg's psychiatrist's office! Raid the Brookings Institute! Plant McGovern materials in Bremer's apartment! Break into the National Archives and steal the secret Vietnam papers of Lyndon Johnson's aides! ("There are ways to do that?" asked the president.) Surrounded by advisors who specialized in "dirty tricks," it never seemed to occur to Nixon that there were limits to what he could get away with. Breaking and entering was simply another tool of the political operative, like spreading rumors.

Nixon had been playing this way for years—leaking information damaging to others and disrupting his political opponents whenever possible. It was no accident that he had carried the nickname "Tricky Dick" since 1950. The president's infamous "Enemies List" was miles long, as was his list of potential punishments. The Committee to Re-elect the President (CREEP) hounded the Democratic frontrunner in the New Hampshire primary, Edmund Muskie, circulating rumors that Muskie's wife, Jane, drank and told dirty jokes, slipping Muskie's pilot a bogus schedule to disrupt the candidate's plans, planting rumors that Muskie planned to name Carl Stokes, the black mayor of Detroit, his running mate. A fake "Harlem for Muskie Committee" phoned white New Hampshire voters in the middle of the night. Banners reading "HELP MUSKIE; SUPPORT BUSING MORE CHILDREN NOW" appeared mysteriously at Democratic rallies. It was unnecessary—Nixon was in no danger of losing his job. But it was amusing, and possibly addictive as well.

On the night of June 17, 1972, five men were arrested for breaking into the Democratic National Committee (DNC) headquarters in Washington's Watergate apartment and office complex. The break-in was undertaken under the auspices of the secret White House Special Investigation Unit, nicknamed the "plumbers," that had been formed to plug government leaks after Daniel Ellsberg's release of the Pentagon Papers. The plumbers operated out of the office of John Ehrlichman, chief domestic advisor to the president. Revealing the layers-within-layers texture of the Nixon White House, one man arrested that night was John McCord, the security director for CREEP.

A month after the break-in and six weeks before the 1972 presidential election, the FBI determined that the head of the Nixon reelection campaign, former attorney general John Mitchell, controlled a secret Republican fund that financed intelligence gathering on Democrats and other "enemies" of the Nixon administration. On October 10, the FBI reported that the Watergate break-in was part of a massive campaign of political spying and sabotage on behalf of Nixon's reelection. None of this was directly connected to the president, however, and therefore did not interfere with Nixon's electoral cakewalk on November 7, when he was reelected by the second-largest popular-vote margin in US history.

BREACH OF FAITH

The Watergate story might have been crushed beneath the weight of the election and a sinking economy if John McCord had been prepared to take a fall for the president. Convicted of participating in the burglary, McCord shocked the nation in March 1973 by alleging that high-ranking government officials had lied during the investigation, that he and others had been pressured by people in high places to hold their tongues and go to jail, and that many participants in the Watergate crime had never been identified. A Senate committee chaired by North Carolina Democrat Sam Ervin was formed to investigate the cover-up. The committee issued a series of subpoenas to White House personnel to compel their testimony.

The Senate Watergate hearings, broadcast live nationally five days a week during the summer of 1973, were watched by millions of incredulous Americans. A central question was whether the president himself had been involved in any of the unlawful conduct. Nixon proclaimed his innocence. When one White House aide revealed the existence of a secret tape-recording system in the Oval Office that preserved the president's conversations, special prosecutor Archibald Cox demanded the tapes. Nixon claimed executive privilege, arguing that White House conversations were confidential. Cox disagreed. Besieged, Nixon ordered Attorney General Elliot Richardson to fire Cox. Richardson resigned. Richardson's deputy William Ruckelshaus, who automatically became the acting attorney general when Richardson resigned, did the same. Solicitor General Robert H. Bork, who was next in line as acting attorney general, argued that *somebody* had to obey the president's orders and fired Cox. This series of events, which came to be known as the "Saturday night massacre," outraged Americans, who demanded the appointment of a new special prosecutor and the release of the tapes.

The president surrendered most of the tapes but held on to others, insisting that executive privilege trumped a subpoena from Congress. Nine months later, on July 24, 1974, the Supreme Court ruled unanimously in *United States v. Nixon* that the president's claim of executive privilege did not control. It is noteworthy that all four of Nixon's appointees to the court ruled against him. At this point, Nixon might have refused to comply with the court's order or just destroyed the most incriminating tapes. To his credit, he turned them over, including a tape that established, beyond doubt, that the president had ordered the Watergate cover-up, if not the burglary itself.

That week the House Judiciary Committee voted that Richard Nixon should be impeached (removed from office) for obstruction of justice. A few days later, the committee added two more grounds of impeachment—abuse of power and contempt of Congress. On August 5, after hearing a newly discovered "smoking gun" tape that determined definitively that the president approved the Watergate cover-up, Nixon's lawyers declared that he had "lied to the nation, to his closest aides, and to his own lawyers for more than two years." Confronted by a delegation of senior leaders of Congress, Nixon addressed the nation in a televised speech on August 8. He announced his resignation—the first and only resignation of an American president—but confessed to only a "few mistakes in judgment." The House of Representatives did not vote on impeachment. Nixon left the White House by helicopter at noon the next day as Vice President Gerald R. Ford was sworn in as president.

ABUSE OF POWER

Watergate is not usually considered a shining moment for the American republic. The president resigned in disgrace, 25 of Nixon's top aides were indicted for criminal activity, the acting head of the FBI was forced to resign (for destroying incriminating documents), and former attorney general John Mitchell was on his way to prison. In an unrelated crisis, Vice President Spiro Agnew had to resign his office in

October 1973 as part of a plea bargain on bribery charges. He was replaced by Michigan congressman Gerald R. Ford, who later succeeded Nixon as president. Watergate disillusioned and alienated millions of Americans from the world of politics. The national mood was one of shock and revulsion. "Don't vote," urged one bumper sticker. "It only encourages them."

However, Congress rose to the occasion and exercised its constitutional responsibility to check the power of the president and ensure the rule of law. The press—known sometimes as the "fourth branch" of government—also distinguished itself in its successful effort to expose government wrongdoing. Executive branch officials like Elliot Richardson and William Ruckelshaus demonstrated a commitment to principle. The Supreme Court reaffirmed the rule that no man is above the law. And of course, when push came to shove, Richard Nixon ultimately obeyed the law and did not destroy the incriminating tapes.

The Watergate investigation led to other troubling revelations about the secret activities of the executive branch. On December 22, 1974, the *New York Times* published an article by Seymour Hersh describing illegal covert activities by the CIA directed against "antiwar forces" and "other dissidents." This report triggered the formation of the Church Committee, chaired by Idaho senator Frank Church. Senate hearings revealed a history of illegal intelligence activities by every administration since the start of the Cold War. The CIA had conducted secret operations to overthrow foreign governments and attempted to assassinate foreign leaders. The FBI and NSA (National Security Agency) had spied on millions of Americans and tried to disrupt both the civil rights and the antiwar movements. The FBI counterintelligence program (COINTELPRO) targeted groups such as the NAACP, SCLC, and SDS, following Director J. Edgar Hoover's command to "expose, disrupt, misdirect, discredit or otherwise neutralize" groups he considered "subversive." The Church Committee concluded, "Groups and individuals have been harassed and disrupted because of their political views and their lifestyles. . . . Unsavory and vicious tactics have been employed—including anonymous attempts to break up marriages, disrupt meetings, ostracize persons from their professions, and provoke or target groups into rivalries that might result in deaths. Intelligence agencies have served the political and personal objectives of presidents and other high officials. . . . Government officials— including those whose principal duty is to enforce the law—have violated or ignored the law over long periods of time and have advocated and defended their right to break the law."

For all but the most cynical Americans, Watergate and later revelations about the CIA and the FBI, on top of the earlier disclosures in the Pentagon Papers, were deeply disillusioning. One post-Watergate poll reported that 70 percent of Americans believed that during the past decade "this country's leaders have consistently lied to the people." When the new president, Gerald Ford, pardoned Richard Nixon unconditionally on September 8, 1974, he only added to "the drop in political trust." Ford rationalized the pardon as necessary to put Watergate "behind us as quickly as possible," but the new president's press secretary, who resigned in protest over the pardon, disagreed: "The pardon tore the scab off the Watergate wound just as it was beginning to heal."

R-E-S-P-E-C-T

In a world characterized by male domination across the social, economic, and political spectrum, women with nothing else in common could nod their heads when black R&B queen Aretha Franklin belted out her 1967 hit "Respect." Even those scandalized by the song's open demand for female sexual satisfaction (with its bouncy command that her man "sock it to me, sock it to me, sock it to me, sock it to me!") could nonetheless identify with its broader plea:

> I gotta have (just a little bit)
> A little respect (just a little bit)

Women brought their own set of social, cultural, and economic concerns to politics in the 1970s. "Respect" meant decidedly different things to different groups of women. For some, it meant equal access to government and the professions, a chance to mold and lead their city, state, or nation. For others, it meant recognition of the crucial contribution made by wives and mothers. Understanding the political history of the last third of the twentieth century requires recognizing the astonishing rise of women.

WOMEN'S WORK

If there was one thing that conservative and liberal women involved in American politics in 1970 could agree on, it was that they were tired of being treated like servants by their male political comrades. On the left, Toni Cade (later Bambara) remarked that "mutinous cadres of women" in all kinds of protest organizations started "getting salty about having to . . . fix the coffee while the men wrote the position papers and decided on policy." On the right, Phyllis Schlafly, whose later political influence matched that of many Republican men, fumed in 1967, "Many men in the [Republican] Party frankly want to keep women doing the menial work, while the selection of candidates and the policy decisions are taken care of by the men in the smoke-filled rooms." Probably no major-party politician would have quipped, as SNCC leader Stokely Carmichael did when confronted by disgruntled women, that the only position for women in politics was prone, but Democrats and Republicans alike would have laughed and told their frustrated female colleagues to "lighten up."

While some women became political activists, others expanded their participation in the market. The paid labor force experienced a massive restructuring in the 1970s, as legions of women between the ages of 20 and 40 entered the job market. Educated women leapt in gladly, happy for the chance, finally, to pursue a profession. Working-class women were more often pushed into the pool by their husbands' declining earnings and the inflation-driven rise in consumer costs. Between 1970 and 1980, six million mothers of infants and school-age children left full-time housekeeping and went to work for wages. By 1980, more than 50 percent of mothers with children under age six worked outside the home. The modern feminist movement both caused and responded to deep social changes—as did the antifeminist movement. Both were, in great measure, rooted in the new reality of the working mother.

Women's lives had been a topic of general conversation since the 1963 publication of Betty Friedan's best seller *The Feminine Mystique*. The suburban mother and former journalist identified what she called "the problem with no name"—the purposelessness felt by many full-time middle-class housewives. Whereas many workingwomen longed to dedicate themselves to their families, educated women like Friedan found domestic life suffocating. Minds broadened by college educa-tion revolted against the idea that motherhood should be a woman's highest ambition and that women were by nature passive, subordi-nate, and nurturing rather than ambitious, creative, and driven.

The new generation of middle-class, white feminists put their edu-cations to work in protesting the reigning culture of womanhood. In September 1968, a group of self-described radical feminists protested the Miss America pageant in Atlantic City by tossing symbols of everyday female oppression such as girdles, false eyelashes, and high-heeled shoes into a "Freedom Trash Can." With a nod to the Yippies and their Pigasus presidential candidate the previous June, the Atlantic City event culminated in the coronation of a sheep as Miss America.

The actions of the new generation of feminists and the unprecedented rise in the number of working mothers vented a more general unease about women's "natural" social role. The more women's social and economic roles changed, the more important it seemed to define women's essential nature. It need not have been a zero-sum game, but for many Americans the more the definition of "women" expanded to include female doctors and lawyers and auto workers, the more the definition of "men" seemed to narrow.

RIGHTS AND OBLIGATIONS

Americans have argued about the relationship among rights, obligations, and entitlements since the first days of the Republic. Was military service a right or an obligation? What about jury service? In 1879, the Supreme Court ruled that the exclusion of men from juries on account of race violated the Fourteenth Amendment's equal protection clause. Although women won the vote through passage of the Nineteenth Amendment in 1920, until the mid-1960s they were denied the opportunity of jury duty in almost every state. Was this exemption a privilege or an unconstitutional exclusion? Was sex like race?

In 1965, a federal appeals court ruled that jury service was "a form of participation in the processes of government, a responsibility, and a right that should be shared by all citizens, regardless of sex." In 1971, in *Reed v. Reed*, the Supreme Court ruled for the first time that discrimination on the basis of sex could violate the Fourteenth Amendment's equal protection clause. Two years later, the court sided with Air Force officer Sharron Frontiero, who wanted to claim dependent's benefits for her husband on the same terms that her male colleagues did for their wives. Invoking a brief written by ACLU lawyer Ruth Bader Ginsburg, Justice William Brennan declared, "There can be no doubt that our Nation has had a long and unfortunate history of sex discrimination. Traditionally, such discrimination was rationalized by an attitude of 'romantic paternalism' which . . . put women, not on a pedestal, but in a cage." Congress itself, he added, had "concluded that classifications based upon sex are inherently invidious."

The congressional action that Justice Brennan referred to in *Fron-*

tiero v. Richardson was the Equal Rights Amendment (ERA), which Congress had approved and submitted to the states for ratification. First proposed in 1923 in honor of the 75th anniversary of the Seneca Falls Convention, the ERA prohibited government from denying or abridging equality of rights under the law on account of sex. Three-quarters of all Americans, including First Lady Betty Ford, supported the ERA. For the amendment to be incorporated into the Constitution, 38 states needed to ratify it. When the court decided *Frontiero*, 30 states already had.

By 1975, however, the ERA was dead in the water. It had been stopped in its tracks by Catholic lawyer, GOP activist, and mother of six Phyllis Schlafly, who founded STOP ERA, a campaign organized around the slogan "Stop Taking Our Privileges," in 1972. A fervent anti-Communist and Goldwater supporter in 1964, Schlafly was a firm believer in difference, between the races and between the sexes. "Why should we lower ourselves to 'equal rights' when we already have the status of special privileges?" she asked in 1972. Enfranchised and emancipated from drudgery by vacuums and self-cleaning ovens, American women were the most privileged women the world had ever seen. Schlafly concluded that "women's libbers" were using the "Extra Responsibility Act" to wage "a total assault on the family, on marriage, and on children" by undermining "the most basic and precious legal right that wives now enjoy, the right to be a full-time homemaker."

As any poor woman could attest, there was no "right" to be a full-time homemaker. The ERA did not impose on wives and mothers the "*legal* obligation to go out to work to provide half the family income," as Schlafly charged. But when Schlafly insisted that the ERA would sever women from their children and force them from the home into the marketplace, she tapped into the broad anxiety many American women felt when they surveyed the world around them. When these women joined ranks to lobby their state representatives to oppose the ERA, it went down to defeat three votes short of ratification in 1982.

"OUR BODIES, OURSELVES"

Pro- and anti-ERA forces had one important thing in common: each recognized the fundamental fact that women have babies and men do not. Each recognized the special vulnerability of women in this regard; both confronted the issue of childcare and wanted increased state support for families. Feminists who wanted to participate fully in the world outside the home wanted state-supported childcare such as women in Western Europe enjoyed. Congress passed legislation in 1971 to provide a system of childcare centers, but President Nixon vetoed it on the grounds that it would substitute "communal approaches to child-rearing" for the traditional "family-centered approach." Women who wanted to labor exclusively in the home in a traditional middle-class marriage wanted society to support them in that, as European nations that paid child and homemaker subsidies did.

Many women recognized the usefulness of planning their pregnancies. Women could control their fertility in three ways: through their sexual behavior, through the use of contraception, and through abortion. Recognizing the importance of the right to control pregnancy, the Supreme Court in 1965 for the first time recognized a constitutionally protected right to privacy that encompassed the right of married couples to use contraceptives in "the sacred precincts of marital bedrooms." Seven years later, the court expanded the right to individuals, whether married or not. "If the right of privacy means anything," wrote Justice William Brennan in *Eisenstadt v. Baird* (1972), "it is the right of the *individual*, married or single, to be free from unwarranted governmental intrusion into matters so fundamentally affecting a person as the decision whether to bear or beget a child."

In the years between *Griswold* and *Eisenstadt*, an estimated one million American women a year had illegal abortions. Physicians performed some of these procedures in secret, but most were done by untrained individuals in illicit spaces dedicated to the task. Women who had "back-alley abortions" risked their lives, their health, and their future fertility. Public health advocates, who favored "therapeutic" abortions in cases where the fetus was severely deformed, had long urged the reform of abortion laws, most of which had not changed since they were first adopted in the late nineteenth century.

Besides lack of access to contraceptives, many women found themselves pregnant because of a lack of knowledge about how their own bodies worked. Women tended not to talk about such things, even to one another, and male doctors monopolized women's health care. In 1970, twelve feminists organized the Boston Women's Health Book Collective and compiled a short book, *Women and Their Bodies*, that focused on topics like menstruation, pregnancy, menopause, and abortion. It sold 250,000 copies and was reproduced in 1973 as *Our Bodies, Ourselves*. This best-selling book reached millions of readers.

In the late 1960s, feminists transformed the movement to reform state abortion laws on medical grounds into a movement to repeal them in the name of female agency. The clarion cry for this movement was "the personal is political," meaning that what happened in the bedroom and other personal relationships reflected broader power dynamics in society. Arguments for liberalizing abortion law in the name of public health gave way to claims of liberty, equality, dignity, and the right of women to make fundamental decisions about their own bodies and futures. The conversation was not really about "choice"—a word that seems to take the issues lightly. Rather, it was about individual freedom and autonomy.

PUSHING BACK

Before the mid-1970s, abortion was not a galvanizing political issue. The Catholic Church, whose doctrine forbade human interference with conception, opposed both contraception and abortion, and worked hard to keep both illegal, but other religious bodies did not concern themselves much with this issue. Southern Baptists, for example, did not consider abortion a categorical wrong, nor did they think that laws regulating abortion should be crafted around any particular religious point of view. In 1971, the Southern Baptist Convention (SBC) called upon its members to "work for legislation that will allow the possibility of abortion under such conditions as rape, incest, clear evidence of severe fetal deformity, and carefully ascertained evidence of the likelihood of damage to the emotional, mental, and physical health of the mother."

Most Americans supported decriminalizing abortion and discussed it in public health terms. A Gallup poll from summer 1972 found that "two out of three Americans think abortion should be a matter for decision solely between a woman and her physician." But as anti-ERA forces coalesced and the 1972 presidential election got underway, abortion became politicized in a very partisan way.

Although out-numbered, abortion opponents were single-issue focused and passionate in moral conviction. Following the lead of the Catholic Church, burgeoning antiabortion organizations reconceptualized their position as "right to life" and encouraged single-issue voting around abortion. This caught the attention of politicians, particularly Republicans. For opponents of abortion, legalization symbolized another corrupting step down the road to immorality—a problematic "permissiveness" that afflicted the nation and was epitomized by the long-haired men and braless women who opposed the war in Vietnam, used drugs and dirty words, and supported George McGovern for president. In the context of that election, "abortion" became shorthand for the erosion of social order and moral standards. McGovern was tarred as the "triple-A" candidate who favored amnesty for draft dodgers, abortion, and acid. Rather than adjusting their arguments against McGovern to reflect the abortion debate, Republicans reframed the abortion debate by associating it with broader social changes they identified with liberals and Democrats.

This reframing of abortion as a partisan issue had barely begun when the Supreme Court invalidated Texas's nineteenth-century abortion statute in *Roe v. Wade* (1973). Resting its decision on the right to privacy enunciated in *Griswold* and *Eisenstadt*, the court held that the individual right at stake could not be overcome merely because the state wished to declare fetuses to be "persons" within the meaning of the Constitution. At the same time, though, the court affirmed the government's legitimate role in regulating abortion for medical reasons and in order to protect potential life in the third trimester of pregnancy. *Roe* therefore held that government could not constitutionally forbid a woman from terminating an unwanted pregnancy, but it could regulate the procedure in the second trimester and could proscribe it after the point of "viability" (when the fetus could survive outside the womb). Together with a companion case, *Doe v. Bolton*, *Roe* declared abortion laws in 46 states unconstitutional. The 7–2 decision was uncontroversial at the time, and addressed a doctor's right to perform abortions without fear of imprisonment more than an individual woman's right to the procedure. Three of the four Nixon appointees to the court joined the decision.

∗

Americans waiting in line for gas in 1974 had plenty of time to consider the state of their nation. What had happened to their government, their economy, their stable and prosperous way of life? What could be done to halt the apparent decline? The combined effects of the government's conduct of the Vietnam War, the revelations of the Pentagon Papers, the Watergate scandal, and the sobering conclusions of the Church Committee caused more than a little despair. In 1968, young people had believed they could change the world. Five years later, a young autoworker reflected on his times, "I think we're in an era where everybody is a kind of spectator. . . . You watch the world around you. You watch the wars. You watch the corrupt politics. You watch the taxes. You're just so small. You can't change anything. I can't change anything out there. How am I going to change the world?"

Young Americans may have been demoralized by 1973, but their parents, especially their mothers, were not. Beating back the ERA, Phyllis Schlafly showed what legions of prayerful, organized, conservative women could accomplish. After *Roe*, the antiabortion and anti-ERA movements merged into a broader campaign to protect what some people called "Judeo-Christian civilization" and others simply "family values." Together, they brought Christianity back into American politics in a way that had not been seen in more than a century.

CHAPTER 11

Right, 1974–1989

In 1979, southern Californian, Baptist, lawyer, and conservative activist Beverly LaHaye founded Concerned Women for America (CWA) to "promote Biblical values for women and families—first through prayer, then education and finally, by influencing our elected leaders and society." CWA focused its efforts on "six core areas of America's modern cultural turmoil: sanctity of life, definition of the family, the fight against pornography, education, religious liberty and national sovereignty." Five years later, LaHaye challenged her many followers—those "truly committed to Jesus Christ"—to "wage warfare against those who would destroy our children, our families, our religious liberties." When the Weathermen or the Black Panthers used such language, governors put the National Guard on alert. But surely this attractive, blonde mother of four did not mean to advocate violence. What *did* she mean, then, and who were these people threatening Christian families and religious liberty across America?

It is a historical commonplace today that American politics was "Southernized" after 1964, meaning that race became politically salient for nonsoutherners and that the political parties flipped: the GOP replaced the Democrats as the party that protected the interests of working-class whites, especially men, while the Democratic Party became the party that protected the interests of minorities, particularly African Americans and women.

This partisan switch is undeniable, but there is more to the story than race, as conservative guru Richard Viguerie, who pioneered political mass mailings and magnified the voices of the conservative grassroots, recognized. Commenting on the successful 1977 campaign to repeal an ordinance passed in Dade County, Florida, that barred discrimination against individuals because of their sexual preference,

FIGURE 11. Aerial photo by Paul Margolies of the AIDS Memorial Quilt, National Mall, Washington, DC, 1996. Photo Courtesy of The NAMES Project.

Viguerie argued that "family" issues were the engine propelling the rise of the New Right. "Conservatives can win," he predicted, "when they're fighting for traditional family values."

The defenders of "traditional family values" defined themselves against their opponents, among whom they numbered feminists, homosexuals, pornographers, abortionists, advocates of busing and affirmative action, and the Supreme Court that protected them while at the same time eroding religious liberty. Their cause was more than righteous—it was holy. When Phyllis Schlafly declared her campaign against the Equal Rights Amendment a "heavenly cause," as she did in 1972, she was in earnest.

The passionate "true belief" of Christian conservatives like Schlafly and LaHaye did not set them apart from other Americans. Passionate certainty was a mark of the times. It was not confined to those motivated by religious faith. People who believed fervently in free-market economics, in the inherent evil of the Soviet Union, in the absolute equality of all citizens under the law, in the dangers of allowing the federal government too much power, in the rightness of their goals regardless of the lawfulness of their means all practiced a form of "true belief" politics that brooked no compromise. Some of these groups sought to protect a world they saw crumbling around their shoulders. Others hoped to create the world anew. Often, if not inevitably, their worlds collided.

True believers' unshakeable faith in the rightness of their cause energized and polarized politics and sometimes burst its bounds. Certain of the righteousness of their cause, some public officials violated their oaths of office and broke the law they had sworn to uphold. Others took the law into their own hands and subverted the democratic process through violence. Because of its unyielding nature, the politics of moral certainty endangers any political system premised on self-governance and mutual respect. As Americans would come to see, the issue was not the issue, whether the cause was abortion, civil rights, or peace. The issue was the democratic process itself.

Harsh Economic Realities

As long as the American economy thrived, as long as it was an economy of abundance and not scarcity, the post-WWII arrangement—whereby corporate America provided relatively high wages and the federal government stimulated investment by borrowing money and spending it on things like highways, universities, and weapons research—created a climate in which it was possible to support social programs like Social Security, Medicare, and Aid to Families with Dependent Children (AFDC) while at the same time enhancing the purchasing power of American workers. This arrangement was premised on American economic global dominance, however, and as that dominance eroded after 1970, the old deal began to dissolve. The American share of gross world product (the combined gross national product of all countries) dropped from 40 percent in 1950 to 23 percent in 1970. Its share of world trade stood at 20 percent in 1950; by 1970, it had declined to 11 percent. This shift reflected the reappearance of Germany and Japan, whose devastated postwar economies had finally recovered (aided by massive infusions of postwar American aid). The time had come for the United States to become integrated into a competitive global economy.

COMPETITION

"Global economic integration" meant competing with foreign firms and foreign workers: in other words, imports. In 1970, 8.3 percent of American gross national product (GNP) was tied to imports and exports; by 1980, that number jumped to 17.4 percent. In the 1970s, key American industries such as autos, steel, and electronics faced, for the first time, quality imports from abroad. Foreign auto producers, which had captured only about 8 percent of the US market in 1970, controlled nearly 22 percent nine years later. In 1970, a foreign car was a Mercedes, driven by a handful of wealthy Americans. By 1973, it was a Honda Civic, suitable for the masses. Dismissed by American automakers as a "tin can car," the inexpensive, fuel-efficient Civic arrived just in time for the oil crisis.

Even during the darkest days of the recession in the mid-1970s, the US economy was weighty: its GDP (gross domestic product) was three times that of Japan's in 1976. But other economic indicators told a story of dwindling American dominance. Exports grew at a rate of 7.3 percent per year after 1974, but imports rose 11.4 percent, leading to an ever-widening trade gap that resulted in significant trade deficits, which jumped from $9.5 billion in 1976 to $31 billion in 1977.

Why care about trade deficits? In part, because of cash flow: it is not in the interest of any nation to pour its financial resources into another country's pocket. But the pressing issue was jobs. The more goods the United States imported, the smaller the domestic manufacturing market became, which meant fewer jobs for Americans. American businesses began investing more and more heavily in foreign manufacturing. Why did this happen? The Ford administration argued that capital fled because of low profits in the United States, which it said reflected the high cost of labor. Unions responded that capital went abroad because of local tax advantages and foreign tariff barriers to US exports. Ford Motor Company had a hard time selling cars made in Detroit in Mexico. But it could easily sell cars made in Mexico in Mexico. It did not take an advanced degree in economics to see the benefit of investing in factories abroad, especially if the federal tax code neither penalized companies that did so nor offered an incentive to stay home.

Like the oil crisis that sparked it, the recession of the mid-1970s was a global phenomenon. Inflation and unemployment were at a postwar high everywhere. While America gobbled up cheap imports, other industrial nations protected jobs by limiting imports. In an effort to expand their export markets, foreign companies subsidized by their governments lowered prices abroad while raising them at home. A Toyota cost more in Japan than it did in the United States. This may have rankled the individual Japanese car consumer, but it protected Japanese jobs—as long as Americans kept on buying their cars. In the

United States, by contrast, Americans consumed more and more imported goods and the market for domestic products shrank accordingly. During the worldwide recession of the 1970s, unemployment in the United States was higher than unemployment in any other industrial nation.

American job loss was not the inevitable result of the economic downturn. As in other nations, policy decisions by the federal government helped define the recession in America. In part, unemployment was higher in the United States than elsewhere because the American government focused on inflation.

INFLATION

Faced with a growing economic crisis, reflected in both rising prices and increasing unemployment, President Ford reduced government spending in an effort to lower inflation. Acknowledging that "unemployment is the biggest concern of the 8.2 percent of American workers temporarily out of work," Ford argued that "inflation [in the form of higher prices] is the universal enemy of 100 percent of our people." These priorities reflected the views of Ford's top economic advisors, who reflected corporate America's belief that the inflation of the 1970s had been caused by the nation's unrealistic "commitment to full employment and maximum production." High wages drove high prices, they charged. The solution? Lower wages and reduce production. "Some people will obviously have to do with less," *Business Week* conceded, adding that "it will be a hard pill for many Americans to swallow."

Everyone agreed that high inflation was a problem, as it drove up both interest rates (the cost of borrowing money, to buy homes and build factories) and the prices of goods and services. But what was its *cause*? Economists and businessmen alike were stumped. Alan Greenspan, the chairman of the Federal Reserve (the nation's federal banking system), thought that government spending caused inflation by injecting cash into the market. Greenspan's solution to the inflation of the mid-1970s was to reduce the amount of money in circulation by raising interest rates, which made it harder for everyone—individuals, businesses, and government at every level—to borrow money. Reduced spending, Greenspan believed, would cause prices to rise and stabilize the economy.

These policies neither ended the recession nor brought inflation under control. Together, the economy and Watergate delivered a one-two punch to the Republican Party and yielded a bumper crop of Democrats in the November 1974 congressional elections.

But the new Democratic Congress was also unable to stop the downward economic spiral. From October 1974 to March 1975, the nation experienced its steepest economic decline since the 1930s. Productivity plunged 2.7 percent. Business profits and wages both fell, while inflation continued to rise. When unemployment hit 7.2 percent in December 1974, President Ford signed legislation that created 100,000 public service jobs and extended unemployment benefits. But he continued to believe that government spending led to excessive consumption, which caused inflation and forced the Federal Reserve to keep interest rates high, which, he insisted, discouraged business growth and investment. "Part of our trouble," explained the president, "is that we have been self-indulgent. . . . For decades, we have been voting ever increasing levels of government benefits—and now the bill has come due." The administration proposed cuts in Social Security, the military, and food stamps as well as a modest stimulus bill. Congress responded with a $23 billion tax cut.

Together, the jobs bill and the tax cuts worked—especially the new earned income tax credit, which protected the poor from rising payroll taxes for Social Security. (Ford denounced this "undesirable welfare type program" but did not veto the bill.) Both retail sales and industrial production rose, and the Federal Reserve began to reduce interest rates. Yet unemployment remained high. No one, including the nation's leading economists, could explain why.

POLITICAL ECONOMY 101, PART 1

Working-class prosperity had been considered synonymous with the national interest since WWII: higher wages stimulated spending, which in turn kept production humming. The period between the end of WWII and 1970 witnessed rapid, robust, and remarkably egalitarian income growth among Americans occupying every rung of the economic ladder. Every income group experienced real income growth between 2.4 percent and 2.7 percent per year. Moreover, these years saw a substantial reduction in income inequality. In 1940, the top 5 percent of earners took home 20.9 percent of total income. That number fell to 16.6 percent by 1968. This trend reversed itself after 1981, however. The share of the top 5 percent rose to 18.6 percent in

1992 and to 21.2 percent in 1994. By 2012, the top 1 percent took home more than 20 percent of total income, and the top 10 percent garnered more than half.

The Great Compression, or the lessening of economic inequality after WWII, was produced by government policies that favored political equality, strong labor unions, and progressive taxation. There was nothing unusual in this. From the earliest days of the Republic, public policy decisions in matters of taxation, debt management, banking, trade and tariffs, and financial rescues (bailouts) had structured US economic growth.

Thus, when unemployment hit 9.2 percent in May 1975—the highest since the beginning of WWII—labor and business leaders alike clamored for government intervention. But President Ford, following the lead of his economic advisors, opposed government intervention at all costs, including wage and price controls of the sort imposed by Richard Nixon in 1971. Framing the question as one of freedom versus authoritarianism, Ford announced that the nation faced a critical choice. "Shall business and government work together in a free economy for the betterment of all?" he asked. "Or shall we slide head-long into an economy whose vital decisions are made by politicians while the private sector dries up and shrivels away?"

Ford's stark opposition between the "private sector" and "decisions made by politicians" suggested that American economic and political spheres operated separately, and spoke to Republicans who had lined up behind Barry Goldwater in 1964. Denounced at that time and later by moderate Republicans for his "extreme opinions," Goldwater thundered, "The good Lord raised this mighty Republic to be a home for the brave and to flourish as the land of the free." It was Americans' job to keep it that way, he announced. "I would remind you," he continued, "that extremism in the defense of liberty is no vice." Attacking the New Deal and the Great Society, Goldwater warned, "Those who seek to live your lives for you, . . . those who elevate the state and downgrade the citizen, must see ultimately a world in which earthly power can be substituted for divine will. And this nation was founded upon the rejection of that notion and upon the acceptance of God as the author of freedom."

Barry Goldwater was crushed that November by Lyndon Johnson. But the note he sounded resonated for decades. The massive grassroots organization that elevated Goldwater to the top in 1964 endured, particularly where it was strongest: in the South and the West, where fervently Christian anti-Communists dedicated to restoring God to government joined anti-tax proponents of limited government in a potent new political alliance. The greatest beneficiary of this New Right coalition was the man who had delivered the speech nominating Barry Goldwater for president at the Republican convention in 1964: conservative California movie star Ronald Reagan.

THE POLITICS OF SCARCITY

Welfare, affirmative action, and other government programs that benefited the underprivileged were always controversial among working- and middle-class whites. As one California Republican declared in the mid-1970s, "Welfare doesn't solve problems, it only produces millions of freeloaders." As wages stagnated after 1973, middling whites increasingly resented the benefits given to poor people—money they thought came directly out of their own pockets. Eleanor Holmes Norton, the head of the New York City Human Rights Commission, was sympathetic. "The poor had access to comprehensive medical care through Medicaid," she noted, while other Americans lacked coverage. "A society that grudgingly buys benefits for its poor, while leaving out others who also cannot afford basic needs, invites class conflict," she wrote.

Economic issues used to unite the Democrats, but by the mid-1970s, they created fissures. When union "last hired/first fired" rules threatened to wipe out black economic gains, the NAACP challenged union seniority plans as perpetuating discriminatory legacies of the past. Litigation that pitted the NAACP against progressive unions like the United Steelworkers of America was bad for the Democrats. Lacking a cohesive center, the party splintered into endless special interest groups (women, African Americans, unions, Jews), each espousing its own form of "identity politics."

With inflation eating away at the wages of the working and middle classes, tax burdens rising, and affirmative action policies diverting opportunities to minorities, arguments about wasteful and misguided government policies gained ground. California led the way in tax revolts and anti–affirmative action pushback. Wages increased by inflation pushed many people into higher income tax brackets, but because of inflation, a family's buying power did not increase. Inflation also increased the assessed value of single-family homes, which meant property taxes skyrocketed. Some people were suddenly unable to afford their own houses.

When California governor Jerry Brown refused to spend any of the $5 billion surplus then residing in state coffers on tax relief, state representatives Howard Jarvis and Paul Gann authored a ballot referendum that cut property taxes by up to two-thirds. Despite warnings of future cuts in government services, two-thirds of Californians voted for Proposition 13 in June 1978. Jarvis interpreted the vote as expressing a broad antigovernment sentiment. "We have a new revolution," he announced. "We are telling the government, 'Screw you!'" Free-market guru and conservative icon Milton Friedman agreed: "The populace is coming to recognize that throwing government at problems has a way of making them worse."

The same year that Californians said "Enough!" to high taxes, the Supreme Court put the brakes on affirmative action programs in higher education. In *Regents of the University of California v. Bakke*, a case involving the medical school at the University of California, Davis, a divided Supreme Court upheld race-based affirmative action in higher education, but narrowed the justifications for it. Before *Bakke*, affirmative action had generally been justified as compensation for past injustice, as a means to increase minority representation in higher education and the professions, and as a way to provide better services to underserved minority communities (in the form of doctors, lawyers, and the like). *Bakke* suggested that the only constitutional justification for affirmative action was the desire to achieve educational "diversity." As one constitutional scholar observed at the time, "This is a landmark case, but we don't know what it marks."

The Californiaization of American Politics

According to most political histories, American politics was Southernerized in the late 1960s. "Southernization" is not a value-neutral term: usually it refers to an intensification of racial conflict, the energetic political participation of organized Christians, assaults on public education, and a decline in public discourse. Accompanied, of course, by fried chicken, sweet tea, country western music, and, not infrequently, violence. The "Southernization of American politics" thesis narrates the rise of the Religious Right in the late 1970s and its capture of the Republican Party, and, after a brief interlude in the desert in 1976, culminates in the election in 1980 of President Ronald Reagan.

The theory is at least half right: the Religious Right *did* muscle in on the traditionally moderate East Coast GOP leadership. The only real problem with the "Southernization of American politics" argument is that very little of this happened in the South. Instead, the action centered on California. *Southern* California, to be sure, but California nonetheless.

HOLY WARRIORS

Postwar California moved to the forefront of American politics in the mid-1960s. A number of factors were involved, including a seismic population shift westward from the South that began during the Depression and accelerated during and after WWII. By 1970, more native southerners lived in southern California than in any other single nonsouthern state.

Southern migrants brought their religion with them. Southern evangelicals, especially fundamentalists, imposed "a distinctive disposition" on the Golden State. They believed in the primacy of individual conversion, the infallibility of the Bible, and the absolute rightness of their doctrine. Combative, inventive, and optimistic, evangelicals were unwilling to compromise their beliefs but always open to new ways of spreading them.

Evangelicals' religious beliefs were accompanied by strong political convictions. Virulently anti-Communist, they believed passionately in free enterprise, limited government, and the Christian roots of the United States. During the 1950s and early 1960s, evangelicals constructed an elaborate network of private religious schools and organizations. Their politics, in California and elsewhere, embodied an unswerving commitment to what they called "traditional family values." Evangelicals opposed abortion, defined a "family" as consisting of a father, a mother, and children, sought to suppress sexually explicit movies, opposed sex education, defended school prayer and the teaching of creationism, condemned homosexuality, and jealously guarded national sovereignty against the influence of the United Nations.

By the mid-1970s, many Christians felt threatened by what they considered a tide of cultural and legal immorality that had risen inexorably since the late 1960s. Everywhere they looked, they saw secularism (defined by one evangelical leader as, simply, "man's attempt to solve his problems independently of God") undermining Christian principles.

Before the 1970s, evangelicals saw their job as saving souls, not drafting government policy. In 1965, Jerry Falwell, a Baptist minister from Virginia, stuck to his denomination's traditional views on politics and religion when he criticized the participation of ministers in the Civil Rights Movement. "The gospel does not clean up the outside but rather regenerates the inside," he preached.

By the time he founded the Moral Majority 14 years later, Falwell had changed his tune—as well as joined the ranks of popular television ministers, or televangelists. The idea that "religion and politics don't mix" he now explained, was "invented by the Devil to keep Christians from running their own country." Although he presented himself as a leader in the escalating culture wars, Falwell in fact followed in the footsteps of "housewife activists" such as Phyllis Schlafly and Beverly LaHaye—LaHaye's Concerned Women for America (CWA) already had 500,000 members. Ministers like Falwell were important, but the energy driving evangelical Christian politics came primarily from suburban housewives already active in local school board battles, Goldwater canvassing, church schools, and—crucially—the anti-ERA campaign.

THE ELECTION OF 1976

One of the lessons of Watergate was the corrupting influence of money on politics. A 1974 amendment to the 1971 Federal Election Campaign Act set a $1,000 limit on direct individual contributions to political candidates and on the amount individuals could spend to help elect candidates. But in 1976, the Supreme Court ruled in *Buckley v. Valeo* that spending money on elections is a constitutionally protected form of free speech. Although it upheld the restrictions on the size of direct contributions to candidates, the court struck down limits on independent expenditures by organizations such as the Chamber of Commerce or big unions like the Teamsters. This had the effect of increasing the influence of political action committees (PACs), which pooled resources from many individuals and then distributed the funds to further their specific agendas. Changes in campaign financing benefited single-issue groups and political outsiders such as newly organized evangelical Christians, and aided the rise into national politics of the relatively obscure former governor of Georgia, James Earl "Jimmy" Carter.

A graduate of the Naval Academy, successful businessman, and Sunday school teacher, Jimmy Carter was a canny politician. Converted to the civil rights cause at approximately the same time that black Georgians finally won access to polling booths, the new Georgia governor

made national headlines in 1971 when he announced at his inauguration that "the time for racial discrimination is over." He hung Martin
Luther King's portrait in the state capitol. Within weeks, Carter's face
adorned the cover of *Time* magazine, Exhibit Number One that the
South was ready at last to rejoin the nation.

Behind the trademark toothy grin lay a calculating politician. (His
own mother, Lillian, who became a sort of republican version of the
Queen Mother during Carter's presidency, described her son as ruthless.) Described by *Newsweek* as "the most unabashed public moralist
to seek the Presidency since William Jennings Bryan," Carter's stump
speeches often seemed more like sermons than campaign talks. His
inability to work with the Georgia state legislature while governor
ought to have sounded warning bells, but the country was ready to be
charmed by a decent man with an Annapolis moral code. Carter's description of himself as a "born-again" Christian was sufficiently mys-
tifying to mainstream Americans in 1976 for reporters to investigate,
but NBC news anchor John Chancellor put the issue to bed when he
assured the nation that being "born again" was "described by other
Baptists as a common experience, not something out of the ordinary."

While Carter plowed ahead in the Democratic primaries, the Republicans suffered through a determined struggle between incumbent
president Gerald Ford and former California governor Ronald Reagan.
More corporate-minded than Nixon, Ford was relatively moderate
when it came to social and cultural issues. Ford supported the ERA,
and although he privately opposed abortion (his wife, Betty, publicly
disagreed with him), he did not consider these issues politically important.

Conservative Republicans, especially evangelicals, hated everything about Ford, including his inability to fix the economy, his refusal to roll back the welfare state, and his continuation of the Nixon-
Kissinger policy of détente toward the Soviet Union. Reagan, on the
other hand, had a certain appeal for the Religious Right. Avowedly
born-again, Reagan was a believer but not an evangelist.

Ford won the 1976 Republican nomination, but Reagan stole the
show with a dynamic speech at the convention. The GOP platform
reflected the power of his supporters, who pushed through a plank
demanding a constitutional amendment prohibiting abortion, and
deleted a plank supporting the ERA. Veteran journalist Murray Kemp-
ton saluted the 65-year-old Reagan, saying he deserved to be "counted
as one of the great candidates in our memory, perhaps the greatest

who never got his chance." Jimmy Carter defeated Gerald Ford by the smallest edge in the Electoral College since 1916, and with the lowest voter turnout in a national election since 1948.

BAD LUCK

Throughout the general election, Carter's primary target was the federal government, which, after Vietnam and Watergate, was associated in the public mind with corruption and incompetence. But Carter was never an antistate conservative. He was a progressive committed to government efficiency, transparency, and honesty. By running as an outsider against Washington, though, Carter helped pave the way for a biting critique of government itself. With the national wounds of Watergate and Vietnam fresh, Carter promised never to lie to the people.

This promise may have been his undoing. Americans were in no mood to be told the truth when the truth consisted of spiraling inflation and skyrocketing unemployment, a crippling energy crisis, and declining international power and prestige. Never mind that the United States relied heavily on foreign oil to fire its factories and heat its homes, and that the price of that oil had doubled since 1973: Americans did not want to be told that the United States was "the most wasteful nation on earth." They did not want to turn down the heat and put on a sweater, as "Jimmy Cardigan" did in 1978, after a revolution in Iran ushered in a second oil crisis. Americans did not want to hear their president say, as Carter did on July 15, 1979, that "all the legislation in the world can't fix what's wrong with America." Americans anxious about stagnant wages and rising taxes did not want to be chastised for spending too much and saving too little. They didn't want their commander in chief to diagnose a national "crisis of confidence." They wanted him to find a way out of the dark.

The year 1978 was capped on either end by revolutions against pro-American regimes on opposite sides of the globe. In Nicaragua, left-wing revolutionaries succeeded in overturning the repressive regime of longtime American friend Anastasio Somoza Debayle. In Iran, Islamic militants led by exiled spiritual leader Ayatollah Ruhollah Khomeini overthrew Shah Mohammad Reza Pahlavi and forced him into exile. Pahlavi, a modernizing autocrat, had been installed by the United States in 1953, after Prime Minister Mohammad Mosaddegh had nationalized Iran's oil industry and petroleum reserves.

The Islamic Republic of Iran was declared on April 1, 1979. Iranians resented the United States for its support of despotism and its disregard of the popular will. When President Carter allowed the deposed shah to enter the United States to receive medical treatment in November 1979 against the advice of Iran's government, a group of revolutionary students shouting "Death to America!" stormed the US embassy in Tehran and held 53 Americans hostage for 444 days. The Iran hostage crisis, described by *Time* magazine as an exercise in "vengeance and mutual incomprehension," humiliated the nation, soured US-Iranian relations for decades, and solidified Jimmy Carter's image as weak and ineffectual.

The Iranian Revolution alarmed more than the Americans. The Soviets, who shared a border with Iran, were concerned about the security of their largely Muslim "republics" in Central Asia. When a Soviet-backed government in Afghanistan looked ready to topple in the face of an Islamic insurgency in late 1979, the Soviet Union invaded.

Carter was stunned. This was the greatest Cold War crisis since the Cubans attempted to install Soviet missiles in 1962. The president embargoed grain shipments to Moscow, suspended Russian fishing rights in American waters, and cancelled American participation in the 1980 Moscow Winter Olympics. But these steps, however decisive, neither got the Soviets out of Afghanistan nor enhanced Carter's reputation. Even worse, a disastrous rescue attempt in April 1980 intended to free the American hostages in Iran resulted in the deaths of eight US servicemen and failed to free any hostages. Plagued by a still-shaky domestic economy and tormented by the Iranians, Carter was defeated decisively in November 1980 by the man who had nearly been the Republican nominee four years earlier: Ronald Reagan.

THE CALIFORNIAN

Ronald Reagan's opponents liked to suggest that the Hollywood actor had gone straight from *Bedtime for Bonzo* (a movie in which Reagan's costar was a chimpanzee) to the presidency. They insisted that he was unqualified for the office. In fact, as a two-term governor (from 1966 to 1974) of the most populous state in the nation, he was better prepared than most new presidents. He was also, as he often was, ahead of the game: Reagan ran against the sixties before most of the rest of the nation had even experienced them. As governor, he came down hard on radical students. He slashed the welfare rolls and raised taxes in an effort to balance the budget. Like others who had prospered during the post-WWII boom years in California, whose extraordinary economic growth had been driven to a large degree by outsized federal defense spending, Reagan's life story seemed to confirm that individual entrepreneurship, hard work, and intelligence paved the road to success. His message—the one that sent him to the White House in 1980—can be summed up in one sentence: high taxes to support big government are morally and economically wrong.

Always optimistic, Reagan radiated confidence in himself, in the nation, and in his core beliefs, which included faith in free enterprise and limited government, and unyielding opposition to Communism. Like Barry Goldwater, who paved the way, Reagan prized liberty over equality. Government's job was to maximize individual liberty by freeing people from needless constraints, not to create a "level playing field," as Lyndon Johnson had argued. Reagan's approach to government, therefore, was to cut taxes and "unleash" business from what he considered burdensome environmental protection regulations and workplace safety rules. Lower taxes, Reagan maintained, would force a reduction of government services while freeing up capital for private investment. This, he believed, combined with less government regulation, would expand the economy, improve efficiency, produce jobs, and ultimately increase tax revenues. Money saved in reduced domestic spending could then be passed to the military to support an aggressively anti-Communist foreign policy. Reagan's program made sense. The fact that Reaganomics never delivered as advertised has had almost no effect on its enduring appeal. Again and again, Americans have turned to Reagan's economic policies, hoping that *this time* they would work.

Reagan's politics were never motivated by social issues, as his more conservative supporters discovered to their chagrin. He was not a moral absolutist, but he appealed to those who were, and his charm was hard to resist. He was open to compromise, which his experience as governor had taught him was essential to effective government. He signed, reluctantly, California's Therapeutic Abortion Act of 1967. Divorced and happily remarried to the also-divorced former actress Nancy Davis, Reagan never joined the "pro-family" crusade. When Christian conservatives in California tried to prevent gay men and women from teaching in the public schools, Reagan resisted, saying, "Whatever else it is, homosexuality is not a contagious disease."

Reagan's later willingness to rely on his staff and his breezy "Don't confuse me with the facts!" approach reinforced liberals' belief that he was not a man of substance. He encouraged this impression, which led his opponents to underestimate him. Derided as an actor playing the part of a president, Ronald Reagan was an extremely successful politician who convinced his foes at home and abroad that he was faking it—not bad for a guy Hollywood producers dismissed as having no leading man potential.

The Reagan Revolution

Reflecting on the conservative wave that had swamped the Democrats and deposited Ronald Reagan in the White House in 1980, conservative columnist Gary Wills remarked shrewdly that "Americans are conservative. . . . What they want to preserve is the New Deal." Ronald Reagan never set out to destroy the social safety net strung by Franklin Roosevelt. As he complained, "The press is trying to paint me as trying to undo the New Deal. I remind them I voted for FDR four times." Instead, he continued unabashedly, "I'm trying to undo the Great Society."

Undoing the Great Society required action on multiple fronts. It meant unraveling the logic and the laws that sustained federal aid to the poor and vulnerable; dismantling regulatory agencies that protected workers, consumers, and natural resources; and reversing policies that protected minority rights and affirmative action. It meant denouncing "activist courts" and appointing conservative jurists who would be "strict constructionists" and adhere to the "original" meaning of the Constitution. It meant restoring God to public life, shoring up nuclear families, and restoring traditional gender roles. Above all, it meant liberating both markets and people from the presence of government in everyday life.

REAGANOMICS

Ronald Reagan swept into Washington touting the theory of supply-side economics. The idea was simple: by reducing federal tax rates, government could bolster the economy by leaving more money in the market, which would in turn generate jobs and goods (supply), increase total income, and ultimately produce enough tax revenue to make up for the initial cut. Critics—including Reagan's former opponent and current vice president George H. W. Bush—called it "voodoo economics," but the plan had high-profile supporters in the government and the academy, including University of Chicago economist and Nobel laureate Milton Friedman. In a speech in February 1981, Reagan predicted that his plan would reverse the budget deficit and produce a surplus by 1984. The public was pleased, but the stock market dipped sharply, indicating that investors were skeptical. It was not clear that the administration's economic program would make it through Congress.

The actions of John Hinkley Jr., the delusional son of an affluent Texas Republican family, changed things on March 30, 1981—only 69 days into Reagan's presidency. Hoping to impress actress Jodie Foster, Hinkley attempted to assassinate the president as he left a reception in Washington. Hinkley failed to hit Reagan directly, but his shots wounded and permanently disabled press secretary James Brady. One bullet ricocheted off the president's limousine, however, and struck the 70-year old president, lodging near his heart. He was nearly killed. Reagan's remark to his stricken wife, Nancy ("Honey, I forgot to duck"), and his good-natured joshing with his doctors ("I hope you are all Republicans!") endeared him to the nation and, along with his injuries, ensured passage of his budget bill.

The Economic Recovery Tax Act of 1981 (also known as the Kemp-Roth Act, for its congressional sponsors, New York representative Jack Kemp and Delaware senator William Roth) cut $750 billion in federal revenue over five years. Individual income taxes were reduced across the board by 5 percent the first year and 10 percent the following two years. The top tax rate was lowered from 70 percent to 50 percent, which was, according to budget director and ardent supply-sider David Stockman, the main goal of the legislation. The government also cut taxes on capital gains (profits from the sale of financial assets like stocks and real estate) and inheritance. Five years later, Reagan's Tax Reform Act of 1986 reduced rates even further, lowering the maximum tax on individual income to 28 percent.

Although Kemp-Roth lowered nearly everyone's federal income tax burden, its chief beneficiaries were wealthy Americans and businesses. Because most Americans paid the bulk of their federal taxes in the form of payroll taxes for Social Security, reduced federal income tax rates did not necessarily increase their well-being. Thanks in great measure to reduced taxes on capital gains, the top 1 percent of American earners saw their incomes grow by 23 percent between 1980 and 1983. Real income for the poorest 20 percent of Americans, however, *declined* by almost 3 percent. Moreover, the bottom half of the population paid a higher share of total taxes in 1983 than it had pre-Reagan.

Reaganomics did not work. The tax reform plan that was designed to stimulate business and produce a budget surplus of $28 billion by 1986 instead drove the United States deeper into debt and triggered a recession. By mid-1982, unemployment stood at 9.7 percent. More than 10 million Americans were without work. Businesses failed right and left. Reagan's approval rating plunged to 35 percent. The federal budget deficit, which had been 2 percent of GDP in 1981 more than doubled by 1985.

GOVERNMENT IS THE PROBLEM

Channeling Barry Goldwater, President Reagan in his first inaugural address in 1981 declared, "Government is not the solution to our problem. Government is the problem." High taxes and excessive regulation were strangling individual initiative and preventing job growth and entrepreneurship; government agents meddled where they did not belong; citizens were soft and un-self-reliant. In layman's terms, it was time to get government off the backs of the people—whether they wanted that or not.

Reagan was determined to free the market from what Republicans considered excessive government regulation. The White House weakened the regulatory reach and authority of several key agencies, including the Occupational Safety and Health Administration (OSHA), the Environmental Protection Agency (EPA), the Federal Trade Commission (FTC), and the Department of the Interior. Although Democrats sometimes favored deregulation in the interest of lower consumer prices (Jimmy Carter deregulated the trucking and airline industries), under Reagan the Republicans turned deregulation into an "all-out business crusade" that drew no distinctions between regulations restraining business competition and those designed to enforce laws protecting working conditions and public health and safety.

Several groups stood between the president and his deregulation plans. Environmental groups like the Sierra Club attacked plans to open federal lands to private developers, and mobilized against EPA efforts to lower clean air and water standards. Labor unions pushed back against rule changes that favored business and eroded the political power of workers. Ronald Reagan was not inherently anti-union; as president of the Screen Actors Guild in 1952, Reagan led his union in a strike. But when the professional air traffic controllers' union, PATCO, threatened to strike in August 1981, Reagan responded privately with the offer of a raise and publicly by threatening to fire all 13,000 controllers who, as federal employees, were forbidden to strike. When the controllers walked out anyway, the president carried through on his promise to replace them with military personnel.

Conservative politicians and pundits cast much of the blame for the nation's economic woes on workers, whom they portrayed as selfish and overpaid, and on unions, which they accused of corruption (many were corrupt, but not all corporate hands were clean either). In decline since the 1950s, the labor movement was an easy target. The percentage of workers in unions declined by a third (from 31 percent to 21 percent) from the mid-1950s to the mid-1970s. Most union members lived in ten states in the industrial Northeast and the West Coast, which limited labor's political muscle. The numbers were much lower for the South, where only about 10 percent of workers were unionized and right-to-work laws existed, which forbade mandatory union membership in union shops and undermined organizing activities and collective bargaining.

Following the example of the federal government, private businesses busted unions rather than negotiate with them. When workers walked off the job at Greyhound Bus Lines and Eastern Airlines, the companies replaced the workers with nonunion labor, who in previous eras had been known as "scabs." Wages fell, strike rates plummeted, and private sector unionization declined yet further. As the recession of 1982 took hold, wage packages shrunk as workers competed desperately for jobs. In January 1983, 20,000 people lined up to apply for 200 automotive jobs in Milwaukee. The federal government offered no jobs program. Instead, it used unemployment to finally break the back of the inflation that had plagued presidents for a decade.

TAKING BACK THE COURTS

Since the early 1960s, conservatives had railed against the Supreme Court and, in particular, Chief Justice Earl Warren. Social issue decisions like *Griswold* (birth control) and *Engel* (forbidding prayer in public schools) recast the boundaries between the public sphere, in which governmental power is supreme, and the private sphere of individual autonomy, the space that is protected from the state's interference. Conservatives complained that the court had engaged in an illegitimate form of "judicial activism" whereby politically liberal justices imposed their political will on the nation in the guise of interpreting the Constitution. This rebalancing of the relative power and autonomy of individuals and the state was, and remains, extraordinarily controversial.

With its decisions on racial discrimination, criminal procedure, school prayer, and abortion, the court acted ahead of both the executive and the legislative branches as an agent of social change. It took heavy fire for its advanced position in what was shaping up to be a full-blown culture war. Outraged Christians who considered the school prayer ban the key to the moral relativism they saw all around them supported 1964 GOP candidate Barry Goldwater, who made much of the "moral rot" of the Supreme Court, and Ronald Reagan in his 1966 gubernatorial campaign in California. In the eyes of these American citizens, the federal government itself had become an agent of secularism and, as such, something to be resisted.

Republicans demanded the appointment of justices committed to "judicial restraint." From 1969 to 1989, Republican presidents made eight consecutive appointments to the Supreme Court, transforming the institution. President Nixon appointed four justices to the Supreme Court—Warren Burger, Harry Blackmun, Lewis Powell, and William Rehnquist. Together, they brought the era of the Warren Court to an end. President Reagan cemented the conservative tenor of the court through his three appointees: Sandra Day O'Connor (the first female justice), Antonin Scalia, and Anthony Kennedy.

Reagan also appointed 368 federal district and appeals court justices—more than any other president in history. To ensure that these new judges and justices would embrace the Reagan perspective on the judiciary, the administration politicized judicial nominations by undercutting the traditional role of the American Bar Association (the leading legal professional association) in evaluating candidates, and by conducting unprecedented interviews with judicial candidates designed to ferret out their views on such issues as abortion, affirmative action, and criminal procedure. Because lifetime appointments to the bench were insulated from shifts in American politics, the Reagan judges could, in the words of longtime Reagan advisor and attorney general Edwin A. Meese, "institutionalize the Reagan revolution so it can't be set aside no matter what happens in future presidential elections." One of Ronald Reagan's most enduring political legacies was to effect a pronounced rightward shift of the federal judiciary through the aggressive appointment of conservative jurists who were far to the right of Nixon's nominees.

POLITICAL ECONOMY 101, PART 2

When he introduced his tax plan in 1981, Reagan declared that taxation "must not be used to regulate the economy or bring about social change." But government policies, whether through taxation, regulation, and enforcement (or not) of the law, do precisely that. Certainly the Reagan tax cuts triggered social change by delivering a "sharp blow," as intended, to the War on Poverty programs. Reagan disappointed die-hard conservatives by sparing entitlement programs like Social Security and Medicare that benefited the middle class along with other Americans, but he cut back or terminated food stamp and Aid for Families with Dependent Children programs for people whose income levels placed them above the government's poverty line. In the early 1980s, the combined real value of food stamps and AFDC was less than the value of AFDC alone in 1969.

Together, the Reagan tax cuts represented the largest tax reduction in American history. They also forced a redistribution of wealth, from the bottom of the heap to the top. Under Reagan, the incomes of the richest 20 percent of Americans rose dramatically, those in the middle rose slightly, and those at the bottom fell. The distance between the top and the bottom—the income gap—widened: the rich got richer while the poor got poorer. By the end of the eighties, 1 percent of American families owned or controlled 37 percent of the country's wealth, which was a degree of concentrated economic power and privilege not seen since the 1920s. Between 1980 and 1983, the percentage of Americans living below the poverty line increased to 15.3 percent—the highest poverty rate in the industrialized world. In 1935, when the New Deal Congress passed Social Security, most poor Americans were elderly. This was no longer the case in 1988. Social Security and Medicare had succeeded in alleviating the poverty of the aged. By the end of Ronald Reagan's tenure, the largest group of poor Americans was children, particularly nonwhite children. One-fifth of American children lived in poverty in 1988.

In addition to widening income inequality in the United States, the Reagan tax cuts, combined with massive increases in defense spending, produced huge federal deficits and dramatically deepened the national debt. Calling for cuts in government spending, Ronald Reagan delivered the largest peacetime budget deficits in the nation's history. Over the eight years of his two-term presidency, President Reagan generated almost twice as much national debt as all his 39 predecessors *combined*. As a result, by 1988 interest on the national debt had skyrocketed to one-seventh of all federal expenditures.

By the mid-1980s, the social effects of Reaganomics were visible, most obviously in America's cities. A new term, "street people," was coined to describe the many homeless people camped out in parks and on sidewalks. "Bag ladies" stuffed their belongings into plastic bags and wheeled them around in purloined shopping carts. Schools and other services declined still further. Street violence and crime sky-rocketed in response to the emergence of "crack," a powerfully con-centrated, highly addictive form of powdered cocaine that plagued neighborhoods overflowing with unemployed young black men. African American infant mortality rates, which had dropped dramatically since the 1970s, soared once crack hit the streets. The achievement gap between white and black schoolchildren, which had been closing since the 1960s, widened. The number of African Americans incarcer-ated tripled. One student of the era has concluded that "black Ameri-cans were hurt more by crack cocaine than by any single cause since Jim Crow."

THE PLAGUE OF THE CENTURY

In the late 1960s, gay men and lesbians began calling openly for the acceptance of homosexuals "as full equals" in society. In 1969, for ex-ample, Carl Wittman, a gay Students for a Democratic Society leader, penned what he termed *A Gay Manifesto* in which he declared: "Our first job is to clear our *own* heads of the garbage that's been poured into them. . . . Liberation for gay people is defining for ourselves who we are. It is time for us to come out."

The 1970s saw gradual, but halting, progress in the cause of gay rights. In 1972, a lesbian was allowed to retain custody of her children in a contested divorce for the first time in American history. In 1973, the American Psychiatric Association renounced its position that homo-sexuality was a mental illness and that gay men and women were by defi-nition diseased. By the end of the decade, 22 states had repealed their laws against consensual sodomy (including any form of oral sex among heterosexuals). Some cities even passed laws that forbade discrimina-tion in housing and employment on the basis of sexual orientation.

These developments sparked a sharp backlash, however, leading to the creation of a new, religion-based antigay movement. Within two years, many of the laws that had been enacted in cities to protect gays from discrimination were repealed. Conservative Christians charged that such laws promoted "child molesting" and "gay recruiting," and the antigay rights crusade saw this struggle as a life-and-death battle for the Christian soul of America.

In the early 1980s, a strange and awful disease struck the gay community. The disease, acquired immuno deficiency syndrome (AIDS), was passed through bodily fluids like blood and semen. As it became associated in the public mind with homosexuality, the Religious Right deemed AIDS God's punishment for homosexual sodomy. Jerry Falwell, who had founded the Moral Majority as an evangelical Christian lobbying organization in 1979, roared that "AIDS is not just God's punishment for homosexuals, it is God's punishment for the society that tolerates homosexuals." Patrick Buchanan, a highly conservative commentator who served as a senior advisor to Ronald Reagan, declared that "AIDS is nature's retribution for violating the laws of nature."

The Reagan administration, which had actively courted the Religious Right, had no interest in devoting public resources to an illness that was thought to threaten only gay men. Over the course of the next decade, AIDS ravaged the homosexual community, killing more than 250,000 gay men and leaving hundreds of thousands more to wonder if they might be next. President Reagan did not even acknowledge the AIDS epidemic publicly until 1985, after his friend and fellow actor Rock Hudson died from the disease.

As so many Americans had before them, AIDS activists organized to gain the attention of the government. In 1987, gay rights activist Cleve Jones created the NAMES Project, which invited people from across the nation to sew a patch for a massive quilt that would commemorate the AIDS epidemic. Each patch, crafted lovingly by family and friends, represented a person who had died of AIDS. In the end, the quilt covered the ground from end to end of the National Mall in Washington, DC. On the ground, the AIDS quilt turned numbers of victims into individuals. From a distance, the sheer size of the quilt demonstrated the magnitude of the plague. Research funding increased under President George H. W. Bush, and the National Institute of Allergy and Infectious Diseases approved several promising drugs for AIDS patients.

Defeating the Evil Empire

From the first days of the Republic, America's leaders walked a fine line between protecting national interests and encouraging democratic ideals of human freedom globally. These goals were not always in tension, but they often were, especially after the United Nations enunciated an international standard of human rights.

Every post-WWII president found himself in the position of having to balance perceived American military and economic interests (not necessarily in sync) against a broader American commitment to support democratic political movements and human rights abroad. For Eisenhower, the defining moment was the Hungarian uprising in 1956; for Kennedy, Johnson, and Nixon, it was Vietnam. Ford signed the 1975 Helsinki Accords reaffirming the incorporation of the Baltic states in the Soviet Union while also recognizing the fundamental right of freedom of thought, which aided dissident (oppositional) movements in the USSR and Warsaw Pact countries. Presidents Carter and Reagan were challenged by events in Latin America and the Middle East.

CONTAINMENT 2.0

When State Department advisor George Kennan wrote his "Long Telegram" explaining the Russians in 1946, his message was that the United States' goal should be to "contain" the Soviet Union. The Soviets were weak, he explained. They did not want war. What the Soviets *did* want, Kennan emphasized, were opportunities to expand their alliance and further their interests. The correct policy for the United States was to prevent opportunities to arise that the Soviet Union could exploit.

Kennan's goal was to provide the United States with a way of being anti-Communist without going to war. His vision of containment stressed diplomacy and economic pressures, not military intervention. Kennan criticized the domino theory on the grounds that not all countries were of equal importance to American interests. Did it really matter if Laos or Cambodia fell to the Communists? He liked to quote John Quincy Adams, who warned that a nation should not go abroad "in search of monsters to destroy."

Guided by Henry Kissinger, whose foreign policy was rooted in an unsentimental assessment of American national interest, presidents Richard Nixon and Gerald Ford hewed to the containment model: détente modulated the tone but did not fundamentally alter the guiding principles of US foreign policy. As long as the Communists stayed in their box, the United States limited its intervention to rhetoric. Wherever there was "Communist aggression," however, the United States pushed back. For example, American intervention to save Israel in the 1973 war "had nothing to do with the merit of the crisis itself,"

Kissinger explained. What was unacceptable was a military victory by states—Egypt and Syria—armed by the USSR.

During Jimmy Carter's presidency, the "the enemy of my enemy is my friend" foreign policy model collided repeatedly with a commitment to American ideals of human freedom. Carter and Secretary of State Cyrus Vance affirmed and expanded America's commitment to human rights as a foreign policy principle, and laid the foundation for renewed American claims to world leadership, especially in Latin America. Denouncing "the inordinate fear of communism that once led us to embrace any dictator who joined us in that fear," Carter refused to defend Nicaraguan ruler Anastasio Somoza Debayle, a longtime friend of the United States, when his government was overthrown by a left-wing popular revolution in 1979. In 1980, the administration suspended military aid to the government of another right-wing anti-Communist ally, El Salvador, after a National Guard "death squad" murdered three American nuns and a missionary. Carter negotiated the transfer of the Panama Canal to local rule against raucous Republican opposition. Remarkably, in the summer of 1979, Carter negotiated a peace treaty between Israel and Egypt that has lasted for more than 35 years.

Jimmy Carter's commitment to transcendent values such as human rights masked a moral arrogance about the assertion of American power that was as broad as it was potentially perilous to American interests. Carter's domestic and foreign policy agendas were suffused with questions of morality and ethics. His faith in the rightness of his policies, his reluctance to explain himself, and his stubborn refusal to compromise reflected his dislike of political give-and-take—the building blocks of democratic process. "Our commitment to human rights must be absolute," he announced in his inaugural address in January 1977.

George Kennan's overriding point about containment was that the most powerful nation on earth needed to be a cold-hearted realist because it could not trust itself to be a moralist. Like powerful individuals, powerful nations could easily present self-interest as benevolence. Containment was intended as "a continual reminder that we do not know what is best for others." Jimmy Carter had no such inhibitions.

Neither did Ronald Reagan.

CONTRA THE CONSTITUTION

Ronald Reagan generally hewed true to the policy of containment. However, the president's rhetorical assaults on détente encouraged radical, even rogue, elements in his administration to pursue an uncompromising anti-Communist agenda that led to significant bloodletting in Latin America, challenged the rule of law in the United States, and eventually triggered a constitutional crisis that nearly brought down the Reagan presidency.

Reagan first flexed his anti-Communist muscles in a dispute involving the tiny Caribbean island of Grenada, where a leftist government had aligned itself with Cuba. Concerned about this new incursion of Communist influence in the Western Hemisphere, Reagan used the War Powers Act to order 1,900 marines to invade Grenada and depose the government. The embarrassingly lopsided affair was cheered at home as well as by most Grenadans and their neighbors in the Caribbean. The military success in Grenada made Reagan look decisive if trigger-happy and sent a message to Latin American revolutionaries elsewhere to watch their backs.

The likeliest next target was Nicaragua, whose Sandinista revolutionaries (after August Cesar Sandino, who had led Nicaraguan resistance to American occupation in the 1930s) had toppled an American-supported dictatorship in 1979. President Carter had held his nose and accepted the Sandinista government. President Reagan did not. Instead, he directed his zealously anti-Communist CIA director, William Casey, to fund and train an antirevolutionary Nicaraguan group that called itself the Contras ("the opposition"). The administration ignored a 1982 act of Congress that prohibited the United States from funding activities aimed at overthrowing the Sandinista regime. When the *Wall Street Journal* reported in March 1983 that the CIA had secretly mined Nicaraguan harbors, politicians from liberal Massachusetts senator Teddy Kennedy to Barry Goldwater were outraged. "I am pissed off," said the eternally frank Goldwater. "This is an act violating international law. It is an act of war."

In June 1984, Congress passed a second law to bar any government intelligence agency from offering assistance of any kind to the Contras, including channeling aid from others. Frustrated, the president gathered together a small group at the White House. Included were Secretary of State George Shultz; CIA head Casey; National Security Council Advisor Robert McFarlane; NSC member Lieutenant

Colonel Oliver North, a marine and Vietnam veteran like McFarlane; and Jeane J. Kirkpatrick, a member of the NSC and Reagan's first US ambassador to the United Nations.

In 1979, Kirkpatrick had published an article called "Dictatorships and Double Standards," which argued that right-wing authoritarian governments were less repressive than revolutionary autocracies and more likely to be open to democratizing pressures from within and without. Following her theory, Kirkpatrick supported CIA chief Casey's plan to obtain third-party money to fund the Contras, in defiance of the new law. Shultz opposed the plan, and warned the president that such a move would be "an impeachable offense." Vice president and former CIA director George H. W. Bush disagreed, arguing that the United States could "encourage" third parties to fund the Contras so long as America offered nothing in exchange. Reagan was adamant about the need to help the Contras. North and McFarlane were charged with coming up with a secret plan. It was risky. Sounding eerily like Robert McNamara after reading the Pentagon Papers, the president warned, "If such a story gets out, we'll all be hanging by our thumbs in front of the White House."

ARMS FOR HOSTAGES

The same month that Reagan ordered North and McFarlane to find a way to keep the Contras in the field, the CIA chief in Lebanon, William Buckley, was kidnapped by Hezbollah, an anti-Israel terrorist organization tied to Iran. Buckley was murdered soon afterward, but Hezbollah continued taking hostages in Beirut. President Reagan had vowed repeatedly never to negotiate with terrorists—including the government of Iran, which he characterized, correctly, as a leading sponsor of state-supported terrorism—but he was obsessed with his duty "to bring those Americans home." In 1985, Iran, at war with Iraq, secretly requested to buy arms from the United States. Congress had strictly forbidden this in 1979 during the Iran hostage crisis. NSC chief McFarlane recommended secretly selling weapons to Iran, with the understanding that Iran would pressure Hezbollah to release the hostages, and the United States could funnel the money Iran paid for the arms to the Contras.

The arms-for-hostages proposal split the administration. Secretary of State Shultz and Secretary of Defense Caspar Weinberger were opposed; President Reagan, new NSC chief John Poindexter, and CIA director Casey approved. By the time the story leaked via a newspaper in Beirut in November 1986, more than 1,500 missiles had been shipped to Iran and millions of dollars passed to the Contras. Three hostages were released, but they were replaced with another three, in what Shultz characterized as "a hostage bazaar." President Reagan denied the entire operation on national television. A week later, he acknowledged that weapons had been sold to Iran but insisted there had been no "arms for hostages" deal. Casey, Poindexter, and Oliver North—who had arranged the money transfer to the Contras—lied under oath to the House and Senate intelligence committees and destroyed every document they could get their hands on, thereby exceeding Richard Nixon's obstruction of justice during Watergate.

Poindexter resigned and North was fired, but questions remained. Had the president known about the illegal activities emanating from the White House? If not, why not? In congressional hearings held in the spring and summer of 1987, Oliver North, handsome and upright in his marine uniform, admitted that he had shredded documents, lied to Congress and the CIA, and falsified financial records. Charged with breaking a slew of laws and subverting the Constitution, North responded that Congress was the real villain for refusing to support the Contras in their valiant fight against Communism. Senator Warren Rudman, a Republican from Vermont who had supported aiding the Contras, chided North for attacking Congress, pointing out that public opinion polls had been strongly against continued aid to the Contras and that "this Congress represents the people." But conservative House Republicans led by Wyoming representative Dick Cheney defended North, attacked Secretary of State Shultz, proclaimed the administration's innocence while rationalizing its lawlessness, and finally condemned Congress for passing the laws violated by the executive branch in the first place. Certain that they were right, Oliver North and his supporters refused to believe that they had ever been in the wrong.

The End of the Cold War

So many momentous German events have occurred on November 9 that the Germans have named it *Schicksalstag* (Day of Fate). The end of the Cold War began when East and West Germans united to bring down the Berlin Wall on November 9, 1989: exactly 71 years after the monarchy was abolished at the end of the First World War, 66 years after the Beer Hall Putsch put Adolf Hitler on the map, and 51 years after Kristallnacht revealed Hitler's agenda. Technically, the Cold War ended during President George H. W. Bush's watch, but it was Ronald Reagan who hastened the end of the Cold War by changing the tone of US-Soviet relations.

REPERCUSSIONS OF IRAN-CONTRA

After the Iran-Contra investigations, the president quietly replaced his inner circle, trading ideologues like Chief of Staff Donald Regan and National Security Council Advisor Poindexter for pragmatists like Tennessee senator Howard Baker and Army Lieutenant General Colin Powell, respectively. Thanks to Oliver North's shredding extravaganza, no documentary evidence existed to directly link the president to the covert operation. Like Nixon and Watergate, the burning question became Reagan's knowledge of the cover-up rather than the events themselves. In the end, 14 members of his administration were indicted, on charges of perjury, obstruction of justice, conspiracy, withholding of evidence, and defrauding the government, and 11 convictions resulted, of which several were vacated on appeal. The rest of the indicted or convicted were pardoned by President George H. W. Bush, who succeeded President Reagan in 1989. Several of those involved in Iran-Contra, such as Latin American specialist Elliot Abrams, who was convicted in 1991 of unlawfully withholding information from Congress, reentered government during the administration of President George W. Bush (2001–2009).

Like Watergate, the Iran-Contra scandal was fundamentally a battle over the balance of power between Congress and the executive. Like Watergate, Iran-Contra revealed the fragility of the rule of law. Unlike Watergate, Iran-Contra cast an unflattering light on a chief executive who was personally appealing even to those who hated his politics and questioned his judgment. Although many Americans were outraged by this latest incident of executive misconduct, few wanted to see the president punished. People *liked* Ronald Reagan. People wanted to believe him.

This personality attribute had its plusses and its minuses. On the one hand, it stayed the hand of justice. Measured by the number of government officials indicted for criminal wrongdoing, Ronald Reagan's two administrations were the most corrupt in American history. On the other, it inspired confidence in the most important and unlikely of partners in forging peaceful coexistence between the United

States and the Soviet Union: Mikhail Sergeyevich Gorbachev, the USSR's eighth and final premier.

Mikhail Gorbachev became general secretary of the politburo and premier of the Soviet Union in March 1985, after the deaths, in quick succession, of premiers Yuri Andropov and Konstantin Chernenko. A lawyer by training and a student by inclination, Gorbachev became premier at a moment in which his nation was on the brink of disaster. The Soviet economy, which had since WWII provided a basic if not luxurious standard of living for its far-flung populace, was crumbling under the pressure of the decade-long war in Afghanistan and the accelerated arms race with the United States. In the early 1980s, upwards of 20 percent of the USSR's annual gross domestic product was earmarked for military spending (compared with approximately 6.2 percent of GDP for the United States). Even hard-liners were beginning to wonder aloud how long the Soviet military would keep "devouring our economy, our agriculture, and our consumer goods."

There were two complementary elements to Gorbachev's plan to modernize the Soviet Union: *glasnost* (openness, including toleration of speech criticizing the government and freedom of worship) and *perestroika* (restructuring, of the economy and of politics). Without sacrificing national security, Gorbachev prodded the military to reconsider its strategy. In August 1985, he imposed a unilateral moratorium on testing nuclear weapons. At the first arms control summit between Reagan and Gorbachev in Geneva in November 1985, each began to believe in the sincerity of the other's commitment to avoiding nuclear war.

PEACEFUL COEXISTENCE

The pursuit of peace began, paradoxically, with a massive military buildup. Defense spending, which had hit low tide under Gerald Ford and began rising during the Carter years, exploded under Reagan. Annual defense outlays rose almost a third during Reagan's first term (from $171 billion to $229 billion). Insisting that America was losing the arms race with the Soviets, Reagan spent billions on the Strategic Defense Initiative (SDI), a missile-defense system designed to destroy enemy missiles before they entered the atmosphere. Dubbed "Star Wars" after the 1978 hit movie, SDI's scientific roots were shallow. Weapons experts on both sides of the Berlin Wall were skeptical about its feasibility. Even so, SDI alarmed Soviets leaders, who insisted that a space shield would increase the risk of a unilateral American nuclear attack. In November 1983, a joint US-NATO war simulation exercise rattled Soviet military leaders enough to put their own nuclear forces on alert.

Two months later, in a nationally televised address on January 16, 1984, President Reagan reiterated his belief that "a nuclear war can never be won and must never be fought," and expressed his hope that he would live "to see the day when nuclear weapons will be banished from the face of the earth." In his speech, Reagan imagined "a better working relationship" between superpowers marked by "cooperation and understanding." Immediately following the speech, Secretary of State George Shultz met for five hours with veteran Russian foreign minister Andrei Gromyko. "The ice was cracked," Shultz reported later.

Ronald Reagan hated everything about Communist nations: their elevation of the state over the individual, their iron grip on the economy, and their denial of personal liberty, including freedom of thought and worship. Unlike Richard Nixon and J. Edgar Hoover, however, Reagan was able to differentiate between the threats posed by external and internal Communists. Reagan was critical of American Communists and their methods (there had been plenty in Hollywood), but realistic about the modest threat they posed.

As president, Reagan pursued victory through strikingly contradictory policies. His attitude toward the Soviets was guided by two principles: first, that the West would, inevitably, triumph in the Cold War; and second, that there could never be a winner in a nuclear war. From his first day in office, Reagan denounced the Soviet Union whenever possible and warned its leaders that their days were numbered. He promised to "roll back" Communism around the globe (the Reagan Doctrine), which translated into aiding anti-Communist insurgencies in Latin America and, following Jimmy Carter, in Afghanistan.

Unlike some of his more apocalyptic and bellicose advisors and supporters, Reagan never came to love the bomb. He always regarded nuclear weapons and nuclear warfare with horror—enough so that he was willing to consider an American-Soviet agreement to eliminate nuclear weapons entirely. The Reagan Doctrine notwithstanding, the president revealed a capacity to recognize and adjust to new geopolitical realities. Disregarding most of his foreign policy advisors and opening himself up to strident criticism from his most fervent anti-Communist supporters, Reagan identified internal shifts occurring within the Soviet Union and exploited them in the interest of peaceful coexistence. Perhaps, he came to believe, American victory did not require Soviet defeat. This most optimistic of American presidents pursued a win-win solution to the Cold War once it was within his sight.

LIGHT AT THE END OF THE TUNNEL

One obstacle overshadowed all others in US-Soviet arms talks: SDI. Reagan's advisors were divided on the usefulness of SDI. Shultz and veteran arms negotiator Paul Nitze (who had authored NSC-68 back in the early days of the Cold War) were willing to trade SDI for the reduction of existing weapons. Secretary of Defense Caspar Weinberger and his assistant Richard Perle were not. Reagan wanted to have things both ways: to progress in arms reduction talks while forging ahead with SDI.

At a two-day meeting in the capital of Iceland, Reykjavik, in October 1986, the Soviets stunned the Americans by proposing to cut long-range ballistic missiles by 50 percent and to ban nuclear testing entirely. When Gorbachev went a step further and suggested eliminating all nuclear weapons, Reagan responded spontaneously, "It would be fine with me." Gorbachev's price for this was the confinement of SDI to laboratory research. Reagan balked. When Gorbachev wondered aloud why a purely defensive system would be necessary if all nuclear weapons were abolished, he offended Reagan, who grabbed Shultz and walked out of the talks.

Reykjavik failed to produce an arms agreement between the two nations. But Gorbachev returned home convinced that the United States would not launch a nuclear first strike against the Soviet Union, which allowed him to cut the military budget and withdraw Soviet troops from Afghanistan. In November 1986, Gorbachev stunned his Warsaw Pact allies by declaring that they could no longer rely on Soviet domestic aid. This gave a green light to democratic reform movements in Eastern Europe. In January 1987, Gorbachev announced the replacement of strict central economic planning in the USSR with greater openness to market forces, and initiated a quiet purge of the military, replacing old cold warriors with officers more open to the West. At the same time, the government released imprisoned political dissidents, or critics, and stopped jamming radio broadcasts by the Voice of America. One of the first dissidents released was physicist and Nobel Peace Prize–winning human rights activist Andrey Sakharov, who reassured Gorbachev by ridiculing SDI as a "Maginot Line in space" and recommended renewed talks with the Americans. In February 1987, Gorbachev uncoupled SDI from future negotiations about intermediate-range missiles in Europe.

In a speech in Berlin on June 12, 1987, President Reagan recalled John Kennedy's visit there nearly 30 years before. Standing before the Brandenburg Gate within steps of the Berlin Wall, Reagan addressed Gorbachev directly: "General Secretary Gorbachev, if you seek peace, if you seek prosperity for the Soviet Union and Eastern Europe, if you seek liberalization: Come here to this gate! Mr. Gorbachev, open this gate! Mr. Gorbachev, tear down this wall!" Although provocative in its own way, Reagan's direct appeal to the Soviet leader was miles away from his earlier stance toward the Evil Empire. At a summit at the White House in December 1987, Reagan and Gorbachev signed the Soviet-American Intermediate-Range Nuclear Forces (INF) Treaty, and displayed the personal warmth the two leaders had developed for each other—warmth that was reflected in the relationship between the Reagans and Gorbachev's stylish and intelligent wife, Raisa, whose presence at the side of the Soviet leader in Reykjavik and Washington softened and humanized American perceptions of the Russians.

*

Returning from his fourth summit with Gorbachev, which was held in Moscow in May 1988, President Reagan was asked if he still considered the Soviet Union an "evil empire." He replied, not quite dismissively, "I was talking about another time, another era." This side of Reagan—his capacity to recognize and embrace change, in others as well as himself—served both him and the nation well in a revolutionary moment. The image of the president speaking at Moscow University before an enormous bust of Lenin captures his fundamental pragmatism and imperturbability, as well as his faith in his own capacity to discern the truth. Ronald Reagan hated Communism but he loved Communists. He reported to be "deeply moved" by his encounters with the Soviet people. He was willing to reconsider his commitments, as he did when he abandoned the party of Roosevelt for the party of Goldwater. He was also willing to bend the rule of law and the political process to the breaking point in pursuit of what he considered to be right. This combination of ideological certainty and flexibility flummoxed Reagan's supporters and opponents alike, and left him, in the end, occupying a one-man no-man's-land of compromise in a political climate of true belief.

FIGURE 12. While US president George W. Bush conducts a reading seminar at the Emma E. Booker Elementary School in Sarasota, Florida, on September 11, 2001, White House chief of staff Andrew Card informs him of a second plane hitting the World Trade Center in New York City. Photographer: Win McNamee. Photo courtesy of Reuters Pictures.

CHAPTER 12

Vulnerable, 1989–2001

The 1990s were marked by political extremism. At the 1992 Republican National Convention, syndicated columnist Patrick Buchanan, a former Nixon speechwriter, delivered a prime-time address in which he warned that abortion, "radical feminism," and "homosexual rights" were destroying the nation, and declared that the United States was in the midst of a religious and cultural "war for the soul of America."

Buchanan was not against the federal government; his goal was to bend it to his will. Others to the right of Buchanan rejected federal power entirely. Also in 1992, federal agents sought to arrest Randy Weaver, a fundamentalist Christian associated with white supremacist militias, at his home in Ruby Ridge, Idaho. One agent was killed in a fierce exchange of gunfire, and Weaver's unarmed wife and 14-year-old son, who had shot the agent, died in the battle. Weaver finally surrendered 12 days later, surrounded by FBI agents, US Marshals, and the Idaho National Guard's armored personnel carriers. It looked like a war zone.

The next year saw a 51-day standoff between federal agents and David Koresh, who claimed to be the "final prophet" of a splinter group of Seventh-Day Adventists in Waco, Texas. Koresh had been stockpiling weapons. The confrontation ended only after another brutal battle that killed 4 agents and 80 other people, including 19 children, who were trapped by fire inside Koresh's compound.

Two years later, on April 19, 1995, two antigovernment militia members, Timothy McVeigh and Terry Nichols, detonated a truck bomb in front of the Alfred P. Murrah Federal Building in Oklahoma City, Oklahoma. Acting in revenge for the Waco battle, they killed 168 people, including many small children and infants in a daycare center located in the building.

During this era, many Americans linked deeply felt convictions about abortion, homosexuality, and women's rights to economic difficulties and challenges to the legitimacy of the federal government. What became known as the "culture wars" pitted defenders of conservative moral norms and claims of patriotism against the forms and agents of cultural change. Conservative politicians, apoplectic over government funding that supported what they considered sacrilegious and repulsive views on sexual freedom, abortion, and homosexuality, cut public funding for the arts and humanities. A group named Advocates for Academic Freedom cast college professors as censorious purveyors of "political correctness" and multiculturalism.

More than any other issue, abortion revealed the depth of the chasm between the two sides of the culture wars. Antiabortion activists charged that *Roe v. Wade* had authorized the legal mass murder of unborn children. Supporters of a woman's legal right to terminate a pregnancy saw the antiabortion movement as an assault on hard-won gains for women's freedom and equality. The election of a pro-choice president in 1992 dismayed antiabortion activists and incited some with extreme fundamentalist Christian beliefs to resort to violence. In 1993, for example, George Tiller, one of only a handful of physicians in the United States who performed legal late-term abortions, was shot outside his clinic in Wichita, Kansas, by Shelley Shannon, an antiabortion activist frustrated by "the inability of the movement to advance its cause in the courts or through elections."

Although Tiller survived the attack, he was subjected to constant threats and abuse, which were broadcast across the nation on new cable television news networks that vastly expanded the viewing options of Americans but also introduced overtly slanted news analysis and bombastic personalities. On his popular television show *The O'Reilly Factor*, Bill O'Reilly persistently referred to George Tiller as "Tiller the Baby Killer," a "murderer on the loose," and guilty of "Nazi stuff."

Tiller was not intimidated. Describing himself as "a general in an epic cultural war to keep abortion legal," he defended his work as saving women's lives and restoring their freedom to determine their own futures. He fortified his clinic and wore a bulletproof vest in public. A lifelong Republican, Tiller regularly attended men's Bible study at Reformation Lutheran Church in Wichita, where his wife, Jeanne, sang in the choir. "The church was the one place he felt safe," Jeanne Tiller said later.

Scott Roeder, a member of a right-wing group known as the Montana Freemen, "saw himself as a foot soldier" in an epic war for righteousness and insisted that murder was a justifiable way to stop abortions. On Sunday, May 31, 2009, in the foyer of Reformation Lutheran, Scott Roeder put a gun to George Tiller's head and executed him. Tiller was the fourth abortion provider, and the eighth person connected to an abortion clinic, to be murdered for their work since 1993. *O'Reilly Factor* contributor Ann Coulter commented crassly, "I don't really like to think of it as murder. It was terminating Tiller in the 203rd trimester."

Scott Roeder was solely responsible for the death of George Tiller. But it would be naïve to imagine that social movements and mass media have no effect on individuals. Characterizing political differences as warfare, and demonizing one's opponents as immoral, can lead to more than rhetorical excess. The democratic political process gives enormous leeway for criticizing the government and fellow citizens. Exceeding it threatens the very basis of the peaceful compact upon which the Republic is built.

The United States in the Post–Cold War World

The collapse of Communist regimes and the transitions in the Soviet Union pursued by Mikhail Gorbachev ended the Cold War and with it the bilateralism that had structured global politics for more than 40 years. The intellectual binaries—totalitarianism versus democracy, managed economy versus capitalism, East versus West—that had structured American politics vanished along with the Communist world. When the Soviet Union ceased to exist in 1992, the compass of US foreign policy lost its magnetic north.

New global circumstances raised new versions of old questions. What was the role of the United States, the only superpower left standing, in the post–Cold War world? Should the United States intervene in what were effectively civil wars? Should the United States act alone (unilaterally), or only in partnership with the suddenly relevant United Nations? What was the relationship between America's national interests and its foreign policy? How would those interests be defined, and by whom?

A NEW WORLD ORDER

President George Herbert Walker Bush, elected in November 1988, inherited a world in transition. He was well-schooled in foreign policy, having been the nation's official emissary to the People's Republic of China and the director of the CIA before becoming vice president under Ronald Reagan. Bush's foreign policy instincts were those of a "pragmatist" in the model of Henry Kissinger, who hesitated to spend American blood or treasure abroad for anything less than a "vital national interest." Preventing the spread of Communism or nuclear weapons met this test. Exporting democracy or defending human rights did not. Bush was an anti-Wilsonian, unwilling to endow American foreign policy with moral content, and disinclined to interfere in the internal affairs of other sovereign states—however misguided they might be.

Other members of the Republican foreign policy establishment were less inhibited. Those who came to be called neoconservatives took a stance associated with Theodore Roosevelt: to fulfill its destiny to guide mankind toward ever-greater freedom, America had a mission to spread democracy across the globe. This purpose had been lost in the 1970s, a dark time of American failure abroad, with the fall of Saigon in 1975 and the disastrous taking of American hostages during the Iranian Revolution in 1979. But with the implosion of the Soviet Union and its Warsaw Pact allies, the moment was ripe for reconceptualization of America's place in the world.

Much of that reconceptualization took place in areas formerly aligned with the Soviet Union. The political map of Central and Eastern Europe was redrawn with breathtaking speed after 1989, as one nation after another pulled free of the Communist orbit. In 1989 and 1990, Estonia, Lithuania, Latvia, Hungary, Poland, Czechoslovakia, and East Germany peacefully shed their Communist governments. Communist regimes in Yugoslavia, Bulgaria, and Romania were overthrown. In 1992, the Soviet Union officially dissolved and was replaced by the Commonwealth of Independent States comprising Russia and 11 former Soviet republics, mostly in the Transcaucasian mountains and peninsula that constituted the old USSR's southern perimeter.

The collapse of the Soviet Union and its allies in Central Europe inspired reformers in other Communist nations, including the People's Republic of China. In the spring of 1989, protesters occupied Tiananmen Square in Beijing. The Chinese government labeled the demonstrators "counterrevolutionaries" and sent in the army to clear the square on June 4, 1989. Searing images of unarmed youths defying tanks and mowed down by machine guns—hundreds were killed and thousands wounded—generated worldwide outrage, but failed to produce freedom in China. Over the next quarter century, China became more integrated into the global market economy, but this new economic openness did not translate into either democratic institutions or an open society.

AFGHANISTAN, 1978–1996

In April 1978, revolutionaries in Afghanistan seized power, declared a secular Communist government, overturned local traditions and kinship ties, and offended Muslim sensibilities. A year later, Islamic fundamentalists, inspired by Iran's revolution, rose up against the new regime, which then appealed to Moscow for help.

This new uprising not only jeopardized the Communist revolution in Afghanistan but also threatened the security of the USSR, whose southern border ran the length of both Afghanistan and Iran—which had recently been reborn as an Islamic state. Two potential outcomes worried the Kremlin: that an Islamic revolution in Afghanistan would unite it with Iran, and that the Americans, already run out of Iran, would intervene in Afghanistan to prevent that outcome. Either way, Soviet interests would be compromised. Reluctantly, the USSR decided to intervene militarily in Afghanistan.

The Soviet invasion of Afghanistan in December 1979 violated the principles of détente and threatened Western access to the oil fields of the Persian Gulf region. Afghanistan became a magnet for Islamic militants, and by the early 1980s a variety of mujahideen groups operating out of Pakistan battled Soviet invaders, Communist infidels, and each other. Just as he had approved of covert aid to the Contras in Nicaragua, President Reagan also sent US aid to the Afghan mujahideen (literally, "those who engage in jihad," or Muslim holy war). The CIA provided the mujahideen with hundreds of millions of dollars, which were matched by Saudi Arabia. Still following traditional Cold War logic, the United States seemed not to care that the anti-Soviet forces were dominated by Islamic fundamentalists whose long-term aspirations conflicted with the interests of America and its allies.

Stalemated in Afghanistan and coming apart at the seams at home, the Soviets retreated in 1988. The nine-year war resulted in more than one million deaths, including 14,500 Soviet soldiers. Beyond that were the uncounted wounded, and the nearly five million refugees who fled to Pakistan and Iran. Afghanistan's capital, Kabul, fell to the mujahideen in February 1992, but peace did not arrive: warlords who had made common cause fighting the Soviets carved out fiefdoms, and former soldiers joined together as armed bandits in gangs that terrorized the countryside.

In southern Afghanistan, groups of religious students known as *talibs* fended off the gangsters and established public order based on an extreme interpretation of Islamic law, or Sharia. The Taliban swept through southern Afghanistan, captured Kabul in 1996, and established the Islamic Emirate of Afghanistan. By 1998, the Taliban controlled 90 percent of the nation. Veterans of the conflict marveled at what could be accomplished with money, Korans, and a few good weapons. An infidel government had been overthrown, and a superpower had been humiliated and defeated. It was inspiring.

IRAQ, 1980–1990

The Kingdom of Iraq was created after World War I by fusing together three Ottoman provinces representing different ethnic and religious groups, and placing them under British control. For the next half century, Iraq passed through periods of British rule, a conjured monarchy, a republican revolution, and Communist intervention. Then, in 1968, Iraq came under the control of the Baath Party, which was inspired by Gamal Abdel Nasser's Egypt and which mixed Arab nationalism and socialism. That year, Baathist political leader Saddam Hussein became vice president. In part because of America's growing alliance with Israel after the Arab world's humiliating defeat in the 1967 War, Iraq, like Egypt, gravitated toward the Soviet sphere.

Throughout the 1970s, Saddam consolidated his power by carefully navigating conflict between the government and the military. The de facto head of government for nearly a decade, Saddam seized dictatorial power in 1979, portraying himself as a secular bulwark against Iran-style Islamic fundamentalism. Most Muslims fall into one of two camps: Sunnis or Shi'ites. Like Iran, but unlike most of the rest of the Muslim world, Iraq's population was predominantly Shi'ite. Saddam and his government, however, like the great majority of the world's Muslims, were Sunni. To demonstrate Iraqi superiority in the Persian Gulf region, and to prevent Iran's Ayatollah Khomeini from inspiring a Shi'ite revolt against Sunni rule in Iraq, Saddam attacked Iran in September 1980.

This was a miscalculation: Iran was disorganized, but it had been energized by its revolution. Horrified by the possibility that Iraq's oil fields might fall into the hands of Ayatollah Khomeini, the United States backed Iraq in the war, sharing intelligence and escorting Iraqi oil tankers with US Navy convoys. Although the Reagan State Department was appalled by Saddam's genocidal use of chemical weapons against rebellious Kurds in northern Iraq, it nonetheless concluded, "Human rights and chemical weapons use aside, in many respects our political and economic interests run parallel with those of Iraq." A national security directive reinforced this message, concluding that "normal relations between the United States and Iraq would serve our longer-term interests and promote stability in both the Gulf and the Middle East." Bolstered by American support, Iraq held its own against Iran. The war ended in 1988 via a UN resolution.

No longer jeopardized by Iran, Saddam became ever bolder. On April 2, 1990, he declared that Iraq possessed chemical weapons and indicated a willingness to use them against Israel. Congress, which until then had deferred to the executive on Iraq policy, denounced Saddam's actions. Senator William Cohen, for example, decried the administration's failure to condemn Iraq: "It is the smell of oil and the color of money that corrodes our principles." On July 27, 1990, the Senate passed a sanctions bill against Iraq. Iraq was already in deep economic distress owing to war-related debt and a drop in petroleum prices caused by oil production in Kuwait, which Saddam contended cost his nation $14 billion per year in lost revenue. He considered Kuwait's refusal to scale back its oil production an act of war, and on August 2, Iraq invaded the kingdom of Kuwait and threatened to strike at Saudi Arabia, an American ally perched atop one-quarter of the world's known oil.

THE GULF WAR

Faced with this crisis, President George H. W. Bush moved more than 400,000 military personnel into the Gulf region in order to deter an Iraqi invasion of Saudi Arabia and pressure Saddam to leave Kuwait. At the same time, Bush and Secretary of State James Baker forged a coalition of over 100 nations to defend Saudi Arabia and the Gulf States. After an intense debate, Congress passed a resolution in January 1991 authorizing the president to use military force against Iraq. After a month-long bombing campaign, the 700,000 ground troops of the US-led coalition went into action in an assault code-named Operation Desert Storm. The Iraqis were overwhelmed and driven from Kuwait, but not before they set the kingdom's oil wells on fire, creating a region-wide ecological disaster.

American troops were welcomed as heroes by grateful Kuwaitis. In northern Iraq, separatist Kurdish militia members known as *peshmerga* drove cars adorned with pictures of President Bush. Such images were transmitted in real time back to the United States by CNN, the new 24-hour cable news network, which became famous for its on-the-spot coverage. Americans still scarred by losses in Vietnam could once again imagine a world in which American military power could be employed effectively in defense of freedom and democracy.

A cease-fire was declared on February 27, 1991, only 100 hours after the ground war began, and before coalition troops reached Baghdad. Removal of the Iraqi leader—"regime change"—was not a war aim, and Saddam Hussein remained in his presidential palace. Many in Washington assumed, however, that the Iraqi military would oust their failed leader, and President Bush urged the people of Iraq "to take matters into their own hands and force Saddam Hussein, the dictator, to step aside." Iraqi Kurds responded by launching a revolt in northern Iraq. Shiʿites, who were fed up with rule by members of the minority Sunni population, rose up in southern Iraq.

Both groups had banked on US military support that was not forthcoming. Both rebellions were crushed by Iraq's Republican Guard. More than one million Kurds fled into the mountains bordering Iran and Turkey. To the horror of the US government, Iraqi helicopters pursued the Kurds relentlessly, massacring tens of thousands.

Saddam had been driven from Kuwait, but no one wanted to risk the breakup of Iraq by intervening there directly. UN inspectors uncovered an Iraqi program to develop biological and nuclear weapons, destroyed the existing cache, and developed a system to prevent their reacquisition. At home, an exultant Bush, sounding suddenly like Woodrow Wilson in Versailles, declared before Congress: "we can see a new world coming into view in which there is the very real prospect of a new world order. . . . A world where the United Nations, freed from cold war stalemate, is poised to fulfill the historic vision of its founders. A world in which freedom and respect for human rights find a home among all nations." Saddam and his Republican Guard remained in place, however, posing a continuing menace to the Gulf region. In Saudi Arabia, US forces settled in to defend America's interests from any Iraqi resurgence.

THE SAUDIS

The assumptions inherent in George Bush's vision—that "freedom" and "human rights" would spread across the globe—betrayed both optimism and cultural and historical ignorance. Few would have guessed in 1991 that Saudi Arabia, then associated with high-spending princes, luxury malls, and five-star hotels, had precisely one well-paved road as late as 1950. Before an American geologist discovered oil in the Arabian Peninsula in 1941, the main source of revenue for the kingdom was the annual stream of pilgrims to the holy cities of Mecca and Medina.

The oil pumped by the Arabian-American Oil Company (ARAMCO) provided Saudi Arabia with sudden wealth and international leverage. This led to cultural dislocation, however, and fueled an intense debate about values. Those Saudis who adhered to the austere dictates of Wahhabism, a fringe version of Sunni Islam that emerged in the eighteenth century, denounced the materialism and corruption of the royal family, and resisted progressive "innovations" such as female education and television, which had been introduced to Saudi Arabia by American-educated princes. To deflect such criticism, the Saudi rulers funded Wahhabist schools and charities at home and around the world—particularly in Pakistan and Afghanistan, where this fiercely fundamentalist version of Islam took hold.

In 1979, the Islamic revolution in Iran reframed the Muslim debate with the West. Iran's Ayatollah Khomeini spoke for Islamic fundamentalists in Saudi Arabia and elsewhere when he rejected "freedom for everything . . . freedom that will corrupt our youth, freedom that will pave the way for our oppressor, freedom that will drag our nation to the bottom." The overnight transformation of Iran, a wealthy, modern nation and an ally of the United States, into an anti-American state governed by clerics under Islamic law demonstrated the attainability of radical Islamic goals, and inspired the seizure of the Grand Mosque in Mecca in 1979 by armed insurgents critical of what they considered lax Saudi enforcement of Islamic law.

Twelve years later, at the end of the Gulf War, the ongoing presence of thousands of non-Muslim American troops in Saudi Arabia deeply offended many religious Saudis, including Osama bin Laden, the scion of a billionaire construction magnate closely associated with the royal family. A strict follower of Wahhabism, bin Laden had earlier joined his Muslim brothers fighting Communism in Afghanistan and funneled Saudi volunteers and money to the Taliban.

After he criticized the Saudi rulers for allowing American troops—including women—to remain in the country, bin Laden was exiled to Sudan. He was stripped of his Saudi citizenship in 1993, expelled from Sudan, and welcomed by the Taliban after their victory in Afghanistan in 1996. There, this reclusive "philanthropist of terror" established himself as the leader of the most powerful Islamic terror organization in the world, al Qaeda, and plotted the destruction of the United States, the world's sole remaining superpower. As the mujahideen had driven out the godless Soviet Communists in the war in Afghanistan, so would al Qaeda destroy the United States—the purveyor of democracy, secular society, materialism, and consumer capitalism. Bin Laden declared holy war, or jihad, "on the Americans" in 1996.

New Republicans and New Democrats

The domestic policies that George H. W. Bush inherited from Ronald Reagan were defined by an economic orthodoxy that stressed the efficiency and wisdom of markets, disdained "big government" taxation, spending, and regulation, and revered a new globalized world of flexible labor pools, free trade, and migratory capital. Once the party of balanced budgets, the Republicans of the 1980s and 1990s revealed a broad streak of "tax-cut populism" and virulent antistatism.

Democrats were equally enamored of market economics and barely more enthusiastic about the possibilities of the engaged state. The party worked tirelessly to distance itself from Republican portrayals of "tax and spend" Democrats. Two-term Democratic president Bill Clinton's signature domestic achievement was to dramatically diminish the welfare system that even Ronald Reagan had not dared touch. By 2000, old notions of governance as an expression of the public good had all but evaporated and been replaced within both parties by ideas championing "limited government."

REPUBLICAN FRACTURE

No longer unified by antipathy to Communism, the Republican Party began to fragment. In 1988, socially conservative Republicans from the South and West challenged the more moderate eastern establishment for control of the party. Although nominally from Texas, Reagan's vice president, George Herbert Walker Bush, an Episcopalian and Yale man, epitomized the Old Guard. Bush was uncomfortable with religious conservatives and unmoved by the Religious Right's antiabortion, pro-school prayer agenda. The vice president's eldest son, George W. Bush, who had sobered up and found God two years earlier, helped the candidate connect with southern and western voters. George W's "goodbye Jack Daniels, hello Jesus" story resonated with conservative voters and helped his father secure the GOP nomination and then the presidency.

In his inaugural address in 1989, Bush moved away from the Cold War rhetoric of the past, pledging to help make a "gentler" world. The new president also distanced himself from the most strident Republican critics of government, promising to foster a "kinder" nation that would be fortified through American traditions of volunteerism. Bush praised "all the community organizations that are spread like stars throughout the nation, doing good," and quietly worried about his debt-ridden government. Indeed, Bush found it difficult to follow a president who had declared, "Government is not the solution. Government is the problem." Ronald Reagan's tax cuts had not powered the economy or generated the increase in revenues he had predicted, but had rather resulted in record growth in the national debt. Furthermore, Reagan's desire to "get the government off our backs" had led to deregulation of multiple spheres of life, including the financial sector, which encouraged reckless behavior in accounting and banking. With Congress controlled by the Democrats, Bush articulated no domestic agenda (he had admitted during the campaign that he was no good at "the vision thing"), relying instead on his veto power to keep Congress in check.

Propelled to office by an alliance of Christian activists and fiscal conservatives, Bush pleased neither. The fiscal conservatives were the first to defect. Before becoming vice president in 1981, Bush had run against Ronald Reagan in the Republican primaries and ridiculed Reagan's fiscal policies as "voodoo economics." How could cutting taxes possibly result in enhanced government revenue? Bush withheld his criticism once he joined the ticket, but the numbers never did add up, and the total federal debt more than tripled during Reagan's two terms in office, in good part because of the enormous tax cuts he pushed through Congress.

When it comes to fiscal policy, American voters do not reward candor, particularly when the issue is increased taxes. Even Franklin Roosevelt promised to lower taxes and cut spending as a presidential candidate in 1932. Following Reagan's example, Bush pledged never to raise taxes, telling delegates to the 1988 GOP convention, "Read my lips: No new taxes." But in 1991, the nation slid into a recession brought on by a combination of the tax giveaway a decade earlier, ill-considered deregulation of the financial sector, which resulted in a government bailout of the savings and loan industry, and mounting national debt (exacerbated by the cost of the Gulf War). The president finally relented. Although pilloried by Republicans, Bush negotiated a budget that combined spending cuts with a modest tax hike for the top income bracket (from 28 percent to 31.5 percent). Republicans vowed to make him pay for his perfidy.

A "NEW DEMOCRAT" AT THE HELM

Despite his success in the Gulf War, President Bush's popularity plummeted because of the rift in the Republican Party, a serious economic recession, and increasing doubts about whether the government had missed an opportunity to stabilize the Middle East by ending the Gulf War with Saddam Hussein's Iraq still on the loose. Although a year earlier Bush had seemed certain of reelection, he lost in November 1992 to Democrat William Jefferson (Bill) Clinton.

Bill Clinton was a born politician: warm, shrewd, ambitious, and emotionally needy. A Rhodes Scholar and graduate of the Yale Law School, Clinton was governor of Arkansas by age 32. His personal magnetism drew vast crowds, into which he would plunge, hugging and shaking hands. Clinton's folksy, southern ways put people at ease and made him "America's first user-friendly president," the junk-food-loving guy next door who battled his weight and deflected charges of marital infidelity.

Born in 1946, and thus the first "baby boomer" presidential candidate, Clinton made the most of media, especially television, in his 1992 campaign. He obliterated incumbent president George H. W. Bush and third-party candidate billionaire Ross Perot in three televised debates, donned sunglasses to play his saxophone on late-night television, and actually answered a woman who asked what form of underwear he favored. (Briefs.)

Clinton was elected as a New Democract, a centrist who combined liberal cultural values, such as equal rights for women and minorities, with conservative economic and social policies. Faced with a skyrocketing cumulative federal deficit of $4.4 trillion, New Democrats sought to slow the expansion of government social programs and bureaucracy and grow the economy. Like President Bush, New Democrats were determined to protect Medicare and Social Security, but tried to temper Republicans' portrayal of their party as addicted to government spending and high taxes by limiting other entitlement programs.

Clinton owed his election in great measure to the faltering economy, and righting that ship was his first priority. In the early 1980s, the Republicans had slashed taxes, arguing that the "release" of capital from government coffers would generate economic growth. Yet inflation peaked at 13.5 percent in 1980, when it finally began to recede, squeezed by record interest rates and unemployment levels higher than at any time since the Great Depression. And in April 1982, the economy collapsed into its sharpest recession since the 1930s.

Growth returned to the American economy during the second half of the 1980s, but the federal deficit remained high. The Omnibus Budget Reconciliation Act of 1993, which passed only when Vice President Al Gore cast the tie-breaking vote, raised the top marginal income tax rate from 31.5 percent to 39.6 percent. Combined with a reviving economy, the tax increases lowered the deficit dramatically. Under President Clinton, the deficit fell from $290 billion in 1992 to $22 billion in 1997, before rising to a budget *surplus* of $236 billion in 2000.

Fueled by the global integration of markets and communications, the 1990s became a "new age of global capitalism," where place and time were virtually annihilated by personal computers, the internet, and satellite-transmitted telephone and television signals. By 1990, the dominant economic ideology of the United States was "faith in the wisdom and efficiency of markets, disdain for big government taxation, spending, and regulation, [and] reverence for a globalized world of flexible labor pools, free trade, and free-floating capital." Lost in the discussion was any consideration of who should bear the social and economic costs of the new global economy.

CLINTON IN OFFICE

Bill Clinton was determined to create a comprehensive national health insurance program so that no American would go without basic medical care. The idea was neither original to Clinton nor especially radical: Harry Truman proposed adding national health care to the New Deal social safety net in 1945, and the rest of the industrialized world included health insurance among their domestic social welfare policies.

Lyndon Johnson's Medicare (1965) covered hospital care and physician services for the elderly and solidified a federal-state program for the indigent (Medicaid). Both programs were expanded under President Reagan. Health care was both an individual necessity and big business: one in every seven dollars spent in the United States was for some aspect of health care, and costs were rising far faster than inflation. The soaring cost of health care in America was an economic as well as a political crisis.

The president entrusted his wife, lawyer Hillary Rodham Clinton, with the assignment of drafting health care legislation. Republicans fulminated at the unseemliness of Mrs. Clinton's leadership on health care, and grumbled that she ought to be strolling the White House rose garden and not sticking her nose into public policy. Mrs. Clinton and her aide Ira Magaziner drafted a bill so enormous and complicated that it became an easy target for private insurance companies, which launched a highly effective television advertising campaign against it. Congressional Democrats, who had not been consulted during the legislative drafting process, had little incentive to support it. Despite having a Democratic majority in Congress, Bill Clinton's health care plan never came up for a vote.

Throughout his two terms in office, President Clinton faced tough Republican opposition. In 1994, the Speaker of the House, Georgia congressman Newt Gingrich, galvanized the midterm elections by convincing nearly every Republican to sign his "Contract with America," a 10-point plan that included tax cuts for the middle class and above, cuts in welfare, a tough anticrime measure, and a balanced-budget amendment. That November, the Republicans swept Congress for the first time since 1954, gaining 9 seats in the Senate and 52 in the House. The 104th Congress would include 73 freshman Republicans, many of them white southerners ideologically to the right of Gingrich.

This new, southern-inflected GOP was personified by Gingrich, whose leadership both reflected and furthered the internal transformation of the Republican Party begun under Ronald Reagan. Unlike the Republican leader of the Senate, Kansan Robert Dole, Gingrich was an ideologue, not a deal maker. His ascendency marked the arrival of a new corps of warrior Republicans who elevated partisan infighting to an art. As veteran political journalist Elizabeth Drew remarked, "The 'Gingrich revolution' of 1994 wasn't just a stunning triumph over the Democrats, but also an assault on mainstream Republicans."

The 104th Congress arrived in Washington fired up and ready to overhaul the welfare system, roll back gun control, limit federal regulatory power, cut taxes, boost the defense budget, and backtrack on foreign aid. When the GOP Congress sent President Clinton spending bills that slashed appropriations for Medicare, Medicaid, and education, he vetoed them. Clinton countered the Republicans' "Contract with America" with his own "Middle-Class Bill of Rights." Every time Gingrich thought he had the president on the ropes, Clinton moved to the right and just out of reach. When a budget impasse led to a six-day shutdown of the government in November 1995, Gingrich was blamed. But Clinton also learned a lesson, vowing never "to get caught in that big-government, big-this, big-that trap again." Stunning his supporters, the president announced in his 1996 State of the Union address that "the era of big government is over."

In 1996, yielding to Republican pressure and New Democrat principles, President Clinton declared that he was ending "welfare as we know it" by limiting the time that recipients were eligible for assistance. The Personal Responsibility and Work Opportunity Act forced the poor to become self-sufficient and to mobilize their own networks of kin, neighbors, and churches to make ends meet. These "little platoons of voluntary assistance" were called on to shoulder the burden borne by the state since the New Deal. Within five years, the number of Americans receiving public assistance dropped by almost half, from 12.2 million to 5.3 million.

CRIME, GUNS, AND RACE

Between 1965 and 1975, the rate of violent crime soared, and by 1980, the murder rate in the United States had doubled. Calls for "law and order" multiplied as crime continued to rise, especially in the cities. Explanations abounded, but the most popular one with policymakers was the trade in illegal drugs, especially marijuana, cocaine, and heroin. The federal government responded with a series of measures intended to address crime.

Early on in the effort to reduce crime, Lyndon Johnson signed into law in 1965 the Law Enforcement Assistance Act, which provided hundreds of millions of dollars in grants for local police departments. Much of the money went toward armored vehicles, tear gas, and other tools of riot control. Then the 1968 Omnibus Crime Control and Safe Streets Act directed billions of dollars to local police departments. By 1981, more than $8 billion had been funneled into an expanding "local" law enforcement system underwritten by the federal government.

Also on the federal government's crime agenda were guns. In 1968, a strong bipartisan majority in Congress passed gun control legislation in an effort to staunch the growth of firearm-related deaths. Such efforts to regulate the use and ownership of firearms were resisted fiercely by the increasingly powerful National Rifle Association that was backed by an increasingly conservative Supreme Court.

"Tough on crime" measures were supported across the partisan aisle. In the 1970s, individual states and Congress introduced mandatory minimum sentencing laws, which dramatically increased the number of prison inmates. Racial minorities, especially young black men, were disproportionately arrested and incarcerated. Bill Clinton preached "personal responsibility" and supported the death penalty (he flew home to Arkansas during the 1992 presidential campaign to preside over the execution of a mentally handicapped African American man). Part of his electoral strategy was to capture for the Democrats the racially coded "law and order" rhetoric that Republicans had used so successfully since Richard Nixon.

Indeed, one of Clinton's greatest domestic policy legacies was a $30 billion crime bill that created dozens of new federal crimes, mandated life sentences for three-time offenders (following the "three strikes and you're out" model pioneered by California), and authorized $16 billion for prison construction and the expansion of state and local police forces. This explosion in prisons had its origins in the "war on drugs," a term introduced by President Nixon and repurposed by President Reagan in 1986. That year, Congress passed the Anti-Drug Abuse Act, which established harsh mandatory minimum prison sentences for low-level drug dealing and far-more-severe sentences for possession and distribution of crack cocaine (a cheaper version of cocaine associated with inner-city blacks) than for powder cocaine (which was associated with whites). Drug arrests rose rapidly after 1980, and account for the majority of the rise in inmate populations. Arrests for marijuana possession (not distribution) accounted for nearly 80 percent of the growth in drug arrests in the 1990s. As law professor Michelle Alexander writes, "The uncomfortable reality is that convictions for drug offenses—not violent crime—are the single most important cause of the prison boom in the United States."

Although crime rates in the United States have declined steadily since 1991, the number of incarcerated Americans has increased from approximately 350,000 in 1990 to more than 2.2 million in 2015. With less than 5 percent of the world's population, by 2015 the United States held nearly 25 percent of the world's prisoners. As of 2015, African Americans are nearly six times as likely to be incarcerated as whites, and Hispanics are more than twice as likely to be incarcerated as whites, leading one student of incarceration, Michelle Alexander, to dub it "the new Jim Crow."

FAMILY VALUES

As a candidate, Clinton promised to issue an executive order to end the long-standing ban against homosexuals in the military. Resistance was stiff: conservative religious groups objected to any policy that might legitimate homosexuality, and the Joint Chiefs of Staff defended the ban on gays in the military as necessary to preserve discipline and morale. The impasse was finally brokered by an unsatisfactory "compromise" that allowed gay men and women to serve as long as they did not reveal their sexual orientation either by word or deed. This policy remained in effect until it was repealed in 2011 under President Barack Obama.

In a similar vein, as issues arose for the first time about the possibility of same-sex marriage, President Clinton signed the 1996 Defense of Marriage Act (DOMA), which denied federal marital benefits to any same-sex couple legally married under state law. In explaining the need for this legislation, the House Judiciary Committee declared that the act was necessary "to reflect and honor a collective moral judgment and to express moral disapproval of homosexuality." DOMA was later declared unconstitutional by the United States Supreme Court in 2013 in *United States v. Windsor*.

Clinton's own family values came under assault by Republicans even before he reached the White House. Republicans took an immediate dislike to Clinton's wife, Hillary Rodham Clinton, that only grew over time. An intelligent and ambitious graduate of Wellesley College, Hillary Rodham met Bill Clinton at Yale Law School. Intending to take the world by storm, Hillary instead spent the first 20 years of her marriage supporting her husband, literally and figuratively. While Bill served as governor of Arkansas, which paid a minimum wage, Hillary supported the family as a corporate lawyer, becoming the first female partner at her firm. As First Lady of Arkansas, Hillary furthered her lifetime interest in children's and family rights and access to legal services for the poor. When the Clintons' daughter, Chelsea, was born in 1980, Hillary's mother moved nearby to help bridge the inevitable work-family divide.

An incorrigible womanizer, Bill Clinton was dogged throughout his two terms as president with accusations of sexual improprieties. When it came to light in 1998 that Clinton had had a sexual relationship with Monica Lewinsky, a 20-year-old White House intern, President Clinton denied details of the relationship during a grand jury investigation. The Republican-controlled House of Representatives voted a bill of impeachment, finding that the president had committed perjury and obstruction of justice and that these offenses constituted "high crimes or misdemeanors" sufficient to warrant impeachment. The Senate, however, failed to convict, and Clinton was therefore able to complete his term of office.

Clinton's sexual life interested average Americans far less than it did members of Congress or Kenneth Starr, the special prosecutor appointed to investigate the Lewinsky case. Many people found Starr vindictive and sanctimonious, motivated by a visceral dislike of the president. They resented how Congress had turned a sex scandal into a constitutional crisis, and that the investigations had cost $60 million of taxpayer money while preventing the president from doing his job. Women, in particular, were disinclined to judge the president harshly, especially since his supposedly radical-feminist career-woman wife had defended him even as his behavior demeaned her.

The Road to the Twenty-First Century

Clinton won reelection handily in 1996, promising to build a "road to the twenty-first century." The bridge to the coming millennium would be invisible, constructed in the netherworld of the new World Wide Web, an information space where documents and other web resources could be accessed via the internet, a global system of interconnected computer networks that linked billions of devices worldwide.

The web was a tangible sign of what was increasingly referred to as "globalization," a sweeping category that emphasized worldwide networks of economic, environmental, and cultural interdependence. The commercial growth of the internet via the World Wide Web invaded and disrupted traditional ways of doing business on a global scale. But it also eroded boundaries, enabling the transmission of knowledge across national, linguistic, and religious borders.

THE "GOLDILOCKS ECONOMY"

Bill Clinton presided over nearly all of the longest continuous economic expansion in modern American history, from 1991 to March

2001. In 1996, 2.8 million new jobs were created, 3.4 million in 1997, 3 million in 1998, and another 3.2 million in 1999. Unemployment fell beneath 4 percent briefly in 2000. The so-called Goldilocks economy was hot enough to advance prosperity, as measured by low unemployment and wealth creation, but cool enough to prevent inflation. As Clinton left the White House in 2000, the federal government was staring at budget surpluses as far as the eye could see.

The prosperity of the 1990s had multiple sources. Consumer demand, plus a willingness of people to take on personal debt, kept the domestic market humming. The fiscal discipline of the Clinton years that ended budgetary deficits encouraged foreign investment. Low oil prices and a weak dollar benefited American exporters, as did lower trade barriers championed by Clinton. Innovation in everything from business models and corporate management to product development and funding structures, what some referred to as "creative destruction," generated opportunity and cleared the ground for new sources of wealth.

The economy of the 1990s was powered by the world of technology and information services set in motion by the personal computer industry during the 1980s. But the entire global economy was not conducted in the ether. The Clinton administration promoted domestic prosperity by expanding foreign trade. After negotiation of the 1993 North Atlantic Free Trade Agreement (NAFTA) among Canada, Mexico, and the United States, intraregional trade flows increased from roughly $290 billion in 1993 to more than $1.1 trillion in 2012. As of 2015, the United States traded more in goods and services with Mexico and Canada than it did with Japan, South Korea, Brazil, India, Russia, and China combined.

NAFTA, which lowered trade quotas and tariffs in agriculture and manufacturing (such as automobiles and textiles), was opposed by trade unions and many congressional Democrats, who predicted that manufacturers would use the free-market trading zone to move production to low-wage Mexico. Manufacturing jobs were in fact lost, but others were gained through exports. The jury is still out on whether free-trade zones benefit the American economy as a whole, and balancing corporate competitiveness and profits with equitable worker compensation and environmental concerns in an age of increasing economic globalization remains a hot-button political issue.

As internet technology and infrastructure spread, more and more people became "hooked into the web." Net-oriented entrepreneurs founded companies right and left. Usually investors will not buy stock in a company until it has proven its worth by producing a desirable and successful product. Because of the "growth over profits" mentality of the dot-com world, in which many companies gave away their services for free to gain present market share, many companies, including Amazon and Google, went public before they had earned a profit. In the exuberant environment of the late 1990s, stock prices soared. The 1995 initial public offering (IPO) of Netscape, the first internet browser, was the greatest stock opening in history. By 2000, the market capitalization of publicly traded corporations in Silicon Valley, the heart of the technology boom, was $750 billion.

But the "get big or get lost" business model was unsustainable, and thousands of internet businesses collapsed under a mountain of debt. A cascade of bankruptcies began in January 2002, and more than $5 trillion of market value was lost between March 2000 and October 2002. As the technology boom receded, consolidation and growth by market leaders caused the tech industry to resemble other traditional economic sectors. As of 2014, 10 information technology firms were among the 100 largest US corporations by revenue, including Apple, Hewlett-Packard, IBM, and Microsoft.

IMMIGRATION

Many Americans' personal experience of globalization came through immigration. Since 1965, the United States has experienced large waves of immigration. More than six million legal immigrants entered the United States during the 1980s. In the 1990s, for the first time, the majority of migrants did not come from Europe. As during the Progressive Era, immigrants composed a growing slice of the population and had a diverse and lasting effect on politics and culture.

The great majority of the newcomers after 1980 came from Asia, Latin America, and the Caribbean. These groups tended to concentrate in a few states, including New York, California, Texas, and Illinois. Metropolitan areas in those states underwent significant change, as new ethnic communities formed. Korean grocers, Indian and Thai restaurants, and Vietnamese nail salons blossomed on city streets. Exotic languages such as Urdu and Arabic joined the linguistic cacophony on the streets of America's largest cities, and enclaves of immigrants in more rural areas, such as upstate New York, prospered.

One person's cosmopolitanism can be another's alienation, however. Surrounded by so many new languages and customs, many native-born Americans felt like strangers in their own land. Many resented what they considered inappropriate accommodation to immigrant ways, such as offering ballots in multiple languages. Others argued that newcomers took jobs from American citizens, flooded public schools with their non-English-speaking children, and overwhelmed already underfunded social services like hospitals. Still others worried that newcomers would reproduce in America the social, political, and economic problems that plagued the regions they had abandoned. Many resisted the desire of immigrants to practice aspects of their ethnic or religious cultures that contradicted mainstream American practices, and criticized them for refusing to "become Americans"— forgetting, perhaps, that their forebears were despised in their own time for all these things.

The argument that cheap immigrant labor reduces the standard of living of all workers has characterized immigration debates since the Civil War. Almost every new group has faced the accusation that they were "stealing jobs from Americans." Economists from both the left and the right have consistently disagreed with that position, arguing that immigration has fostered economic growth. Many new immigrants performed low-wage work that native-born Americans avoided, such as agricultural and domestic labor. Others, such as foreign-born nurses and computer programmers, brought with them education and skills.

What one historian called "the turn against immigration" began in earnest during the 1990s. The timing was puzzling. Anti-immigration sentiment usually correlates with a contracting economy, growing unemployment, and perceived external threats. These characteristics described the 1980s, but not the 1990s. Yet public opinion had clearly changed. Although general anti-immigrant sentiment increased, most native-born anger was directed toward the many undocumented immigrants who entered the United States illegally by crossing the border with Mexico.

The shift in public mood was evident in California in 1994, which enacted an overtly anti-immigrant ballot proposition that denied illegal immigrants access to any public social services, health care, or education. Proposition 187 was immediately challenged as unconstitutional (the Fourteenth Amendment speaks of equal protection under the law for all *people*, not all citizens) and was never fully implemented. Believing that the nativism on display in California spoke for other Americans, politicians, including President Clinton, fell into line. Three federal statutes passed before the 1996 presidential election indicate the perceived threats posed by immigrants: the Antiterrorism and Effective Death Penalty Act, the Personal Responsibility and Work Opportunity Reconciliation Act (which denied public assistance such as food stamps to unnaturalized immigrants and their American-born citizen-children), and the Illegal Immigration Reform and Immigrant Responsibility Act.

THE UNIPOLAR MOMENT:
FOREIGN POLICY UNDER CLINTON

The United States entered the new millennium with unmatched economic and military power. America's unrivaled strategic position allowed for great freedom of action — action that most Americans discouraged. Congress in particular was unmotivated to intervene in the world's problems. Dubbed the "half-hearted hegemon" by the journal *Foreign Affairs*, the United States under President Clinton undertook to define the boundaries of its power and the shape of its vulnerabilities.

Since Vietnam, US generals had opposed US military involvement in virtually all wars and almost never favored intervention on humanitarian grounds. General Colin Powell, a decorated Vietnam combat veteran and chairman of the Joint Chiefs of Staff until 1993, vehemently opposed deploying US troops in harm's way "for unclear purposes" in foreign nations. In the 1990s, the United Nations became the forum for collective activity. By 1994, 17 international UN peacekeeping missions were underway — more in that one year than in all of the preceding half century. The UN's new vitality was partnered with the creation of a new borderless Europe in the form of the European Union (EU).

In 1992, the Bush administration sent 28,000 US troops to help distribute international famine relief in war-torn Somalia. Warlord Mohamed Farrah Aidid objected to outside interference, and his men slaughtered two dozen Pakistani troops operating under UN command in June 1993. In response, President Clinton deployed Army Rangers against Aidid, who shot down two American helicopters on October 3, killing 18 US airmen. A video of rejoicing Somali militia members dragging the naked corpse of a US soldier through the streets of Mogadishu helped convince Clinton to end the mission six months later. Elsewhere in Africa, the United States was reluctant to bolster UN efforts to stop a genocide in Rwanda that left 800,000 Tutsi Rwandans dead in a little over three months.

American presidents have occasionally undertaken humanitarian interventions, but as Samantha Power, the US ambassador to the United Nations under President Obama has written, "the United States has consistently refused to take risks in order to suppress genocide." After a Serb invasion of Srebrenica, a Bosnian Muslim enclave under the nominal control of UN troops, and the subsequent slaughter of its civilian inhabitants in July 1995, however, the United States finally took action. NATO, backed by the United States, began intensive bombing of Bosnian Serb positions. This forced a cease-fire in October and brought all parties to the negotiating table in Dayton, Ohio.

This first move toward a more interventionist foreign policy stance was bolstered by the appointment in 1996 of UN ambassador Madeline Albright as the first female secretary of state. The daughter of a Czech diplomat who escaped both the Nazis and the Communist takeover, Albright was the leading hawk among Clinton's advisors. In early 1999, Albright convinced a still-wary administration to intervene in Kosovo, a province of Serbia populated mainly by Muslims, where the Serbs again engaged in civilian massacres. Once again, a NATO bombing campaign forced the concession of Serbia, whose brutal leader Slobodan Milosevic was subsequently tried for war crimes before the International Criminal Tribunal for the Former Yugoslavia.

Despite his initial hesitation to use US force abroad, in the end Clinton employed military forces 84 times in eight years. His foreign policy legacy includes the enlargement of NATO, collaboration with Russia to reduce nuclear inventories, and the beginning of a diplomatic dialogue with North Korea. First Lady Hillary Clinton collaborated with Secretary of State Albright to monitor and promote women's rights internationally, and declared in a major speech in Beijing that "women's rights are human rights."

TERRORISM

Barely one month after Clinton's inauguration, in February 1993, a truck bomb parked in the underground garage of the World Trade Center in New York City exploded, killing six people and injuring more than one thousand. Within two weeks of the bombing, the FBI had captured four members of the group behind the attack and revealed a broad network of support that centered on a blind Egyptian spiritual leader, Omar Abdel Rahman. The bomb maker, Ramzi Yousef, escaped, but he was eventually captured by the FBI in a "snatch" carried out in Pakistan.

In 1996, Saudi agents of Hezbollah, a terrorist organization supervised and supported by Iran, struck a high-rise housing complex that was home to US soldiers in Saudi Arabia, killing 19 American soldiers and injuring nearly 400 other people. Terrorist violence against American targets was clearly on the rise, but no clear pattern was discernable.

After his reelection, Clinton placed terrorism first in a list of challenges facing the country, but encountered an unresponsive Congress, which considered terrorism "a second- or third-order priority." In a time of decreasing federal expenditures, the Clinton administration nearly doubled the federal counterterrorism budget between 1995 and 2000, from $5.7 billion to just over $11 billion. For the first time in 40 years, the executive designed and funded a major program for homeland defense.

The need for such measures was made tragically clear on August 7, 1998, when American embassies in Tanzania and Kenya were struck by car bombs, resulting in carnage in Nairobi: 257 people, including 12 Americans, were killed, and 5,000 others were wounded. This time, the signs pointed clearly to Osama bin Laden's al Qaeda organization, which had declared war on the United States in 1996 and again earlier in 1998. In addition to the loss of life, the terrorists' capability to coordinate two nearly simultaneous attacks on US embassies in different countries suggested their growing operational capacity.

In response, the United States bombed al Qaeda training camps in Afghanistan and Sudan, extended sanctions levied on al Qaeda to the Taliban government in Afghanistan, and issued an order allowing American intelligence forces to capture or kill Osama bin Laden. Diplomatic outreach to Pakistan and Afghanistan had no effect. As one National Security Council note put it, "Under the Taliban, Afghanistan is not so much a state sponsor of terrorism as it is a state sponsored by terrorists." The CIA spread the word among the leaders of the tribal border region between Afghanistan and Pakistan that the United States wanted bin Laden stopped. The president wanted him dead.

Undeterred, on October 12, 2000, al Qaeda operatives in Yemen bombed and nearly sank a billion-dollar American guided missile destroyer, the USS *Cole*, killing 17 servicemen and wounding at least 40. The Clinton administration was divided about what action to take in response. Although it seemed clear to Clinton's counterterrorism crew that this latest attack against Americans abroad was the work of al Qaeda, the CIA and FBI were unconvinced. An angry Michael Sheehan, the State Department's counterterrorism coordinator, demanded of his counterpart at the NSC, Richard Clarke, "Does al Qaeda have to attack the Pentagon to get their attention?"

Regime Change

By most measures, the Clinton presidency was a great success. But after eight years, many Americans suffered from "Clinton fatigue" brought on by the endless congressional inquiries into Bill and Hillary's private life, and the "sleaze factor" associated with Bill Clinton's affair with Monica Lewinsky. Although he escaped impeachment, many Americans felt that Clinton had tarnished the office of the presidency and were open to new leadership.

THE 2000 ELECTION

As second-in-command under a popular two-term president in a time of prosperity, Al Gore ought to have won the election easily. Both he and his Republican adversary, George W. Bush, were the products of political dynasties. But whereas Gore had served as a congressman and senator from Tennessee from 1977 to 1993 before becoming vice president, Bush was a latecomer to politics whose entire political career consisted of serving as a two-term governor of his adopted home state of Texas.

In contrast to Gore, whose campaign persona was described variously as "wooden," faltering, and "stiff," Bush was an energetic and organized campaigner, optimistic and upbeat. Like Ronald Reagan, "Dubya" (he was often referred to by his middle initial to distinguish him from his father) was unpretentious and likeable. Both he and Gore had attended prestigious East Coast boarding schools and Ivy League universities, but where Gore was pedantic, lecturing people on the environment, Bush reveled in his lack of academic achievement. Bush was the candidate more people would feel comfortable having a beer with. Gore was the candidate no one wanted to be stuck in a corner with.

Conscious that many Americans considered Republicans to be hard-hearted in their social policies, Bush extolled his brand of "compassionate conservatism," and vowed to be "a uniter, not a divider" as president. He was openly religious on the campaign trail (as president, Bush would open every cabinet meeting with prayer—crossing the crevasse between church and state in a single "amen"). Like Clinton in 1992, Bush appealed to the moderate center, and he vowed to end partisan gridlock in Washington. With the economy purring and the federal budget actually showing a surplus, Bush called for huge tax cuts, insisting that the surplus was "the people's money," not "the government's money." Gore opposed Bush's proposed tax cut, which he said was irresponsible and a handout to the wealthy, and failed to emphasize the Clinton administration's role in the economic gains of the late 1990s.

Neither Bush nor Gore focused much on foreign policy, although Bush was strongly critical of Clinton's use of American soldiers abroad, especially for the dubious goal of "nation-building." "I would be very careful about using our troops as nation-builders," he said in a presidential debate. Although both candidates called for higher defense spending, neither said much about terrorism or nuclear proliferation.

There was a third candidate in 2000, Green Party nominee Ralph Nader. A longtime consumer advocate and environmentalist, Nader's position that both parties were beholden to the rich appealed to many—and most of them were Democrats. His argument that a President Bush or a President Gore would be equally bad for the planet obscured the differences between the two—such as the fact that George Bush was a Texas oil man, and Al Gore was a firm believer in global warming and the need to address it. The votes cast for Nader in New Hampshire, where Gore lost by only 7,000 votes, and in Florida, likely tipped the election to the Republicans.

Although the campaign was hard-fought, barely half of all Americans bothered to cast a ballot. Bush appealed strongly to rural and suburban whites, especially in the South, and to churchgoers and married men. Gore won the cities and the coasts, 54 percent of women's votes, and 90 percent of African American votes. Nader picked up 2.7 percent of the popular vote. When Americans went to bed early on November 3, 2000, Al Gore led George W. Bush, 48.4 percent to 47.9 percent.

INDECISION 2000

By the next morning, it was clear that Gore had won the popular vote by more than 500,000 votes. The Electoral College vote was another matter, however: there, the candidates were in a dead heat. On election night, many states were too close to call, including, critically, Florida, which had 25 electoral votes and George Bush's brother Jeb in the governor's mansion. Whoever won Florida would become the 43rd president of the United States. Because of the closeness of the Florida election—Bush led Gore by 1,784 votes—automatic recounts were scheduled to commence in two days. So began the saga of the 2000 presidential election. Over the next five weeks, Florida officials and an army of lawyers raked through piles of ballots set aside for a variety of reasons, including "undervotes" (partially punched ballots from ancient punch card machines) and "overvotes" (in which voters confused by the ballot punched more than one hole). After the automatic recount, Bush's margin of victory had shrunk to 327 votes. The presidency hung in the balance.

Gore's legal team petitioned the Florida Supreme Court for a manual recount in four counties whose electoral processes were particularly confused. Republicans resisted, insisting that the Florida state legislature, which was controlled by the Republicans, had the power to appoint presidential electors when an election was in dispute.

The Florida Supreme Court ruled in favor of Gore and allowed the recount. The Republicans appealed to the Supreme Court of the United States, which agreed to hear the GOP challenge to the Florida Supreme Court's decision. On December 12, in a 5–4 decision in *Bush v. Gore*, the court halted the recount, holding that the process approved by the Florida Supreme Court violated the right of Florida voters to have their votes counted consistently and fairly, and therefore violated the equal protection clause of the Fourteenth Amendment. All five of the justices in the majority had been appointed by Republican presidents. The dissenting justices, including two who had been appointed by Republican presidents, complained that the position adopted "by the majority of this Court can only lend credence to the most cynical appraisal of the work of judges throughout the land."

The 2000 election was a constitutional crisis of the first magnitude. The appearance of political partisanship was inescapable. In the words of Justice John Paul Stevens, who had been appointed to the court by President Ford and who dissented in the case, the court's decision undermined "the Nation's confidence in the judge as an impartial guardian of the rule of law." One of the justices in the majority, Sandra Day O'Connor, admitted 15 years later that it might have been better if the court had refused to hear the case.

Vice President Gore conceded the election on December 13. "The U.S. Supreme Court has spoken," Gore declared. "Let there be no doubt, while I *strongly* disagree with the Court's decision, I accept it. . . . Tonight, for the sake of our unity as a people and the strength of our democracy, I offer my concession." Democrats were despondent and angry. But the transfer of power from one president to the next proceeded smoothly, and President George W. Bush was inaugurated on a cold and wet January 20, 2001. And since the domestic policies Bush and Gore had campaigned on were not, in the end, all that different (both supported deregulation, economic globalization, and education), did it really matter who was in the White House?

THE BUSH ADMINISTRATION

The new George Bush's administration looked very much like his father's old one. At its core was Vice President Dick Cheney, who had served the first President Bush as Defense Secretary during the Gulf War. A mild-mannered man of strong beliefs, Cheney calmed Republicans anxious about the younger Bush's lack of experience in foreign affairs. The Secret Service code name for Cheney in the Ford White House was Backseat, which captured his powerful but largely obscured role in the Bush White House. Karl Rove, the mastermind behind all of George W's campaigns and senior advisor and deputy chief of staff to Bush, was more forthright: he called Cheney "the management." An advocate of expanded executive power, Cheney became the most powerful vice president in American history.

Vice President Cheney was joined in the administration by his old friend Donald Rumsfeld, who became Secretary of Defense. Cheney and Rumsfeld's working partnership went back to the Nixon administration. Both had served in Congress; both had held cabinet positions under several Republican presidents. Both were well-connected in Republican foreign policy circles and affiliated with an anti-détente cohort that argued for a strong, unilateral American presence in the world. Rumsfeld, whose business career was in pharmaceuticals and broadcast transmission (i.e., cable, satellite, and high-definition television), championed a pared-down, high-tech military that would keep soldiers out of harm's way through development and deployment of advanced weapons systems.

During his first months in office, President George W. Bush focused almost exclusively on domestic politics, leaving foreign relations to

Secretary of State Colin Powell and National Security Advisor Condoleezza Rice, the first African Americans to serve in these positions. The
former head of the Joint Chiefs of Staff, Powell was skeptical about
the influence of US military power and cautious about its deployment.
Rice, an expert on Soviet politics, was Bush's closest advisor in the
White House.

To the consternation of the CIA and Bush's own counterterrorism
head, Richard Clarke, a holdover from the Clinton administration,
neither Bush nor his national defense team paid much attention to
the danger that had so occupied Bill Clinton during his second term:
foreign terrorism. Efforts by Clarke and CIA director George Tenet to
brief the new president and his cabinet on al Qaeda were brushed off,
even as the CIA picked up worrisome intelligence, such as al Qaeda
members talking of "very good news to come" and "preparations to
strike the idol of the world." Vice President Cheney and Under Secretary of Defense Paul Wolfowitz rejected the idea that an independent
organization could pull off major terrorist acts like the 1993 World
Trade Center bombing and the 1998 attacks on the East African embassies without a state sponsor, by which they meant Iraq.

In an effort to capture the attention of the new administration, CIA
analysts wrote a series of reports with titles like "Bin Ladin Attacks
May Be Imminent" and "Bin Ladin Planning High-Profile Attacks."
When asked by a skeptical Cheney and Rumsfeld whether the intelligence on which they were relying might be purposely deceptive, the
CIA responded with a report, titled "UBL Threats Are Real." President Bush's daily briefer from the CIA delivered the report personally.
This was followed up by yet another report, issued on August 6, 2001,
titled "Bin Ladin Determined to Strike in US." Yet no precautions were
taken.

COMPASSIONATE CONSERVATISM IN ACTION

As governor of Texas, George Bush had governed from right-of-
center, and, like Clinton, he had campaigned as a centrist determined
to unite, not divide, the country. During his first months in Washington, Bush cooperated with congressional Democratic leaders to pass
the No Child Left Behind Act, which raised educational testing standards and increased federal funding for schools. Bush also supported
the Democratic plan to expand Medicare to cover prescription drugs.
His appointments demonstrated a commitment to racial inclusion: his

was the first Republican administration in which African Americans, women, and Latinos held significant power.

In Texas, George Bush had distributed government funds to successful Christian programs that dedicated themselves to rehabilitating drug addicts and prisoners. As president, Bush intended to promote social programs run by religious organizations through government-funded "faith-based initiatives." President Clinton had signed a similar law, "Charitable Choice," in 1996, and the first director of the Office of Faith-Based and Community Initiatives, political scientist John DiIulio, a conservative Democrat, believed a bipartisan faith-based bill was an attainable goal. Unfortunately for DiIulio, the White House staff had little interest in the program. Referencing a popular 1960s television show, DiIulio referred to White House staffers as "Mayberry Machiavellians" who steered legislative initiatives or policy proposals "as far right as possible" to satisfy the political influence of conservative Christians and libertarians.

The number one Mayberry Machiavellian was Karl Rove, whose Office of Strategic Initiatives had "effective oversight over Bush's domestic policy shop." Under Rove's watchful eye, the White House was subordinated to the political arm of the GOP. To woo Republican constituencies, Rove steered policy on issues ranging from global warming (the coal industry) to tax cuts (the wealthy) to fetal stem cell research (Catholics and evangelicals). He stiffed the advocates of small government by advising the president to expand federal funding for pet projects of important voting blocs. He replaced public officials with political hacks, most disastrously in the case of the head of the Federal Emergency Management Agency. Cabinet secretaries like Treasury Secretary Paul O'Neill had less clout than Rove. More conservative than President Bush, Rove steered the entire GOP ship of state starboard.

The keystone of the Bush domestic agenda was tax reform, including two major cuts, in 2001 and 2003, which lowered income taxes for all Americans, especially for those at the top of the income scale. The idea was that the tax cuts would spur economic activity and increase tax revenue. This was precisely the magical economic thinking that George Bush Senior had dismissed in 1980 as "voodoo economics." But the idea that tax cuts translated into increased tax revenues, rather than increased budget deficits and cuts in government services, appealed despite overwhelming evidence that the lower rates would generate only enough new economic growth to cover half the lost tax revenue.

In addition to lost government revenue, the Bush tax cuts exacerbated income disparities. Congressional Budget Office data showed that income gaps widened appreciably between 2003 (the year of the second Bush tax cut) and 2004. Economists Peter Orszag and William Gale described the Bush tax cuts as reverse government redistribution of wealth: "Because high-income households received by far the largest tax cuts, the tax cuts have increased the concentration of income at the top of the spectrum," and shifted "the burden of taxation away from upper-income, capital-owning households and toward the wage-earning households of the lower and middle class."

CATASTROPHE

When four passenger jets were hijacked in the United States on the morning of September 11, 2001, there was no reason for the passengers to doubt the hijackers when they said they were diverting the flights and all would be well if their demands were met. Jetliners had been commandeered before. In the 1960s, so many hijackers had demanded that flights be rerouted to Cuba that American airlines routinely stocked instructions for approaching the then-forbidden island. In the 1970s, planes—and their passengers—became part of extortion attempts by various anti-Israel organizations in the Middle East. After Palestinian militants hijacked four planes on a single day in 1970, President Nixon ordered that armed federal marshals rotate among flights. To deter hijackers, metal detectors were installed in airports in 1973.

Beginning in 1976, after the successful Israeli commando raid on an Air France jetliner in Entebbe, Uganda, some terrorists began to blow up planes rather than hijack them. In 1988, Libyan intelligence agents planted a bomb on an American jet that exploded over Lockerbie, Scotland, killing all 259 passengers and 11 people on the ground. But until September 11, 2001, no one had ever hijacked a plane as part of a suicide mission, turning the plane itself into a weapon.

The four airliners hijacked on September 11 were part of a coordinated attack on the United States by al Qaeda. At 8:46 a.m., American Airlines Flight 11, en route from Boston to Los Angeles, crashed into the North Tower of the World Trade Center in New York City. At 9:03 a.m., United Airlines Flight 175 barreled into the South Tower, the second of the Twin Towers. At 9:37 a.m., American Airlines Flight 77 slammed into the Pentagon, in Washington, DC.

A fourth hijacked plane, United Airlines Flight 93, was on its way to Washington, aimed at either the White House or the Capitol Building. Passengers on this flight were able to contact families and officials on the ground, and learned of the other attacks. Gathered at the rear of the plane, the passengers decided to assault the cockpit. The last recorded words of the hijackers suggest a struggle for control of the airplane, which crashed into a field near Shanksville, Pennsylvania, killing all 44 people aboard, but no others.

Nearly 3,000 people were killed in the September 11 attacks (soon known as 9/11). In addition to the 19 hijackers, the dead included 246 plane passengers, 271 people at the Pentagon, and 2,606 people at the World Trade Center, including 72 law enforcement officers and 342 firefighters, who ran to their own deaths trying to save others. At least 200 people fell or jumped to their deaths, sickening already horror-struck witnesses on the ground and those watching on television.

The president was visiting an elementary school in Florida when the 9/11 terrorists struck the World Trade Center. By the time Bush was evacuated in Air Force One, the Pentagon had been hit. After stops at air force bases in Louisiana and Nebraska, where the president conferred with top officials via videoconference, he returned to Washington under the watchful eyes of two F-16 fighter escorts. Back in the White House, Bush addressed the nation, promising that the United States would overcome this terrible tragedy, and vowing revenge on the perpetrators. Speaking to Afghanistan, whose Taliban leaders had hosted al Qaeda since 1996, Bush announced that the United States "would make no distinction between terrorists and nations that harbor them."

*

The events of September 11 provoked an outpouring of sympathy for the United States from its allies — and even from its competitors such as Russia and China — many of whom had also lost citizens in the attacks. The moment was over, however, by September 20, when President Bush spoke before both houses of Congress. According to the president, the United States had passed from a war on al Qaeda to a "war on terror." This global "war on terror," Bush explained, "begins with Al Qaeda, but it does not end there. It will not end until every terrorist group of global reach has been found, stopped, and defeated." The United States had dedicated itself to this course of action, and the rest of the world would have to choose sides: "Every nation, in every region, now has a decision to make. Either you are with us or you are with the terrorists."

The difference between retaliating against al Qaeda and declaring war on terror, investigative journalist Nicholas Lemann has written, "is the difference between a response and a doctrine." George W. Bush effected "the most revolutionary changes in U.S. foreign policy since the Truman Doctrine of 1947." In the process, instead of the "uniter" he aimed to be, George W. Bush became one of the most divisive presidents in American history.

FIGURE 13. Barack Obama takes the oath of office and is sworn in as the 44th president of the United States next to his wife, Michelle Obama, by chief justice of the United States John G. Roberts Jr. in Washington, DC, January 20, 2009.

CHAPTER 13

Forward, 2001–2016

Like many rural southerners of her generation, Lilly McDaniel was born into a home with no electricity or running water. Work was always a part of her life growing up in Possum Trot, Alabama, in the 1940s, even after she married Charles Ledbetter in 1956. In addition to raising two daughters, Lilly worked as a manager at H&R Block and as a financial aid advisor at Jacksonville State University. As she recalled later, "If you lived in the country in those years, you worked."

In 1979, Lilly got her dream job: a management position on the tire-production floor at a local Goodyear factory. Like many wage workers, she was required to sign a contract that prohibited her from discussing pay rates with other employees. Not that Lilly had much opportunity to engage in conversation with her coworkers, who were overwhelmingly male and hostile to the entrance of a woman manager. "I realized going in that these people had never adjusted to being around a woman, so I tolerated a lot of discriminatory things," she said. Assigned to the night shift, she often worked overtime.

Shortly before she retired from Goodyear in 1998, Lilly found an anonymous note in her locker that disclosed significant pay differentials between Lilly and her male colleagues. Despite her seniority, Lilly was paid less than the lowest-paid man doing the same job, which translated to a monthly wage difference of nearly $2,000. She was "emotionally let down" when she saw the difference in pay, and she understood the long-term effect on her retirement benefits. "I could not let it slide," she said.

Helped by a local Equal Employment Opportunity Commission (EEOC) office, Lilly charged Goodyear with sex discrimination, and calculated that the difference between what she had made over the course of her career and what she would have gotten if she had been paid as much as the lowest-paid man was $60,000. Goodyear offered to settle the case for $10,000. Lilly went to court. The jury awarded her more than $3 million in damages, which was reduced by the judge to $360,000, the greatest amount a worker could get for pay discrimination under federal law. Goodyear appealed, arguing that federal law required Lilly to have filed a complaint within 180 days of the time the discrimination occurred—not when it came to light.

When the case came before the Supreme Court in 2007, the EEOC argued that few employees would discover within six months of their employment that their salary differed from that of their peers, and insisted that the clock on the 180-day rule should restart each time a discriminatory paycheck was issued. But the court sided with Goodyear, 5–4. Justice Samuel Alito, who had just replaced Sandra Day O'Connor, cast the deciding ballot.

Justice Ruth Bader Ginsburg, who had spent her career before joining the court fighting for women's rights, was livid. In a rare departure from custom, she read her dissent from the bench. "In our view," she said, speaking for the minority, "the Court does not comprehend, or is indifferent to, the insidious ways in which women can be victims of pay discrimination." Ginsburg pointedly invited Congress to amend the Civil Rights Act of 1964 to address the issues raised in the Ledbetter case, and in 2009 Congress did just that, passing legislation that restarted the 180-day time clock each time a discriminatory paycheck was issued.

The Lilly Ledbetter Fair Pay Act was the first bill signed into law by President Barack Obama. She was thrilled. After 2009, Lilly became a vocal activist for pay equity and antidiscrimination. "I had no idea this was such a national problem," she reflected. "This is not only a person like myself, this is professional people as well. I've heard it from physicians, teachers, nurses, every job you can imagine."

Indeed: in 2014, female full-time workers earned only 79 cents for every dollar earned by a man, a gender wage gap of 21 percent. Lilly Ledbetter never set out to become an activist or to set a precedent. She merely tried to right the wrong she experienced at the hands of Goodyear. Her loss in the courts led to a gain for all workingwomen in America and a new career for the retired tire manufacturing manager as an advocate for women's equality.

The Post-9/11 World

The terrorist attack of September 11, 2001, was the deadliest foreign act of destruction on US soil since Pearl Harbor in 1941. The terrorists' targets—the Capitol Building, the Pentagon, and the World Trade Center—symbolized the foundations of American power: democratic governance, military might, and the global economic influence of Wall Street.

All three institutions faced tremendous challenges in the years that followed. At first, the catastrophic events of 9/11 and the heroic responses of government officials, first responders, and ordinary citizens unified the nation. But the administration of President George W. Bush soon divided Americans. Two wars, in Afghanistan and Iraq, strained the military capacity of the United States and reversed the financial stability that had been achieved by the administration of President Bill Clinton. An economy already faltering after a crash in technology stocks in 2000 was damaged further. The aggrandizement of executive power resulted in secret policymaking, serious breaches of civil liberties, and human rights violations. Worst of all, the Bush administration's misrepresentations about the threat posed by Iraq resulted in a US invasion that triggered a civil war there and destabilized the entire Middle East.

HYPERPOWER

When Japan bombed Pearl Harbor, President Franklin Roosevelt asked Congress to declare a state of war between the two nations. Because the 9/11 attacks were carried out by nonstate actors, it was not clear what the correct response was. Osama bin Laden was in Afghanistan, sheltered by the Taliban. Advised by the State Department to demand that the Taliban turn him over, President Bush responded, "Fuck diplomacy. We are going to war." But who, exactly, was the enemy?

The CIA and the counterterrorism experts in the Office of National Intelligence (ONI) were unanimous that al Qaeda, and therefore bin Laden, was behind the 9/11 attacks. Vice President Dick Cheney, Defense Secretary Donald Rumsfeld, and Under Secretary of Defense Paul Wolfowitz agreed, but they also insisted that Saddam Hussein's Iraq stood behind al Qaeda. All three had been architects of the 1990 Gulf War under the previous President Bush, and they considered Saddam Hussein a continuing threat to regional stability in the Middle

East and a menace to his own people. Now they insisted that Iraq had played a role in the September 11 attacks, and they maintained that Iraq possessed weapons of mass destruction (WMD) that either Iraq or al Qaeda might use against America.

Intelligence officials were flummoxed by the administration's focus on Iraq. There was no evidence at the time (and none was found later) that Saddam Hussein had any connection with al Qaeda. There were no links between bin Laden and Iraq. A CIA report, "Iraqi Support to Terrorism," produced in the summer of 2002, found no evidence of any working relationship between Iraq and al Qaeda before, during, or after 9/11, and no evidence of Iraqi complicity in or foreknowledge of 9/11. Counterterrorism chief Richard Clarke erupted in one meeting that attacking Iraq made about as much sense as bombing Mexico after Pearl Harbor.

Bombing Afghanistan, on the other hand, made sense. In October 2001, US and British forces bombarded Afghanistan in an effort to destroy al Qaeda and capture or kill bin Laden. Rather than send US ground forces, Defense Secretary Rumsfeld relied on proxy Afghan fighters, who invaded Taliban territory. By December 2002, this joint effort had destroyed the Taliban government and al Qaeda's mountain headquarters at Tora Bora. Unfortunately, however, hundreds of al Qaeda operatives, including bin Laden, escaped into the mountainous no-man's-land across the Pakistani border.

In the absence of verifiable links to al Qaeda, the administration turned to Iraq's desire and capacity to manufacture and use weapons of mass destruction, thereby linking the global war on terror with nuclear proliferation. It was true that in 1998 Saddam had ejected the UN weapons inspectors posted there since the Gulf War, and it was likely that he had resumed his effort to develop a nuclear weapon. But there was no evidence that he had made any progress on this front, and no reason to think that an Iraqi attack on the United States was plausible. Nonetheless, in the summer of 2002, a high-ranking British officer reported to his government that the Bush administration was determined to go to war with Iraq and that "intelligence and facts were being fixed around the policy." Top officials, including Secretary of State Colin Powell in an address before the United Nations in February 2003 and President Bush in his 2003 State of the Union speech, continually cited documents describing the sale of uranium from Niger to Iraq long after the reports had been discredited as fraudulent by the CIA.

"A STRATEGIC ERROR OF THE FIRST MAGNITUDE"

Despite the consensus of the intelligence community that Iraq had nothing to do with 9/11, Bush administration officials, particularly Vice President Cheney, continued to assert publicly that there was an ongoing link between Iraq and al Qaeda. Much of the public was convinced. A *Washington Post* poll conducted in August 2003 revealed that 70 percent of respondents believed it was likely that Saddam Hussein had been involved in the 9/11 attacks. When Lawrence Lindsey, Bush's National Economic Council director, warned in the *Wall Street Journal* that a war in Iraq would cost between $100 and $200 billion, he was forced to resign. Donald Rumsfeld soothed these troubled waters by insisting that the war would cost under $50 billion and that most of the cost would be paid for with Iraqi oil revenue.

Beginning in the fall of 2002, administration officials kept up a steady drumbeat for war. There was "no doubt" that Saddam Hussein had weapons of mass destruction, Cheney reported. He and National Security Advisor Condoleezza Rice insisted that Saddam would acquire nuclear weapons "fairly soon." Did it make any sense, Rice asked provocatively, "for the world to wait . . . for the final proof, the smoking gun that could come in the form of a mushroom cloud?"

There was little debate about the merits of preemptive war. With midterm elections approaching, only a handful of Democrats dared question the war rationale or oppose the president. The venerable Robert Byrd, Democratic senator from West Virginia, delivered a lonely dissent: "There is no debate, no discussion, no attempt to lay out for the nation the pros and cons of this particular war. We stand passively mute . . . paralyzed by our own uncertainty, seeming stunned by the sheer turmoil of events."

On March 19, 2003, the United States attacked Iraq. Military victory came quickly, and triumphant American troops entered Baghdad on April 9. As public order broke down, however, Saddam Hussein escaped, at least for the time being. On May 1, President Bush, dressed in a fighter-pilot jacket, proclaimed the end of the Iraq War on an aircraft carrier under an enormous banner reading "MISSION ACCOMPLISHED."

The liberation of Iraq came faster, with fewer casualties and less destruction, than even the optimists had foreseen. The Iraqi army melted away before General Tommy Franks's 160,000 troops. There was only one problem: there was no plan for postwar Iraq. An inadequate number of US troops stood by as electricity failed and food and water ran short. Looters ransacked government buildings as the US administrator, Paul Bremer, dismissed the entire Iraqi army. In this climate of chaos, an anti-American insurgency developed. The war became an occupation, and Iraq descended into sectarian warfare between Sunni and Shi'ite Muslims. Though the administration had promised a quick and simple intervention in Iraq, by the end of 2003 the victory already proclaimed was nowhere in sight. Looking back at the Iraq War, an Army War College Strategic Studies Institute paper declared the war "a strategic error of the first magnitude."

OPERATION IRAQI FREEDOM

The US invasion of Iraq was almost universally condemned by America's European allies and across the Arab world. The stated causes for war—weapons of mass destruction and links to international terrorism—proved to be either greatly exaggerated or false. The argument that the war was justified as an effort to bring freedom and democracy to Iraq was offered only *after* it turned out that there were no weapons of mass destruction there. The Iraqi political parties that emerged were sectarian (religious in nature), not national, and did not further the secular democracy desired by the United States.

Experts on postwar rebuilding from across the political spectrum were unanimous that security and reconstruction in Iraq would require large numbers of troops for a long period, as well as international cooperation to rebuild basic infrastructure, keep the peace, and nurture democratic leadership among Iraqis. The natural agency to manage postwar Iraq was Colin Powell's State Department, which was stocked with experts on the Middle East. But Donald Rumsfeld was determined that postwar Iraq would be administered by the Defense Department, whose top priority seemed to be leaving as soon as possible. Rumsfeld insisted that it was not America's job to reconstruct Iraq: "The Iraqi people will have to reconstruct that country over a period of time." Secretary Rumsfeld's spokesperson, Larry Di Rita, announced, "We're going to stand up an interim Iraqi government, hand power over to them, and get out of there in three to four months. All but twenty-five thousand soldiers will be out by September."

But there was no state—Saddam had fled, the Americans were thin on the ground, and the purported government-in-exile of Ahmed Chalabi that had been flown in by the United States to run the country was both inadequate to the task and illegitimate in the eyes of its putative people. The Iraqis, recalled an American advisor, "were losing faith in us by the second." Without Saddam's totalitarian rule, Iraq became a place of competing ethnic claims and hatreds that fragmented, neighborhood by neighborhood, into thousands of pieces. Insurgents murdered police recruits to demonstrate the inability of the new, American-backed institutions to protect them. The Iraqi army might have restored order, but it had been disbanded wholesale as part of the process of dismantling Saddam's Baath Party. Overnight, at least 250,000 Iraqi men—armed, angry, and with military training—were humiliated and unemployed. Many of the suddenly unemployed Iraqi soldiers took up arms against the United States.

Apart from the decision to go to war in the first place, the decision to dissolve the Iraqi army, recalled one senior advisor, was "probably the single most catastrophic decision of the American venture in Iraq. In a stroke, the Administration helped enable the creation of the Iraqi insurgency." The insurgency became a sectarian civil war, out of which al Qaeda in Iraq emerged as the most powerful and violent wing. Its operatives drove truck bombs into mosques and weddings and beheaded their captives. By the time the last American soldiers departed in 2011, the group, now calling itself the Islamic State of Iraq (ISI), had been defeated. But as the Americans left Iraq, a great uprising began in Syria against that nation's ruthless dictator, Bashar al-Assad. The remnants of the ISI joined the fight against Assad, and became the Islamic State of Iraq and Syria—ISIS. Many ISIS leaders were once soldiers in Saddam Hussein's army.

By 2012, nearly 4,500 US soldiers had died in Operation Iraqi Freedom, and more than 32,000 had been wounded, many grievously. At home, the "war on terror" polarized American politics, undermined faith in democratic institutions, and endangered the core values of the American republic. In 2007, retired lieutenant general Ricardo Sanchez, who had commanded US forces in Iraq from 2003 to 2004, declared the Bush war plan "catastrophically flawed."

NOT A BLANK CHECK

The "war on terror" announced on September 20, 2001, was more than a rhetorical device to rally the American people. It enabled the Bush administration to claim the extraordinary powers reserved to the executive in wartime. The administration repeatedly declared that the terrorists had taken "advantage of the vulnerability of an open society" and that Americans must therefore accept encroachments on their freedoms. The centerpiece of Bush's antiterrorism strategy was the USA PATRIOT Act, a complex statute passed by Congress only six weeks after September 11. The legislation sailed through Congress with no hearings, no debate, no deliberation, and almost no opposition.

Among other things, the PATRIOT Act authorized the National Security Agency (NSA) to obtain information about individuals considered relevant to a terrorist investigation. This was interpreted by the Foreign Intelligence Surveillance Court (FISC), which operates in secret in order to protect classified information and programs, to permit the collection and storage of the telephone records of millions of Americans in a massive government database. The existence of this secret program came to light in 2014 after a low-level employee of the National Security Agency, Edward Snowden, released a large cache of classified material. Following the recommendations of a presidential panel created to consider the relationship between liberty and security, Congress sharply restricted the metadata program by enacting the USA Freedom Act in 2015.

Even more problematic was President Bush's secret authorization of the NSA to conduct surveillance of the *content* of the phone calls and emails of American citizens without probable cause and without obtaining a warrant from the FISC. This program clearly violated both the Foreign Intelligence Surveillance Act and the Fourth Amendment, which protects American citizens from "unreasonable searches and seizures."

The war on terror also raised questions about the detention of persons suspected of being terrorists or of acting in complicity with such persons. In the months and years after 9/11, the US government imprisoned more than one thousand alleged "enemy combatants" who had been captured in Afghanistan and elsewhere in a special detention facility created in Guantanamo Bay, Cuba, without granting them a hearing to challenge the legality of their detention. The Supreme Court later held that the federal courts could review the legality of the confinement of detainees at Guantanamo even if they were not technically on American soil.

The Bush administration even went so far as to claim that it could detain *American citizens* as "enemy combatants" without giving them a hearing. The Supreme Court resoundingly rejected the government's contention. Justice Sandra Day O'Connor, speaking for eight justices, made clear that "a state of war is not a blank check for the President when it comes to the rights of the Nation's citizens." The court thus reaffirmed Justice Robert Jackson's conclusion, made after President Truman had tried to nationalize the steel industry to end a strike during the Korean War, that the Constitution makes the president commander in chief of the army and navy, not of the nation.

Perhaps the most dangerous policy adopted by the Bush administration following 9/11 was its attempt to conceal its policies from the American public. The executive branch evaded the constraints imposed by the separation of powers, judicial review, checks and balances, and democratic accountability. Some measure of secrecy is, of course, essential to the effective operation of government during wartime. Overbroad government assertions of secrecy, however, cripple informed public debate. As New York senator Daniel Patrick Moynihan once observed, "Secrecy is the ultimate form of regulation because people don't even know they are being regulated."

THE SHAME OF AMERICA

In 2004, photographs emerged of US troops sexually humiliating and torturing suspected Iraqi insurgents in Abu Ghraib prison in Baghdad. Americans were stunned by the images, which showed, among other things, a hooded man apparently wired with electrodes balancing precariously on a block. Word also began to leak out about secret detention facilities in eastern Europe where CIA interrogators used "enhanced interrogation techniques" (EITs) such as waterboarding (simulated drowning), sleep deprivation, ice baths, rectal "feeding," and threats against family members to gather intelligence. Similar treatment characterized the government's prison in Guantanamo Bay, which the Bush administration argued was beyond the reach of American law because it was on foreign soil. When the Supreme Court disagreed, Bush's public opinion ratings plummeted, and the administration's torture and detainment policies became live issues in the 2004 election.

Torture at Abu Ghraib was made possible by the Bush administration's decision, at the start of the war, to ignore the 1949 Geneva Conventions on the treatment of prisoners of war. The administration justified EITs as necessary to obtain vital information about future terrorist attacks. The Justice Department's Office of Legal Counsel offered a highly controversial legal rationale that defined torture as, in practical terms, equivalent to death. The "torture memos" allowed broad scope for actions, such as waterboarding, that were illegal under the terms of the Geneva Conventions, which establish standards of international law for humanitarian treatment in war.

As far as the CIA was concerned, EITs were legal and had been approved by the commander in chief. The congressional oversight committees charged with monitoring the CIA were briefed. More to the point, the CIA believed that EITs worked in some cases: intelligence gained through the use of EITs revealed the knowledge that al Qaeda desired to bring down suspension bridges in America, and detainees subject to EITs divulged the first clues as to Osama bin Laden's whereabouts. Although top CIA officials were personally leery about the use of EITs, especially waterboarding, they also acknowledged their effectiveness.

In 2014, the Senate Select Committee on Intelligence published a 6,700-page report on the CIA's detention and interrogation program. The report confirmed that enhanced interrogation practices were known to National Security Advisor Condoleezza Rice and Vice President Cheney, who were briefed by CIA Director George Tenet in summer 2002. Senior Democrats were briefed on the program as well. President Bush gave formal permission for the torture but was unaware of its extent until 2005.

The Senate report was highly critical of the American use of EITs on both practical and moral grounds. Upon the release of the report, Republican senator from Arizona John McCain, who was tortured as a POW in Vietnam, praised its conclusions: "Our enemies act without conscience. We must not. This [report] . . . makes clear that acting without conscience isn't necessary, it isn't even helpful, in winning this strange and long war we're fighting. We should be grateful to have that truth affirmed."

In addition to the American lives lost and shattered, the wars in Afghanistan and Iraq cost an estimated $800 billion. Conservative estimates of Iraqi deaths due to war-related injuries hover between 100,000 and 200,000. When combined with the Bush tax cuts, the wars in Afghanistan and Iraq produced soaring deficits, as well as a sober reckoning with the trade-offs between national security and national values. The war in Iraq tarnished America's image abroad, destabilized the Middle East, and incited anti-American sentiment in the Muslim world. This undermined Washington's efforts to combat global terrorist operations. In the end, the chief beneficiary of the war was Iran, which no longer faced a strong nation to the west.

The Great Recession

The Great Recession, which began in 2008, swept away eight million jobs and forced more than four million home foreclosures. House prices fell $5.5 trillion. (This is an enormous number, considering that the annual economic output of the US economy was roughly $14 trillion.) The recession was precipitated by no natural disaster, no war, no technological innovation that made workers and their knowledge redundant. What there *was* beforehand was a tremendous run-up in household debt. Large run-ups in household debt are closely related to banking crises and broader economic disasters. Large increases in household debt and economic disasters seem, in turn, to be related to collapses in spending. The American economy in 2008 was a perfect storm of debt, lending, and increasingly restrained spending.

THE GREAT BUBBLE TRANSFER

The dot-com bust in 2000 seemed to presage a serious economic decline. But business losses were cushioned and wider economic disruptions curtailed by a real estate bubble, and only a minor recession resulted in 2001. Financial analyst Stephanie Pomboy dubbed this phenomenon "the great bubble transfer," in which a speculative bubble in the home mortgage market compensated for the bursting of the dot-com stock bubble.

A primary reason for the housing boom was the decision of many people to park their money in real estate, which looked safer than the stock market after the tech bubble burst. Also, interest rates dropped, which enticed more people to join what President George W. Bush, reelected in 2004, called the "ownership society." Cheap financing expanded the number of mortgage borrowers despite the increasing cost of houses. First-time buyers were encouraged by banks offering adjustable-rate mortgages that required no down payment and featured low interest rates that would rise after a few years. Those who already had mortgages refinanced at a lower interest rate, which provided cash that could be spent on college tuition or remodeling the kitchen. During these years, the ratio of household debt (home mortgages, credit card debt, etc.) to disposable personal income rose steadily. By 2007, the average household's debt reached almost 130% of disposable income. American families were running their own personal deficits.

Believing that housing prices would continue to rise and that interest rates would remain low, Americans took on too much debt and bought houses they could not afford. Banks made loans that seemed destined to default—such as so-called NINJA loans, which were granted to people with *no income, no jobs,* and no *assets.* The number of subprime mortgages—loans to people likely to default—surged, and the market in mortgage-backed securities that included subprime mortgages skyrocketed from $56 billion in 2000 to $508 billion in 2005.

Banking crises and large expansions in household debt are closely related. Indeed, as economists have shown, severe economic disasters are almost always preceded by a large increase in household debt. Why? Because unless someone is crazy or completely irresponsible, debt acts as a brake on spending. Indeed, a massive decline in spending predated the banking crash in the fall of 2008. The collapse in residential investment was already evident in 2006. Economists Atif Mian and Amir Sufi have determined that consumption was the key driver of the recession. By the summer of 2008, auto purchases—always a bellwether of the American economy—were already down 35 percent.

Regulatory breakdown was a vital factor in both precipitating and explaining the financial crisis. President Clinton's Treasury secretary, Robert Rubin, was a veteran of the investment bank Goldman Sachs. In 1999, Rubin and Assistant Secretary of the Treasury Lawrence Summers convinced Congress to repeal the Glass-Steagall Act of 1933, which had separated investment banking from commercial banking. This allowed the development of the mortgage-backed securities market whose meltdown in 2007 marked the beginning of the global financial crisis. (A security is a tradeable financial asset of any kind. A mortgage-backed security's value is tied to the value of the mortgages that underpin it.) In 2000, Rubin, aided by Alan Greenspan (chairman of the Federal Reserve) and Arthur Levitt (chairman of the Securities and Exchange Commission, the SEC), beat back a congressional effort to regulate derivatives, a highly complex form of wagering on certain outcomes—such as the mortgage default rate. In the instance of mortgage lending and the financial products built on it, regulatory failure proved calamitous.

MORAL HAZARDS

Housing prices peaked in 2006, by which time the average home cost four times what the average family earned. As the low "teaser" mortgage interest rates expired on adjustable-rate mortgages, high-risk borrowers defaulted in droves. The first tremors of the coming crisis were felt in July 2007, when two hedge funds of the investment bank Bear Stearns that held nearly $10 billion in mortgage-backed securities suddenly imploded.

In March 2008, in an effort to stabilize the crisis, the US government brokered a shotgun marriage between Bear Stearns and JPMorgan Chase, investing $29 billion of government financing to cover dubious Bear Stearns assets. In early September, the Treasury Department rescued the government-backed private mortgage agencies Fannie Mae and Freddie Mac by pledging up to $200 billion. As many noted at the time, "Such interventions put taxpayer money at risk and made a mockery of the notion of 'moral hazard,' a guiding principle of economics which posits that unless actors bear the consequences of their actions they will act recklessly."

Treasury Secretary Henry Paulson and Federal Reserve System Chairman Ben Bernanke were pummeled, both by Republicans averse to any tampering with markets and by liberal Democrats outraged by a government rescue of what they deemed Wall Street's overpaid, irresponsible bankers. Republican senator Jim Bunning insisted that the bailouts were socialist, while the economist Nouriel Roubini observed that, as in the Great Depression, bankers were once again the first group "to go on the 'dole' in America."

On September 11, 2008, less than a week after the rescue of Fannie Mae and Freddie Mac, Timothy Geithner, the president of the Federal Reserve Bank of New York, reported to Paulson and Bernanke that Lehman Brothers, the largest underwriter of subprime-mortgage-backed securities, was on the brink of bankruptcy. The expectation was that Lehman, like Bear Stearns, was "too big to fail," and would thus be bailed out by the federal government. It was not. The bank filed for bankruptcy on September 14.

The decision to allow Lehman to fail was praised widely. "The government had to draw a line somewhere," editorialized the *Wall Street Journal*. The stock market was less certain about the wisdom of the Lehman bankruptcy. The Dow Jones Industrial Average dropped by 4.4 percent—the biggest one-day percentage drop since the 9/11 attacks. The shares of American International Group (AIG), which had guaranteed more than $500 billion of mortgage-backed securities, dropped 61 percent, as traders realized the insurance firm's huge vulnerability. By September 13, AIG was facing $40 billion in claims.

AIG did business in 130 countries and had 74 million customers, including 30 million in the United States. If AIG failed to honor its guarantees, it could spark a global bank run that would be even more disastrous than the failure of Lehman. AIG, it was decided, was too interconnected to fail.

While the public praised Henry Paulson for allowing Lehman's demise, he and Timothy Geithner rescued AIG with an $85 billion loan that would be collateralized by all of AIG's other insurance assets. The government would receive a 79 percent equity stake in AIG, which effectively nationalized it. "We'd just crossed another boundary," recalled one participant in the negotiations. "No one had any idea what would happen if we let a company this size fail." On September 16, Paulson and Bernanke informed the House and Senate leadership that the Federal Reserve had exercised its emergency powers to seize control of AIG and loan it $85 billion.

MELTDOWN

By October 2008, the total losses of financial institutions from mortgage-related securities reached $500 billion. In the grand scheme of things, this is not such a large number. In fact, it is dwarfed by the more than $5 *trillion* of losses in the value of shares on the US stock markets when the technology bubble burst. Why then was the subprime crisis so much more damaging than the technology bust a few years earlier? How could the loss in value of mortgage-related securities have such a large effect on the global financial system and the broader economy?

The bursting of the tech bubble resulted in a huge loss of household wealth but had little effect on household spending because tech stocks were owned by rich households that carried little debt. In 2001, almost 90 percent of all stocks in the United States were owned by the top 20 percent of the net-worth distribution. The rich lost money in 2000, but that did not produce a decline in spending. The housing crash was a disaster because while it hit across the board, it hit the poor especially hard — and triggered a massive decline in spending that sent shockwaves throughout the economy.

What could be done to prevent a complete global financial meltdown? Paulson and Bernanke proposed that the government stabilize the money-market funds by guaranteeing them in the way the government stood behind banks through the FDIC. This would amount to a $4 trillion guarantee, though, and at a far higher risk level than securing bank funds to individual depositors. President Bush gave the plan the go-ahead, saying that he would take care of the politics of the decision.

Early on the morning of September 19, 2008, before the US markets opened, Henry Paulson issued a statement that the federal government would adopt a "comprehensive approach" to resolve the financial crisis. Later that morning, President Bush addressed the nation from the Rose Garden. Declaring that "this is a pivotal moment for America's economy," Bush continued: "Our system of free enterprise rests on the conviction that the federal government should interfere in the marketplace only when necessary. Given the precarious state of today's financial markets—and their vital importance to the daily lives of the American people—government intervention is not only warranted; it is essential."

The secretary of the Treasury was grateful. "There were plenty of people around the President" who just wanted to trust the free market, Paulson recalled later. "He freed me from all of that. He wanted there to be a free market left for all of us to work with." Bush, Paulson recounted, abandoned free-market orthodoxy and instead "focused on what was best for the country." The news that the government had a plan to deal with the crisis was received with relief on Wall Street, where the Dow Jones average rose 400 points.

Congress balked, however, at injecting $700 billion into the banks. Senators and representatives from both parties were besieged by angry constituents, who resented injecting billions of taxpayer dollars into the institutions that had caused the crisis in the first place. On September 29, the House rejected the emergency legislation. Global markets convulsed, the Dow dropped 778 points, and credit markets froze. Henry Paulson was beside himself. After energetic lobbying, the bill passed on October 3, 2008.

RECESSION

Facing a possible global economic meltdown, President George W. Bush, like his counterparts in Europe, allowed the government to use the tools it had to intervene in and stabilize the free-falling market. After nearly 30 years of Republican recitation of the magic of free markets and the perniciousness of government intervention, Bush underscored the role of the federal government in regulating the economy to protect the public interest.

The expected recession following the financial panic hit the United States hard during 2009, as a new president, Barack Obama, took office. Unemployment reached 9.7 percent. The worst economic crisis since the Depression destroyed household and retirement savings, pensions, and institutional endowments. Stabilizing AIG cost taxpayers $180 billion. Before the economy hit bottom, the auto industry had to be bailed out along with the banks. Lenders foreclosed on nearly three million homes between October 2008 and September 2009.

The idea behind the government relief program was that banks would use the infusion of taxpayer money to beef up lending, which would bolster the economy and help people at risk of losing their homes to refinance and jump-start consumer spending. Instead, many banks used the cash to pay down their own debts to each other and to reward themselves richly. Banks that received bailout money compensated their top executives nearly $1.6 billion in 2008. Banks also put government money to use during the 2008 election in which companies that had received $295 billion in bailout money spent $114 million on lobbying and campaign contributions.

The cascading financial crisis brought the mighty US economy to its knees. It cost millions of Americans their livelihoods and their homes, bankrupted thousands of businesses, destroyed roughly $4 trillion of wealth, and left government at every level desperate for tax revenue necessary to carry out basic functions. Three-quarters of a million jobs were lost *per month* in the first quarter of 2009. Total employment peaked in January 2008 and then fell for 25 consecutive months—the longest losing streak since the 1930s. A total of about 8.8 million jobs disappeared during this period. Behind these lost jobs lay a decline in consumption most apparent in the states hit hard by the housing crash.

The Great Recession left what appears to be a permanent scar on the household net worth of three generations of Americans. From 2007 to 2010, the average net worth of the poorest 20 percent of homeowners in the United States fell from $33,000 to $2,000. It rose from 2010 to 2013—to $7,000. For the middle 20 percent, the average net worth rose from $193,000 to $200,000. This is far below the average $230,000 this group had in 2004. Only the top 20 percent of homeowners have seen their wealth exceed 2004 levels.

Sluggish income growth has limited economic recovery. Output per worker has increased since the recession, but the share of output going to labor in the form of wages and salaries is at an all-time low in postwar America. The banks are healthy, but the recovery is not. Saving the banks did not save the economy. The politics of economic under-performance would erupt in 2011 and remain onstage for the follow-ing years.

Of the People, by the People, for the People?

Between 2000 and 2016, America experienced constant conflict and confusion in the realm of electoral politics. This was due to a combina-tion of factors, including two highly contested presidential elections, increasing political polarization, and the growing impact of money on the electoral process. It was an era of sharp division over such issues as voter registration, redistricting, and campaign finance, raising serious questions about the nature of American democracy.

VOTING RIGHTS: ACCESS AND BOUNDARIES

Among the many consequences of the contested 2000 presidential election was a renewed battle over voting rights. In the pivotal state of Florida, for example, thousands of voters had been denied access to the polls because of long, slow lines, registration inconsistencies, and Florida's particularly harsh felony disenfranchisement laws.

A 2001 task force chaired by former presidents Gerald Ford and Jimmy Carter concluded that voter registration laws in the United States were "among the world's most demanding." As a result, Ameri-can voter turnout was "near the bottom of the developed world." In 2000, only 70 percent of Americans were registered to vote. This re-mained the case in 2012, when more than 50 million otherwise eligible Americans still were not registered to vote.

This state of affairs was not by chance. Between 2000 and 2015, Republican-controlled state legislatures made it more difficult for poor people to vote by passing a series of laws that, for example, re-quired voters to possess a state-issued photo ID and eliminated same-day voter registration. The purported goal was to prevent voter fraud, but there was no evidence of significant voter fraud anywhere in the United States. Since 2000, half the states, all controlled by the Re-publican Party, have enacted laws making it harder for citizens to vote, leading one election specialist to conclude that the framing of "elec-tion law has become part of a political strategy."

Voter registration laws are one way to manage the electorate. Redistricting is another. Computer software has enabled intricate partisan manipulation of district lines, with distorting effects. A state legislature controlled by one party can easily create districts that enable, say, 40 percent of a state's citizens to control a majority of its legislative districts. Such gerrymandering reduces political competition within districts, perpetuates the tenure of incumbents, and creates legislative majorities, in Congress and the states, that often do not reflect the views of the majority of citizens. The United States is the only major democracy in the world that allows politicians to pick their own voters through the process of drawing district lines.

Democrats have redistricted in their favor in the past. Ronald Reagan had to work with a House of Representatives weighted in the Democrats' favor. Recent partisan redistricting, however, has benefited Republicans and done so in ways intentionally difficult to undo. "Through artful drawing of district boundaries, it is possible to put large groups of voters on the losing side of every election," neuroscientist and good-government guru Sam Wang explained in an op-ed titled "The Great Gerrymander of 2012." That year, Democratic candidates for Congress received more votes than Republican candidates. Yet because of GOP redistricting, for the first time in 40 years, the party that won the most votes failed to take control of the House. In Pennsylvania, for example, the Democrats received 51 percent of the vote to the GOP's 49 percent. This bare Democratic majority translated to a congressional delegation of 13 to 5 — Republicans to Democrats. When electoral majorities are consistently set aside, when a political party wins 51 percent of the vote but receives only 30 percent of the representation, as in Pennsylvania, democracy suffers.

In 2015, former US senator Tom Harkin of Iowa reflected on the state of gerrymandering across the nation and the ever-more-extreme politics it encouraged. Other states, according to Harkin, should follow the lead of Iowa and California and adopt an independent district line–drawing commission. "The whole system now is really bad," he said. "I don't know what's going to change it. . . . Maybe it will take a calamity. Something big's going to have to happen to get it righted again."

CAMPAIGN FINANCE REFORM, PART 1

Like redistricting, concern over the role of money in politics dates to the early Republic, when ordinary citizens began to challenge upper-class Americans for public office. In the absence of personal wealth, this new breed of politicians financed their campaigns by offering government jobs to their contributors. The 1883 Pendleton Civil Service Reform Act forbade the selling of government jobs, ended patronage as a source of political funds, and had the unintended consequence of driving politicians toward a new revenue source: big business.

The great new corporations of the Gilded Age poured money into political campaigns in pursuit of industry-friendly policies. An 1889 cartoon, *The Bosses of the Senate*, depicted enormous, bloated men, named "Steel Trust," "Copper Trust," and so forth, looming over Congress. In the 1896 presidential election, Mark Hanna—the prototypical political operative—raised $16 million for Republican William McKinley, more than 20 times what Democrat William Jennings Bryan had in his coffers. "All questions in a democracy," Hanna expounded, "are questions of money."

The influence of money on politics was demoralizing and often infuriating to ordinary people—some of whom made their unhappiness known through mass demonstrations and violence. The first campaign finance laws were passed under Theodore Roosevelt in 1907, at a moment of outsized business influence, political venality, financial crisis, and great economic inequality. Despite the fact that, in the words of the *Washington Post*, "Boodle is become an indispensable factor in our elections," Congress passed campaign finance legislation that prohibited monetary contributions to political campaigns by corporations.

Congress adjusted the campaign-finance regime six decades later, after Watergate revealed the extent of financial corruption involved in President Richard Nixon's 1972 reelection campaign. For example, in acts that were effectively bribery, donors contributed to Nixon's campaign in exchange for ambassadorships, and the federal subsidy for milk was raised after the Associated Milk Producers pledged $2 million to the campaign. New laws limited the amount that individuals and corporations could contribute to candidates and regulated the amount they could spend independently to effect a candidate's election.

In 1974, in *Buckley v. Valeo*, the Supreme Court struck down part of that law, deciding that money spent to influence elections was a form of constitutionally protected free speech. The court upheld limits on contributions to candidates, deciding that government has a substantial interest in avoiding the appearance as well as the reality of corruption and undue influence. But it invalidated the limits on independent expenditures to support a candidate's election, because the court considered them less likely to have a corrupting effect.

In the years between 1974 and 2002, corporations and wealthy donors increasingly found ways to circumvent the line between contributions and independent expenditures in ways that enabled them once again to gain undue influence on the political process. Thus, in 2002, Congress enacted the bipartisan McCain-Feingold Campaign Reform Act, which was signed into law by President George W. Bush. The act closed a series of loopholes involving such devices as soft money and issue ads that had enabled corporations and wealthy individuals to funnel large amounts of money into the electoral process through independent expenditure groups. In *McConnell v. Federal Election Commission*, decided in 2003, the Supreme Court, in a 5–4 decision, upheld the constitutionality of the McCain-Feingold legislation and concluded that the national interest in avoiding both the reality and the appearance of corruption justified campaign finance regulations.

CAMPAIGN FINANCE REFORM: PART 2

By limiting the impact of corporations and wealthy donors, the new campaign finance laws worked to the advantage of Democrat Barack Obama in 2008. His campaign pioneered the use of social networking sites in politics and translated grassroots excitement into money. In February 2008, the Obama campaign reported that 94 percent of its donations had come in increments of $200 or less. This was celebrated by one writer as having "realized the reformers' . . . big goal of ending the system whereby a handful of rich donors control the political process. [Obama] has done this not by limiting money but by adding much, much more of it—democratizing the system by flooding it with so many new contributors that their combined effect dilutes the old guard to the point that it scarcely poses any threat."

This was not to last. Two years into the Obama presidency, a reconstituted Supreme Court reconsidered its prior opinion on campaign finance law. The critical shift in personnel was the replacement of Justice Sandra Day O'Connor, who had voted with the majority in *McConnell*, by the far more conservative Samuel Alito in 2006. In a momentous 5–4 decision, the court effectively overturned *McConnell* and held, in *Citizens United v. Federal Election Commission* (2010), that the McCain-Feingold Act violated the First Amendment. In essence, the court held that the government could restrict political expenditures, even by corporations, only to the extent necessary to prevent actual quid pro quo corruption—that is, outright bribery.

The justices in the majority dismissed the concerns that unlimited corporate expenditures might distort the American electoral process, or unduly influence the views of elected officials, or create the appearance of undue influence and thus undermine the confidence of citizens in the democratic process. In a dissenting opinion, Justice John Paul Stevens maintained that the majority had overturned "the common sense of the American people, who have recognized a need to prevent corporations from undermining self-government since the founding."

Following the *Citizens United* decision in 2010, vast sums of money flooded national politics. Between 2000 and 2012, the amount of money poured into elections grew nearly tenfold, from an inflation-adjusted $100 million in 2000 to $980 million in 2012. Moreover, under existing law many so-called super PACs (political action committees) have no obligation to disclose the identities of their contributors, thus shielding their efforts to shape the political process from public view. Political spending by such groups rocketed from less than $5 million in 2002 to $300 million in 2012.

The dynamic grassroots fundraising pioneered by the Obama campaign in 2008 was overwhelmed in the 2012 election, as both parties raced to take advantage of what *Citizens United* had unleashed. That year, 99 Americans (mostly billionaires, representing less than .00001 percent of the American people) provided 60 percent of all the independent expenditure money spent by candidates. As the nonpartisan Sunlight Foundation concluded after the election, "One ten-thousandth" of America's population, or "1% of the 1%," was "shaping the limits of acceptable [political] discourse."

Rejecting the judgment of Congress, which has direct experience with the effect of money on the political process, the court in *Citizens United* insisted that "the appearance of influence or access . . . will not cause the electorate to lose faith in our democracy." But by 2013, the percentage of Americans convinced that corruption was "widespread throughout the government of this country" had risen to almost 80 percent, and more than three-quarters of Americans disapproved of the *Citizens United* decision. As one election-reform advocate has observed, Americans increasingly regard the current American political process as "an accepted system of legal corruption."

Land of Opportunity?

It was a commonplace among social scientists of the post-WWII era that modernity would be a great economic equalizer. The idea was that as productive capacity grew, it would steadily erode the enormous economic inequalities of developing nations (such as Bangladesh) and narrow the gap between rich and poor in advanced capitalist nations. As long as the pie kept getting larger, many people thought, no one had to worry about portion size: everyone's piece grew, albeit not at the same rate. Because of the correlation between economic growth and social mobility, the American Dream of moving upward, through hard work, conservative family finances, and government policies aimed at enlarging a middle class through progressive taxation, seemed well within reach.

THE GREAT U-TURN

The era of widely shared postwar prosperity came to a sudden end in the mid-1970s, with the collapse of the high-wage, high-benefits economy of the post-WWII era. There were many reasons for the economic transformations of the 1970s: a massive restructuring of the paid labor force, including the entrance of millions of women; intensifying pressure from low-wage foreign labor markets, especially in manufacturing, and from a transnational, mobile labor force competing for jobs in the globalized economy; and the collapse of labor unions and the breakdown of the system of accommodation forged between big labor and big business.

Because of these and other factors, most Americans have experienced a drop in their standard of living since the late 1970s. The main sources of income growth for the middle class in the last 30 years have been increased hours and the rise of dual-earner households. Between 1948 and 2011, productivity increased by 254 percent, but hourly compensation grew by only 113 percent. In short, the average American in 2012 was working more but earning less.

Where did the gains from productivity go, if not to workers? The obvious answer is that they went to owners, managers, and investors. Since 1979, the wealthiest 5 percent of Americans have taken home more than half of the total income growth in the nation. More than 20 percent of total income growth has gone to the top 1 percent. Between 1979 and 2007, the middle class, those in the 40–60 percent level, saw real wages *decline* by 17 percent, and income for the bottom 20 percent dropped by almost 60 percent. Nothing like this has happened since the Great Depression.

How did this happen? About 60 percent of the increase in the top 1 percent's share of total income has come from the expansion of the financial sector and an explosion in executive pay. Public policy has also played a role. At the same time that their incomes have skyrocketed, effective tax rates on the super-rich have fallen. The Bush tax cuts of 2001 and 2003 reduced the taxes paid by the wealthiest 1 percent of Americans by 17 percent, and cut the taxes of all other Americans together by an average of 5 percent. As *Business Insider* magazine said bluntly: "America's companies and company owners—the small group of Americans who own and control America's corporations—are hogging a record percentage of the country's wealth for themselves."

From 2007 to 2009, the recession produced a 17.4 percent decline in average real income—the largest drop since the Great Depression. The bottom 90 percent of Americans saw one-third of their wealth wiped out. From 2009 to 2012, the United States experienced a significant economic recovery, in which average real income growth jumped by 6 percent. Nearly all of that increase, however—95 percent of it—accrued to those already in the top 1 percent of the income distribution. By 2015, the richest 1 percent of all Americans had more net worth than the bottom 90 percent combined, and the 400 wealthiest Americans had more net worth that the bottom 50 percent of all Americans combined.

AT LAST

The growing financial crisis on Wall Street proceeded apace with the 2008 presidential campaign, which was highly competitive. The Republicans settled on Arizona senator John McCain, who eventually chose Sarah Palin, the lively former governor of Alaska, as his running mate. New York senator and former First Lady Hillary Rodham Clinton was the presumptive Democratic presidential candidate—until she was challenged in the primaries by a first-term senator from Illinois with an unusual name, Barack Hussein Obama.

Barack Obama first came to national attention in 2004, while a candidate for the Senate, when he gave an electrifying speech at the Democratic National Convention. The son of a foreign student from Kenya and a white Kansan who met and married in Hawai'i, Obama explained that his first name, Barack, meant "blessed," adding that his parents believed "that in a tolerant America, your name is no barrier to success." A graduate of Columbia University and Harvard Law School, he continued: "In a generous America you don't have to be rich to achieve your potential. . . . I stand here knowing that my story is part of the larger American story, that I owe a debt to all of those who came before me, and that in no other country on Earth is my story even possible."

The future junior senator from Illinois reached beyond the Democratic audience that evening when he asserted that "there's not a liberal America and a conservative America; there's the United States of America. There's not a black America and a white America and Latino America and Asian America; there's the United States of America." Rejecting political pundits' tendency to "slice and dice our country into red states and blue states," Obama dwelt on the commonalities among people. "In the end," he concluded, "that's what this election is about. Do we participate in a politics of cynicism, or do we participate in a politics of hope?"

Obama's story was compelling, and his message of unity, hope, and change inspired many in the 2008 presidential election, including many first-time voters. One message in particular seemed to galvanize voters: the notion that America could change for the better—what Obama called "the audacity of hope." In a heartfelt speech on race in Philadelphia in March 2008, Obama expressed his belief in the politics of the possible. "This union may never be perfect," he concluded, "but generation after generation has shown that it can always be perfected."

Barack Obama was not the first African American to run for president. Jesse Jackson, a civil rights leader from Chicago, campaigned for the Democratic nomination in 1984 and 1988. Jackson did not prevail, but he energized minority Americans to register to vote. When he won nearly 30 percent of primary voters in 1988, he demonstrated the willingness of white Democrats to vote for a black candidate for president.

On November 4, 2008, Obama and his running mate, Senator Joe Biden from Delaware, won decisively, capturing both the popular vote and the Electoral College. Obama received 69.5 million votes, the largest total ever recorded for a presidential candidate. The Democrats won the coasts, the Great Lakes industrial region, and Colorado and New Mexico. Republicans took the lower and upper South, the mountain West, and Utah, Arizona, and Kansas. Obama's election meant that the Democrats, who had captured both the House and the Senate in 2006, were in control of all three branches of government for the first time since 1994.

BLOWBACK

No president since Franklin Roosevelt faced the domestic challenges that awaited Barack Obama as he entered office in January 2009. In terms of job loss and GDP (gross domestic product) decline, the 2008–2009 period was the worst in 70 years. The implosion of the economy in 2008 resembled the crash of 1929, but the political circumstances the two presidents faced were very different. FDR took office after three years of failed efforts by Republicans to revive the economy. By 1932, even Herbert Hoover had given up relying exclusively on the private sector to cope with the crisis. This gave Roosevelt an opportunity to innovate—to try virtually any policy solution. Obama, by contrast, inherited the crash of 2008 as it unfolded. He had little choice but to continue the stabilization policies handed off to him by Henry Paulson and Ben Bernanke, who had saved the global financial system by transferring the banking and mortgage systems' massive risk and volatility to the government that rescued them.

As people felt the effects of the recession—as they lost their jobs, their retirement savings, and, in many cases, their homes, their anger grew. Rather than direct their rage at the financial institutions that precipitated the collapse, or at the Republican administration that inaugurated their rescue, many Americans instead targeted a nebulous "government" in Washington, DC, and the man newly at its helm.

The election of Barack Obama and a Democratic Congress further energized an obstreperous wing of the Republican Party that came to be known as the Tea Party. The appearance of the Tea Party was triggered by dissatisfaction with Republican leaders, above all President George W. Bush. Its ideology, such as it was, was rooted in an earlier reaction against the redistributive policies of the New Deal. The anti–New Deal American Liberty League, for example, denounced Franklin Roosevelt's economic policies in language familiar to contemporary politics. "You can't recover prosperity," it announced in 1934, "by seizing the accumulation of the thrifty and distributing it to the thriftless and unlucky."

Initially viewed by GOP party leaders as a flash in the pan, the Tea Party instead grew in influence until, by 2012, it represented the core of the Republican Party, powerful enough to dethrone the Speaker of the House and install in his stead its own favorite son. It was, in large degree, a regional phenomenon: its followers clustered heavily in the South, particularly the Deep South, and, to a far lesser extent, the mountain and desert West. Although representing only 42 percent of House Republicans, by 2014 a full 60 percent of the House Tea Party Caucus hailed from the South. By 2010, the white South had emerged as the pillar of the GOP. Like other southern conservatives before them, Tea Party Republicans were uniformly white, overwhelmingly male, and disproportionately old.

The Tea Party's ire was initially directed at President Obama's $75 billion relief plan to aid homeowners by reducing monthly mortgage payments through refinancing. Like bankruptcy law, which reduces debts that cannot be paid in order to serve a broader economic interest (such as saving jobs), the housing relief program was designed to prevent the abandonment and disintegration of entire neighborhoods, especially in working-class and poor areas.

To many conservative Republicans, however, mortgage relief looked like a massive government handout. This reinforced the suspicion of Tea Party supporters that President Obama, once in office, would reward the undeserving. Fifteen years after Bill Clinton cut welfare to the bone, Tea Party activists still differentiated between entitlements like Social Security, which were earned, and welfare, which was not. Recalling Ronald Reagan's "welfare queens" living high on the hog, Tea Party supporters remained forever on guard against economic redistribution to moochers who jumped the line.

A POSTRACIAL SOCIETY?

Barack Obama's election resulted in a rapturous but premature declaration that the United States had entered a "postracial" era in which racial identity would cease to be a salient factor in politics. Obama himself worked hard to prove this true. Yet although Obama was raised by his white grandparents in multiethnic Hawai'i, conservative television talk show host Glenn Beck still insisted that the new president had "a deep-seated hatred for white people."

Other politicians, and other presidents, have been roughed up by the media and their fellow citizens. John Tyler, who assumed the presidency after the death of William Henry Harrison, was ridiculed as "His Accidency." Critics of the New Deal attacked FDR as an "un-American radical." At the height of the Vietnam War, Lyndon Johnson was excoriated by his opponents as a "murderer" and a "war criminal."

But no president in the nation's history has been treated as disrespectfully by the media and other elected officials as Barack Obama.

Cartoons circulated depicting the president and his family as monkeys. He was accused (falsely) of being a "secret Muslim," having been a Black Panther, refusing to recite the Pledge of Allegiance, being a socialist, and lying about just about everything. Real estate developer and reality television personality Donald J. Trump's baseless but ceaseless assertion that Obama had been born in Kenya, and was thus ineligible for the presidency, created a fringe political movement. An exasperated president produced his Hawai'ian birth certificate in 2010, but this had no effect on "the Birthers," as they were now called. In 2009, the president was interrupted during a major speech on health care to both houses of Congress by South Carolina congressman Joe Wilson, who cried out, "You lie!" In the nineteenth century, such an assault on honor would have triggered a duel.

Although a vocal group of Democrats persisted in questioning the legitimacy of President George W. Bush after the contested 2000 election, Democratic members of Congress rallied behind the president after 9/11. Despite the Democrats' resounding victory in the 2008 election, however, there was a noteworthy reluctance by many Republicans to acknowledge that the new president was, in fact, the president. GOP Senate leader Mitch McConnell of Kentucky set the tone by declaring that his main agenda for the next four years was to prevent the reelection of Barack Obama. This was not an unreasonable goal for the losing side in a presidential election, but the tone of the political vituperation that followed, the palpable sense of Republican outrage, suggested a deeper source of injury—as when South Carolina senator Jim DeMint spoke of trying to "break" the president.

What role, if any, did race play in the tenor of the personal and political invective that showered President Obama for his eight years in office? It is impossible to say with certainty. But the fact that only one other president in American history was the target of similar, though more subdued, personal attacks sheds some light. In his day, this president was castigated by the press and his political opponents as a "liar," a "despot," a "usurper," a "thief," a "monster," an "ignoramus," a "pirate," and a "king." He was charged with being "cunning," "heartless," "filthy," and "fanatical." He was accused of being "adrift on a current of racial fanaticism," and labeled by his enemies "Abraham Africanus the First." But even Abraham Lincoln was never portrayed as an ape eating a banana.

Change We Can Believe In

Barack Obama campaigned in 2008 on the slogan "Change We Can Believe In." He had a long list of items that needed changing that included improved schools, a reconfigured tax code that would shift the burden of supporting the government from the bottom to the top, an end to the war in Iraq, better relations with America's foreign allies, and expanded social services. At the very top of his list was that elusive trophy that American presidents had chased since 1946: national health care. In an inaugural address before 1.6 million people packed into the National Mall, the new president struck a nonpartisan tone when he declared, "On this day, we come to proclaim an end to the petty grievances and false promises, the recriminations and worn-out dogmas that for far too long have strangled our politics."

EXPANDING THE SOCIAL SAFETY NET:
HEALTH CARE

Although the United States led the world in health care expenditures, which accounted for more than 17 percent of the national GDP, approximately 50 million Americans, or 15 percent, lacked health insurance in 2008. The passage of the Patient Protection and Affordable Care Act (ACA) in March 2010 signaled the most progressive expansion of US government social policy since the 1960s, when Medicare and Medicaid were added to the basic social safety net established by the New Deal.

Universal health care was a longstanding goal in the United States. President Obama's plan was modeled on one first developed by conservative policy analysts at the Heritage Foundation and implemented in Massachusetts under Republican governor Mitt Romney—Obama's future Republican opponent in the 2012 presidential election. Opposed by a disciplined and unflinching Republican Party stocked with ever-more-oppositional Tea Party members, "Obamacare," as it was dubbed, passed with no Republican votes after a fierce GOP filibuster in the Senate.

Some opposition to Obamacare was spurious. Critics claimed that the legislation would create "death panels" that would decide the fate of elderly Americans, and insisted, falsely, that Americans would have to pay for health care for illegal immigrants. The Tea Party movement cried "socialism." But opponents also put forth more substantive objections, including the concern that the ACA violated the principle of federalism by authorizing the federal government to intrude into matters traditionally left to the states, unduly restricted the freedom of individuals to decide for themselves whether to purchase health insurance and of employers to decide whether to provide it, compelled employers to provide insurance coverage for things (such as contraception) that were incompatible with their religious beliefs, and would add to the national debt.

Between 2011 and 2015, even as millions of Americans enrolled in the new insurance program, Republicans in the House of Representatives voted on 67 occasions to repeal the ACA. The GOP campaign led to a disastrous government shutdown in 2013 but failed to affect the ACA. Meanwhile, ACA opponents challenged the constitutionality of the act in the federal courts.

In 2012, the Supreme Court upheld the Affordable Care Act, but also ruled that the states could not be compelled to participate in a proposed expansion of Medicaid designed to reach the working poor. Although the federal government paid 100 percent of the cost of Medicaid expansion in the states until 2020, and 90 percent after that, Republican-led states rushed to opt out of the expanded Medicaid program, leaving about 4 million poor, uninsured Americans in a coverage gap. Of adults in the coverage gap, 89 percent lived in the South, the epicenter of the Tea Party revolt.

The initial rollout of Obamacare in 2011 was an administrative disaster. But a crack team of "technocrati" in Washington re-created the ACA software platform and soon had the enrollment process up and running smoothly. In 2015, five years after passage of the ACA, 16 million more Americans had health insurance than before.

While spending on health care continued to rise, the rate of increase slowed markedly, and the cost of implementing the ACA was less than anticipated. More paying customers means more jobs: far from being the "Job-Killing Health Care Law" predicted by its critics, after the ACA was signed into law, the health care industry gained nearly one million jobs.

MARRIAGE EQUALITY

For most of American history, the notion that a man could marry a man, or a woman could marry a woman, seemed absurd. But when the Hawai'i Supreme Court ruled in 1993 that the state's law restricting same-sex marriage might violate the Hawai'i constitution, other states rushed to amend their own constitutions to define marriage explicitly as between one man and one woman. With the American people at the time opposed to same-sex marriage by a margin of 68 percent to 27 percent, Congress passed in 1996, and President Bill Clinton signed, the Defense of Marriage Act (DOMA). The act provided, among other things, that if any state recognized marriages between persons of the same sex, those people would be ineligible for the multitude of federal benefits that were otherwise available to married couples. Since same-sex marriage was not legal in any state in the nation, DOMA was more symbolic than substantive.

Seven years later, though, in 2003, Massachusetts legalized same-sex marriage when its Supreme Court held that laws denying same-sex couples the freedom to marry violated the Massachusetts constitution. In response, another 13 states amended their state constitutions to *forbid* same-sex marriage. By 2013, more than 30 states had enacted state constitutional amendments expressly outlawing same-sex marriage.

Then in 2013, in the landmark case *United States v. Windsor*, the Supreme Court found DOMA unconstitutional in a bitterly divided 5–4 decision bolstered by two recent Obama appointments, Associate Justices Sonia Sotomayor and Elena Kagan. In his opinion for the court, Justice Anthony Kennedy, a Reagan appointee, emphasized that a state's decision to give same-sex couples the right to marry "conferred upon them a dignity and status of immense import," and that a central purpose of DOMA was to undermine "the equal dignity" of gays and lesbians. Indeed, DOMA's "principal effect," he maintained, was to discriminate against legally married same-sex couples in a way that "demeans the couple" and "humiliates tens of thousands of children now being raised by same-sex couples."

Only two years later, in another contentious 5–4 decision authored by Justice Kennedy, the Supreme Court held in *Obergefell v. Hodges* that, because the right to marry is fundamental, no state can constitutionally deny same-sex couples the freedom to marry. Although there was some resistance to the court's decision, within a matter of hours same-sex couples were able to marry in every state in the nation.

Between the 1990s and 2015, the transformation in public opinion regarding same-sex marriage was unprecedentedly swift. In 1996, when DOMA was passed, only 27 percent of Americans thought that same-sex marriage should be recognized as valid, with the same rights as traditional marriages. By 2015, that number stood at 60 percent. A majority of Republicans in that year still opposed same-sex marriage (68 percent), while Democrats overwhelmingly supported it (74 percent). Among younger Americans (age 30–48), 62 percent supported marriage equality.

Obergefell left many fundamental questions unaddressed. For example, can a state discriminate against gays and lesbians in contexts other than marriage? Can states refuse to allow same-sex couples to adopt children? Should private individuals opposed to same-sex marriage for religious reasons be exempted from a state's antidiscrimination requirement? These are the sorts of questions that the nation will continue to struggle with for some years to come.

"DOUBT IS OUR PRODUCT"

Environmental debates should be placed in the broader context of growing energy production and consumption. In 1950, the United States produced 334 billion kilowatt hours of electricity; by 2000, it produced 3.802 trillion kilowatt hours, an increase of more than tenfold. Electricity ran furnaces, air conditioners, televisions, computers, and refrigerators. But the power plants that generated all this electricity polluted the air and the water, and combined with automobiles and other consumers of fossil fuels, they led to global warming: a problem caused by the burning of fossil fuels such as coal and oil to produce other forms of energy, like electricity.

Some of the earliest research on climate change was conducted by the petroleum industry. In the mid-1970s and 1980s, Exxon (later ExxonMobil) employed top scientists who worked side by side with university researchers and the Department of Energy. In 1977, an Exxon senior scientist informed the company's management committee that there was "general scientific agreement" that what was then called the greenhouse effect was likely caused by human-made carbon dioxide.

In 1978, another Exxon researcher reported to the company that doubling the amount of carbon dioxide in Earth's atmosphere would increase temperatures two to three degrees Celsius, with disastrous environmental repercussions. "Present thinking," he wrote, "holds that man has a time window of five to ten years before the need for hard decisions regarding changes in energy strategies might become critical." During the 1980s, Exxon scientists continued to research climate change, and they concluded that stopping "global warming would require major reductions in fossil fuel combustion." In 1988, the head of NASA's Goddard Institute for Space Studies, James Hansen, took climate change to the broader public and testified before Congress that the planet was warming.

Rather than respond to this testimony with its own independent research that supported NASA's findings, Exxon instead worked with veterans of the tobacco industry to organize and fund extreme climate-denial campaigns. In the early 1960s, the tobacco industry's own scientists had determined that smoking caused cancer and that nicotine was addictive. What to do? A 1969 industry memo recommended attacking the science behind the antismoking studies: "Doubt is our product since it is the best means of competing with the 'body of fact' that exists in the mind of the general public. It is also the means of establishing a controversy."

Like the tobacco industry, oil and coal producers transformed an emerging scientific consensus on climate change into a raging scientific "debate," insisting that there was "no proof" of global warming and lecturing media on the need to offer a "balanced presentation of all the facts." In 1997, on the eve of the Kyoto conference on global warming, Exxon CEO Lee Raymond, who had been a senior executive throughout the decade that Exxon had studied climate science, gave a speech to Chinese leaders and oil industry executives. He said that the globe was cooling and that government action to limit carbon emissions "defies common sense."

After a decade of highly partisan dispute over the existence and causes of climate change, the majority of Americans believed by 2015 that global warming was occurring. The experience of catastrophic storms like Hurricanes Katrina and Sandy in 2005 and 2012 combined with the fact that all but one of the years between 2000 and 2015 were the hottest on record globally helped drive this shift. But a minority of the public and Republican politicians have continued to disagree strongly about whether human activity is the dominant cause of global warming.

GERONIMO

In December 2009, President Obama flew to Oslo to receive the Nobel Peace Prize, which he had been awarded for, effectively, being the first African American US president. The timing was less than ideal: Obama had ordered automated drone attacks in Pakistan and was preparing to send tens of thousands of American troops to Afghanistan. Indeed, the US launched more missile strikes against al Qaeda targets inside Pakistan during Obama's first year in office than in all eight years of George W. Bush's presidency. Obama had not closed the Guantanamo Bay prison, either, despite his campaign promise.

As a candidate for president, Barack Obama had been asked if he would be willing to pursue al Qaeda leaders inside Pakistan, even if that meant invading an ally nation. He answered, "If we have Osama bin Laden in our sights and the Pakistani government is unable, or unwilling, to take [him] out, then I think we have to act and we will take [him] out. We will kill bin Laden. We will crush Al Qaeda. That has to be our biggest national security priority."

On the night of May 1, 2011, two Black Hawk helicopters lifted off from an airfield in eastern Afghanistan on a covert mission into Pakistan to kill Osama bin Laden, or "Geronimo," as he was referred to for the mission. Inside the helicopters were 23 Navy SEALS, a Pakistani translator, and a Belgian Malinois dog named Cairo. Fifteen minutes after taking off, the aircraft slipped, undetected, into Pakistani airspace.

Just past 11:30 p.m. in the eastern United States, President Obama informed the country that Special Operations forces had completed a "targeted operation" to kill bin Laden in a compound in northern Pakistan. The operation was supported strongly by his hawkish Secretary of State Hillary Clinton. Bin Laden's death gave the White House the political capital it needed to begin to remove troops from Afghanistan. The president announced a timetable for withdrawal while simultaneously stepping up drone attacks in Pakistan.

The president's bin Laden strategy was more successful than his economic programs. The economy improved only gradually during Obama's first term in office. Unemployment levels began to fall in 2009, but the new positions were often low-wage service jobs that were a poor substitute for lost jobs in manufacturing or offices. The rich prospered: between 2009 and 2012, incomes of the top 1 percent grew by almost a third. For the remaining 99 percent, however, incomes grew by only .04 percent—not even enough to keep up with inflation.

Anger at inequality and a perceived constriction of opportunity inspired political discontent on the left. Occupy Wall Street, which got its name when a loose group of protesters occupied a park in the southern tip of Manhattan, took up the cause of income inequality.

Their slogan "We are the 99%" highlighted the distance between the top 1 percent of earners and everyone else and injected income inequality into the 2012 presidential election.

Barack Obama was reelected as president in November 2012 by a large margin. There were many reasons for his success, including the weakness of his Republican opponent, former Massachusetts governor Mitt Romney. But two issues were paramount: national security and the economy, which was slowly recovering from its near-death experience in 2008. Vice President Joe Biden distilled the issues into one pithy slogan: "Bin Laden is dead and General Motors is alive."

The Rise of the Radical Right and the Election of 2016

Mitt Romney's 2012 loss to Barack Obama was not mirrored in Congress. (Obama beat Romney by some five million popular votes.) Republicans remained in control of the Senate, which is tilted by design toward the lesser-populated parts of the nation, a compromise initiated by the Founders to protect the interests of the smaller and slaveholding states. And because of the major overhaul of congressional districts that the Republican Party carried out in 2010 through its control of state legislatures, the Democrats carried fewer House districts than the Republicans, even when the statewide popular vote broke in favor of the Democrats. For the first time in 40 years, the party that received the most votes failed to take control of the House of Representatives.

All those gerrymandered "safe" GOP congressional seats resulted in the most conservative Republican caucus ever. Bolstered by an infusion of members in 2014, the expanded Tea Party organized against the party leadership the next year and ejected the Republican Speaker of the House, Ohio representative John Boehner—who could not control his own party despite having a 246-to-188 GOP majority, the largest Republican advantage since 1947.

This is the predictable result of a congressional electoral system rigged through political gerrymandering. There is no competition in such a system, which encourages extremism. And not only is there no price paid for extremism; it is rewarded.

A case in point: in February 2016, Supreme Court justice Antonin Scalia, a hero to the Right, died. President Obama nominated Chief Judge Merrick Garland to succeed Scalia. This was a conciliatory move on the part of the president toward the Republicans who controlled the Senate. Rather than put forth a much younger nominee known as a committed liberal, Obama nominated a 64-year-old moderate who was highly qualified, morally upright, and universally respected in Washington.

Knowing that a court with Justice Garland rather than Justice Scalia would tilt in a more liberal direction, Senate Republicans refused to exercise their constitutionally mandated duty to "advise and consent" on nominations to the Supreme Court and denied Garland a hearing. They justified this unprecedentedly partisan move by arguing that the Senate should not confirm a justice nominated in the last year of a president's term. This argument was disingenuous at best. A long list of presidents, including George Washington, Thomas Jefferson, Andrew Jackson, Abraham Lincoln, William Howard Taft, Woodrow Wilson, Herbert Hoover, Franklin Roosevelt, and Ronald Reagan had Supreme Court nominees ratified in their last year in office. The Republican senators' dereliction of duty represented disdain for the president of the United States, for the people who elected him, and, most worrisomely of all, for the Constitution.

It is too soon to analyze the 2016 presidential election, which pitted a Democratic establishment candidate, the former First Lady, United States senator, and secretary of state Hillary Rodham Clinton, against a wealthy real estate developer and reality television star, Donald J. Trump. Clinton won the popular vote by a healthy 2.1 percentage points, or nearly three million votes. But in an upset victory, Trump won the presidency with a majority in the Electoral College, which, by design, favors small states and sparsely populated regions over densely populated areas. Donald Trump thus became one of five American presidents to assume the office despite having lost the popular vote.

This was the second time in four elections that a candidate won the popular vote but lost the office. This is, to put it mildly, a problem. When the will of the majority of the people is thwarted, faith in the political system is eroded. When the will of the majority is steamrollered in Congress, when the privileges of a duly elected president are blocked, when the candidate favored in the popular vote still loses the election, this is bad for democracy—no matter which party holds the reins of power.

This is precisely the sort of situation that worried Justice Oliver Wendell Holmes. When the institutions of government are undermined or break down, the Republic is endangered. As Holmes and

his Civil War generation understood, participatory government—
government of the people, by the people, and for the people, as Lincoln put it at Gettysburg—*is* the Republic, not a means to it. Lose one
and the other disappears. This is especially true with respect to the
impartial rule of law. The fundamental unity of the people must be
maintained through the democratic process. Threats to that process,
whether violence, corruption, unchecked power, overbearing wealth,
disrespect for the Constitution, disenfranchisement, or manipulation
of the rules of the game, endanger that sense of unity. Holmes understood that today's losers have to believe that victory is possible tomorrow. Disrespect of or loss of faith in the system imperils the Republic
itself.

Acknowledgments

This book has taught us both many things, none more fundamental than the need for help along the way. Foremost, we are grateful to each other for friendship, patience, inspiration, and good humor in numerous trials along the way. Timothy Mennel, executive editor at the University of Chicago Press, believed in the project and made it stronger, always giving us his unstinting confidence, encouragement, discipline, and, above all, patience. Rachel Kelly, Kelly Finefrock-Creed, and the entire staff of the press brought indispensable technical guidance and attentive concern for every detail. Geri Thoma of Writers House steered us wisely and warmly at crucial stages. And we could have had no better developmental editor than Ann Hofstra Grogg, who kept the book moving through endless drafts with her invaluable judgment, deep gifts for communication and organization, and unlimited supplies of wit, warmth, and insight.

Friends, colleagues, and sharp-eyed professionals have made *Building the American Republic* much stronger with their comments and criticisms. Anonymous reviewers at the press enriched its content, analysis, and accuracy throughout. The early chapters of volume 1 benefited immeasurably from a deeply generous and learned reading by Professor Kathleen DuVal. The hard work and sharp insights of the research assistant for volume 1, Robert Richard, show on every page, and Gabriel Moss created excellent maps. Professor Geoffrey R. Stone of the University of Chicago Law School read every word of volume 2. He cut a lot of them, improved the rest, and shared his wisdom and knowledge freely. Any remaining flaws, errors, or misjudgments are our fault alone.

Above all, we are both enormously grateful to our families, who supported this project with guidance, reassurance, and love for more years than we like to remember.

Harry L. Watson
University of North Carolina at Chapel Hill

Jane Dailey
University of Chicago

For Further Reading

Chapter 1. Incorporation, 1877–1900

Edward L. Ayers, *The Promise of the New South: Life After Reconstruction* (1992)

William Cronon, *Nature's Metropolis: Chicago and the Great West* (1992)

Gary Gerstle, *Liberty and Coercion: The Paradox of American Government from the Founding to the Present* (2015)

Doris Kearns Goodwin, *The Bully Pulpit: Theodore Roosevelt, William Howard Taft, and the Golden Age of Journalism* (2013)

Karl Jacoby, *Shadows at Dawn: A Borderlands Massacre and the Violence of History* (2008)

Patricia Nelson Limerick, *The Legacy of Conquest: The Unbroken Past of the American West* (1987)

Louis Menand, *The Metaphysical Club: A Story of Ideas in America* (2002)

Christine Stansell, *The Feminist Promise, 1792 to the Present* (2013)

Alan Trachtenberg, *The Incorporation of America: Culture and Society in the Gilded Age* (1982)

Richard White, *Railroaded: The Transcontinentals and the Making of Modern America* (2012)

Chapter 2. Interconnected, 1898–1914

Glenda Elizabeth Gilmore, *Gender and Jim Crow: Women and the Politics of White Supremacy in North Carolina, 1896-1920* (1996)

George C. Herring, *From Colony to Superpower: U.S. Foreign Relations since 1776* (2011)

Michael Kazin, *A Godly Hero: The Life of William Jennings Bryan* (2007)

Paul Kennedy, *The Rise and Fall of the Great Powers* (1989)

Michael McGerr, *A Fierce Discontent: The Rise and Fall of the Progressive Movement in America, 1870-1920* (2005)

Edmund Morris, *Theodore Rex* (2002)

Robert J. Norrell, *Up from History: The Life of Booker T. Washington* (2011)

Nell Irvin Painter, *Standing at Armageddon: A Grassroots History of the Progressive Era* (2008)

Daniel T. Rodgers, *Atlantic Crossings: Social Politics in a Progressive Age* (2000)

Elizabeth Sanders, *Roots of Reform: Farmers, Workers, and the American State, 1877–1917* (1999)

Christine Stansell, *American Moderns: Bohemian New York and the Creation of a New Century* (2000)

Michael Willrich, *Pox: An American History* (2011)

Chapter 3. War, 1914–1924

Christopher Capozzola, *Uncle Sam Wants You: World War I and the Making of the Modern American Citizen* (2010)

Lynn Dumenil, *The Modern Temper: American Culture and Society in the 1920s* (1995)

Adam Fairclough, *Better Day Coming: Blacks and Equality, 1890–2000* (2002)

Beverly Gage, *The Day Wall Street Exploded: A Story of America in Its First Age of Terror* (2009)

George C. Herring, *From Colony to Superpower: U.S. Foreign Relations since 1776* (2011)

Michael Kazin, *A Godly Hero: The Life of William Jennings Bryan* (2007)

David M. Kennedy, *Over Here: The First World War and American Society* (1979)

William E. Leuchtenburg, *The Perils of Prosperity, 1914–1932* (1993)

Lisa McGirr, *The War on Alcohol: Prohibition and the Rise of the American State* (2015)

Daniel T. Rodgers, *Atlantic Crossings: Social Politics in a Progressive Age* (2000)

Geoffrey R. Stone, *Perilous Times: Free Speech in Wartime from the Sedition Act of 1798 to the War on Terrorism* (2005)

Chapter 4. Vertigo, 1920–1928

Anthony J. Badger, *FDR: The First Hundred Days* (2008)

Brooke L. Blower, *Becoming Americans in Paris: Transatlantic Politics and Culture between the World Wars* (2013)

George Chauncey, *Gay New York: Gender, Urban Culture, and the Making of the Gay Male World, 1890–1940* (1995)

Nancy F. Cott, *The Grounding of Modern Feminism* (1987)

Roger Daniels, *Guarding the Golden Door: American Immigration Policy and Immigrants since 1882* (2005)

Philip Dray, *At the Hands of Persons Unknown: The Lynching of Black America* (2003)

Thomas C. Holt, *Children of Fire: A History of African Americans* (2011)

David M. Kennedy, *Birth Control in America: The Career of Margaret Sanger* (1971)

David M. Kennedy, *Freedom from Fear: The American People in Depression and War, 1929–1945* (2001)

Edward J. Larson, *Summer for the Gods: The Scopes Trial and America's Continuing Debate over Science and Religion* (1997)

William E. Leuchtenburg, *The Perils of Prosperity, 1914–1932* (1993)

Kristin Luker, *Abortion and the Politics of Motherhood* (1985)

Nancy MacLean, *Behind the Mask of Chivalry: The Making of the Second Ku Klux Klan* (1995)

Patricia Sullivan, *Lift Every Voice: The NAACP and the Making of the Civil Rights Movement* (2010)

Chapter 5. Depression, 1928–1938

Lizabeth Cohen, *Making a New Deal: Industrial Workers in Chicago, 1919–1939* (1990)

Doris Kearns Goodwin, *No Ordinary Time: Franklin and Eleanor Roosevelt: The Home Front in World War II* (1995)

Ira Katznelson, *Fear Itself: The New Deal and the Origins of Our Time* (2014)

David M. Kennedy, *Freedom from Fear: The American People in Depression and War, 1929–1945* (2001)

William E Leuchtenburg, *Franklin D. Roosevelt and the New Deal, 1932–1940* (2009)

William E. Leuchtenburg, *Herbert Hoover* (2009)

Mark Mazower, *Dark Continent: Europe's Twentieth Century* (2000)

Chapter 6. Assertion, 1938–1946

Allan Bérubé, *Coming Out Under Fire: The History of Gay Men and Women in World War II* (1990)

John Morton Blum, *V Was for Victory: Politics and American Culture during World War II* (1977)

John Dittmer, *Local People: The Struggle for Civil Rights in Mississippi* (1995)

John W. Dower, *War without Mercy: Race and Power in the Pacific War* (1987)

Adam Fairclough, *Better Day Coming: Blacks and Equality, 1890–2000* (2002)

Adam Fairclough, *Race and Democracy: The Civil Rights Struggle in Louisiana, 1915–1972* (1995)

David M. Kennedy, *Freedom from Fear: The American People in Depression and War, 1929–1945* (2001)

Michael Klarman, *From Jim Crow to Civil Rights: The Supreme Court and the Struggle for Racial Equality* (2006)

Paul Gordon Lauren, *The Evolution of International Human Rights: Visions Seen* (1998)

Paul Gordon Lauren, *Power and Prejudice: The Politics and Diplomacy of Racial Discrimination* (1996)

Steven F. Lawson, *Black Ballots: Voting Rights in the South, 1944–1969* (1976)

Deborah E. Lipstadt, *Beyond Belief: The American Press and the Coming of the Holocaust, 1933–1945* (1992)

Mae M. Ngai, *Impossible Subjects: Illegal Aliens and the Making of Modern America* (1994)

Geoffrey R. Stone, *Perilous Times: Free Speech in Wartime from the Sedition Act of 1798 to the War on Terrorism* (2005)

Chapter 7. Containment, 1946–1953

Margot Canaday, *The Straight State: Sexuality and Citizenship in Twentieth-Century America* (2011)

Lizabeth Cohen, *A Consumers' Republic: The Politics of Mass Consumption in Postwar America* (2003)

Steven M. Gillon, *The American Paradox: A History of the United States since 1945* (2006)

Laurie B. Green, *Battling the Plantation Mentality: Memphis and the Black Freedom Struggle* (2007)

Peter Guralnick, *Last Train to Memphis: The Rise of Elvis Presley* (1994)

David Hajdu, *The Ten-Cent Plague: The Great Comic-Book Scare and How It Changed America* (2008)

George C. Herring, *From Colony to Superpower: U.S. Foreign Relations since 1776* (2011)

Barbara Dianne Savage, *Broadcasting Freedom: Radio, War, and the Politics of Race, 1938–1948* (1999)

Ellen Schrecker, *Many Are the Crimes: McCarthyism in America* (1999)

Geoffrey R. Stone, *Perilous Times: Free Speech in Wartime from the Sedition Act of 1798 to the War on Terrorism* (2005)

Chapter 8. At Odds, 1954–1965

John Dittmer, *Local People: The Struggle for Civil Rights in Mississippi* (1995)

Adam Fairclough, *Better Day Coming: Blacks and Equality, 1890–2000* (2002)

Steven M. Gillon, *The American Paradox: A History of the United States since 1945* (2006)

Thomas C. Holt, *Children of Fire: A History of African Americans* (2011)

Elizabeth Jacoway, *Turn Away Thy Son: Little Rock, the Crisis That Shocked the Nation* (2008)

Danielle L. McGuire, *At the Dark End of the Street: Black Women, Rape, and Resistance — a New History of the Civil Rights Movement from Rosa Parks to Black Power* (2011)

Anne Moody, *Coming of Age in Mississippi: The Classic Autobiography of Growing Up Poor and Black in the Rural South* (1992)

Charles M. Payne, *I Got the Light of Freedom: The Organizing Tradition and the Mississippi Freedom Struggle* (2007)

Barbara Ransby, *Ella Baker and the Black Freedom Movement: A Radical Democratic Vision* (2005)

Thomas J. Sugrue, *Sweet Land of Liberty: The Forgotten Struggle for Civil Rights in the North* (2009)

Chapter 9. Riven, 1965–1968

John Morton Blum, *Years of Discord: American Politics and Society, 1961–1974* (1991)

Mark Philip Bradley, *Vietnam at War* (2012)

H. W. Brands, *American Dreams: The United States since 1945* (2011)

William H. Chafe, *The Unfinished Journey: America since WWII* (2014)

Jefferson R. Cowie, *Stayin' Alive: The 1970s and the Last Days of the Working Class* (2012)

Doris Kearns Goodwin, *Lyndon Johnson and the American Dream: The Most Revealing Portrait of a President and Presidential Power Ever Written* (1991)

David Maraniss, *They Marched into Sunlight: War and Peace, Vietnam and America, October 1967* (2004)

William L. O'Neill, *Coming Apart: An Informal History of America in the 1960s* (2004)

Rick Perlstein, *Nixonland: The Rise of a President and the Fracturing of America* (2009)

Thomas J. Sugrue, *Sweet Land of Liberty: The Forgotten Struggle for Civil Rights in the North* (2009)

Stephen Tuck, *We Ain't What We Ought to Be: The Black Freedom Struggle from Emancipation to Obama* (2011)

Chapter 10. Breakdown, 1968–1974

Larry M. Bartels, *Unequal Democracy: The Political Economy of the New Gilded Age* (2010)

Dan T. Carter, *The Politics of Rage: George Wallace, the Origins of the New Conservatism, and the Transformation of American Politics* (1996)

William H. Chafe, *The Unfinished Journey: American since WWII* (2014)

Jefferson R. Cowie, *Stayin' Alive: The 1970s and the Last Days of the Working Class* (2012)

David Farber, *The Rise and Fall of Modern American Conservatism: A Short History* (2012)

Steve Fraser and Gary Gerstle, *The Rise and Fall of the New Deal Order, 1930–1980* (1990)

Linda Greenhouse and Reva Siegel, *Before* Roe v. Wade: *Voices That Shaped the Abortion Debate before the Supreme Court's Ruling* (2010)

Laura Kalman, *Right Star Rising: A New Politics, 1974–1980* (2010)

Stanley Kutler, *Abuse of Power: The New Nixon Tapes* (1997)

Rick Perlstein, *Before the Storm: Barry Goldwater and the Unmaking of the American Consensus* (2009)

Jason Sokol, *There Goes My Everything: White Southerners in the Age of Civil Rights, 1945–1975* (2007)

Judith Stein, *Pivotal Decade: How the United States Traded Factories for Finance in the Seventies* (2011)

Thomas J. Sugrue, *Sweet Land of Liberty: The Forgotten Struggle for Civil Rights in the North* (2009)

Chapter 11. Right, 1974–1989

William C. Berman, *America's Right Turn: From Nixon to Clinton* (1998)

Jefferson R. Cowie, *Stayin' Alive: The 1970s and the Last Days of the Working Class* (2012)

Darren Dochuk, *From Bible Belt to Sunbelt: Plain-Folk Religion, Grassroots Politics, and the Rise of Evangelical Conservatism* (2012)

David Farber, *The Rise and Fall of Modern American Conservatism: A Short History* (2012)

Laura Kalman, *Right Star Rising: A New Politics, 1974–1980* (2010)

Lisa McGirr, *Suburban Warriors: The Origins of the New American Right* (2002)

Samuel Moyn, *The Last Utopia: Human Rights in History* (2012)

Daniel T. Rodgers, *Age of Fracture* (2012)

Judith Stein, *Pivotal Decade: How the United States Traded Factories for Finance in the Seventies* (2011)

Sean Wilentz, *The Age of Reagan: A History, 1974–2008* (2009)

Chapter 12. Vulnerable, 1989–2001

Michelle Alexander, *The New Jim Crow: Mass Incarceration in the Age of Colorblindness* (2012)

Alan S. Blinder, *After the Music Stopped: The Financial Crisis, the Response, and the Work Ahead* (2013)

Richard A. Clarke, *Against All Enemies: Inside America's War on Terror* (2004)

Gail Collins, *When Everything Changed: The Amazing Journey of American Women from 1960 to the Present* (2010)

George C. Herring, *From Colony to Superpower: U.S. Foreign Relations since 1776* (2011)

Melvyn P. Leffler, *For the Soul of Mankind: The United States, the Soviet Union, and the Cold War* (2008)

Michael Morell and Bill Harlow, *The Great War of Our Time: The CIA's War against Terrorism—from al Qa'ida to ISIS* (2015)

George Packer, *The Assassins' Gate: America in Iraq* (2006)

James T. Patterson, *Restless Giant: The United States from Watergate to Bush v. Gore* (2007)

Samantha Power, *"A Problem From Hell": America and the Age of Genocide* (2013)

Daniel T. Rodgers, *Age of Fracture* (2012)

Jacob Weisberg, *The Bush Tragedy* (2008)

Chapter 13. Forward, 2001–2016

Anat Admati and Martin Hellwig, *The Bankers' New Clothes: What's Wrong with Banking and What to Do about It* (2014)

Alan S. Blinder, *After the Music Stopped: The Financial Crisis, the Response, and the Work Ahead* (2013)

Richard A. Clarke, *Against All Enemies: Inside America's War on Terror* (2004)

Gail Collins, *When Everything Changed: The Amazing Journey of American Women from 1960 to the Present* (2010)

David Daley, *Ratf**ked: The True Story Behind the Secret Plan to Steal America's Democracy* (2016)

E. J. Dionne Jr., *Why the Right Went Wrong: Conservatism—from Goldwater to Trump and Beyond* (2016)

George C. Herring, *From Colony to Superpower: U.S. Foreign Relations since 1776* (2011)

Jane Mayer, *Dark Money: The Hidden History of the Billionaires behind the Rise of the Radical Right* (2016)

Bill McKibben, *Oil and Honey: The Education of an Unlikely Activist* (2014)

Atif Mian and Amir Sufi, *House of Debt: How They (and You) Caused the Great Recession, and How We Can Prevent It from Happening Again* (2014)

Michael Morell and Bill Harlow, *The Great War of Our Time: The CIA's War against Terrorism—from al Qa'ida to ISIS* (2015)

George Packer, *The Assassins' Gate: America in Iraq* (2006)

Rick Perlstein, *Before the Storm: Barry Goldwater and the Unmaking of the American Consensus* (2009)

Geoffrey R. Stone, *Top Secret: When Our Government Keeps Us in the Dark* (2007)

Geoffrey R. Stone, *War and Liberty: An American Dilemma: 1790 to the Present* (2007)

Index

Page numbers in italics refer to illustrations.

Plan, 203, 205–6; mutually assured destruction (MAD), 299; research and development during, 242; Suez crisis, 243–44

colonization, 42, 179. *See also* American imperialism

Colored Farmers' Alliance, 21

Colson, Charles, 298, 301, 307

comic books, 225–26

Comintern, 204

Commission for Relief in Belgium, 77, 141, 146

Commission on Interracial Cooperation, 98

Committee on Public Information (CPI), 85, 87

communications: government takeover during World War I, 90; internet, 367, 372, 373–74; telegraph system, 4

Communism, 204, 215–16, 219–20. *See also* anti-Communism; Cold War

Communist Labor Party, 100

Communist Party of the United States (CPUSA), 100, 139, 140, 158–60, 159, 204, 215, 218, 219

compassionate conservatism, 379–80, 383–84

Compton, Arthur, 174

Comstock, Anthony, 115–16, 116–17

Comstock Act (1873), 115–16, 117

Conant, James B., 174

Concerned Women for America (CWA), 321, 331

Congress of Industrial Organizations (CIO), 162, 163, 216, 237, 287, 308

Congress of Racial Equality (CORE), 253, 277, 280

Connor, Eugene, 253, 254

conscription: during the Vietnam War, 262, 281, 282, 301; during World War I, 76, 79, 81, 84, 100

Constitution. *See* Amendments to the Constitution

Consumer Product Safety Act, 294

containment, 203, 204–5, 208–9, 344–45

contraception. *See* birth control

Coolidge, Calvin: businessmen's government of, 109; election of, 109, 125; lack of success in domestic reform, 142; reaction to police strike, 97; support for National Origins Act, 124; veto of McNary-Haugen Bill by, 111

corporations, 11–14, 47–49. *See also* antitrust policies

corruption, 17–18, 108–9, 407, 408, 409

Cortelyou, George B., 64

Coulter, Ann, 357

Council of Christians and Jews, 196

Cox, Archibald, 310

Cox, James, 102

Coxey, Jacob, 25, 26

Coyle, James, 105

Creel, George, 85, 87

criminal justice system: African Americans in, 35, 370–71; death penalty, 370; drug laws, 369, 370; family courts, 62; juvenile courts, 62; minimum sentencing laws, 370; parole, 62; probation, 62; progressive reforms in, 62; Supreme Court decisions affecting, 257–58; three strikes laws, 370

Cronkite, Walter, 275, 283, 292

Cuba: Bay of Pigs Invasion, 245–46; Cuban missile crisis, 247; Guantanamo Bay, 43, 46, 396; Jewish refugees to, 174; Platt Amendment, 43; rebellion against Spanish rule, 41–43; revolution of 1933, 170; Spanish-American War in, 42–43; sugar cultivation in, 41; Wilson's military intervention in, 72

culture wars, 225–28, 356. *See also* Religious Right

currency: creation of US dollar, 69; exchange of greenbacks for gold, 19; free silver demands, 19, 22, 27–28